TERRA MAXIMA

AMAZING FACTS OF NATURE

The Great Barrier Reef, off the coast of Queensland, Australia, is the world's largest single structure made by living organisms.

TERRA MAXIMA

AMAZING FACTS OF NATURE

Marble Canyon in northern Arizona marks the beginning of the magnificent Grand Canyon. Downstream from Glen Canyon Dam, 6 km (4 miles) south of the city of Page, the striking shape drawn by the course of the Colorado River is known as Horseshoe Bend.

ABOUT THIS BOOK

TERRA MAXIMA is a tour of our planet's most impressive natural features – from the darkest depths of its seas and oceans to its highest mountains, largest monoliths, longest rivers, most spectacular waterfalls, and deepest meteor craters, valleys, canyons, and caves.

The book seeks out nature's most remarkable plants and animals in their natural habitats, including the largest whales, fish, and seals, the most dangerous predators, fastest land animals, biggest and smallest birds, and longest migratory routes. We will admire the world's greatest flowering plants, discover its astonishing ancient trees, ferns, and cacti, explore its thickest coniferous woodlands, mangroves, rainforests, and bamboo woods, and cross its driest deserts.

Illustrated with superb images taken by the world's leading landscape and wildlife photographers, this book documents the natural world at its

most spectacular – from Antarctic glaciers, bubbling volcanoes, and deep gorges to incredible animals like those of the Pantanal, Serengeti, and Okavango Delta. The many impressive satellite images reveal some of our planet's most remote regions – places such as the Siberian taiga, the rainforests of the Amazon Basin, the dune fields of the Namib Desert, or the snow-capped peaks of the Andean volcanoes, for example. The lists provide a quick overview of key facts, with a fascinating, more detailed account of the Earth's greatest natural features presented in the short and informative accompanying texts.

Join us on this great voyage of discovery.

Walruses are the Arctic's largest pinniped species. The one shown here is in the Arctic Ocean, near the Franz Josef Land archipelago.

CONTENTS

The twin peaks of Gros Piton and Petit Piton are located on St Lucia, not far from the town of Soufrière. Together with areas of tropical and subtropical rainforest, the two mountains are part of a protected area inscribed on the UNESCO World Heritage list for its geological diversity.

CONTENTS

Our blue planet in all its beauty. Until the 16th century, we believed it to be the focal point of the universe, at its very center, a place subsequently assigned to the Sun by Copernicus and Kepler. We now know that even the Sun is just a mid-sized star on the edge of the Milky Way – one of some 300 billion. The discovery that the magnificent Milky Way is itself just one of many similar galaxies was made less than a hundred years ago, and today's modern telescopes allow us to observe billions of galaxies. Over time, our planet has occupied an increasingly peripheral position in our understanding of the universe. In the grand scheme of things, it is merely a tiny speck, yet planet Earth remains the sole basis of our existence. We cannot seek refuge anywhere else in space, so it is absolutely vital that we look after our planet carefully. The Earth may well be unique, and living on it is a stroke of chance and good fortune to which we owe our very existence.

Earth as seen from the Moon. Through the protective veil of the atmosphere, you can see the Atlantic Ocean, with the American continent to the west and Europe and Africa to the east.

THE SOLAR SYSTEM

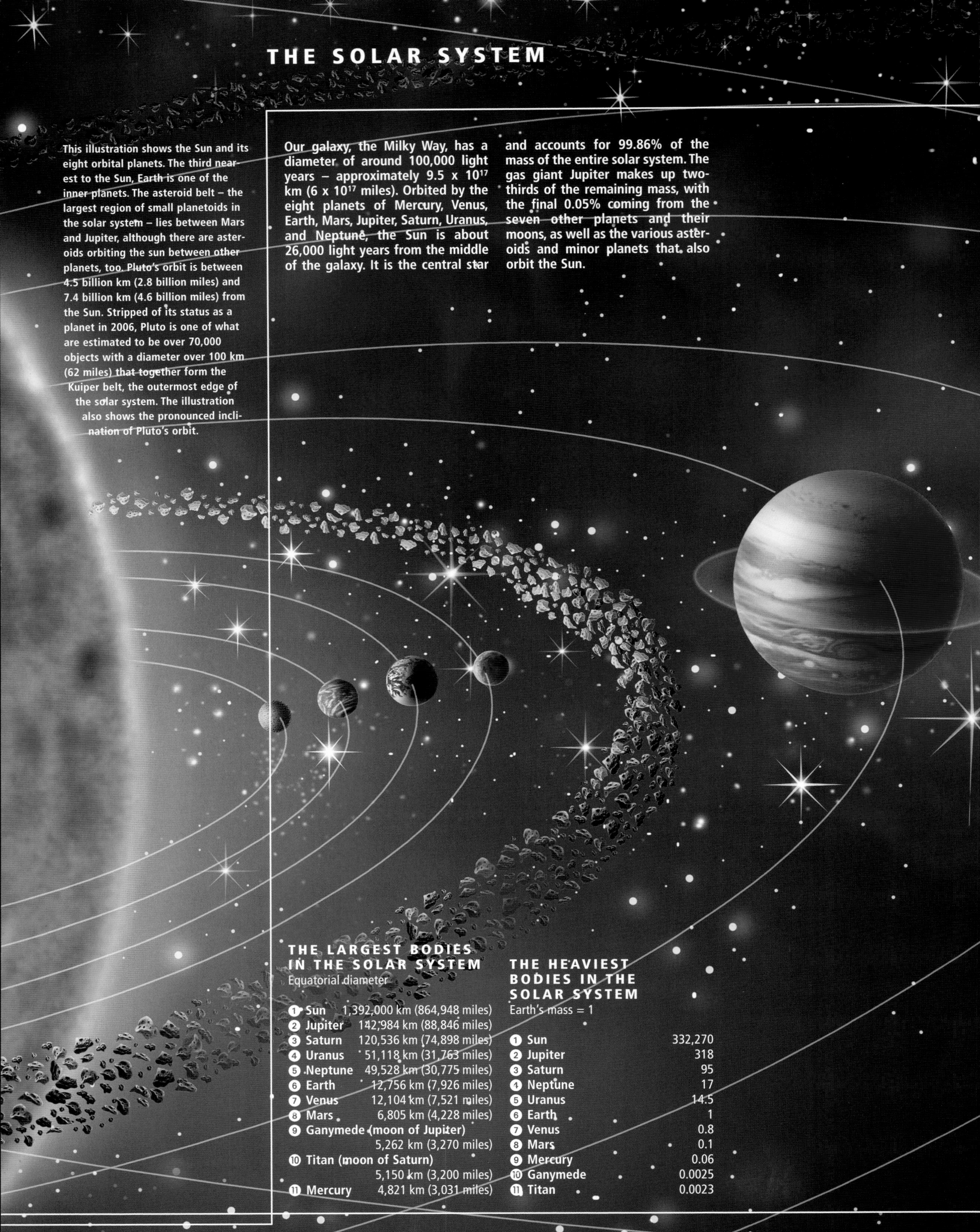

This illustration shows the Sun and its eight orbital planets. The third nearest to the Sun, Earth is one of the inner planets. The asteroid belt – the largest region of small planetoids in the solar system – lies between Mars and Jupiter, although there are asteroids orbiting the sun between other planets, too. Pluto's orbit is between 4.5 billion km (2.8 billion miles) and 7.4 billion km (4.6 billion miles) from the Sun. Stripped of its status as a planet in 2006, Pluto is one of what are estimated to be over 70,000 objects with a diameter over 100 km (62 miles) that together form the Kuiper belt, the outermost edge of the solar system. The illustration also shows the pronounced inclination of Pluto's orbit.

Our galaxy, the Milky Way, has a diameter of around 100,000 light years – approximately 9.5×10^{17} km (6×10^{17} miles). Orbited by the eight planets of Mercury, Venus, Earth, Mars, Jupiter, Saturn, Uranus, and Neptune, the Sun is about 26,000 light years from the middle of the galaxy. It is the central star and accounts for 99.86% of the mass of the entire solar system. The gas giant Jupiter makes up two-thirds of the remaining mass, with the final 0.05% coming from the seven other planets and their moons, as well as the various asteroids and minor planets that also orbit the Sun.

THE LARGEST BODIES IN THE SOLAR SYSTEM
Equatorial diameter

1. Sun   1,392,000 km (864,948 miles)
2. Jupiter   142,984 km (88,846 miles)
3. Saturn   120,536 km (74,898 miles)
4. Uranus   51,118 km (31,763 miles)
5. Neptune   49,528 km (30,775 miles)
6. Earth   12,756 km (7,926 miles)
7. Venus   12,104 km (7,521 miles)
8. Mars   6,805 km (4,228 miles)
9. Ganymede (moon of Jupiter)   5,262 km (3,270 miles)
10. Titan (moon of Saturn)   5,150 km (3,200 miles)
11. Mercury   4,821 km (3,031 miles)

THE HEAVIEST BODIES IN THE SOLAR SYSTEM
Earth's mass = 1

1. Sun   332,270
2. Jupiter   318
3. Saturn   95
4. Neptune   17
5. Uranus   14.5
6. Earth   1
7. Venus   0.8
8. Mars   0.1
9. Mercury   0.06
10. Ganymede   0.0025
11. Titan   0.0023

JOHANNES KEPLER (1571–1630)

Born in the town of Weil der Stadt, south-west Germany, Johannes Kepler discovered the laws of plan-

Portrait of Johannes Kepler, *circa* 1620.

etary motion that now bear his name. Kepler was able to show that the planets orbit not in circles – as Copernicus suspected – but in ellipses. He also demonstrated that the Sun is always at one of the focal points of the ellipse. Alongside Galileo, Kepler is considered to be one of the fathers of modern science.

With the Sun at its center, the solar system has a diameter of 14 billion km (8.7 billion miles). It takes the Sun's rays more than six hours to reach the Kuiper belt, but they get to Earth in just eight minutes.

THE SUN

As far as astronomy is concerned, the Sun is a pretty average star. The temperature on its surface can exceed 5,500°C (9,932°F), and it is over 15 million °C (27 million °F) at its core. Our central star consists of up to 70% hydrogen and 28% helium, with heavier elements – primarily oxygen and carbon – accounting for just 1.5–2% of its mass. Quite how the Sun derived its energy remained a mystery for a very long time. It could not have been a chemical process like carbon combustion, since that would only have created enough energy to last for 100,000 years. The answer only emerged after the discovery of atomic energy. In 1938, the German-American physicist Hans Bethe described the process known as the proton-proton chain, a fusion reaction whereby the Sun's hydrogen is converted into helium. The generation of energy relies upon the fact that the larger nucleus created by nuclear fusion has a slightly lesser mass than the original particles. This difference – known as the "mass defect" – is

JUPITER
778 million km (483 million miles)

A planet's distance from the Sun is usually measured along the longest semi-major axis of its orbit. In Jupiter's case, this is 778 million km (483 million miles). Jupiter is the largest planet by some margin, and is primarily composed of hydrogen and helium. It has various satellites, the four largest of which – Io (the red dot you can see on the right of the image), Europa, Ganymede, and Callisto – were first discovered by Galileo in 1610. The temperature of Jupiter's ever-changing bands of cold gas is around –50°C (–58°F). Their light and dark tints come from small amounts of phosphorus and sulfur. The Great Red Spot – a persistent anticyclonic storm – is a particularly intriguing feature (below left on the image). As well as being the largest planet, Jupiter also has the quickest rotation – lasting just 9 hours and 55 minutes.

NEPTUNE
4,497 million km (2,794 million miles)

It was the fact that something appeared to be disturbing Uranus' orbit that first led scientists to suspect the existence of an eighth planet. Neptune was first observed through a telescope in 1846. Methane forms a very significant part of Neptune's atmosphere, where the temperature is -218°C (-360°F). Like Jupiter, Neptune has numerous satellites. It also has mysterious dark spots.

URANUS
2,870 million km (1,783 million miles)

The seventh planet was discovered in 1781. It too is a gas planet. When Voyager 2 passed Uranus in 1986, the space probe's images revealed hardly any visible features. The planet's system of rings was, however, confirmed. Some 14.5 times the size of Earth in terms of mass, this cold giant has some 27 satellites, including Titania and Oberon.

SATURN
1,427 million km (887 million miles)

The sixth planet is also a gas planet. Saturn has the lowest mean density of all the planets, and is mainly made up of hydrogen. Like Jupiter, Saturn exhibits a system of different bands and zones. First observed as far back as 1655, its distinctive rings are its most striking feature. Of the numerous satellites orbiting Saturn, the largest is Titan, with a diameter of 5,150 km (3,200 miles).

EARTH
150 million km (93 million miles)

Third in line and everything here is exactly right – from the size of planet Earth to its mean density and distance from the Sun. The development of the Earth's atmosphere, the accumulation of its water, and the existence of life on Earth are the result. The atmosphere both protects us from dangerous radiation and ensures that most of the objects crashing toward Earth from space are burnt to harmless ashes. Unlike the outer gas giants, Earth is one of the inner, or terrestrial, planets. The Moon, one light second away, is the only satellite to orbit our planet. Earth is not a perfect sphere, being slightly flatter at the North and South Poles, and the distance between the two poles is thus 43 km (27 miles) shorter than the Earth's diameter at the equator.

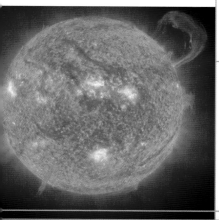

released as energy according to Einstein's $E=mc^2$ equation. The square of the speed of light (c^2) results in a very large figure, but the process is an immensely slow one. Even at the Sun's extremely hot core, only one in every 100 million protons reaches the necessary speed for a collision. Nonetheless, there are enough protons inside the sun for some 5 million tonnes (5.5 million short tons) of mass to be converted into energy every second. Though this has been going on for some 4.5 billion years, less than 4% of the Sun's hydrogen has so far been used up – leaving enough for a good few billion years to come. Thanks to its powerful effect on Earth, it has been worshiped as a deity by some cultures.

The Sun is a very active star. Spots – the darker areas shown on this image – appear regularly, but usually disappear again after a few days. With temperatures of 4,300°C (7,772°F), the interior of such spots is somewhat cooler than other parts of the Sun. Prominences – violent plasma eruptions – are particularly spectacular (left).

(Large image) The eight planets of our solar system from left to right and from top to bottom: (illustrations not to scale) Jupiter, Neptune, Uranus, Earth, Saturn (middle), Venus, Mars, and Mercury.

Olympus Mons: The Highest Volcano In The Solar System

Named after the seat of the Greek gods, Mars' 27-km (16½-mile) high Olympus Mons volcano is consid-

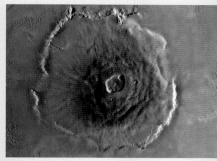

Olympus Mons.

ered to be the highest volcano in the known solar system. Its crater has a diameter of 80 km (50 miles). This is an example of a shield volcano, comparable with Hawaii's Mauna Loa.

Valles Marineris: The Largest Canyon In The Solar System

Mars is also the location of the solar system's largest known canyon. Up to 600 km (370 miles) wide and as much as 10 km (6 miles) deep, this

Valles Marineris' curved graben system.

vast rift (graben) system runs along Mars' equator for over 4,000 km (2,500 miles) – equivalent to the distance between the east and west coasts of North America.

VENUS
108 million km (67 million miles)

Venus is the second-nearest planet to the Sun. It is one of the Earth-like planets, and its orbit comes closer to Earth than that of any other planet. Venus' atmosphere, made up mostly of carbon dioxide, is completely opaque. Thanks to the greenhouse effect, the surface temperature is over 460°C (860°F) – far too hot for there to be any water. Venus has no moons.

MARS
228 million km (142 million miles)

Fourth from the Sun, Mars looks red from Earth. It, too, is a similar planet to Earth, and it even has a thin atmosphere (95% of which is composed of carbon dioxide). Craters and extinct volcanoes have both been discovered on the surface of Mars, but there is no sign of water in liquid form so far. Mars is considerably smaller than Earth and has two moons, Deimos and Phobos.

MERCURY
58 million km (36 million miles)

Mercury, the nearest planet to the Sun, is another Earth-like planet. It is, however, extremely small, its mass being just 6% of the Earth's. Though it appears to have a very thin atmosphere, this can provide little protection from temperatures that range from extremes of 425°C (797°F) by day to -170°C (-274°F) by night. Mercury's landscape is similar to that of our Moon.

On 24 August 2006, astronomers met in Prague, in the Czech Republic, to redefine the way we see space. They stripped Pluto of its status as a planet and reclassified it as a "dwarf planet". The decision was based upon the idea that the major planets have cleared away most of the other objects in their orbit. This reasoning was somewhat controversial, as there are still thousands of other objects in the orbits of both Earth and Jupiter, albeit relatively small ones compared to the mass of the planets themselves. The term "plutoid" is used to describe the small objects that orbit the Sun in the Kuiper belt area beyond Neptune's orbit. Eris and Pluto are the two largest Trans-Neptunian objects.

This page: Discovered in 2005, Makemake is the third largest plutoid after Eris and Pluto. It is named after Makemake (pronounced "MAH-kay MAH-kay"), the creator god in the mythology of Easter Island.

ERIS

The dwarf planet of Eris was only discovered in 2005. With a diameter of approximately 2,400 km (1,500 miles), it is slightly larger than Pluto, and was initially hailed as the "tenth planet". Eris has at least one satellite, which was named Dysnomia in 2006. This satellite has a diameter of some 240 km (149 miles).

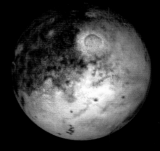

PLUTO

Discovered as recently as 1930, the object once thought to be the ninth planet has since been downgraded to a dwarf planet. Pluto has a diameter of approximately 2,390 km (1,485 miles), making it slightly smaller than both Eris and even our own Moon. Charon is the largest of Pluto's three satellites. At around 1,200 km (750 miles), its diameter is unusually large.

Satellites – also known as moons – are bodies that orbit a planet or dwarf planet without themselves being orbited. According to current knowledge, the planets of the solar system have a total of 167 natural satellites. Two of these are in fact bigger than the planet Mercury, topping its 4,878-km (3,031-mile) diameter. With its 67 moons, Jupiter has the most satellites. Saturn, in second place, has 61, while Mercury and Venus have no moons at all.

This page: The Io moon of Jupiter with Jupiter itself in the background. Io is the innermost and third largest of Jupiter's many moons.

THE LARGEST MOONS IN THE SOLAR SYSTEM

(J=Jupiter, S=Saturn, U=Uranus, N=Neptune)
Equatorial diameter

① Ganymede (J)
5,262 km (3,270 miles)
② Titan (S)   5,150 km (3,200 miles)
③ Callisto (J)   4,821 km (2,996 miles)
④ Io (J)   3,643 km (2,264 miles)
⑤ The Moon   3,476 km (2,160 miles)
⑥ Europa (J)   3,122 km (1,940 miles)
⑦ Triton (N)   2,707 km (1,682 miles)
⑧ Titania (U)   1,578 km (981 miles)
⑨ Rhea (S)   1,528 km (949 miles)
⑩ Oberon (U)   1,523 km (946 miles)
⑪ Iapetus (S)   1,436 km (892 miles)
⑫ Charon (Pluto)
1,207 km (750 miles) km

Orbiting the planet Jupiter, Ganymede (top) is the largest moon in the solar system. It is covered by a thick layer of ice and is even believed to have a thin atmosphere. Earth's own moon (bottom), is captured here during a total lunar eclipse.

Ice, liquid water, and possibly even primitive life are believed to exist on Saturn's moon Enceladus (top, with the impressive crescent of another of Saturn's moons, Titan, in the foreground). Europa (bottom) is one of Jupiter's four largest satellites.

The icy surface of Callisto (top), Jupiter's second largest moon, is completely covered with impact craters. The average surface temperature is −139°C (−218°F). Triton (bottom), the largest of Neptune's satellites, is completely covered with a layer of ice.

Io (top) is the innermost of Jupiter's four large moons. It has a level of volcanic activity that is unmatched anywhere else in the solar system. Discovered in 1787, Oberon (bottom) is a rocky moon pitted with craters orbiting Uranus. It, too, is covered by ice.

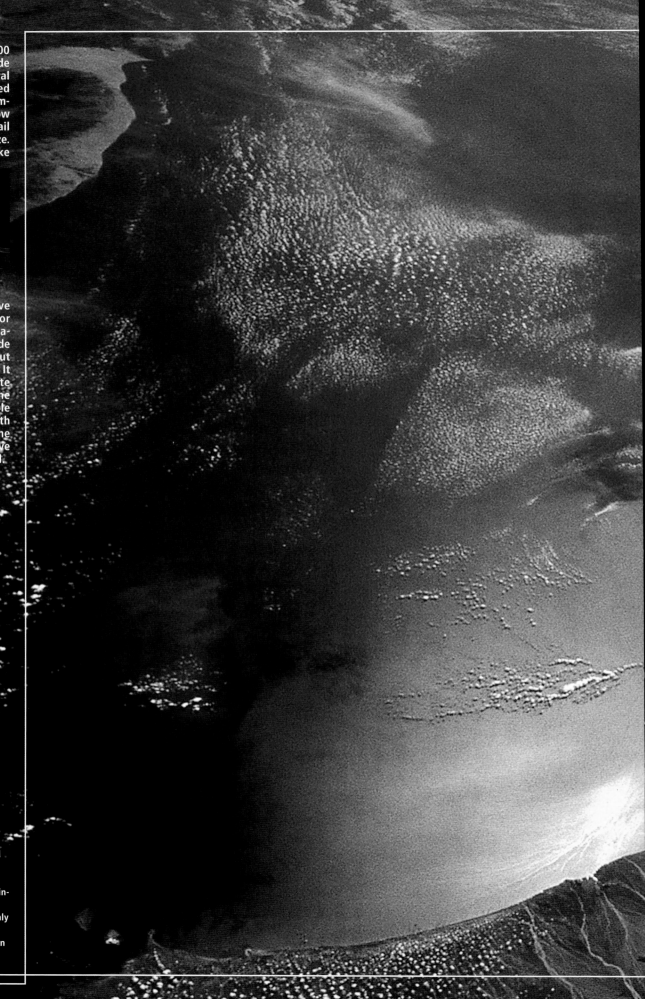

Moving at altitudes of 400–600 km (250–370 miles), manmade satellites orbit the Earth several times a day. Some are equipped with sophisticated digital cameras whose resolution is now high enough to capture detail of less than 1 m (3 feet) in size. Large-scale satellite images like

Earth rises above the Moon.

the one shown here have become important tools for meteorologists and cartographers, and they also provide important information about the state of the environment. It was, for example, satellite imagery that confirmed the existence of the ozone hole above the North and South Poles, and showed up the destruction of the protective ozone layer all over the world.

In eastern Africa, the wedge-shaped Somali Peninsula juts out into the Indian Ocean south of the Gulf of Aden. Because of its shape, the peninsula is also known as the Horn of Africa. Though its boundaries are only roughly defined, the peninsula does take in both Somalia and the eastern part of Ethiopia.

LIVING EARTH

Those parts of Alaska that are not covered by ice quickly develop a rich vegetation.

A member of Ethiopia's Kara people.

Flying high: the bald eagle.

On land: a white-tailed deer fawn.

At sea: a humpback whale and its young.

Life on Earth goes back some four billion years. The first life forms were single cell microorganisms like bacteria, archaea, and eukaryotes. Evolution – the development of inherited genetic code through mutation and natural selection – saw these simple life forms become ever more complex creatures, better adapted to the world around them. Over the course of the geological eras, this gradual evolutionary process led to the differentiation of the plant and animal worlds into algae, spore and flowering plants, gymnosperms, and magnoliophyta, and fish, amphibians, reptiles, insects, and mammals respectively.

Man only appeared on the scene right at the end of this process, some two million years ago. *Homo habilis* rapidly evolved into *Homo erectus* before finally becoming dominant on Earth as the modern *Homo sapiens*.

As far as we know, Earth is the only body in space to have supported life. It is only on Earth that a delicate interplay of different factors has nurtured a flora and fauna that has successfully evolved to adapt itself to a huge variety of contrasting environments.

Our own Moon has a diameter of some 3,476 km (2,160 miles), making it the fifth largest moon in the entire solar system. Covering barely 38 million sq. km (15 million sq. miles), its surface area is equivalent to 7.4% of that of the Earth – smaller

The Moon rises above the Isle of Wight, England.

than the combined 42 million sq. km (16 million sq. miles) of North and South America. The Moon's volume is 2% and its mass about 1.2% of the Earth's. It is this low mass that explains the Moon's low gravity. A man weighing 80 kg (176 lb) on Earth weighs in at just 13.3 kg (29 lb) on the Moon, and a long-jumper who can jump 8 m (26 feet) on Earth would jump almost 50 m (164 feet) on the Moon. Even a heavily laden astronaut can move around with the lightness of a ballerina.

This image of the Moon was taken by the Galileo space probe. The Mare Imbrium is visible in the top left, with the Mare Serenitatis below it in the middle left of the picture. The lighter strip between the two lunar *maria* is the Montes Caucasus mountain range.

THE LARGEST MARIA (SEAS)
Mean diameter

The darker areas of the Moon's surface were once thought to be seas. There is, of course, no trace of water, but the term has stuck nevertheless.

① Oceanus Procellarum 2,568 km (1,596 miles)
② Mare Frigoris 1,596 km (992 miles)
③ Mare Imbrium 1,123 km (698 miles)
④ Mare Fecunditatis 909 km (565 miles)
⑤ Mare Tranquillitatis 873 km (542 miles)
⑥ Mare Nubium 715 km (444 miles)

THE LARGEST TERRAE (HIGHLANDS)
Length

The Moon's mountain ranges are visible as lighter areas, often between *maria*. Their names are often borrowed from mountain ranges on Earth.

① Montes Rook
    791 km (492 miles)
② Montes Cordillera
    574 km (357 miles)
③ Montes Haemus
    560 km (348 miles)
④ Montes Caucasus
    445 km (277 miles)
⑤ Montes Jura
    422 km (262 miles)
⑥ Montes Apenninus
    401 km (249 miles)

THE LARGEST CRATERS
Mean diameter

Craters are created by meteor strikes. The largest-known crater in the solar system is the South Pole-Aitken Basin on the Moon.

① South Pole-Aitken Basin
    2,240 km (1,392 miles)
② Apollo 537 km (334 miles)
③ Birkhoff 345 km (214 miles)
④ Poincaré 319 km (198 miles)
⑤ Planck 314 km (195 miles)
⑥ Schrodinger
    312 km (194 miles)

THE MOON LANDING

Top: The US flag and Lunar Module. Above: The LRV moon buggy from Apollo 15 (1971).

Followed by a global television and radio audience of almost half a billion people, man's first steps on the moon on 21 July 1969 were the event of the century. The Saturn V rocket carrying the Apollo 11 capsule and astronauts Neil Armstrong, Buzz Aldrin, and Michael Collins had taken off from Kennedy Space Center, Florida, four days earlier. It was three days before Apollo 11 reached the Moon's orbit, and the Eagle Lunar Module with Neil Armstrong and Buzz Aldrin on board landed in the Mare Tranquillitatis on 20 July. At 02:56:58 UTC on 21 July (still 20 July in America), Armstrong was the first of the two astronauts to emerge from the Lunar Module, uttering the immortal words about one small step for a man and one giant leap for mankind. Two and a half hours later, man's first moonwalk was over. The astronauts had completed all their tasks, and even collected 21.6 kg (48 lb) of rock samples. The return flight to the Command Module in lunar orbit passed off without incident, and the return to Earth went equally smoothly. When the capsule splashed down in the Pacific on 24 July, the returning astronauts received a hero's welcome.

Astronaut and geologist Harrison Hagan Schmitt examines a rock in the Taurus highlands during the Apollo 17 mission of 1972. Together with fellow astronaut Eugene Cernan, Schmitt completed the longest lunar exploration of all the Apollo missions.

Comets and asteroids are two of the objects that can collide with other bodies in space – including with Earth. Scientists estimate that there could be more than 1,000 bodies in orbit with a diameter of over 1 km (½ mile) that might one day come crashing down to Earth as meteorites,

Comet over Stonehenge, England.

a third of which are comets. Earth has already had numerous collisions in its history, and there are over 100 craters with diameters of 100–300 km (62–186 miles) that are known to have been caused by impacts with extraterrestrial bodies. The consequences of these collisions could be calamitous. The extinction of the dinosaurs and much of the plant and animal life of the Mesozoic era has been linked to the meteor strike that created Mexico's Chicxulub Basin crater 65 million years ago. The meteorite in question had a diameter of some 10 km (6 miles), and the force of the impact is believed to have been five times the explosive power of the world's entire nuclear arsenal. The dust and gases thrown up in the explosion completely blocked out the Sun's rays, leading to catastrophic climate change.

THE HOBA METEORITE

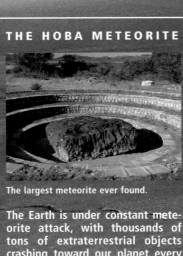

The largest meteorite ever found.

The Earth is under constant meteorite attack, with thousands of tons of extraterrestrial objects crashing toward our planet every day. Most meteorites are small enough to burn up on entering the Earth's atmosphere, and it is extremely rare for large meteorites to actually strike the ground. There are three main types of meteorite: stony meteorites, iron meteorites, and stony-iron meteorites. The largest intact meteorites belong to the iron category. Top of the list is the Hoba meteorite, which weighs in at some 60 tonnes (66 short tons). Found in Namibia in 1920, it is believed to have smashed into Earth approximately 80,000 years ago. Its crater is no longer visible, but the iron and nickel meteorite itself still remains at the exact spot at which it first came to rest. The site is open to the public, and visitors can walk around the meteorite on the tiered walls that have been built around it – rather like an amphitheater.

THE LARGEST METEORITE FINDS
Mass in tonnes (short tons)

1 **Hoba**, Namibia
60 tonnes (66 short tons)
2 **Campo-del-Cielo**, Argentina
37 tonnes (41 short tons)
3 **Cape York**, Greenland
31 tonnes (34 short tons)
4 **Armanty**, China
28 tonnes (31 short tons)
5 **Bacubirito**, Mexico
22 tonnes (24 short tons)
6 **Cape York**, Greenland
20.1 tonnes (22 short tons)
7 **Mbosi**, Tanzania
16 tonnes (17.5 short tons)
8 **Campo-del-Cielo**, Argentina
14.9 tonnes (16.4 short tons)

THE LARGEST METEORITE FINDS AND CRATERS

THE LARGEST METEORITE CRATERS ON EARTH

In Antarctica, the Wilkes Land crater is, with a diameter of 500 km (311 miles), the world's largest known crater site. The truly awesome meteorite that created it landed here about 250 million years ago. The crater itself is buried under 1.5 km (1 mile) of ice. It was discovered in 2006 using readings of the Earth's fluctuating gravitational field taken by the GRACE satellite. Radar measurements confirmed the find.

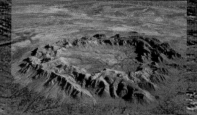

The Gosses Bluff crater in Australia.

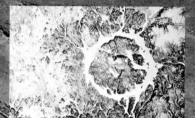

Canada's Manicouagan crater.

Mean diameter

1. **Wilkes Land,** Antarctica
   500 km (311 miles)
2. **Vredefort,** South Africa
   300 km (186 miles)
3. **Sudbury,** Canada
   250 km (155 miles)
4. **Chicxulub,** Mexico
   170 km (106 miles)
5. **Popigai,** Russia   100 km (62 miles)
6. **Manicouagan,** Canada
   100 km (62 miles)
7. **Acraman,** Australia   90 km (56 miles)
8. **Chesapeake Bay,** USA
   90 km (56 miles)
9. **Puchezh-Katunki,** Russia
   80 km (50 miles)
10. **Morokweng,** South Africa
    70 km (43 miles)
11. **Kara,** Russia   65 km (40 miles)
12. **Beaverhead,** USA   60 km (37 miles)

The Barringer crater (left) in Arizona, USA, lies between Flagstaff and Winslow. It is about 1.5 km (1 mile) wide and some 170 m (558 feet) deep. The iron meteorite that created it struck around 50,000 years ago. The meteorite had a diameter of roughly 50 m (164 feet), and was moving at a speed of approximately 40 km (25 miles) per second when it hit Earth.

VREDEFORT DOME – THE WORLD'S LARGEST PROVEN METEORITE CRATER

Vredefort crater lies about 120 km (75 miles) south-west of Johannesburg. Dating back over two billion years, it is the world's oldest crater, and until the discovery of the Wilkes Land crater in 2006 it was also the largest.

Giant meteor strikes have been responsible for the greatest catastrophes in the Earth's natural history, and their influential role in both the evolution of the planet's plant and animal life and its geological development is now accepted. Exactly what struck this spot over two billion years ago in what is now South Africa is difficult to ascertain. It may have been a 12-km (7-mile) wide asteroid, moving at 20 km (12 miles) per second. But it could also have been the smaller head of a comet, crashing toward Earth at an even faster speed. On impact, a meteorite releases its energy as heat within fractions of a second, causing both the meteorite and large areas of the earth it hits to immediately vaporize. In Vredefort's case, scientists estimate that some 70 cu. km (17 cu. miles) of rock were vaporized in this way. This leads to the huge explosion that creates a meteor crater, with the earth that is thrown up out of the ground forming the crater wall. The energy of the impact also causes reactions in the minerals below ground, the ultra high pressures turning quartz into stishovite and coesite. The creation of

shatter cones – rocks bearing striped markings on their surface – can also be explained by the shock waves of a meteorite impact, the stone literally shattered into small, sharp-edged pieces. Once the rock has set again, it is known as a breccia. The breccia found at the Vredefort crater is particularly special – known as pseudotachylite, it is the subject of great scientific interest. The meteor strike also allowed hornfels – usually only found in deeper layers of rock – to come to the surface. The Vredefort Dome became a UNESCO World Heritage Site in 2005, taking into account the site's age (it is the oldest) and size (it is the largest and the most deeply eroded), and the wealth of geological features that it contains.

The name Vredefort Dome refers to the bulge created in the middle of the crater by the impact (left). Below: An aerial view reveals the semicircular shape of the Vredefort Dome meteor crater.

Major meteorite strikes are mercifully rare, and two strikes right next to each other are even more unusual. The Clearwater Lakes, in the Canadian province of Quebec, are believed to be the result of one such near simultaneous double impact. Scientists

Canoeist on Clearwater Lake.

believe that the two asteroids must have been orbiting around each other in a similar way to binary stars. Forming two almost perfect circles, the lakes have diameters of 26 km (16 miles) and 36 km (22 miles).

There is hardly a cloud in the sky above the barren tundra of the Labrador Peninsula, Quebec, Canada. The two meteor craters look like giant eyes. The western lake features a striking ring of islands, with the eastern lake to its side.

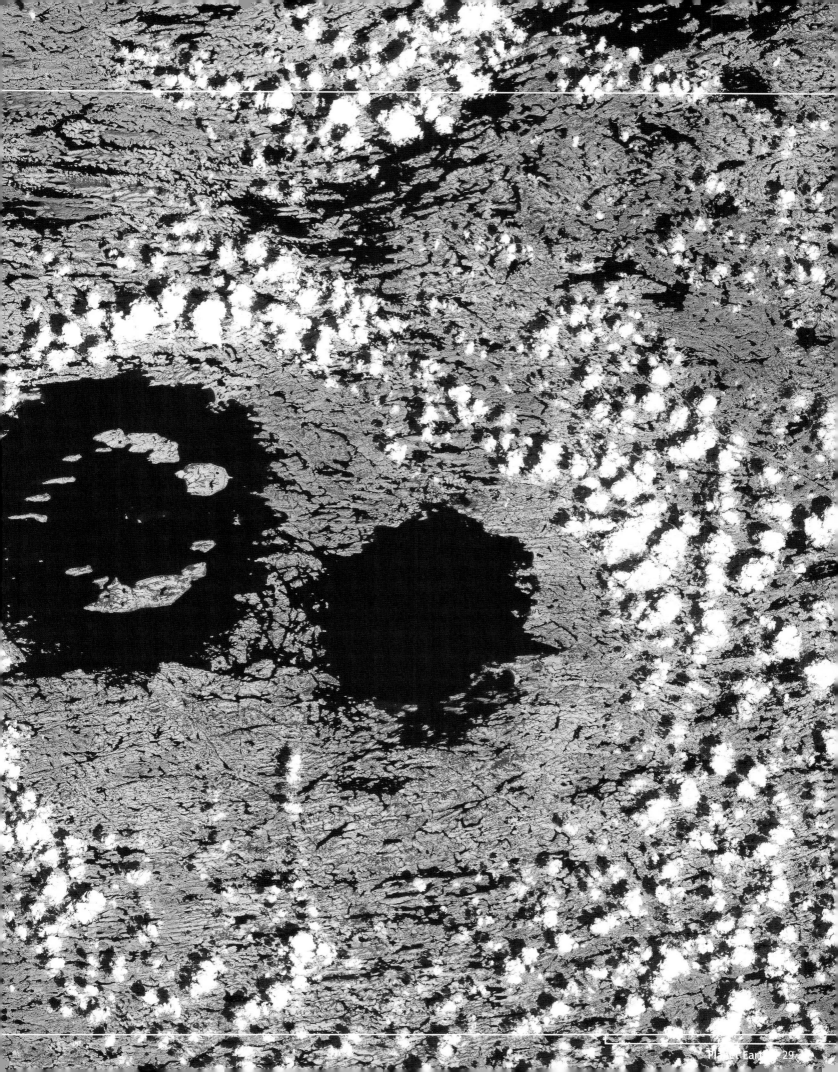

OCEANS

The oceans cover some 71% of the Earth's surface. Spanning 361 million sq. km (139 million sq. miles), they form a body of water that makes our planet look blue when seen from space. The Pacific, Atlantic, and Indian Oceans are the world's three largest seas, and together account for approximately 90% of its surface water – the Arctic Ocean and Southern Ocean make up the remaining 10%. Oceans make up 97.5% of all the Earth's water, with mainland freshwater accounting for just 2.5%. The sea has a salt content of around 3.5%, and its average depth is 3,000–4,500 m (9,800–14,750 feet). There are different types of transition from the seabed to the continents and islands, depending on the prevailing tectonics. Shelf seas are no more than 200 m (660 feet) deep, whereas escarpments and oceanic trenches can be as deep as 11,034 m (36,191 feet).

Waves are mainly created by wind. They cause the water to move in a swaying motion, without actually transporting any significant amounts of water. In a hurricane, waves can reach heights of up to 20 m (66 feet).

OCEANS BY LENGTH OF COASTLINE

❶ Pacific Ocean
135,664 km (84,298 miles)
❷ Atlantic Ocean
111,866 km (69,510 miles)
❸ Indian Ocean
66,526 km (41,337 miles)
❹ Arctic Ocean
45,387 km (28,202 miles)
❺ Southern Ocean
17,968 km (11,165 miles)

OCEANS BY SURFACE AREA AND AVERAGE DEPTH

❶ Pacific Ocean
Surface area   181,340,000 sq. km
(70,020,00 sq. miles)
Average depth 4,188 m (13,740 ft)
❷ Atlantic Ocean
Surface area   106,400,000 sq. km
(41,080,400 sq. miles)
Average depth 3,339 m (10,955 ft)
❸ Indian Ocean
Surface area   73,556,000 sq. km
(28,400,000 sq. miles)
Average depth 3,400 m (11,155 ft)
❹ Southern Ocean
Surface area   20,327,000 sq. km
(7,848,000 sq. miles)
Average depth 4,500 m (14,750 ft)
❺ Arctic Ocean
Surface area   14,090,000 sq. km
(5,440,000 sq. miles)
Average depth   1,500 m (4,900 ft)

Oceans support many different species of fish, which often swim around in large schools. *Rhinoptera* fish are found in subtropical waters. Up to 2 m (6½ feet) long, they swim in schools that can number hundreds of fish.

ARCTIC OCEAN

Perilous, inhospitable, and covered by ice, the Arctic Ocean spans an area of 14,090,000 sq. km (5,440,000 sq. miles) – making it the smallest of the world's five oceans. It is almost completely surrounded by the mainland of northern Asia,

The foaming East Siberian Sea.

North America, and Europe. Its northernmost point is an ice cap, and the ice has an average thickness of 2–4 m (6½–13 feet)

all year round. The ice is not static but drifting, its constant movement primarily caused by the sea currents and the Earth's rotation. The outer reaches of the ice cap are characterized by the weird and wonderful pack-ice landscape created by the additional factors of wind and sea erosion. Moving south, this turns into a much more open drift-ice zone of floating icebergs. Strong seasonal variations play an important role in all of these processes.

The narrow Bering Strait separates North America and Asia and connects the Arctic Ocean to the Pacific, while the Norwegian Sea provides a link to the Atlantic. Broad, flat shelf areas – especially off the Siberian coast – typify large parts of the seabed beneath the Bering Strait.

THE LARGEST MARGINAL SEAS

❶ **Barents Sea** 1,521,878 sq. km (587,600 sq. miles)
❷ **Greenland Sea** 1,084,000 sq. km (418,500 sq. miles)
❸ **Kara Sea** 880,000 sq. km (339,800 sq. miles)
❹ **Laptev Sea** 623,000 sq. km (240,500 sq. miles)
❺ **Chukchi Sea** 580,000 sq. km (224,000 sq. miles)
❻ **East Siberian Sea** 527,000 sq. km (203,500 sq. miles)
❼ **Beaufort Sea** 508,000 sq. km (196,000 sq. miles)

THE DEEPEST SEA DEPTHS

❶ **Molloy Deep** 5,608 m (18,399 feet)
❷ **Litke Deep** 5,449 m (17,877 feet)
❸ **Canadian Basin** 4,994 m (16,385 feet)
❹ **Central Arctic Basin** 3,290 m (10,794 feet)

THE BARENTS SEA: THE LARGEST MARGINAL SEA IN THE ARCTIC OCEAN

The tranquil and untouched Hornsund fjord, Spitsbergen, in Norway's Svalbard archipelago.

Mainland Europe and the Svalbard, Franz Josef Land, and Novaya Zemlya archipelagos all border the Barents Sea. The expanse of water between Norway's North Cape and Svalbard – in other words the area where the Barents Sea meets the Norwegian Sea – is large enough to allow the remnants of the warm Gulf Stream to reach this shelf sea. As a result, the Barents Sea is almost completely free of ice, and ports like Murmansk remain accessible to shipping even in winter. It is for this reason that Murmansk is the most important base of the Russian Northern Fleet.

By comparison with other parts of the Arctic Ocean, the water temperature here is relatively high. In spring, this accelerates the production of phytoplankton and so boosts the growth of zooplankton, the organisms (many invisible to the naked eye) that drift in the sea and form the primary food of the cod that are the object of large-scale fishing by both Russian and Norwegian fleets.

In the outer reaches of the Arctic Ocean, summer sees the solid layer of ice break up into ice floes, creating a drift-ice zone. Polar bears, the world's largest land-based predators, spend most of their time on the drift ice.

The geographic North Pole, in the Arctic Ocean, is the most northerly point on Earth. It is located not on dry land but on a 2–3-m (6½–10-foot) thick layer of ice that is forever moving over the 4,000-m (13,100-feet) deep ocean – making it impossible to map

An icebreaker in the Arctic Ocean.

the pole at a fixed location. This is the north end of the Earth's axis. From here, you can only look south – it is impossible to look to the east or west. The geographic North Pole is not to be confused with the magnetic North Pole, which is located in northern Canada. The phenomenon of polar day – when the Sun never sets – lasts for six months every year (21 March–23 September), with a short transition phase at the beginning and end of this period. The rest of the year experiences polar night, which means that the Sun never rises.

In summer, cracks start to appear in the layer of ice over the Arctic Ocean, creating areas of open water.

THE RACE TO THE POLE

The history of polar exploration goes back a long way. A host of researchers and adventurers were determined to be the first to reach the pole, and there was no shortage of drama and intrigue in the competition that ensued between them.

Whether or not Robert E. Peary (1856–1920) and Matthew A. Henson (1866–1955) were really the first to reach the North Pole on 6 April 1909 is a subject of considerable academic debate. The explorer Frederick Cook (1865–1940), for one, claimed to have beaten them to it by a year, although this is equally questionable.

What is certain is that Umberto Nobile, Roald Amundsen, and Lincoln Ellsworth flew over the geographic North Pole in their airship *Norge* in May 1926. In 1958, the USS Nautilus was the first submarine to get under the solid layer of ice at the North Pole – thus disproving the notion of an Arctic continent once and for all.

Polar explorer Robert Edwin Peary.

Illustration of Peary's expedition.

Polar explorer Matthew A. Henson.

Amundsen and Ellsworth look on as the *Norge* flies overhead.

A submarine emerges between the ice floes at the North Pole.

Covering an area of 106,400,000 sq. km (41,080,000 sq. miles), the Atlantic is the world's second largest ocean. It spans about a fifth of the Earth's surface, reaching from the Arctic Ocean all the way to the Southern Ocean.

The Mid-Atlantic Ridge lies more or less in the middle of the ocean. Running from north to south, at a length of some 11,000 km (6,835 miles), it is the world's longest unbroken mountain chain. In the northern hemisphere, the mountains rise above the water to form the islands of Jan Mayen and the Azores. In the southern hemisphere, the relatively small Ascension Island, Tristan da Cunha, Gough Island, and Bouvet Island are also all part of the Mid-Atlantic Ridge.

Originally, the Mid-Atlantic Ridge was no more than a small crack in the former super-continent of Pangaea. Over the course of the last 200 million years, plate tectonics have seen the continents drift further apart, so that the Atlantic Ocean has grown to a width of 5,000 km (3,100 miles), and this process is still very much ongoing. The underwater mountains are traversed by a 25–50-km (15½–31-mile) wide rift valley, where magma emerging on to the Atlantic sea floor causes it to spread out to the east and west. In the northern hemisphere, this process is occurring at a rate of around 2–3 cm (¾-1¼ inches) every year. In the southern hemisphere, the figure is approximately 4 cm (1½ inches).

THE DEEPEST SEA DEPTHS

1. **Milwaukee Deep**
   9,219 m (30,246 feet)
2. **Meteor Deep**
   8,264 m (27,113 feet)
3. **Romanche Gap**
   7,730 m (25,361 feet)
4. **Cayman Trench**
   7,686 m (25,217 feet)
5. **Cape Verde Basin**
   7,292 m (23,924 feet)
6. **Calypso Deep**
   5,267 m (17,280 feet)

Rocky cliffs like these, on the Isle of Skye in Scotland, are typical of the coastlines of western Europe.

THE LARGEST MARGINAL SEAS

1. **Sargasso Sea**   4,500,000 sq. km
   (1,737,000 sq. miles)
2. **Mediterranean Sea**
   2,966,000 sq. km
   (1,145,000 sq. miles)
3. **Caribbean Sea** 2,754,000 sq. km
   (1,063,000 sq. miles)
4. **Gulf of Mexico** 1,600,000 sq. km
   (617,700 sq. miles)
5. **Labrador Sea** 1,115,000 sq. km
   (430,500 sq. miles)
6. **Norwegian Sea** 1,100,000 sq. km
   (424,700 sq. miles)
7. **North Sea**   575,000 sq. km
   (222,000 sq. miles)
8. **Black Sea**   424,000 sq. km
   (163,700 sq. miles)
9. **Baltic Sea**   413,000 sq. km
   (159,500 sq. miles)

Drifting icebergs in the Labrador Sea, an arm of the Atlantic.

Black sand along the Norwegian Sea coast of southern Iceland.

The List-East Lighthouse on the North Sea island of Sylt.

A skerry island on the Baltic Sea coast in Södermanland, Sweden.

Mediterranean sunset on the Aegean island of Santorini.

Trunk Bay on the American Virgin Islands in the Caribbean.

THE SARGASSO SEA: THE LARGEST MARGINAL SEA IN THE ATLANTIC OCEAN

In the Sargasso Sea, warm sea currents circulate the water in a clockwise motion like a giant whirlpool. Here, calm and tranquil conditions can give way to powerful waves with very little warning. It is this fact that makes the region – which includes the Bermuda Triangle – so unpopular with seafarers.

The Sargasso Sea south of the Bermuda Islands and east of Florida.

SCORESBY SUND – THE WORLD'S LONGEST FJORD

Created by glacial movement, fjords are sea inlets that can stretch for considerable distances inland. Fjords, straits, and bays characterize the Greenland coastline.

At 314 km (195 miles), Scoresby Sund, in eastern Greenland, is the world's longest fjord. It is also the world's largest fjord system, its many subsidiary fjords and arms spanning a total area of 38,000 sq. km (14,672 sq. miles). The surrounding mountains reach elevations of up to 2,200 m (7,200 feet). To the west, Scoresby Sund spreads out into numerous smaller fjords.

Milneland is one of the islands here. Covering roughly 3,900 sq. km (1,500 sq. miles), it is Greenland's third largest island, its landscape heavily fissured and mostly glaciated. The climate in this region is truly Arctic, with long, cold winters and violent storms. The low temperatures mean that the fjord – surrounded by the mosses and lichen that are typical of the coastal tundra

vegetation – remains frozen over as late as June. Inland, giant glacial tongues sweep through the valleys, and huge icebergs that have broken off the ice drift through the fjord system. The climate of the inner Scoresby Sund is rather milder, allowing a more abundant flora to develop. Berries, heather plants, grasses, and moorland plants all flourish here.

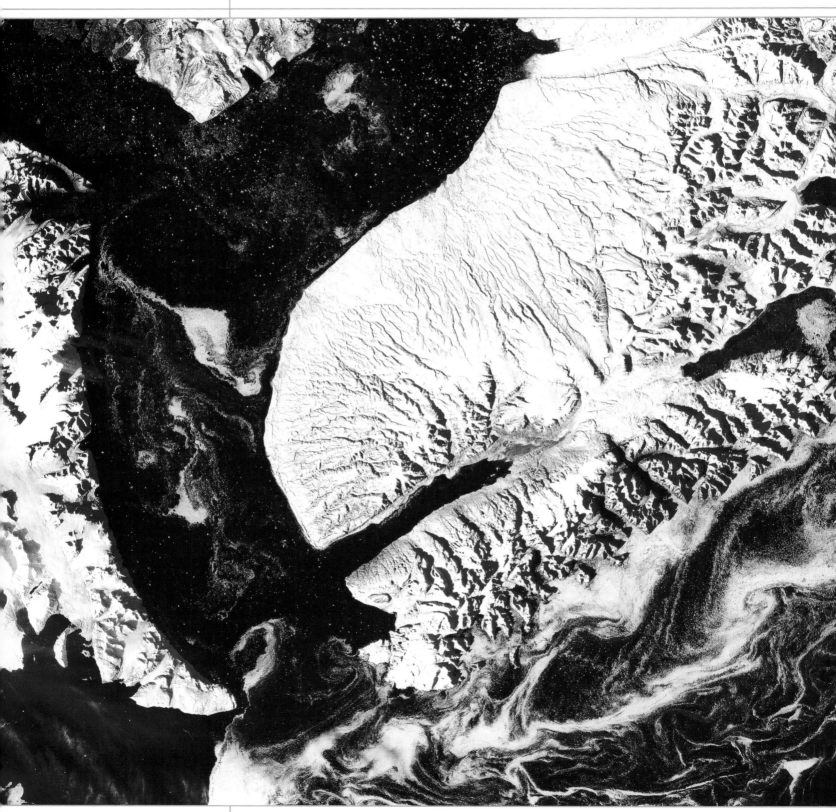

Below: This satellite image shows a section of the east coast of Greenland. Scoresby Sund is visible on the extreme left of the picture (toward the south). The Hurryfjord side arm cuts deep into the Jameson Land peninsula. Only in summer are the waters of Scoresby Sund free of ice (left).

SOGNEFJORD

SOGNEFJORD: THE WORLD'S DEEPEST FJORD

At a depth of some 1,308 m (4,291 feet), Sognefjord, in western Norway, is the world's deepest fjord. Stretching 204 km (127 miles), it is also the longest fjord system in Europe. Of its many branches, the very narrow Nærøyfjord, a UNESCO World Heritage Site, is notable for its sheer rock walls, which reach a height of 1,700 m (5,577 feet).

The Sognefjord fjord system.

Cloudy skies above the Aurlandsfjord.

The Aurlandsfjord forms the southern end of the large Sognefjord system, of which the famous Nærøyfjord is also a branch. The water is deep enough for cruise ships to sail far inland.

THE NORWEGIAN COASTLINE: THE WORLD'S LONGEST FJORD COAST

Norway has one of the world's longest and most spectacular coastlines, with countless fjords cutting into the mainland all the way from the far north of the country right down to the south. Geirangerfjord and Nærøyfjord – both UNESCO World Heritage Sites – are two of the most famous inlets. Hardangerfjord is often dubbed the queen of Norway's fjords, while the Sognefjord, Lysefjord, Nordfjord, and Trondheimfjord – all on the west coast – are also notable. Porsangerfjord and Varangerfjord are the best-known fjords in Norway's extreme north.

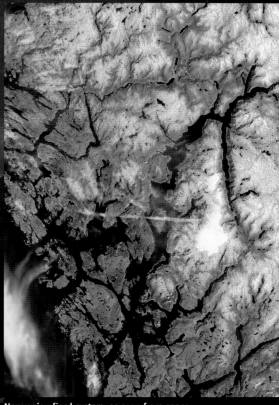

Norwegian fjord system, as seen from space.

The Wadden Sea is a part of the North Sea that stretches from the port of Den Helder in the north-west of the Netherlands to Esbjerg in western Denmark. Covering an area some 450 km (280 miles) long and 40 km (25 miles) wide, this area constitutes the world's largest unbroken system of mudflats.

Almost all of this undisturbed landscape enjoys protected status. The seabed is extremely flat, and there are long sections with hardly any inclines. The average depth of the water is 100 m (328 feet), running completely dry at low tide. Tidal gullies are a typical feature of the Wadden Sea, allowing water to flow in and out. Deposits from the rivers, the changing tides, and the almost

Morsum Cliff on the Wadden Sea on the eastern coast of Sylt has been protected since 1923.

ever-present wind mean that the sea's sediments and nutrients are constantly shifting. This ongoing process creates the sandbanks, dunes, and islands that are home to countless birds and seals, including gray seals. The loose, sandy terrain also supports many different types of plant, which help to stabilize the ground.

View of North and East Friesland, showing German Bight. The North Frisian Islands of Sylt, Föhr, Amrum, and Pellworm, as well as the Halligen islands, lie to the north. To the south, the Elbe and Weser Rivers flow into the sea. The East Frisian Islands and the Dutch Wadden Islands are further west. The light blue patches between the islands and the mainland are areas of the Wadden Sea's fine sediment, separated by the darker tidal gullies and river mouths. The very light, almost white areas are the sandbanks, beaches, and dunes along the North Sea side of the islands.

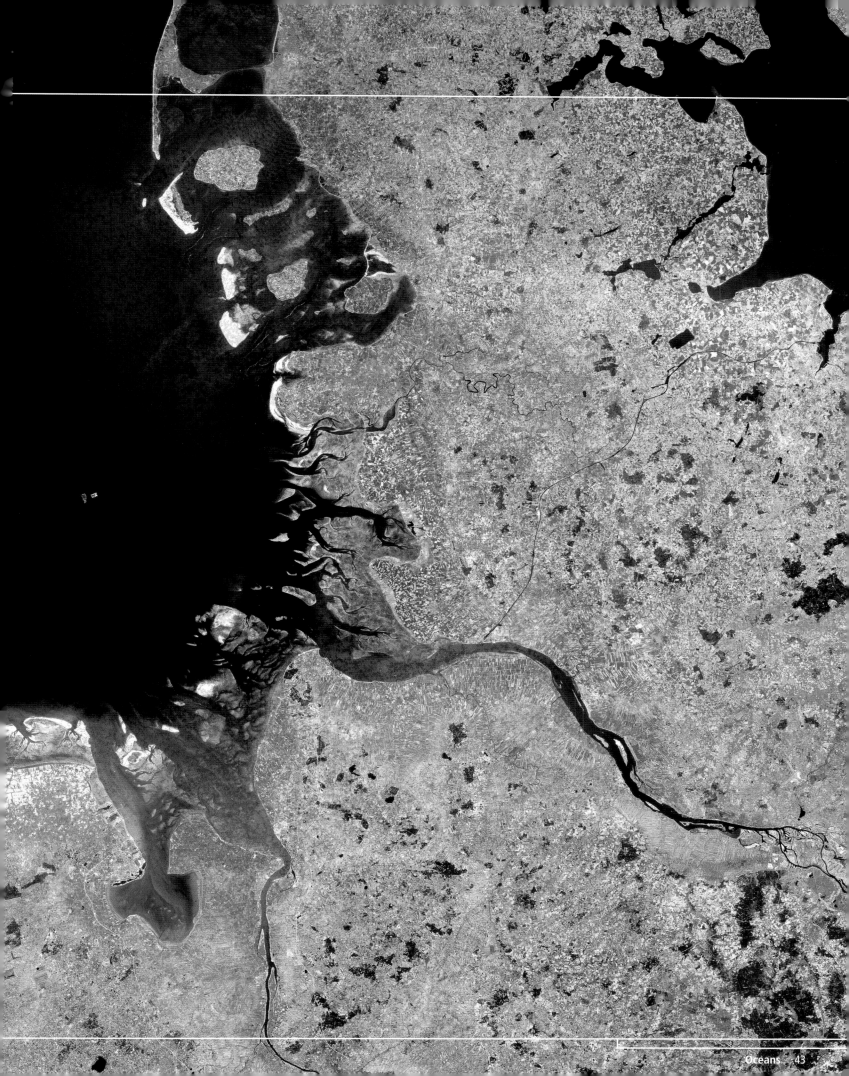

THE BAY OF FUNDY: THE WORLD'S LARGEST TIDAL RANGE

The Bay of Fundy lies between the provinces of Nova Scotia and New Brunswick on the Canadian east coast, at the end of the Gulf of Maine. It shares

Hopewell Rocks in the Bay of Fundy.

the title of the world's largest tidal range with Ungava Bay in the north of the Labrador Peninsula. At high tide, the water level in the Bay of Fundy is generally around 15–16 m (49–52 feet) higher than it is at low tide. At spring tide, this figure can rise to as much as 21 m (69 feet).

SAINT-MALO

At Saint-Malo, Brittany, France, the difference between high and low tide is about 12 m (39 feet). This tidal range is harnessed to generate electricity at the world's biggest tidal power station, which opened here on the Rance River in 1967. The 750-m (2,461-foot) long dam captures energy from the water flowing in and out of the estuary, powering 24 bulb turbines.

The estuary of the Rance River in the bay of Saint-Malo.

THE SEVERN ESTUARY

In south-west England, the River Severn flows into the Bristol Channel. At 15 m (49 feet), the tidal range in the Severn Estuary is second only to that of the Bay of Fundy. On around 130 days of every year, the tides combine with the strong south-westerly winds to create "bores" – up to 3-m (10-foot) high waves that surge up the river at speeds of up to 20 kph (13 mph).

Low tide on the Severn Estuary, Gloucestershire.

Twice a day at high tide, Hopewell Rocks disappear beneath the water. Dubbed the Flowerpot Rocks, these formations owe their characteristic shape to ongoing tidal erosion.

SALTSTRAUMEN: THE WORLD'S STRONGEST TIDAL CURRENT

Where only a narrow channel connects the sea to large bays and inlets, and where there is a relatively high tidal range, the water tries to level out. It forces its way through the channel as if breaking through a dam, forming what look like horizontal waterfalls. This phenomenon, known as a maelstrom, can be observed near Bodø in northern Norway. Saltstraumen is the world's strongest tidal current. The raging water rushes in and out of the bay at high and low tide respectively, creating powerful whirlpools. It is not unusual for volumes of up to 400 cu. m (14,000 cu. feet) of water to reach speeds of up to 40 km/h (25 mph). Further north, the Mokstraumen lies between the islands of Moskenesøya and Værøy in the Lofoten archipelago. It is the world's second strongest tidal current.

Not far from the city of Bodø, Saltstraumen is the world's strongest tidal current.

INDIAN OCEAN

The Indian Ocean is the world's third largest ocean, and the topography of its sea floor is complex. The seabed is divided into large basins by the plate boundaries along the Central, Southwest, and Southeast Indian Ridges. These basins are themselves divided into a

The Seychelles, Indian Ocean.

series of smaller plateaus and trenches.

Water currents in the Indian Ocean vary. North of the equator, monsoon winds drive the current toward Africa in the winter and toward India in the summer – bringing heavy downpours. South of the equator, there is almost no wind in the "Horse" latitudes, but the so-called "Roaring Forties" latitudes, lying at 40–50° south, fall within the West Wind Drift. Here, the prevailing westerly winds range from strong to stormy.

THE LARGEST MARGINAL SEAS

① **Arabian Sea** 3,862,000 sq. km
(1,491,000 sq. miles)
② **Bay of Bengal** 2,127,000 sq. km
(821,200 sq. miles)
③ **Great Australian Bight**
1,306,000 sq. km
(504,250 sq. miles)
④ **Andaman** 798,000 sq. km
(308,100 sq. miles)
⑤ **Red Sea** 527,000 sq. km
(203,500 sq. miles)
⑥ **Gulf of Aden** 279,000 sq. km
(107,700 sq. miles)
⑦ **Persian Gulf** 239,000 sq. km
(92,300 sq. miles)
⑧ **Gulf of Oman** 108,000 sq. km
(41,700 sq. miles)
⑨ **Timor Sea** 61,500 sq. km
(23,750 sq. miles)

THE DEEPEST SEA DEPTHS

① **Diamantina Deep**
8,047 m (26,401 feet)
② **Sunda Trench**
7,258 m (23,812 feet)
③ **North-west Australian Basin**
7,000 m (22,966 feet)
④ **North Australian Basin**
6,840 m (22,441 feet)
⑤ **Madagascar Basin**
6,500 m (21,325 feet)
⑥ **Fosse de Jeffreys**
5,998 m (19,678 feet)

There are countless tropical islands in the Indian Ocean. This one is in the Maldives.

THE ARABIAN SEA: THE LARGEST MARGINAL SEA IN THE INDIAN OCEAN

The Arabian Sea covers an area of approximately 3.86 million sq. km (1.49 million sq. miles) between the Arabian Peninsula, the Horn of Africa, and the Indian subcontinent. In summer, the difference between the temperature on the mainland and at sea causes the south-west monsoon – giving the countries of India and Pakistan some of the heaviest downpours on Earth.

View of Goa's Konkan Coast, on the Arabian Sea. Goa is the smallest of India's states.

Boats in the Gulf of Thailand, a shallow inlet of the South China Sea.

The coast of Sinai on the Red Sea. The sea separates the Arabian Peninsula from Africa.

The Twelve Apostles, limestone pillars on Australia's south coast, are up to 60 m (197 feet) high.

PACIFIC OCEAN

THE LARGEST MARGINAL SEAS

❶ **Australasian Mediterranean Sea,**
Western Pacific   9,080,000 sq. km
(3,506,000 sq. miles)

❷ **Philippine Sea,**
Western Pacific   c. 5,000,000 sq. km
(c. 1,930,000 sq. miles)

❸ **Coral Sea,**
South-west Pacific   4,791,000 sq. km
(1,850,000 sq. miles)

❹ **Bering Sea,**
North Pacific   2,300,000 sq. km
(888,000 sq. miles)

❺ **Tasman Sea,**
South-west Pacific   2,300,000 sq. km
(888,000 sq. miles)

❻ **Gulf of Alaska,**
North Pacific   1,533,000 sq. km
(592,000 sq. miles)

❼ **Sea of Okhotsk,**
North Pacific   1,530,000 sq. km
(590,700 sq. miles)

❽ **East China Sea,**
Western Pacific   1,250,000 sq. km
(482,600 sq. miles)

❾ **Sea of Japan,**
Western Pacific   1,049,000 sq. km
(405,000 sq. miles)

❿ **Gulf of California,**
Eastern Pacific   160,000 sq. km
(61,800 sq. miles)

THE AUSTRALASIAN MEDITERRANEAN SEA: THE LARGEST MARGINAL SEA IN THE PACIFIC OCEAN

Junks in Ha Long Bay, in the Gulf of Tonkin, Vietnam.

The Australasian Mediterranean Sea refers to all the marginal seas of the Pacific Ocean in Southeast Asia. It includes the Java, Banda, South China, and Sulu seas, among others. Its islands border the Indian Ocean, and its broad straits meet the Pacific Ocean. These are tropical waters, with a correspondingly diverse flora and fauna, and there are coral reefs of varying size throughout. The western part of the Australasian Mediterranean Sea features large, relatively shallow shelf areas, whereas large basins with depths of up to 7,440 m (24,409 feet) dominate its eastern part.

The mountainous Aleutian Islands on the southern edge of the Bering Sea.

Cabo San Lucas lies at the southern tip of the Baja California peninsula.

The Pacific Ocean and its marginal seas cover a total area of 181,340,000 sq. km (70,020,000 sq. miles) – a little over a third of the Earth's surface. The marginal seas, divided from the rest of the ocean by islands and island chains, are almost all located in the western part of the Pacific, where the sea floor – with its deep-sea trenches and oceanic ridges – is particularly interesting. Challenger Deep, in the Mariana Trench, is the deepest point of all the world's oceans. The eastern Pacific seabed, meanwhile, lacks the variety found in the west. Its main feature, the East Pacific Rise, runs from southern California to the Antarctic, but beyond this there are only a series of fracture zones and a small number of islands.

The 200–300 islands of Palau form the westernmost island group of the Caroline Islands archipelago, in the Pacific Ocean.

THE DEEPEST MANNED DIVE

In January 1960, the bathyscaphe *Trieste* – a diving vessel specially designed for deep-sea exploration (right) – reached a depth of 10,916 m (35,814 feet) in the Mariana Trench. Aboard were the Swiss scientist Jacques Piccard and his American companion Don Walsh. The floating bathyscaphe descends below the water surface when its tanks are filled with seawater. The small white chamber at the bottom of the vessel accommodates the crew, withstanding vast pressures of more than 1 tonne per sq. cm (7 short tons per sq. inch). Following Piccard and Walsh's expedition, the place at which they dived was named Trieste Depth.

THE DEEPEST SEA DEPTHS

① Vitiaz Deep I	11,034 m	
Mariana Trench	(36,201 feet)	
② Trieste Depth	10,916 m	
Mariana Trench	(35,814 feet)	
③ Challenger Deep	10,899 m	
Mariana Trench	(35,758)	
④ Vitiaz Deep II	10,882 m	
Tonga Trench	(35,701)	
⑤ Horizon Deep	10,542 m	
Tonga Trench	(35,702 feet)	
⑥ Galathea Deep	10,540 m	
Philippine Trench	(34,580 feet)	

Corals look like little underwater flowers and their colorful variety captivates divers; however, they are not submarine plants but fixed colonies of tiny organisms, deriving nourishment from micro-plankton, which they filter from seawater with their tentacles. The corals

Stony corals on the Great Barrier Reef.

that create reefs are called *Scleratinia*, and these form a kind of skeleton from deposits of calcium carbonate. Discarded skeletal material is continually overgrown with fresh coral and complicated reef systems soon build up. The colonies require clear water with a maximum depth of about 60 m (200 feet) and sea temperatures between 18 and 35°C (64 and 95°F). Such conditions are only found in the tropical and subtropical zones between the 25th parallels north and south of the equator. The largest and most famous coral reef of this kind is the Great Barrier Reef off the east coast of Australia. Apart from the stony, reef-forming corals there is a myriad of soft coral species, some of which are also found in deep water.

Soft corals are just one of 6,000 subspecies of the so-called cnidarians (*Anthozoa*). These four pictures from the Red Sea and the Western Pacific hardly do justice to the astonishing diversity of the world of corals.

Large image: *Anthomastus ritteri* is a deep-water coral living off the coast of California and Mexico at depths between 400–1,200 m (1,300–4,000 feet).

The ecological diversity and importance of coral reefs often invites comparison with tropical rainforests. To understand their significance, you need only consider two remarkable statistics: coral reefs make up just 0.015% of the world's oceans, yet they are home to

Coral reefs are home to many fish.

over 25% of its marine life. The complexity of this fascinating marine ecosystem stems not just from the diverse corals of many hues, but also the algae, fish, crabs, mussels, and other organisms with which they share the biotope. Their neighbors are often their prey, and life in this symbiotic system is finely balanced. The various hues serve to lure, deceive, and disguise – either as a means of finding food, or to avoid becoming it. This is a world of hunting and shameless feasting. Each species has developed its own survival and procreation strategy, and this is what makes the coral reefs so complicated and, at the same time, so vulnerable. The rising sea level and water temperature are particular grounds for concern, since these can lead to the dreaded phenomenon of coral bleaching – the whitening of coral reefs under stress.

THE WORLD'S LARGEST CORAL REEFS

❶ Great Barrier Reef,
Australia   348,700 sq. km
                      (134,600 sq. miles)
❷ New Caledonia Barrier Reef,
New Caledonia   15,743 sq. km
                      (6,077 sq. miles)
❸ Andros,
Bahamas   6,000 sq. km
                      (2,316 sq. miles)
❹ Belize Barrier Reef,
Belize   963 sq. km
                      (372 sq. miles)
❺ East Rennell,
Solomon Islands   370 sq. km
                      (143 sq. miles)
❻ Tubbataha Reef,
Philippines   332 sq. km
                      (128 sq. miles)

THE GREAT BARRIER REEF: THE WORLD'S LARGEST CORAL REEF

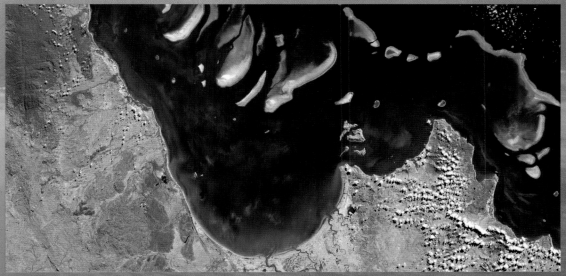

Satellite image showing a section of the Great Barrier Reef north of Princess Charlotte Bay and Cape Melville.

There are some 3,000 individual reefs and about 900 islands off the coast of Queensland, in north-eastern Australia. What the Australian Aborigines called Waga Gaboo (meaning "The Big Reef") stretches out for over 2,500 km (1,550 miles). It covers an area almost as large as Germany, spanning 348,700 sq. km (134,600 sq. miles). This is the largest structure on Earth built by microscopically small creatures. Countless polyps produce some 4 tonnes (4.4 short tons) of skeletal limestone every day. This giant biotope supports over 4,000 mollusk species, 300 types of coral, some 1,500 species of fish, and countless shear-waters, brown boobies, frigate birds, and other bird species.

The Great Blue Hole is an incredible feature of the Belize Barrier Reef. The vertical reef walls create a submarine doline with its associated caves.

ATOLLS

An atoll is a circular coral reef that surrounds a lagoon. Found only in the tropical waters of the Pacific and Indian Oceans, most atolls are the result of volcanic activity and plate tectonics. Atolls only have a small land area, with little or no freshwater, and the small islands within them are almost all uninhabited.

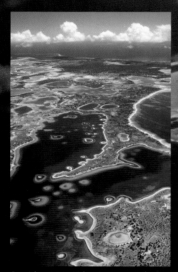

Covering 321 sq. km (124 sq. miles), Kiritimati (or Christmas Island) has a larger land area than any of the world's other atolls. Located close to the equator, it is part of the Republic of Kiribati in the Line Islands.

Bora Bora is one of the Society Islands of French Polynesia. This aerial image shows the mountain in the middle of the atoll and the circular coral reef around it. The numerous long, narrow islands are called *motu* – the Polynesian word for "island".

THE LARGEST ATOLLS
Total area (lagoon and reef)

① **Thiladhunmathi-Miladhunmadulu Atoll,** Maldives   3,850 sq. km
(1,486 sq. miles)

② **Chesterfield Islands,** New Caledonia   3,500 sq. km
(1,351 sq. miles)

③ **Huvadhu Atoll,** Maldives   3,152 sq. km
(1,217 sq. miles)

④ **Chuuk Atoll,** Caroline Islands   3,130 sq. km
(1,208 sq. miles)

⑤ **Sabalana Inlands,** Indonesia   2,694 sq. km
(1,040 sq. miles)

⑥ **Lihou Reef,** Coral Sea   2,529 sq. km
(976 sq. miles)

⑦ **Ardasier Reef,** Spratly Islands   2,347 sq. km
(906 sq. miles)

⑧ **Kwajalein Atoll,** Marshall Inlands   2,304 sq. km
(889 sq. miles)

⑨ **Namonuito Atoll,** Caroline Islands   2,267 sq. km
(875 sq. miles)

⑩ **Ari Atoll,** Maldives   2,252 sq. km
(869 sq. miles)

THE MALDIVES

There are some 1,200 coral islands in the Maldives, spread over 26 atolls. The islands are formed from the now extinct volcanoes along the Central Indian Ridge, and none rise more than 2 m (6½ feet) above the ocean surface. The atolls line up alongside one another like a marine string of pearls. The deepest waters look dark blue, the shallower areas turquoise. There are still large areas of coral beneath the water's surface. Each atoll has a light, coral sand beach on the side facing out to sea. Inside, the atolls surround lagoons. Even at night, average temperatures do not drop below 25°C (77°F), and this tropical climate promotes the growth of corals. This complicated ecosystem is also a very fragile one, however, and the Asian tsunami of 2004 caused devastating damage to the underwater world. If the water temperature becomes too high, the process known as coral bleaching sets in, and the anthozoans die out.

The enormous Thiladhunmathi-Miladhunmadulu Atoll in the Maldives is the world's largest. With its lagoon and reef, the atoll covers an area of 3,850 sq. km (1,486 sq. miles). The total land area is 51 sq. km (20 sq. miles).

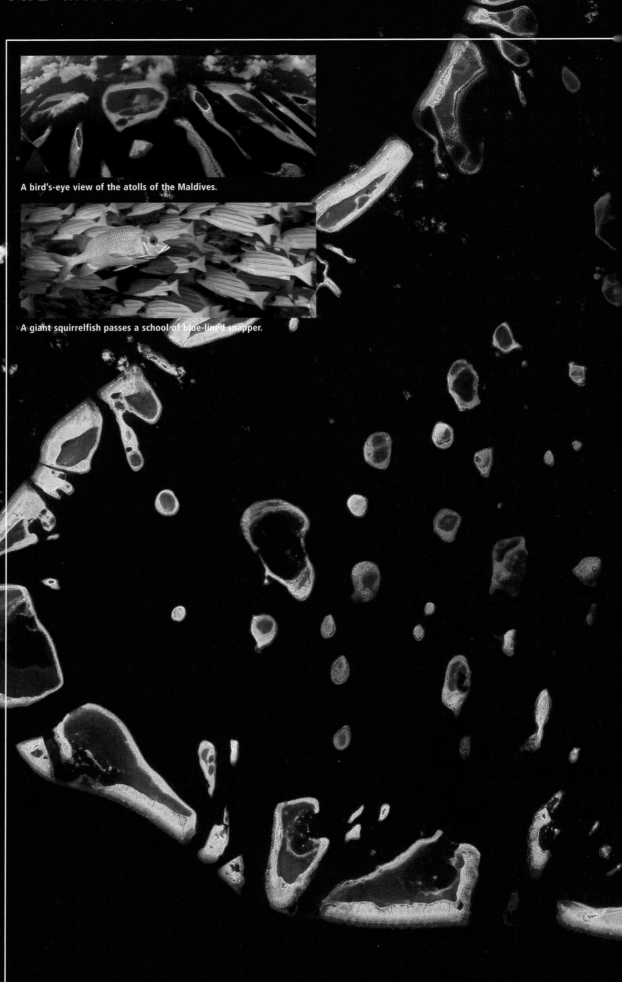

A bird's-eye view of the atolls of the Maldives.

A giant squirrelfish passes a school of blue-lined snapper.

This view from space shows part of the
North Male Atoll, north of Male, the
capital of the Maldives. It has a total
area of 1,565 sq. km (604 sq. miles).

Seals in the Weddell Sea.

Strange as it may seem, the Southern Ocean has only been delimited since the year 2000, when the International Hydrographic Organization defined it as the waters south of the 60th parallel, which were areas previously considered part of the Atlantic, Pacific, and Indian Oceans. The Southern Ocean covers an area of 20,327,000 sq. km (7,848,000 sq. miles), making it the second smallest of the world's oceans. It completely surrounds the fifth and coldest of the continents, namely Antarctica.

THE LARGEST MARGINAL SEAS

1. Weddell Sea   2,800,000 sq. km
(1,081,000 sq. miles)
2. Bellings-   1,500,000 sq. km
hausen Sea   (579,000 sq. miles)
3. Ross Sea   960,000 sq. km
(370,600 sq. miles)
4. Dumont-   950,000 sq. km
d'Urville Sea   (366,800 sq. miles)
5. Davis Sea   900,000 sq. km
(347,500 sq. miles)
6. Amundsen Sea   770,000 sq. km
(297,300 sq. miles)
7. Cooperation Sea   230,000 sq. km
(88,800 sq. miles)

THE DEEPEST SEA DEPTHS

1. Bellingshausen Sea
4,830 m (15,846 feet)
2. Dumont d'Urville Sea
4,725 m (15,502 feet)
3. Amundsen Sea
4,460 m (14,633 feet)
4. Ross Sea
4,175 m (13,698 feet)
5. Weddell Sea
4,037 m (13,245 feet)
6. Cooperation Sea
3,500 m (11,483 feet)
7. Davis Sea
3,082 m (10,112 feet)

Icebergs are a typical feature of the Southern Ocean, especially the tabular icebergs that calve off ice shelves. They are the first port of call for hungry penguins, but they can also hinder birds searching for food.

THE WEDDELL SEA: THE LARGEST MARGINAL SEA IN THE SOUTHERN OCEAN

The Weddell Sea and part of the Ronne ice shelf, east of the Antarctic Peninsula.

Covering an area of 2.8 million sq. km (1.08 million sq. miles), the Weddell Sea is the largest marginal sea of the Southern Ocean. It spans a distance of 2,000 km (1,250 miles) between the Antarctic Peninsula in the west and the coast of Coats Land in the east, meeting the Ronne-Filchner ice shelf to the south. It reaches depths of up to 4,037 m (13,245 feet). Much of the surface is permanently covered by pack ice, especially on the lee side of the Antarctic Peninsula. The currents of the Weddell Sea move ice toward the peninsula, the tides turning clockwise to push ice coming from the north first toward the south, and then west toward the peninsula.

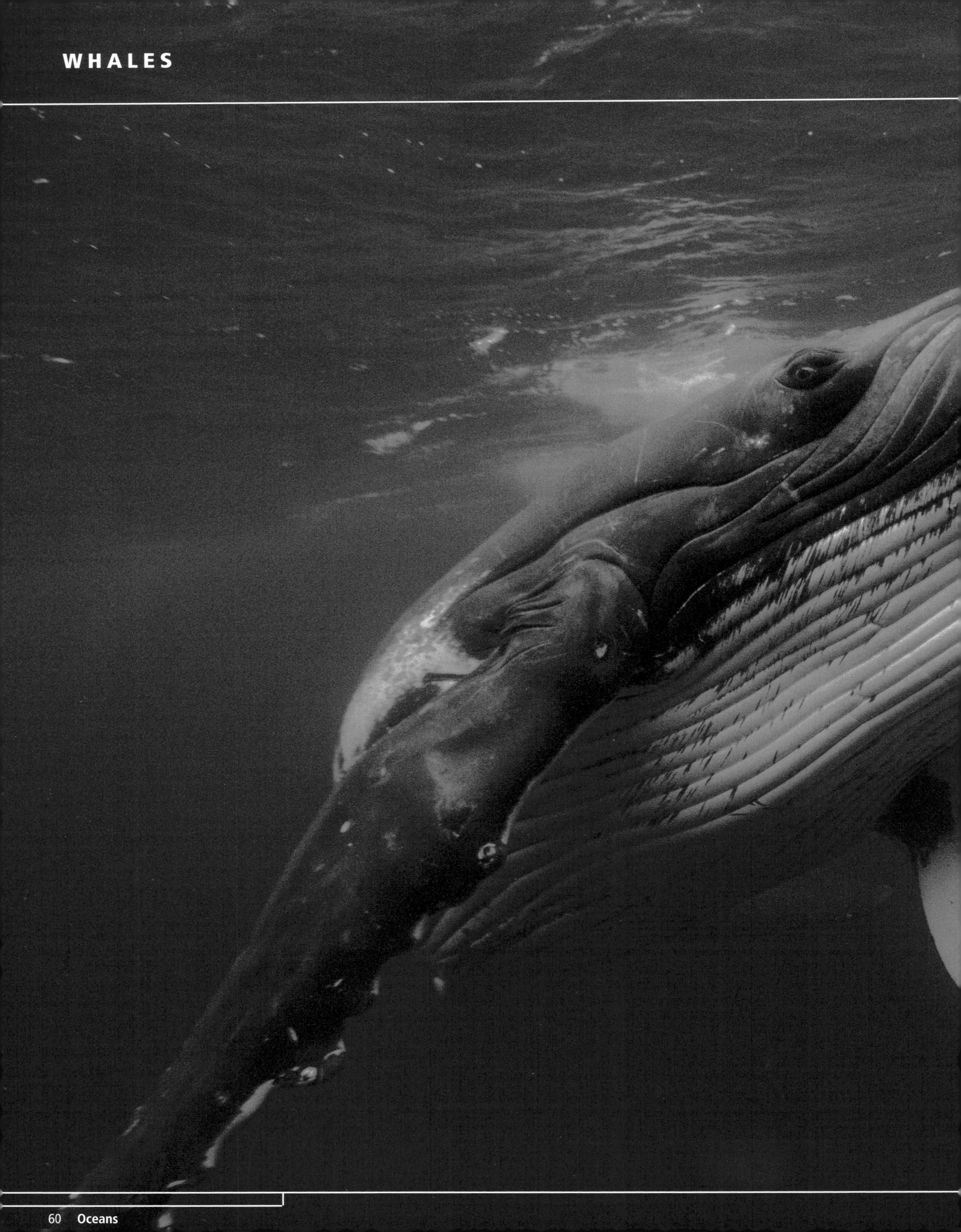

Two majestic blue whales off the Pacific coast of California.

DIVING RECORD

Whales are magnificent divers, and blue whales can reach depths of up to 300 m (980 feet) – despite surfacing for air after 20 minutes. The real record holder is the sperm whale, which can dive 3,200 m (10,500 feet) and stay submerged for 90 minutes. Usually, though, it dives to depths of 300–600 m (980–1,970 feet) – about the same depth as reached by submarines.

The sperm whale holds the world record for deep-sea diving. This one is about to go up for air on the sea surface.

There are nearly 90 different species of whale, divided into the suborders of baleen and toothed whales – the latter of which also includes dolphins. The largest whales, however, all come under the baleen *(Mysticeti)* category, notably the blue whale, which – at lengths of up to 33 m (108 feet) – is the largest animal on Earth. These animals use their beards to filter the small crustaceans that are the mainstay of their diet from the seawater. Toothed whales *(Odontoceti)*, meanwhile, use their teeth to catch their prey – although not to break it up into smaller pieces or chew it. Toothed whales mostly eat fish. All whales are mammals, breathing air and giving birth to fully developed calves. They are highly social creatures and live in groups, communicating with one another by means of their mysterious whale song.

THE LARGEST WHALES

❶ Blue whale
Length	24–33 m (79–108 ft)
Weight	100–120 t (110–132 sts)

❷ Fin whale
Length	18–22 m (59–72 ft)
Weight	30–80 t (33–88 sts)

❸ Bowhead whale
Length	11–18 m (45–59 ft)
Weight	20–50 t (66–110 sts)

❹ Right whale
Length	14–18 m (36–59 ft)
Weight	60–100 t (33–88 sts)

❺ Sperm whale
Length	11–18 m (36–59 ft)
Weight	30–80 t (22–55 sts)

❻ Sei whale
Length	12–16 m (39–52 ft)
Weight	20–30 t (22–33 sts)

❼ Gray whale
Length	12–15 m (39–49 ft)
Weight	14–35 t (15-38 sts)

❽ Humpback whale
Length	11–15 m (36–49 ft)
Weight	25–30 t (28–33 sts)

The humpback whale has unusually long and narrow pectoral fins. This great mammal often has barnacles on both its fins and head.

* Weight   t= tonnes   sts= short tons

BASKING SHARK

Length	up to 15 m (50 feet)
Weight	up to 7 tonnes
	(7.7 short tons)

Despite their terrifying size, basking sharks (*Cetorhinus maximus*) are not predators and present no danger to humans. They are the second-largest fish species on earth after whale sharks, and feed on the plankton they passively filter from seawater, which flows through their open mouths and over their gills. Up to 2,000 tonnes (2,200 short tons) of seawater an hour can flow through a basking shark's mouth. The outsize gill slits required for this almost completely encircle the head and are a distinguishing feature of the species. The basking shark is principally to be found in the temperate to warm waters of the Atlantic and Pacific Oceans and has been recorded both as single specimens and in groups of up to a hundred or more. The basking shark population is much threatened by hunting, and the animal's liver, which can make up to 30% percent of its weight, is the greatest prize. A fully grown specimen can yield up to 1,500 l (400 US gallons) of shark liver oil.

The basking shark (*Centorhinus maximus*) throws open its mouth to filter plankton and tiny organisms from the water that flows across its gills (above and large image).

WHALE SHARK

Length	up to 18 m (60 feet)
Weight	up to 13 tonnes (14.3 short tons)

The whale shark (*Rhincodon typus*) is the world's largest fish and a giant among marine animals. Living in groups known as "shivers" in the tropical and subtropical ocean regions to the north and south of the equator, it has the most fearsome dentition of any creature on earth, with many hundreds of teeth arranged in 300 rows. Quite what these are for is unclear, as it is a plankton-eater like the basking shark. The only difference is that the whale shark actively draws water into its mouth, for which purpose it often swims into a vertical position and closes its mouth to swallow its prey. Whale sharks can live to an age of 100, reaching sexual maturity at 10. Little is known of their reproductive habits, but it has been conjectured that a female can carry in her body up to 300 young at various stages of development.

GREAT WHITE SHARK

Length	up to 8 m (27 feet)
Weight	up to 3 tonnes (3.3 short tons)

After starring in Steven Spielberg's dramatic film *Jaws*, the great white shark (*Carcharodon carcharias*) is regarded as the most fearsome and frightening of all the shark species. Seen from below, surfers and swimmers look like seals, the shark's natural prey, and the resulting "shark attacks" are not a question of aggression or malice on the part of the shark – it is merely following its hunting instinct. The endangered great white shark is to be found in small concentrations in all the world's oceans, and its social conduct is only imperfectly understood.

Whale sharks patrolling (top), with their young (middle), and feeding on plankton (below).

The great white seeks its prey just beneath the surface of the water (top); (below) its terrifying jaws.

THE ORCA

An orca cow with her young calf. Orcas can swim at speeds of up to 55 km/h (34 mph), making them the oceans' fastest known mammal.

The orca *(Orcinus orca)* is the largest species of dolphin, and also a member of the suborder of toothed whales. Weighing in at 5–9 tonnes (5.5–10 short tons), they are 6–8 m (20–26 feet) long, and have a tall dorsal fin. They are found throughout the world's oceans, but are mostly concentrated in cooler waters. Orcas live for approximately 50 to 80 years and are divided into sedentary and migratory groups. Sedentary orcas stick to familiar waters, often in groups of over 50 animals, and primarily feed on fish. Migratory orcas, meanwhile, roam the seas in small groups of five to ten animals. Fast swimmers, they are adept at catching large prey, and do not hesitate to hunt blue whales – even though these are much bigger than the orcas themselves. Working in teams, the animals' hunting techniques are quite astounding. In the Antarctic, they catch penguins and seals by literally tipping them off the ice sheets. In Patagonia, they throw themselves on to the beaches to catch sea lions, and in the waters around New Zealand, they can even overcome sharks with a powerful blow of their tail fin. It is these daring hunting methods that have earned the orca the names "killer whale" and even "murder whale".

During the breeding period, the bulls leave their groups. They will return to their families at a later date, but this strategy ensures that inbreeding is avoided. Conflicts between bulls are not a feature of orca society, and, in the course of their evolution, the orcas have apparently learned to resolve their conflicts without violence, cooperating with one another instead.

Orcas live in matriarchal family groups. Once sexually mature, they breed every five or six years. The matriarch carries her young for 15 months. Having given birth to her calf, the mother then teaches it a wide range of hunting methods. Though the orcas are highly intelligent creatures, it still takes several years to turn the young animal into a daring and successful hunter. The high-frequency clicking and whistling sounds commonly known as whale song are orcas' means of acoustic communication.

Top: An orca off the Kenai Peninsula, Alaska. Above: A sea lion on the beach is easy pickings for an orca.

Orcas jumping out of the water are said to be "breaching". Scientists suspect this to be a display of power.

...ne area of the Earth that rises above sea level – and makes up 30% of the planet's surface – can be divided into landmasses that are more or less completely sepa-rated from each other by expans-es of water, and these masses are referred to as continents -– derived from the Latin *terra continens*, meaning "continuous land". Although there is essentially no difference between an island and a continent – both are areas of

...ropical landscape in Costa Rica.

...and surrounded by water – geo-scientists have agreed to use the term "continent" for areas of land above a certain size. However, there is no consensus to date on the number of continents that exist. Those who consider Europe and Asia – the separation of which is purely historical and cultural – and North and South America as continuous landmasses count five continents (Eurasia, Africa, Amer-ca, Australia, and Antarctica), while others think there are six, counting North and South America as separate continents. For many, seven regions are commonly regarded as continents: Europe, Asia, Africa, North America, South America, Australia, and Antarctica. While the distribution of oceans and landmasses seems relatively stable today, geologically their current position represents just a snapshot in time as the continen-tal plates are continually moving.

CONTINENTS BY SURFACE AREA

1	Asia	44.4 million sq. km (17 million sq. miles)
2	Africa	30.3 million sq. km (11.7 million sq. miles)
3	North America	24.9 million sq. km (9.6 million sq. miles)
4	South America	17.8 million sq. km (6.9 million sq. miles)
5	Antarctica	13.2 million sq. km (5.1 million sq. miles)
6	Europe	10.5 million sq. km (4.1 million sq. miles)
7	Australia	8.5 million sq. km (3.3 million sq. miles)

CONTINENTS BY LENGTH OF COASTLINE

1	North America	75,600 km (47,000 miles)
2	Asia	69,000 km (42,900 miles)
3	Europe	37,900 km (23,500 miles)
4	Africa	30,500 km (19,000 miles)
5	South America	28,700 km (17,800 miles)
6	Australia	25,000 km (15,500 miles)
7	Antarctica	18,000 km (11,200 miles)

Mesa Arch in Canyonlands National Park, south-eastern Utah, one of the many natural stone arches created through the process of erosion. The national park covers an enormous expanse of desert mesa consisting primarily of horizontal sandstone layers between 150 and 300 million years old. The density of the sandstone varies, so it erodes at different rates, giving rise to impressive stone formations such as arches and columns. The canyons were created by river, soil, and vertical erosion.

EUROPE

With a total surface area of around 10.5 million sq. km (4.1 million sq. miles), Europe is the second smallest continent and makes up 7% of the Earth's land area. The nations of Europe are home to around 12% of the world's population, or approximately 700 million people.

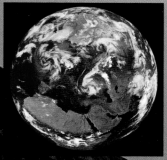

View of Europe and North Africa.

Europe is located in the northern hemisphere and the continent is bordered to the north by the North Sea, to the west by the Atlantic Ocean, and to the south by the Mediterranean. Its coastline measures a total length of 37,900 km (23,500 miles).

EUROPE'S GEOGRAPHIC SUPERLATIVES

❶ Expanse:
North–south
  3,800 km (2,400 miles)
East–west 6,000 km (3,700 miles)

❷ Northernmost point:
Cape Nordkinn, Norway
71° 8′ N, 27° 39′ E

❸ Southernmost point:
Punta de Tarifa, Spain
36° 0′ N, 5° 36′ W

❹ Westernmost point:
Cape Roca, Portugal
38° 46′ N, 9° 30′ W

❺ Easternmost point:
Ural Mountains, Russia – 67° E

❻ Highest mountain:
Caucasus Mountains, Mount Elbrus
  5,642 m (18,510 feet)
Alps, Mont Blanc 4,807 m
  (15,771 feet)

❼ Lowest point:
Caspian Sea -28 m (-92 feet)

❽ Longest river:
Volga 3.534 km (2,196 miles)

❾ Largest lake:
Lake Ladoga 17,703 sq. km
  (6,835 sq. miles)

❿ Deepest lake:
Hornindalsvatnet, Norway 514 m
  (1,686 feet)

⓫ Largest island:
Great Britain 229,883 sq. km
  (88,758 sq. miles)

The European continent is part of the Eurasian landmass and accounts for one-fifth of its western surface area. However, historically and culturally Europe is perceived as an independent continent. While the other continents have marine borders, no eastern boundary to Europe has been internationally defined, making it a matter of convention – generally, the eastern limit of Europe is accepted as the Ural Mountains. Geographically, either the Kuma-Manych Depression, 300 km (186 miles) north of the Caucasus Mountains, or the Caucasus Mountains themselves are considered to be the border with Asia in the south-east. The topography of the European continent – the most subdivided continent – is so heterogeneous that this relatively small continent can be separated into many different natural landscapes: mountain ranges and valleys, lowlands and uplands, and jagged coastlines with many islands – Europe is the continent with most peninsulas – all are found here. The landscape of northern Europe was mainly formed during the ice ages and is characterized by jagged coasts in the north-west, barren plateaus, mountain ranges, and flat lake-dotted regions. It is linked to the mid-European ridge, with the wooded uplands, hilly countryside, and dells of western and central Europe. The southern European peninsulas – the Peloponnese, Iberian, and Apennine – are home to the high fold mountains of the Pyrenees, Alps, and Carpathian Mountains. Highlands and plateaus are also found in the south. The landscape of eastern Europe features the East European Plain, which stretches to the Ural Mountains and river, and as far as the Arctic Ocean in the north. Europe is the continent with the greatest variety of landscapes in the smallest area.

Its striking shape makes the Matterhorn, a Swiss landmark, one of the most famous mountains in the world.

Cliffs, small bays, and coastal islands typify the west coast of Ireland.

ASIA

With a surface area of 44.4 million sq. km (17 million sq. miles), or almost one-third of the land surface area of the Earth, Asia is the largest of the continents. Asia is also the most densely populated, with more

View of Asia and the Indian Ocean.

than 3.7 billion inhabitants – around three-fifths of the global population. Most of Asia is in the northern hemisphere, with only the Southeast Asian island area extending over the equator. Asia is bordered to the north by the Arctic Ocean, to the west by the Pacific Ocean, to the south-east toward Australia by the Molucca Sea and Banda Sea, and to the south by the Indian Ocean.

ASIA'S GEOGRAPHIC SUPERLATIVES

❶ Expanse:
North–south
8,500 km (5,300 miles)
East–west 11,000 km (6,800 miles)
❷ Northernmost point:
Cape Chelyuskin, Russia
77° 43' N
❸ Southernmost point:
Cape Buru, Malaysia – 1° 25' N
❹ Westernmost point:
Cape Baba, Turkey – 26° 3' E
❺ Easternmost point:
Cape Dezhnev, Russia – 169° 4' W
❻ Highest mountain:
Himalayas, Mount Everest
8,850 m (29,035 feet)
❼ Lowest point:
Dead Sea   -400 m (-1,312 feet)
❽ Longest river:
Yangtze River
6,380 km (3,964 miles)
❾ Largest lake:
Caspian Sea   371,000 sq. km
(143,245 sq. miles)
❿ Deepest lake:
Lake Baikal, Russia   1,637 m
(5,371 feet)
⓫ Largest island:
Borneo   748,168 sq. km
(288,869 sq. miles)

Asia is separated from America by the Bering Strait, the link between the Arctic Ocean and the Pacific, and is connected to Africa by the Isthmus of Suez. Asia is a continent of superlatives and contradictions, home to both the highest mountain and the deepest basin on the planet: Mount Everest and the Dead Sea. As the geography of the continent ranges from the polar regions in the north to the inner tropics in the south, the large-scale landscapes, and the vegetation and climatic zones typical of these, are correspondingly varied. The north is primarily characterized by the lowlands of western and northern Siberia, and the central Siberian mountain region. The south-west is dominated by a fold-mountain system, which extends from the islands in the Mediterranean to the Himalayas, whose eight-thousanders are the highest peaks. Highlands and lowlands spread out to the south of these (Deccan Plateau and Tibet, Turan Lowland), alternating with valleys (Tarim valley) and other

plains. From north to south, you will find tundra and taiga (the largest wooded region in the world), boreal coniferous forest, forest steppe, steppe, deserts (Gobi, Rub' al-Khali), dry savannas, tropical rainforest, and monsoon forest.

Impressive karst landscapes cover large areas of south-west China (weathered limestone formations). The Lijiang River, here near Xingping (main image), winds its way between the cities of Guilin and Yangshuo through karst towers reaching up to 300 m (984 feet) in height.

Steep limestone rocks are a feature of the Koh Phi Phi island group in the Andaman Sea off the west coast of Thailand.

While the Indian subcontinent, which includes India, Bangladesh, Bhutan, Nepal, Pakistan, and Sri Lanka, belongs to Asia geographically, it forms its own continental plate that was once part of the southern continent of Gondwana. For millions of years, this continent drifted through the Indian Ocean. When it collided with the Eurasian Plate, the Himalayas were created. The subcontinent extends from their base as far as the triangular peninsula that comes to a point to the south in the Indian Ocean. It can be divided into three landscape regions: The Himalayas, followed by the Indus and Ganges plains, which rise in the south to the Deccan Plateau, a raised area intersected by rivers that is bordered at the coasts of the peninsula by wide plains. The vegetation is correspondingly varied: the north and north-east are dominated by rainforests and plantations. The Indus and Ganges plains are characterized by subtropical vegetation, which changes to mangroves in the Ganges delta. The upland consists mainly of savannas, with further desert and steppe regions in the west. The Laccadive, Andaman, and Nicobar island groups are also part of India. At the end of 2004, an undersea earthquake in the Indian Ocean caused a tsunami that caused devastation on Sri Lanka, the Andaman and Nicobar Islands, as well as in Southeast Asia.

With a surface area of more than 3.2 million sq. km (1.2 million sq. miles), India is the seventh largest nation in the world. The subcontinent's other countries are relatively small, but unique. Bangladesh is typified by the delta region of the Brahmaputra, Ganges, and Meghna Rivers. The Kingdom of Bhutan is the location of the 7,541-m (24,741-foot) high Gangkhar Puensum, the highest as-yet unconquered mountain in the world. Mount Everest, the "Throne of the World", rises in Nepal. The three highest mountain ranges in the world meet in the north of Pakistan: the Hindu Kush, Karakoram, and Himalaya mountains. The 65,610-sq.-km (25,332-sq.-mile) island state of Sri Lanka, is world-renowned for its Ceylon tea.

Main image: At 8,091 m (26,545 feet), Annapurna I in the Nepalese Himalayas is one of the highest mountains in the world. Far left: Phewa Lake and the peaks of the Annapurna range at Pokhara in Nepal (top); the Aravalli Range is a 600-km (373-mile) long range of mountains up to 1,722 m (5,650 feet) high in northern India (bottom). Left: Paddy fields in southern India (top); a lighthouse on the Malabar Coast in south-west India (bottom).

DEPRESSIONS – THE WORLD'S LOWEST LAND REGIONS

Depressions or geomorphologic basins are regions on dry land with a water level below sea level. Basins with a base lower than sea level are called crypto-depressions.

JORDAN RIFT VALLEY

Dead Sea	-400 m (-1,312 feet)
Lake Tiberias	-212 m (-696 feet)

The Jordan Rift Valley, some 400 km (249 miles) long and 10 km (6 miles) wide, is the northern part of the Great Rift Valley. Two of the deepest depressions in the world are found here: Lake Tiberias (Sea of Galilee), which is the largest potable water reservoir of Israel and the lowest freshwater lake in the world at 212 m (696 feet) below sea level, and the Dead Sea. The River Jordan, the lowest river in the world, flows through the Jordan Rift Valley and opens into the Dead Sea, which has no outlet and is the lowest-lying inland lake in the world. The water level of this salt lake falls every year, as many projects along the river extract water from the Jordan and the tropical climate (with average annual temperatures around 30°C/86°F, never falling below 18°C/64°F) also ensures a high rate of evaporation. The concentration of minerals is extraordinarily high: while other seas have a salt content of around 3%, the Dead Sea's salinity is around 30%.

THE WORLD'S DEEPEST DEPRESSIONS
Depth of water level below sea level

1. **Bentley Subglacial Trench**
   Antarctica -2.496 m (8,189 feet)
2. **Dead Sea**
   Jordan Rift Valley
   -400 m (1,312 feet)
3. **Lake Tiberias**
   Jordan Rift Valley
   212 m (696 feet)
4. **Turfan Depression**
   China -155 m (509 feet)
5. **Lake Assal**
   Africa -153 m (502 feet)
6. **Laguna del Carbón**
   South America -105 m (345 feet)
7. **Death Valley**
   North America -85,5 m (282 feet)
8. **Lake Qarun**
   Egypt -42 m (138 feet)
9. **Caspian Sea**
   Western Asia -28 m (92 feet)
10. **Lake Eyre**
    Australia -17 m (56 feet)

THE WORLD'S DEEPEST CRYPTODEPRESSIONS
Depth of ground below sea level

1. **Lake Baikal**
   Central Asia -1.181 m (3,875 feet)
2. **Lake Tanganyika**
   East Africa -688 m (2,257 feet)
3. **Lake Garda**
   Northern Italy -281 m (922 feet)
4. **Lake Como**
   Northern Italy -228 m (748 feet)
5. **Lake Maggiore**
   Northern Italy -179 m (587 feet)
6. **Lake Iseo**
   Italy -66 m (217 feet)
7. **Lake Lugano**
   Switzerland/Northern Italy
   -17 m (56 feet)

ASIA
Turfan Depression (Aydingkol Lake)
-155 m (-509 feet)
The basin-like Turfan Depression is a fault in the foothills of several mountain ranges in the northwest of China. The Ala River is the largest feeder of water into the 50,000-sq.-km (19,300-sq.-mile) Turfan Depression, which has no outlets. The lowest point of the basin is at Aydingkol Lake, where the banks of the lake are 155 m (509 feet) below sea level.

AUSTRALIA
Lake Eyre **-17 m (-56 feet)**

When full of water, Lake Eyre is the largest lake in Australia and the lowest point on that continent. However, the water level of this salt lake is extremely dependent on climatic conditions: the volume of rain during the monsoon determines how deep the lake will be – at most up to 4 m (13 feet), around once every ten years; otherwise around 1 m (3 feet).

Turfan Depression in China.

Sunrise on Lake Eyre.

The satellite image shows the Jordan Rift Valley, part of the Great Rift Valley (far left). The Dead Sea is the lowest inland lake in the world (left). Below: Death Valley, the lowest point in North America, is one of the driest areas in the world.

AFRICA
Lake Assal   -153 m (-502 feet)

Salt deposits by Lake Assal.

Salt mining by Lake Assal, Danakil Desert.

Measuring some 54 sq. km (21 sq. miles), Lake Assal – in the Danakil Depression in the middle of East African Djibouti, to the west of the Gulf of Aden – is the saltiest body of water in the world (outside Antarctica, where some lakes in the dry valleys contain even more salt). It has a salt content of nearly 35%, ten times that of the oceans and even higher than that of the Dead Sea. At around 153 m (502 feet) below sea level, Lake Assal is the lowest point on the African continent. The lake is fed by underground springs, which are in turn supplied with water by the Indian Ocean. The high salt content of the lake is largely attributable to the high temperatures and the resulting extreme rate of evaporation. Salt pans surround the lake to the west and northwest.

NORTH AMERICA
Death Valley   -86 m (-282 feet)

Around 225 km (140 miles) long, most of Death Valley in California is below sea level. Its lowest point is -86 m (-282 feet) in Badwater Basin, the lowest point in North America and the northern hemisphere. Temperatures in the "Valley of Death" occasionally exceed 51°C (124°F) and rarely fall below 21°C (70°F), making it one of the hottest regions in the world.

Badwater Basin in Death Valley.

SOUTH AMERICA
Laguna del Carbón   -105 m (-345 feet)

Sparsely populated, inhospitable Patagonia in the south of Argentina is the site of the lowest point in South America 105 m (345 feet) below sea level: Laguna del Carbón, near Puerto San Julian, Santa Cruz. Many fossils have been discovered in its petrified primeval forests.

ANTARCTICA
Bentley Subglacial Trench
     -2.496 m (-8,189 feet)

Bentley Subglacial Trench, which is roughly the size of Mexico, is the world's lowest point outside of an ocean at 2,496 m (8,189 feet) below sea level. A layer of ice and snow 3,000-m (9,800-feet) thick covers this geological valley in West Antarctica. It was named after US geophysicist Charles Bentley.

At 8.5 million sq. km (3.3 million sq. miles), the smallest of the world's continents includes the main landmass of Australia, the island of Tasmania off its

Australia as seen from space.

south-east coast, some smaller islands, and the Great Barrier Reef, the largest coral reef in the world. The name of the continent comes from the Latin *terra australis*, meaning "southland", due to the location of the continent in the southern hemisphere on both sides of the tropic of Capricorn, at the boundary of the Indian and Pacific Oceans.

AUSTRALIA'S GEOGRAPHIC SUPERLATIVES

❶ **Expanse:**
North–south
3,700 km (2,300 miles)
East–west 4,000 km (2,500 miles)

❷ **Northernmost point:**
Cape York, Queensland
10° 41' S

❸ **Southernmost point:**
Wilson Promontory, Victoria
39° 8' S

❹ **Westernmost point:**
Steep Point, Western Australia
113° 9' E

❺ **Easternmost point:**
Cape Byron, New South Wales
146° 22' E

❻ **Highest mountain:**
Great Dividing Range, Mount
Kosciuszko 2,228 m (7,310 feet)

❼ **Lowest point:**
Lake Eyre, South Australia
-17 m (-56 feet)

❽ **Longest river:**
Murray-Darling
3,370 km (2,094 miles)

❾ **Largest lake:**
Lake Eyre, South Australia
9,500 sq. km (3,700 sq. miles)

❿ **Deepest lake:**
Lake St Clair, Tasmania
200 m (656 feet)

⓫ **Largest island:**
Tasmania 64,519 sq. km
(24,911 sq. miles)

The Australian continent is bordered to the north by the Timor Sea, the Arafura Sea, and the Torres Strait, to the east by the Coral Sea and Tasman Sea, to the south by the Bass Strait, and to the west by the Indian Ocean. In comparison to other continents, the coast of Australia is relatively undifferentiated as far as the Gulf of Carpentaria in the north. The Australian continent can be subdivided into three main regions: the western Australian tableland, which typically features bizarre rocky landscapes (Kimberley region) and vast deserts (Great Sandy Desert); the Great Dividing Range, which runs along the entire eastern coast; and the central Australian valley, the lowland region also known as the Outback, which links west to east and contains expansive deserts (Great Victoria Desert). The most striking elevations in the middle of the country are Uluru and Kata Tjuta (the Olgas).

New Zealand consists of two islands. The South Island was created around 100 million years ago when two continental plates collided. Hills and plains, lakes and fjords were formed by ice age glaciers. The North Island is home to many volcanoes, thermal springs, and geysers, which are situated along the seam of the Australian and Pacific tectonic plates. New Zealand is often called the "green island" due to its sparse population and unique, virtually untouched natural landscape.

Mitre Peak (above), at 1,692 m (5,551 feet) high, is a mountain close to Milford Sound fjord on New Zealand's South Island.

The term "Oceania" is used to classify the island world of the Pacific culturally and economically, grouping Melanesia, Micronesia, and Polynesia into one subcontinent with New Guinea and New Zealand, and sometimes Australia. Tectonically this is incorrect, as the regions are all located on different plates (the Australian, Pacific, and some smaller plates). Discounting Australia, around 15 million people live on the 7,000-plus islands, which have a land surface area of around 1.3 million sq. km (502,000 sq. miles).

Some of the 36 domes of Kata Tjuta ("many heads"), also known as "the Olgas", in the heart of Australia.

The landmass of the African continent lies between the Indian Ocean and Atlantic Ocean. It is the second largest continent in the world in terms of surface

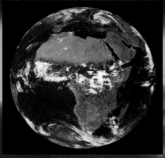

Africa as seen from space.

area (30.3 million sq. km/11.7 million sq. miles, 20% of the world's land surface area) and population (around 967 million, 14.4% of the global population). Africa spans both sides of the equator and terminates to the south at the Cape of Good Hope. The European Mediterranean forms its northern boundary. At the Strait of Gibraltar, the continent extends 14 km (8½ miles) into Europe. The Red Sea forms the natural boundary with Asia; the Suez Canal has existed as an artificial boundary since 1869.

Its geographic position across the equator determines Africa's climatic conditions: 75% of its surface area is between the tropics, making it the largest contiguous tropical landmass in the world. To the north and south (Sahelian Zone) there are subtropical savanna and semi-desert regions. While the Namib Desert in the south is a smaller example, the Sahara, the largest desert region in the world, covers almost the entire northern third of the continent. The topography of Africa is characterized by flat mountain ridges and vast basins. The Maghreb region in north-west Africa is bordered by the Sahara Desert, Mediterranean Sea, and the

Atlas Mountains. Niger and Chad form large basins in the north, while the Congo and Okavango Rivers form delta regions in central and southern Africa. Apart from Madagascar in the east, there are only a few coastal islands in the Gulf of Guinea – otherwise the coast of the African continent is generally undifferentiated.

Granite blocks on Anse Source d'Argent beach, La Digue in the Seychelles.

AFRICA'S GEOGRAPHIC SUPERLATIVES

❶ Expanse:
North–south
7,500 km (4,700 miles)
East–west 6,000 km (3,700 miles)

❷ Northernmost point:
Bizerta, Tunisia
37° 16' S, 9° 52' E

❸ Southernmost point:
Cape Agulhas, South Africa
34° 49' S, 20° 0' E

❹ Westernmost point:
Cape Verde Peninsula, Senegal
14° 44' N, 17° 31' W

❺ Easternmost point:
Ras Hafun, Somalia
10° 25' N, 51° 16' E

❻ Highest mountain:
Kilimanjaro, Tanzania
Kibo 2,228 m (7,310 feet)

❼ Lowest point:
Lake Assal, Djibouti
-153 m (-502 feet)

❽ Longest river:
Nile 6,671 km (4,145 miles)

❾ Largest lake:
Lake Victoria, East Africa
68,870 sq. km (26,590 sq. miles)

❿ Deepest lake:
Lake Tanganyika, East Africa
1,470 m (4,823 feet)

⓫ Largest island:
Madagascar 587,042 sq. km
(226,658 sq. miles)

View of Kilimanjaro from Amboseli
National Park in south-west Kenya,
with an umbrella thorn acacia in
the foreground.

GREAT RIFT VALLEY

The Great Rift Valley (or Great African Rift Valley) runs southward from Syria to Mozambique for a total of approximately 6,000 km (3,700 miles). The Rift Valley was created by the spreading apart of the Earth's crust, volcanic eruptions, and the movements of the African

The Rift Valley in Kenya.

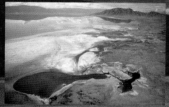
Lake Natron in Tanzania.

and Arabian continental plates over the course of the last 35 million years. Over the millions of years to come, the continuing movement of the Rift Valley tectonic plates will probably split eastern Africa from the rest of the continent. Along the Rift Valley, tectonic activity gave rise to numerous volcanoes including Mount Kenya, Kilimanjaro, and Mount Meru. The still-active Ol Doinyo Lengai volcano in Tanzania is the only carbonatite volcano in the world.

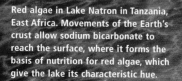
Red algae in Lake Natron in Tanzania, East Africa. Movements of the Earth's crust allow sodium bicarbonate to reach the surface, where it forms the basis of nutrition for red algae, which give the lake its characteristic hue.

Lava flow on the Ol Doinyo Lengai volcano in Kenya.

Salt deposits on the Dallol volcano in Ethiopia.

By Lake Abbe, Djibouti, hot springs form travertine chimneys.

A hot spring in the Danakil Depression, Ethiopia.

North America is the third largest continent, and the largest continent in the western hemisphere. It stretches from the glacial world of Alaska as far as the Caribbean, and together with Greenland,

North and Central America.

Mexico, the states of the Central American isthmus, and the Caribbean islands, it encompasses almost 25 million sq. km (9.6 million sq. miles) – representing more than 16% of the world's landmass. Two countries, USA and Canada, account for more than three-quarters of its surface area. North America is bordered to the north by the Arctic Ocean, to the east by the Atlantic Ocean, and to the west by the Pacific.

NORTH AND CENTRAL AMERICA'S GEOGRAPHIC SUPERLATIVES

① **Expanse:**
North–south 7,000 km (4,350 miles)
East–west 6,000 km (3,700 miles)

② **Northernmost point:**
Cape Murchison, Canada
71° 59' N, 94° 32' W

③ **Southernmost point:**
Punta Mariato, Panama
7° 12' N, 80° 53' W

④ **Westernmost point:**
Cape Prince of Wales, Alaska
65° 35' N, 168° 5' W

⑤ **Easternmost point:**
Cape St. Charles, Newfoundland
and Labrador   52° 13' N, 55° 37'W

⑥ **Highest mountain:**
Mount McKinley (USA)
6,194 m (20,322 feet)

⑦ **Lowest point:**
Death Valley, California
-85.5 m (-281 feet)

⑧ **Longest river:**
Mississippi (with Missouri)
6,051 km (3,760 miles)

⑨ **Largest lake:**
Lake Superior, Canada
82,414 sq. km (31,820 sq. miles)

⑩ **Deepest lake:**
Great Slave Lake, Canada
614 m (2,014 feet)

⑪ **Largest island:**
Greenland   2,166,086 sq. km
(836,330 sq. miles)

Together with South America, North America forms the double continent of America, which stretches about 16,000 km (10,000 miles) from the far north to the extreme south.
North America extends from the Arctic Ocean to the Caribbean Sea. It is connected to South America by the land bridge of Central America, which is just 50 km (31 miles) wide at its narrowest points, and is physically and geographically part of the North American landmass, together with the islands of the American Mediterranean (Caribbean Sea and

The Tolimán and San Pedro volcanoes rise up beyond Lago de Atitlán in the uplands of Guate

Gulf of Mexico) and Greenland. The east–west expanse measures approximately 6,000 km (3,700 miles) from Alaska to Nova Scotia. The topography of North America is very varied, from the glacial world of Alaska to mountain ranges and broad expanses of prairie and desert. Three extensive landscapes running from north to south can be distinguished: firstly in the west, the American Cordillera extend across the entire double continent from Alaska to Tierra del Fuego, encompassing almost continuous mountain ranges, and at

15,000 km (9,300 miles) are the longest fold mountains in the world. Formed about 70 million years ago, the Rocky Mountains comprise the main mountain range in the North American Cordillera. The Appalachians in the east form the second main landscape, comprising forested upland bordered by broad coastal lowland. The Appalachians are around 400 million years old and so are among the oldest mountains in the world. Thirdly, the inner plains between the mountain ranges consist of vast, open areas (Great Plains) and the

five Great Lakes, which at a total of 244,000 sq. km (94,210 sq. miles) are the largest body of inland freshwater in the world.

Deep bays (including Hudson Bay, Gulf of Mexico, and Gulf of Alaska) are typical features of the North American coastline. The Caribbean Islands, consisting of the Greater and Lesser Antilles, lie in a great arc from Cuba to South America. The continent is tectonically very active as the North American Plate meets the Pacific Plate here, therefore volcanic eruptions and earthquakes occur frequently.

More than 500 million people inhabit North and Central America, of which over 300 million live in the United States. The average population density is low compared with European industrialized nations, and heavily populated conurbations are only found on the east coast of the USA.

In the evening light, the red rocks in Arches National Park shine so brightly that they seem to be on fire. Frost and desert wind have created over 200 natural stone arches, such as Delicate Arch shown here.

EARTHQUAKES

Earthquakes are natural tremors of the Earth's crust and mantle. Particularly at the boundaries between the continental plates where these move away from or toward each other (faults), stresses are generated that are eventually discharged through erratic movements of the planet's

San Andreas Fault, California.

crust – resulting in tectonic quakes. The San Andreas Fault in California, for example, where the Pacific Plate drifts past the North American Plate, is the site of recurring earthquakes. The Richter scale is used to measure the strength of earthquakes, and the energy discharged during a tremor is recorded using seismographs.

THE WORLD'S STRONGEST EARTHQUAKES
Strength on the Richter scale

❶	Chile (Valdivia) 1960	9.5
❷	Alaska ("Good Friday Earthquake") 1964	9.2
❸	Undersea earthquake off the coast of Sumatra 2004	9.1
❹	Russia (Kamchatka) 1952	9.0
❺	Earthquake off the coast of Ecuador 1906	8.8
❻	Alaska (Andreanof Island) 1957	8.8
❼	Alaska (Rat Island) 1965	8.7
❽	North Sumatra 2005	8.6
❾	India (Assam) 1950	8.6
❿	Indonesia (Banda Sea) 1938	8.6

The San Andreas Fault stretches more than 1,100 km (680 miles) from Mexico as far as San Francisco.

HISTORIC EARTHQUAKES

On 1 November 1755, an earthquake and subsequent fires destroyed the Portuguese capital of Lisbon. The quake, which cost the lives of 30,000 to 100,000 people, is believed to have measured 8.5–9.0 on the Richter scale. This catastrophe was the impetus that led to the development of modern seismology.

One of the worst natural disasters to take place in the USA was the San Francisco earthquake of 18 April 1906, in which around 3,000 people lost their lives. Its strength was between 7.8 and 8.8 on the Richter scale, and it shook the area along the San Andreas Fault for hundreds of miles.

Lisbon, 1755.

San Francisco, 1906.

THE WORLD'S MOST
VIOLENT EARTHQUAKES

EARTHQUAKES OF MODERN TIMES

Mexico City is located in a tectonically active region where repeated earthquakes are experienced. In September 1985, an earthquake measuring 8.1 on the Richter scale struck this heavily populated city and more than 10,000 people were killed. In 1994, an earthquake in California measuring 6.7 killed 60 people, and the following year in January 1995, the ground in Kobe, Japan shook at 7.3 on the Richter scale – costing 6,433 people their lives. One of the most catastrophic earthquakes, known as the "Great Wenchuan Earthquake", struck the Chinese province of Sichuan on 12 May 2008. The effects of the quake, measuring 8.0 on the Richter scale, could be felt 1,550 km (960 miles) away in Beijing, as well as in Shanghai and Bangkok. The earthquake claimed the lives of 86,000 people. Worst affected was the town of Beichuan, where around half of the population died.

Beichuan, 2008.

California, 1994.

Kobe, 1995.

Mexico, 1985.

Sichuan, 2008.

After Asia, Africa, and North America, South America is the fourth largest continent on our planet. With a total surface area of 17.8 million sq. km (6.9 million

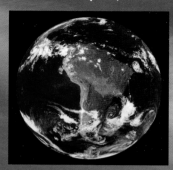

South America as seen from space.

sq. miles), it constitutes around 12% of the land surface area of the world. In the north, South America is linked to North America by the Central American land bridge; in the south, it comes closer to Antarctica than any other continent.

SOUTH AMERICA'S GEOGRAPHIC SUPERLATIVES

① **Expanse:**
North–south
          7,500 km (4,700 miles)
East–west   6,000 km (3,700 miles)
② **Northernmost point:**
Punta Gallinas, Colombia
12° 28' N
③ **Southernmost point:**
Cape Froward, Chile
55° 59' S
④ **Westernmost point:**
Punta Pariñas, Peru
4° 40' S, 81° 19' W
⑤ **Easternmost point:**
Ponta do Seixas, Brazil
7° 8' S, 34° 47' W
⑥ **Highest mountain:**
Andes
Aconcagua   6,963 m (22,845 feet)
⑦ **Lowest point:**
Laguna del Carbón,
Argentina   -105 m (-345 feet)
⑧ **Longest river:**
Amazon   6,448 km (4,007 miles)
⑨ **Largest lake:**
Lake Maracaibo, Venezuela
     13,300 sq. km (5,135 sq. miles)
⑩ **Deepest lake:**
Lago General Carrera, Chile,
Argentina   590 m (1,936 feet)
⑪ **Largest island:**
Isla Grande de Tierra del Fuego,
Chile, Argentina
     48,185 sq. km (18,604 sq. miles)

The Torres del Paine are landmarks in the eponymous national park in the south of Chile.

Compared with other continents, South America appears compact – the coast is less segmented by bays and the topography is relatively uniform, apart from the mountain regions of the Andes. Three large areas dominate the surface topography of the continent: the highlands of the Andes in the west, three river plains, and three mountainous regions to the east of the Andes. The steep American Cordillera continues along the Pacific coast in the southern part of the American double continent. With the Andes, the second highest mountain system in the world after the Himalayas, it reaches its greatest width: around 700 km (435 miles) from east to west at the latitude of the tropic of Capricorn. The Andes run the length of the entire South American continent from north to south and are the longest mountain range in the world. Plateaus open out between the mountain ranges of the Cordillera, with lowlands to the east. Between the mountainous areas of Guyana in the north and Brazil lies the Amazon Basin, through which the Amazon flows. The lowland covers 4 million sq. km (1.5 million sq. miles) and is the largest tropical rainforest region in the world. This is followed by the alluvial plains of Gran Chaco and the Pampas, which lead to Patagonia, the third mountainous region. The lowland of the Orinoco Basin is located in the extreme north of the continent, and in the south is the floodplain of the Paraguay and Paraná river system, which eventually becomes a subtropical alluvial landscape.

The vast north–south expanse of the continent causes extreme climatic differences. For example, the hot, damp rainforest regions of Amazonia in the south are very different from the cool, temperate region of Patagonia and the polar-influenced Tierra del Fuego. The 12 South American states, including the Galapagos Islands and the English and French overseas territories of the Falkland Islands and French Guyana, are home to more than 370 million people, a good 5% of the global population.

Tropical rainforest – here, along the Amazon in Brazil – is South America's primary form of vegetation.

ANTARCTICA

The continent of Antarctica has a surface area of 13.2 million sq. km (5.1 million sq. miles). Of this area, 200,000 sq. km (77,000 sq. miles) is land not

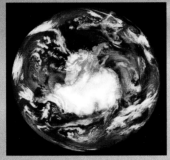
Antarctica as seen from space.

covered by ice. A landmass 30% larger than Europe is covered by a layer of ice approximately 2 km (1¼ miles) thick. Toward the middle of the continent, this layer can be as much as 4.5 km (2¾ miles) thick, which also makes Antarctica the highest continent.

ANTARCTICA'S GEOGRAPHIC SUPERLATIVES

The Antarctic region extends as far as the Antarctic Circle at 66° 33' S. Its boundary is marked by the Antarctic Convergence (see text right) at approximately 50° S. The size of the continent fluctuates according to the season: in the winter months, it more or less doubles in size as the ice mass increases.

❶ **Highest mountain:**
 Sentinel Range, Mount Vinson
  4,892 m (16,050 feet)

❷ **Lowest point:**
 Bentley Subglacial Trench,
 West Antarctica
  -2,496 m (-8,189 feet)

❸ **Longest river:**
 Onyx River 30 km (19 miles)

❹ **Largest lake:**
 Lake Vostok (subglacial),
 East Antarctica
  15,690 sq. km (6,058 sq. miles)

❺ **Deepest lake:**
 Lake Vostok (subglacial),
 East Antarctica 670 m (2,198 feet)

❻ **Largest island:**
 Alexander I Island
  49,070 sq. km (18,946 sq. miles)

Antarctica, also known as the south polar region, is the southernmost part of the world lying almost completely within the Antarctic Circle. The Antarctic borders are indicated not by the coastline of the landmass but by the Antarctic Convergence, a well-defined zone at the southern edges of the Atlantic, Indian, and Pacific Oceans. The Convergence lies between 48° and 60° south. At this location, colder water flowing northward from the Antarctic meets warmer water flowing in a southerly direction. If

the ice shelves at the edge of the land regions, the sea, and the islands are included in the surface area calculations, the total surface area of the Antarctic is some 53 million sq. km (20.5 million sq. miles). The Weddell Sea on the Atlantic side and the Ross Sea on the Pacific side advance far into the landmass of Antarctica. These bays split the continental mass into East Antarctica, measuring more than 10 million sq. km (3.8 million sq. miles), and West Antarctica, with an area of 2.3 million sq. km (888,000 sq.

miles). The coastline of the entire Antarctic region is almost 18,000 km (11,200 miles) long. More than 90% of the world's ice masses are concentrated around the South Pole in the coldest continent. The volume of the continental ice sheet is estimated to be 24 million cu. km (5.8 million cu. miles), making it the largest contiguous ice mass in the world. The enormous layer of ice covering Antarctica shifts at its edges as an ice shelf or flows off into icebergs and as drift ice ("calving"). The Transantarctic Mountains extend

3,500 km (2,175 miles) between East and West Antarctica (the fifth longest mountain range in the world), reaching heights of more than 4,500 m (14,765 feet). The range includes the dry valleys of Antarctica – an area of almost 5,000 sq. km (1,900 sq. miles) in East Antarctica that has been free of ice for millions of years.

Above: The Filchner Mountains in Antarctica's Queen Maud Land are named after the leader of the second German South Polar Expedition, explorer of the Antarctic and Asia Wilhelm Filchner.

Bizarre icebergs, sculpted by wind and water, are a common sight south of the Antarctic Circle.

The geographic South Pole in the interior of Antarctica is the most southerly point on Earth, at a latitude of precisely 90°. The ice sheet, 2,804 m (9,200 feet) above sea level, is around 2,700 m (8,860 feet) thick at the South Pole, and in winter it receives no daylight whatsoever, while in summer the sun never sets – though it remains just above the horizon. For this reason and due to its altitude, the South Pole is one of the coldest places in the world and is much colder than the North Pole: temperatures fluctuate between a maximum of -25°C (-13°F) and a minimum of

Flags of nations at the South Pole.

-65°C (-85°F) during the year. Since 1956, the USA has maintained a permanent science station at the South Pole, the Amundsen-Scott Station, named after the first expedition leaders to reach the pole.

The US Amundsen-Scott Station is situated on the continental ice sheet at an altitude of 2,853 m (9,360 feet).

ROALD AMUNDSEN AND ROBERT SCOTT

Together with their respective expedition teams, English Robert Falcon Scott (1868–1912) and Norwegian Roald Amundsen (1872–1928) raced each other to the South Pole in 1911. The winner of this exciting but tragic contest was Amundsen, who reached the South Pole with his four companions on 14 December 1911 and named his camp there Polheim. When Scott arrived on 17 January 1912, he found a tent bearing a

Amundsen and Scott did not arrive for another 45 years: in 1956, Admiral George Dufek arrived by plane to prepare for the construction of the US Amundsen-Scott research station.

One of Amundsen's dogsleds.

Roald Amundsen (1892–1928).

The goal is reached: 14 December 1911.

Norwegian flag – he was too late and had come second. On the return journey, all members of the British expedition died from malnutrition and frostbite, including Scott himself. The next person to set foot on the South Pole after

Scott finds Amundsen's tent at the Pole.

PENINSULAS

EUROPE'S LARGEST PENINSULAS

Geirangerfjord, Norway.

① Scandinavia 770,000 sq. km
(297,000 sq. miles)

② Iberian
Peninsula 580,000 sq. km
(224,000 sq. miles)

③ Balkan
Peninsula 560,000 sq. km
(216,000 sq. miles)

④ Apennine
Peninsula 301,000 sq. km
(116,000 sq. miles)

ASIA'S LARGEST PENINSULAS

Kronotsky stratovolcano on Kamchatka.

① Arabian
Peninsula 3,000,000 sq. km
(1,158,000 sq. miles)

② Indochinese
Peninsula 1,011,000 sq. km
(390,000 sq. miles)

③ Asia Minor 757,000 sq. km
(292,000 sq. miles)

④ Chukchi
Peninsula 721,000 sq. km
(278,000 sq. miles)

⑤ Kamchatka 370,000 sq. km
(143,000 sq. miles)

AUSTRALIA'S LARGEST PENINSULAS

Water lilies on a billabong, Australia.

① Cape York
Peninsula 137,000 sq. km
(53,000 sq. miles)

② Arnhem land 97,000 sq. km
(37,500 sq. miles)

AFRICA'S LARGEST PENINSULA

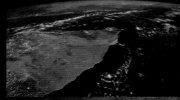
The wedge-shaped Horn of Africa.

① Horn of Africa 2,000,000 sq. km
(772,000 sq. miles)

NORTH AND CENTRAL AMERICA'S LARGEST PENINSULAS

Glaciated mountains, Alaska Peninsula.

① Labrador
Peninsula 275,000 sq. km
(106,000 sq. miles)

② Yucatán 180,000 sq. km
(69,500 sq. miles)

③ Florida 170,000 sq. km
(66,000 sq. miles)

④ Baja California 143,000 sq. km
(55,000 sq. miles)

⑤ Melville
Peninsula 65,000 sq. km
(25,000 sq. miles)

⑥ Alaska Peninsula c. 60,000 sq. km
(c. 23,000 sq. miles)

⑦ Nova Scotia 55,200 sq. km
(21,300 sq. miles)

⑧ Kenai Peninsula 23,000 sq. km
(9,000 sq. miles)

SOUTH AMERICA'S LARGEST PENINSULA

Coast of Valdés Peninsula, Argentina.

① Valdés Peninsula 3,625 sq. km
(1,400 sq. miles)

ANTARCTICA'S LARGEST PENINSULA

Drift ice off the coast of West Antarctica.

① Antarctic c. 340,000 sq. km
Peninsula (c. 131,000 sq. miles)

THE WORLD'S LARGEST PENINSULAS

① **Arabian**
   Peninsula   3,000,000 sq. km
                       (1,158,000 sq. miles)
② **Horn of Africa**   2,000,000 sq. km
                       (772,000 sq. miles)
③ **Indochinese**
   Peninsula   1,011,000 sq. km
                       (390,000 sq. miles)
④ **Scandinavia**   770,000 sq. km
                       (297,000 sq. miles)
⑤ **Asia Minor**   757,000 sq. km
                       (292,000 sq. miles)
⑥ **Chukchi**
   Peninsula   721,000 sq. km
                       (278,000 sq. miles)
⑦ **Iberian Peninsula**   580,000 sq. km
                       (224,000 sq. miles)
⑧ **Balkan Peninsula**   560,000 sq. km
                       (216,000 sq. miles)
⑨ **Kamchatka**   370,000 sq. km
                       (143,000 sq. miles)
⑩ **Antarctic**
   Peninsula   c. 340,000 sq. km
                       (c. 131,000 sq. miles)
⑪ **Apennine**
   Peninsula   301,000 sq. km
                       (116,000 sq. miles)
⑫ **Labrador**
   Peninsula   275,000 sq. km
                       (106,000 sq. miles)

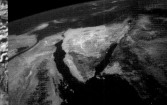

The Sinai Peninsula with the Red Sea.

Peninsulas are large areas of land that project into a body of water, while still being connected to the mainland. Many peninsulas are simply higher sections of the Earth's crust that rise above the sea with the surrounding area covered by water. If the width is much larger than the length, as in the case of Wales, for example, it is not referred to as a peninsula. Using the example of Great Britain and Ireland, you can see that islands also have peninsulas.

Kamchatka, between the Bering Strait and the Sea of Okhotsk, at 370,000 sq. km (143,000 sq. miles) is the largest peninsula in East Asia.

ARABIAN PENINSULA –
THE WORLD'S LARGEST PENINSULA

The Arabian Peninsula is the westernmost of the large south Asian peninsulas And, unlike India, is quite sparsely populated.

The Arabian Peninsula in the extreme south-west of the Asian continent is the largest peninsula on the planet at almost 3 million sq. km (1.2 million sq. miles). It has borders with Jordan and Iraq in the north, the Persian Gulf and Gulf of Oman in the east, the Arabian Sea and Gulf of Aden in the south, and the Red Sea in the west. With a population of around 70 million (estimate from 2008) on the enormous expanse of land, the Arabian Peninsula is also one of the most sparsely populated regions in the world. Its inhabitants are spread across the states of Saudi Arabia, the United Arab Emirates, Bahrain, Yemen, Qatar, Kuwait, and Oman. Saudi Arabia is by far the largest of these countries, with a surface area of 2.24 million sq. km (865,000 sq. miles). In the west and south, the Arabian Peninsula features high, inaccessible mountain regions that gradually level out eastward toward the Persian Gulf. With its extremely hot, dry climate – very few areas record annual precipitation exceeding 178 mm (7 inches), and in summer temperatures can reach 55°C (131°F).

The peninsula is largely covered by the Arabian Desert, with the large, sandy deserts of Rub' al-Khali and an-Nafud. Tectonically, the peninsula is part of the Arabian Plate. From a geological perspective, it is part of the old African continental mass, although it is now separated from Africa by the Red Sea. It contains large reserves of natural gas and oil.

The satellite image shows East Africa, Yemen, the Red Sea, and the Gulf of Aden (left). Below: The Rub' al-Khali ("Empty Quarter"), at around 780,000 sq. km (300,000 sq. miles) the largest sand desert in the world, covers a third of the Arabian Peninsula. The lonely desert roads are lined by sand dunes.

THE MOUNTAIN REGIONS OF THE ARABIAN PENINSULA

The rugged 1,500–2,500 m (4,900–8,200 feet) mountainous region of Yemen, which makes up over a third of the country, rises in the country's interior. The highest mountain is the Jabal an-Nabi Shu'ayb (3,760 m/12,336 feet). The main Sarawat mountain range has a truly mild climate for the peninsula, which explains why many villages can still be found at an altitude of up to 2,500 m (8,200 feet). In the Sultanate of Oman, the generally rugged Al Hajar or Oman Mountains extend from the border with the United Arab Emirates toward the Indian Ocean for around 450 km (280 miles), framing the coast along the Gulf of Oman. The highest peak is Jabal Shams (3,020 m/9,908 feet).

The village of Al Karn in the mountains of Yemen.

The Al Hajar Mountains in the Sultanate of Oman.

ISLANDS

The world's largest islands are several times larger than all the Benelux countries put together. Between them, they cover the full spectrum of climate zones, from the thick layer of ice that covers Greenland to the dense tropical rainforests of New Guinea – and everything in

Drift ice on the coast of Greenland.

between. Common to them all is the fact that they are completely surrounded by water, and some are large enough to mark the boundaries between the world's oceans, marginal seas, and other bodies of water.

THE WORLD'S LARGEST ISLANDS

① **Greenland,** Denmark
2,166,086 sq. km (836,330 sq. miles)

② **New Guinea,**
Indonesia/Papua New Guinea
785,753 sq. km (303,381 sq. miles)

③ **Borneo,**
Indonesia/Malaysia/Brunei
748,168 sq. km (288,869 sq. miles)

④ **Madagascar**
587,042 sq. km (226,658 sq. miles)

⑤ **Baffin Island,** Canada
507,451 sq. km (195,928 sq. miles)

⑥ **Sumatra,** Indonesia
443,066 sq. km (171,069 sq. miles)

⑦ **Honshu,** Japan
230,316 sq. km (88,926 sq. miles)

⑧ **Great Britain,** United Kingdom
229,883 sq. km (88,758 sq. miles)

⑨ **Victoria Island,** Canada
217,291 sq. km (83,897 sq. miles)

⑩ **Ellesmere Island,** Canada
196,236 sq. km (75,767 sq. miles)

Lighthouse at Cape Reinga, the most north-westerly point on the North Island of New Zealand. This is where the Tasman Sea meets the Pacific.

Greenland is the world's largest island. Covering an area of 2,166,086 sq. km (836,330 sq. miles), it is roughly 2,650 km (1,650 miles) long and approximately 1,000 km (620 miles) wide at its broadest point. The magnificent, thick sheet of ice that covers some 80% of the island's surface reaches

Drift ice and stormy conditions around Cape Farvel make these waters extremely hazardous.

altitudes of up to 3,000 m (9,800 feet) and is a hangover from the last ice age. The southern and south-western coasts are, by contrast, largely ice free. Polar bears, reindeer, musk oxen, and more than 200 different bird species all live in this subpolar and polar climate. The only trees are in a very small area in the extreme south of the island. Those sections of the coast that are not covered by ice are instead characterized by tundra vegetation.

The thaw along the east coast of Greenland, including Scoresby Sund – the world's longest fjord. The olive-green areas indicate plant growth.

Greenland's many magnificent glaciers reach all the way down to the sea. The large chunks of ice that calve off the glaciers along the coast drift through the bays and out into the open sea as icebergs.

The top image above shows the glaciers edging toward the coastline between the rocks. The lower image shows a section of Disko Bay, in western Greenland, which is literally teeming with icebergs.

ARCTIC OCEAN

Also known as the North Polar Sea, the Arctic Ocean is the smallest of the world's oceans. Numerous islands sit on its shelf edges.

BAFFIN ISLAND
Canada
507,451 sq. km (195,928 sq. miles)

This is the largest of the many islands in the Canadian Arctic Archipelago of northern Canada, and the world's fifth largest island overall. It is traversed by a heavily glaciated mountain chain that spans almost its entire length. The numerous fjords that typify the coastline along Baffin Bay feature only sparse vegetation, while the south and south-west parts of the island – whose lowlands were formed during the ice age – exhibit a tundra vegetation. Over to the east, Mount Thor is a geological highlight, its 1,250-m (4,101-foot) high vertical rock face the highest of its kind anywhere on Earth. The islands' few settlements are home to some 11,000 inhabitants, most of them Inuit. More than half of the population lives in Iqaluit, the capital of Nunavut territory. Created in 1999, this new territory takes in many of the islands of northern Canada, as well as a large section of the northern Canadian mainland and the entire Hudson Bay area. Its population survive by fishing, hunting, and – increasingly – tourism.

VICTORIA ISLAND
Canada
217,291 sq. km (83,897 sq. miles)

Canada's second largest island is part of the Canadian Arctic Archipelago. Its western part lies in the Northwest Territories, its eastern side in Nunavut. The Dolphin and Union Strait, Prince of Wales Strait, Dease Strait, Victoria Strait, Coronation Gulf, and Queen Maud Gulf separate it from the mainland. The landscape is the result of glacial activity. The Shaler Mountains – rising to 665 m (2,182 feet) – mark its highest point. The island is named after the British Queen Victoria.

DEVON ISLAND
Canada   55,247 sq. km (21,331 sq. miles)

This second largest of the Queen Elizabeth Islands is part of Nunavut territory. Covering an area of 55,247 sq. km (21,331 sq. miles), it is the largest uninhabited island in the world. The Devon ice cap, which rises to 1,920 m (6,300 feet) in the Treuter Mountains, accounts for a third of the island's entire surface area. Devon Island is famous for the Haughton impact crater, the diameter of which measures some 20 km (12 miles). Thanks to its climate, the island was chosen as the location of a simulated Mars habitat in preparation for a manned mission to Mars.

The tundra vegetation of Victoria Island.   Ice floes off Ellesmere Island.

ELLESMERE ISLAND
Canada
196,236 sq. km (75,767 sq. miles)

Part of the Queen Elizabeth Islands, Ellesmere Island lies off the north coast of Greenland. Its northern tip, Cape Columbia is the most northerly point of North America. The jagged east and west coasts are shaped by fjords, and more than a third of the surface is glaciated. There are no trees in the tundra, but lichen, mosses, and Arctic plants all thrive here. The average temperature is around 12°C (54°F). Quttinirpaaq National Park spans about one-fifth of the island.

NOVAYA ZEMLYA SEVERNY ISLAND
Russia   48,904 sq. km (18,882 sq. km)

Severny Island (the northern isle) is Europe's fourth largest island. Together with Yuzhny Island (the southern isle) and numerous smaller islands, it forms the Novaya Zemlya archipelago, which separates the Barents Sea to the west from the Kara Sea to the east. The narrow Matochkin Strait lies between the two islands. While tundra dominates the southern isle, the northern isle is heavily glaciated. Both islands are the location of research stations.

BANKS ISLAND
Canada
70,028 sq. km (27,038 sq. miles)

The westernmost island of the Canadian Arctic Archipelago is named after the English naturalist Sir Joseph Banks and belongs to the Northwest Territories. The Prince of Wales Strait, McClure Strait, and Amundsen Gulf separate the island from the surrounding islands of Victoria Island, Prince Patrick Island, and Melville Island. This is an essentially low-lying landscape dominated by tundra vegetation, and it is only in the east that the Durham Heights reach altitudes of up to 730 m (2,395 feet).

AXEL HEIBERG ISLAND
Canada   43,178 sq. km (16,671 sq. miles)

One of the Queen Elizabeth Islands, this is Canada's seventh largest island. It lies just west of Ellesmere Island, from which it is separated by Nansen Sound. Fjords have given the island its heavily indented shape. At 2,211 m (7,254 feet), Outlook Peak is the highest point. The island is uninhabited, and glaciers and ice cover a third of it. In 1985, an Eocene forest was discovered in the east of the island. The fossils it yielded dated back 40–50 million years, and its swamp cypress and dawn redwood trees grew up to 50 m (164 feet) high and could live a thousand years.

Left: Baffin Island is the largest island of the Canadian Arctic Archipelago. The northern part of the island is mountainous and glaciated, but the west is a swampy landscape.

Devon Island is partially glaciated.

A glacial tongue on Axel Heiberg Island.

MELVILLE ISLAND
Canada   42,149 sq. km (16,274 sq. miles)

This hilly and uninhabited island in the Canadian Arctic Archipelago is the fourth largest of the Queen Elizabeth Islands. Its highest point rises to 776 m (2,546 feet). The island meets the Hazen Strait to the north, the Byam Martin Channel to the north-east, and the Viscount Melville Sound and McClure Strait to the south. Its western side belongs to the Northwest Territories, its eastern side to Nunavut. There is only sparse vegetation in the central area, which is partly covered by ice. Melville Island was discovered by the British explorer Sir William Edward Parry.

SOUTHAMPTON ISLAND
Canada   41,214 sq. km (15,913 sq. miles)

Surrounded by Roes Welcome Sound and the Frozen Strait, Evans Strait and Fisher Strait, Southampton Island lies in the northern end of Hudson Bay. Its landscape is essentially flat. The Porsild Mountains, to the north-east, are the exception, at more than 600 m (1,970 feet). Mathiasen Mountain is, at 625 m (2,051 feet), the highest peak. The tundra is home to numerous mammals, including polar bears, caribou, lemmings, and Arctic hares. Coral Harbour is the main settlement, and most of its 800-strong population are Inuit.

SPITSBERGEN
Norway   37,673 sq. km (14,546 sq. miles)

Spitsbergen is the largest island of the Norwegian Svalbard archipelago, and the name is sometimes used to refer to the entire archipelago. The island's Arctic flora is almost entirely composed of mosses, lichen, and ferns, though large areas of the island are entirely barren. Ny-Ålesund, on the west coast, is home to an international Arctic research facility that includes the world's most northerly marine research laboratory and an observatory dedicated to the study of the Northern Lights, the extraordinary play of lights best seen at night.

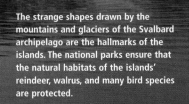

The strange shapes drawn by the mountains and glaciers of the Svalbard archipelago are the hallmarks of the islands. The national parks ensure that the natural habitats of the islands' reindeer, walrus, and many bird species are protected.

The islands of the Atlantic Ocean together exhibit the full range of climate zones, from the sub-polar regions to the temperate latitudes, Mediterranean, and tropical areas.

GREAT BRITAIN
United Kingdom
229,883 sq. km (88,758 sq. miles)

Europe's largest island is the world's eighth largest island overall. For its size, the landscape is extremely diverse, and the contrasts between different areas are often quite striking. Geographically speaking, Great Britain can be broadly divided into a highland and lowland region. The former comprises Scotland, Wales, and northern, north-west, and south-west England. The Scottish Highlands are the most mountainous part of the United Kingdom, followed by the Scottish lowlands and the Southern Uplands. Wales is spanned by the Cambrian Mountains, eastern and south-eastern England by broad low-lands. Heavily eroded lowland mountains dominate the landscape of northern England, while the undulating slopes and hills of the Pennines typify the scenery heading south. The landscape of southern England is similarly subtle, its appearance almost park-like. Magnificent, sheer cliffs alternate with sandy beaches along the ragged coastline.

NEWFOUNDLAND
Canada
108,860 sq. km (42,031 sq. miles)

The vast estuary of the Gulf of St Lawrence separates Newfoundland from mainland Canada. This rocky island is, in geological terms, an extension of the Appalachian Mountains. Characterized by low mountains, the island rises to 814 m (2,671 feet) at its highest point. The island has a fjord coastline, with woods and moors dominating inland. Its terrain was formed during the ice age.

At the northern extreme of the Appalachians, Newfoundland is mountainous.

IRELAND
Ireland/United Kingdom
81,638 sq. km (31,521 sq. miles)

The "Emerald Isle" is divided between the Republic of Ireland and British Northern Ireland. The central Irish lowlands are notable for their many moors and lakes, and the small beech and oak groves lend the terrain here a park-like character. Mountainous areas surround this lowland plain, and Carrauntoohil – at 1,038 m (3,406 feet) – is the highest point. Unlike the east coast, the west has many bays and some steep cliffs.

Right: Stormy weather over the lighthouse at Fanad Head, north-west Ireland.

CUBA
Cuba   105,806 sq. km (40,852 sq. miles)

Cuba, part of the Greater Antilles, is the largest island in the Caribbean. It separates the Gulf of Mexico from the Caribbean and is 1,200 km (745 miles) long and 120 km (75 miles) wide. Broad lowland plains divide Cuba's three mountain ranges, with one in the west, one in the central region, and one in the east. The island's highest point, at 1,974 m (6,476 feet), is in the Sierra Maestra.

The Malecón promenade runs along the beach in Havana, Cuba.

HISPANIOLA
Dominican Republic/Haiti
73,929 sq. km (28,544 sq. miles)

Hispaniola is the second largest of the Greater Antilles islands. The western part of the island is the republic of Haiti, while the Dominican Republic spans the eastern side. The island is traversed by five mountain chains, taking in the five highest summits in the Caribbean – notably the 3,175-m (10,417-foot) high Pico Duarte. The vegetation includes rainforests and cloud forests.

Right: Palm trees line this idyllic beach in the Dominican Republic.

ICELAND
Iceland
103,000 sq. km (39,768 sq. miles)

This so-called "island of fire and ice" marks a real hot spot on the Mid-Atlantic Ridge. There are some 130 active volcanoes, as well as geysers, steam vents, and sulfuric springs. There are also a large number of glaciers, which together cover some 11% of the island's surface. Most of the island, however, is a 300–1,000-m (980–3,280-foot) high plateau, its terrain a barren rock desert.

A mighty torrent of water cascades down the Godafoss.

TIERRA DEL FUEGO
Argentina/Chile
48,185 sq. km (18,604 sq. miles)

The Strait of Magellan separates Tierra del Fuego from the South American mainland. Here, the Cordillera Darwin marks the end of the Andes mountain range. The climate in this region is subpolar, humid, maritime in character, and frequently stormy. The islands' inland forests give way to the shrubs, mosses, and lichen of the tundra that is principally concentrated along the coast.

Right: Tierra del Fuego's leaning trees bear witness to the strength of the wind.

Left: In Dorset and Devon, the fossils found along Britain's "Jurassic Coast" provide a unique overview of 185 million years of natural history.

SICILY
Italy   25,662 sq. km (9,908 sq. miles)

Just off the "toe" of Italy, Sicily is the largest island in the Mediterranean. It is separated from the mainland by the narrow Strait of Messina. Mountains and hills are the dominant feature, often without any trees. Sicily's only major lowland plain lies on its eastern coast, near Catania. Rising 3,323 m (10,902 feet) above it, Mount Etna is Europe's highest active volcano, a truly awe-inspiring sight. Even in winter, the island enjoys a very mild Mediterranean climate that makes it an ideal place to grow citrus fruits.

SARDINIA
Italy   23,949 sq. km (9,247 sq. miles)

Sardinia is the second largest island in the Mediterranean, and its terrain is extremely varied. The central part of the island is mountainous. Punta la Marmora – which rises to 1,834 m (6,017 feet) – is its highest point, and there are some heavily fissured rock features in the north-eastern mountains. The Campidano lowland plain is a vast graben that runs diagonally across the south-west of the island, marking the edge of the mountains in the former mining region of Iglesiente. Sardinia has several smaller offshore islands.

JAMAICA
Jamaica   10,991 sq. km (4,244 sq. miles)

The third largest of the Greater Antilles islands, Jamaica is separated from Cuba, 145 km (90 miles) further north, by the Cayman Trench. Jamaica is essentially mountainous, and the Blue Mountains traverse the island from west to east. To the south lie extensive coastal swamplands. At altitudes of up to 900 m (2,953 feet), limestone plateaus account for some 60% of the island's surface, and karst formations are therefore a characteristic feature. Except for a few rainforests and cloud forests, most of Jamaica's indigenous vegetation has been destroyed by human intervention.

The land that splits off from the edges of the five tectonic plates beneath the Indian Ocean breaks through the water's surface as islands, island chains, and island arcs.

MADAGASCAR
Madagascar
587,042 sq. km (226,658 sq. miles)

The wide Mozambique Channel separates the world's fourth largest island from the African continent. Madagascar is some 1,600 km (1,000 miles) long and up to 580 km (360 miles) wide. Its eastern coast is so straight that it might almost have been drawn with a ruler, and there are only a few bays. The west coast, by contrast, is much more varied, and its bays and estuaries extend right into the alluvial plains. Rising above it all, the mountains that form the backbone of the island reach heights of up to 2,876 m (9,436 feet), descending in sharp vertical steps as you move further east. The relatively large distance between Madagascar and mainland Africa means that endemic species constitute a large proportion of the island's flora and fauna. The lemur – a type of primate that comes in all different shapes and sizes – is the best known. Some of Madagascar's many other species, however, have had very little scientific research. Deforestation means that their natural habitat is in real danger.

SUMATRA
Indonesia
443,066 sq. km (171,069 sq. miles)

The sixth largest island on Earth stretches for some 1,700 km (1,050 miles). The Barisan Mountains – a series of extinct and active volcanoes – run parallel to the island's west coast. Rising to a height of 3,805 m (12,484 feet), Mount Kerinci marks their highest point. To the east, the mountains give way to a marshy alluvial plain. Lake Toba, in the north-west, is the world's largest volcanic lake, spanning 1,146 sq. km (442 sq. miles). It was formed by a supervolcano some 74,000 years ago.

JAVA
Indonesia
138,794 sq. km (53,587 sq. miles)

Java, the most densely populated of Indonesia's islands, lies to the east of Sumatra. It stands out for its fertile soil and large number of volcanoes. One of these, Mount Merapi, is among the most dangerous on Earth. South of Java, the Sunda Trench marks the subduction zone of the Australian Plate. It is here that the Australian Plate is slowly edging beneath the Eurasian Plate, causing the high level of volcanic activity and earthquakes.

SRI LANKA
Sri Lanka
65,610 sq. km (25,332 sq. miles)

This tropical island off the southern tip of India is just a few degrees north of the equator. Some 6,000 years ago, it was probably still connected to India via Adam's Bridge. The mountains of the central highlands reach to over 2,500 m (8,200 feet). The famous tea plantations are a legacy of British colonial rule. The mountains divide the island into two climate zones. While the south-west has a perpetually humid monsoon climate, the north-east is semi-humid, with a distinct dry period.

TASMANIA
Australia
64,519 sq. km (24,911 sq. miles)

The Bass Strait separates Tasmania from the Australian mainland. Much of the western part of the island is still untouched wilderness, consisting of rainforests and moorlands that are home to many endemic plants. The island's fauna includes a significant number of endemic species, notably the Tasmanian Devil. National parks protect almost half of the island, and a quarter of it enjoys UNESCO World Heritage status.

Bush and rainforest vegetation on the rainy Tasmanian west coast.

Antongil Bay is Madagascar's largest (left). Humpback whales come to mate here every year at the end of June.

Palm-lined beaches, tropical rainforests, and mountainous woodlands are typical features of Sri Lanka's sunny south-western coast.

TIMOR
Indonesia/East Timor
28,418 sq. km (10,972 sq. miles)

The island of Timor is about 500 km (300 miles) long and 80 km (50 miles) wide. Politically, it is divided. All but a small enclave of its western side belongs to Indonesia, while East Timor has been independent since 2002. Rising to a height of 2,963 m (9,721 feet), the extinct Tatamailau volcano is the highest point. Little remains of Timor's vast sandalwoods and tropical rainforest, and secondary forests and grasslands are now dominant in the non-agricultural areas. The island has a semi-humid, tropical climate with a distinct dry period.

SUMBAWA
Indonesia
14,386 sq. km (5,554 sq. miles)

Sumbawa lies between the islands of Lombok and Flores. It is traversed by several mountain chains, and there are still sections of tropical rainforest on the slopes. The Tambora volcano in the north of the island erupted in 1815, devastating Sumbawa and claiming more than 100,000 lives. It also had a significant impact on the world's climate. Some 100 cu. km (24 cu. miles) of magma came to the surface and 400 million tonnes (441 million short tons) of sulfuric gases were released into the atmosphere, causing a temporary cooling of the Earth.

FLORES
Indonesia
13,540 sq. km (5,228 sq. miles)

Flores is Portuguese for flowers, and the name is a hangover from the time when Portuguese colonists ruled over the island – before being supplanted by the Dutch. The island is some 400 km (250 miles) long and, at its broadest point, 70 km (43 miles) wide. Its terrain is mostly mountainous, with small lowland areas along the coast. The Kelimutu volcano and its trio of crater lakes – one red, one blue, and one a shade of turquoise – are particularly noteworthy. The volcano, which rises to a height of 1,639 m (5,377 feet), last erupted in 1968.

SUMBA
Indonesia
10,711 sq. km (4,135 sq. miles)

Sumba lies slightly removed from the Lesser Sunda Islands. Its mountainous western side has a humid climate, with enough rainfall to sustain the irrigated rice paddy fields. By contrast, the climate in the east is dry, and the terrain – with its high grasses and few surviving trees – more like a savanna in character. There are no active volcanoes here. Deforestation has seen the island's once rich sandalwood forests dwindle to a far more modest area, but the island's isolated location means that traditional rituals and customs are still alive and well.

PACIFIC OCEAN

Most of the Pacific islands fall within either the tropical or subtropical climate zone. The South Pacific and Polynesian islands in particular are the very epitome of a tropical island paradise.

NEW GUINEA
Indonesia/Papua New Guinea
785,753 sq. km (303,381 sq. miles)

North of Australia, the world's second largest island is almost on the equator. Politically, it is divided between Indonesia in the west, and Papua New Guinea in the east, which became an independent state in 1975. Stretching from the west to the south-east, a high mountain range runs right across the island. Puncak Jaya, the highest peak, lies in the west, rising 4,884 m (16,024 feet) above sea level in the Maoke Mountains. The highest summit in the east is Mount Wilhelm, at 4,509 m (14,793 feet), and there are several more mountains rising to over 4,000 m (13,100 feet) between it and Puncak Jaya. An extensive, flat, lowland area lies to the south of the mountains. Traversed by meandering rivers, it often floods in the rainy season. The northern lowlands are closed in by a long band of mountains along the coast, forcing extensive sections of the main rivers of northern New Guinea to flow parallel to the highlands before finally reaching the sea. Tropical rain-

BORNEO
Indonesia/Malaysia/Brunei
748,168 sq. km (288,869 sq. miles)

The world's third largest island straddles the equator in the perpetually humid tropics. Its central mountains are surrounded by rainforest-covered hills and lowlands. Borneo remains relatively inaccessible, so is not heavily populated. Mount Kinabalu, which rises to 4,095 m (13,435 feet), is its highest point. The island is home to an extremely diverse range of plant and animal species, although large-scale deforestation has placed the orangutan's natural habitat in grave danger.

SOUTH ISLAND
New Zealand
145,836 sq. km (56,308 sq. miles)

The Southern Alps and their foothills span the western side of the island, becoming hills and lowlands to the east and south. Right in the middle of the island, Aoraki (Mount Cook) is its highest point. To the south, the many glacial lakes and characteristic fjord coast testify to the fact that this landscape was formed during the ice age. Heavy rainfall is a signature feature of the cool, temperate climate.

Thick clouds gather over Nugget Point, South Otago, Catlins (right, inset).

HONSHU
Japan
230,316 sq. km (88,926 sq. miles)

Separated from Hokkaido by the Tsugaru Strait, Honshu is Japan's largest island. It lies within the Ring of Fire around the Pacific Ocean, and has numerous active volcanoes. These counterbalance the pressure built up by the Pacific Plate as it slides beneath the Eurasian Plate. Earthquakes are not unusual on this densely populated island. At 3,776 m (12,388 feet), Mount Fuji is Japan's highest volcano, but the chances of it erupting are low.

NORTH ISLAND
New Zealand
111,583 sq. km (43,082 sq. miles)

The 35-km (21½-mile) wide Cook Strait separates the North Island from South Island. The volcanic highlands around Lake Taupo form the core of the subtropical North Island, and there are thermal springs, steam vents, fumaroles, mud pools, and geysers around the edge of this area. There are mountains along the eastern coast. The north of the island is a narrow swathe of land with numerous bays and islands to the east but none on the western coast, and the sandy beaches here seem to stretch forever.

SULAWESI
Indonesia
189,216 sq. km (73,058 sq. miles)

This volcanic island was called Celebes and is notable for its irregular shape. Temperatures here are tropical, and lush rainforests and mountain woodlands are the main vegetation features. Sulawesi shares its climate and flora with that of Borneo, on the other side of the Makassar Strait. Sulawesi's terrain exhibits a complex structure. Mountains cover 70% of the island's surface, Mount Rantemario – which rises to a height of 3,440 m (11,286 feet) – being the highest peak.

LUZON
Philippines
109,965 sq. km (42,458 sq. miles)

Luzon, the largest island in the Philippines, is one of the most densely populated islands on Earth. It lies between the South China Sea, the Philippine Sea, and the Luzon Strait. The terrain is mountainous, the Cordilleras that run from north to south meeting wide lowland plains inland. The island's numerous active volcanoes include Pinatubo and Mayon. The latter is a textbook example of a stratovolcano, and its perfect shape has made it well known. Laguna de Bay is the second biggest freshwater lake in Southeast Asia, after Sumatra's Lake Toba.

The red torii marks the entrance to the Itsukushima Shinto shrine, on the island of Miyajima. Located off the coast of Honshu on the Seto Inland Sea, the island boasts some of Japan's most beautiful landscapes.

forests are the dominant feature of the island's terrain, and woodlands account for 75% of its surface area. New Guinea boasts one of the ten most diverse ranges of plant species on Earth, and a similar diversity characterizes the islands' animal life, including some endemic species. One, the bird of paradise, is the national emblem of Papua New Guinea.

Not far from Rabaul, Papua New Guinea, Mount Tavurvur is one of this region's many active volcanoes (left). Papua New Guinea is the world's third largest island nation after Indonesia and Madagascar.

MINDANAO
Philippines
97,530 sq. km (37,657 sq. miles)

Lying to the north of the Celebes Sea, Mindanao is the Philippines' second largest island. Its terrain is mountainous, and its summits include the highest mountain in the Philippines, Mount Apo. Rising to 2,954 m (9,692 feet), this extinct volcano towers above the capital city of Davao in the south of the island. Mindanao's tropical rainforests are home to many endemic and some rare species – notably the Philippine eagle, whose wingspan can be as much as 2.2 m (7 feet).

HOKKAIDO
Japan
78,719 sq. km (30,394 sq. miles)

Cool summers and snowy winters are the hallmarks of Japan's second largest and most northerly island. The plateaus in the central part of the island are the result of volcanic activity. The surrounding lowland plains stretch down to the coast. The island has a high level of seismic activity. Some of its volcanoes are active, and powerful earthquakes are a frequent occurrence. Like Honshu, Hokkaido falls within the Ring of Fire that encircles the Pacific.

SAKHALIN
Russia
72,943 sq. km (28,163 sq. miles)

This long tract of land off eastern Russia is the country's largest island. It is almost 1,000 km (620 miles) long, but just 24–160 km (15–100 miles) wide. A chain of low mountains runs its entire length, and Mount Lopatin – which rises to 1,609 m (5,279 feet) in the central part of the island – is the highest point. Sakhalin's main rivers are the Poronai and the Tym, while taiga accounts for much of its vegetation. The island has significant oil and natural gas reserves.

SOUTHERN OCEAN

The Southern Ocean, Earth's second smallest ocean, is the meeting point of the Atlantic, Pacific, and Indian Oceans. Its islands include both those located off the coast of Antarctica, and therefore south of the 49th parallel south, as well as the more remote islands scattered across the ocean. The latter – including South Orkney, Heard Island, South Georgia, and South Sandwich – are mostly of volcanic origin, and the extreme nature of the Antarctic climate means that they are mostly glaciated and uninhabited. The Antarctic Peninsula is another feature of the Southern Ocean, taking in the smaller, coastal islands of the Southern Shetlands such as Elephant Island and King George Island.

THE LARGEST ISLANDS IN THE SOUTHERN OCEAN

❶ Alexander I Island
   49,070 sq. km (18,946 sq. miles)
❷ Berkner Island
   43,837 sq. km (16,925 sq. miles)
❸ Thurston Island
   15,700 sq. km (6,062 sq. miles)
❹ Carney Island
   8,500 sq. km (3,282 sq. miles)
❺ Roosevelt Island
   7,910 sq. km (3,054 sq. miles)
❻ Siple Island
   6,390 sq. km (2,467 sq. miles)
❼ Adelaide Island
   4,463 sq. km (1,723 sq. miles)
❽ Spaatz Island
   4,100 sq. km (1,583 sq. miles)

Sunrise above the mountain chains. The terrain of the Antarctic Peninsula is extremely mountainous, reaching heights of up to 2,800 m (9,186 feet).

In winter, large parts of the Southern Ocean's surface are covered by ice and ice floes.

POLAR REGIONS

The Arctic and Antarctic Circles lie at about the 66th parallel north and 66th parallel south respectively. The Arctic lies to the north of the former, and the Antarctic to the south of the latter. This polar landscape is one of ice, snow, rocks, and boulders where the temperature can drop as low as -70°C (-94°F) and periods of several months pass in complete darkness. That this harsh, inhospitable environment might support life seems improbable, if not impossible, yet humans, animals, and a variety of plants all survive here. The northernmost significant settlement – with a resident population of nearly 2,000 people – is

A walrus on the drift ice near Spitsbergen.

Longyearbyen on the island of Spitsbergen; which is part of the Svalbard archipelago.

Drift ice off the coast of West Antarctica. These ice floes and small icebergs drift through the sea having broken off the glaciers and inland ice.

The Antarctic is the world's largest surviving, fully intact ecosystem. The Arctic, too, is largely untouched.

THE ARCTIC

The Arctic covers 26.4 million sq. km (10.2 million sq. miles), only 30% of which is terra firma. It is the Arctic Ocean that forms the core of the Arctic. Spanning 14 million sq. km (5.4 million sq. miles), this is a marginal sea of the Atlantic Ocean. Greenland is the largest island in the Arctic and in the world overall. Cold, severe winters and cool summers typify the Arctic climate, and the frozen ground only ever thaws at the surface. The Arctic has more animal species than the Antarctic, including musk oxen, reindeer, caribou, Arctic foxes, polar bears, Arctic hares, lemmings, walruses, whales, and birds. Thanks to the Arctic Ocean, the climate is less raw than that of the Antarctic, which explains why the Arctic's coldest point is found not at the North Pole, but in eastern Siberia, where temperatures plunge to -77.8°C (-108°F). Greenland has the Arctic's thickest ice, some 3,400 m (11,155 feet) deep. The geomagnetic North Pole – where the Earth's magnetic field points directly downward – is near Qaanaaq.

THE ANTARCTIC

Antarctica is the only continent whose size changes according to the time of year. Its actual landmass is about 30% larger than that of Europe. The thick layer of ice that covers it is, on average, 2,000 m (6,600 feet) deep, but its maximum depth can be as much as 4,000 m (13,100 feet). The South Pole lies in the middle of this high plateau. There are valuable natural resources beneath the ice, but the Antarctic Treaty of 1959 forbids its signatories from claiming this territory and instead ensures that is reserved for peaceful, scientific research. The polar area is divided into several main regions, namely the Sub-Antarctic Islands, the shelf-ice areas, the Transantarctic Mountains, Antarctic mountains, and the Kerguelen Islands. The 3,500-km (2,175-mile) long Transantarctic mountain range marks the boundary between East and West Antarctica. The highest point on the continent is Mount Vinson in the Sentinel Range of the Ellsworth Mountains,

Ice floes drifting along the coast of the Antarctic Peninsula.

which – including the ice that covers it – reaches a height of 4,892 m (16,050 feet). With its harsh climate, the Antarctic explorer Robert F. Scott (1868–1912) once said of the Antarctic, "Great God! This is an awful place…". Temperatures here remain firmly below freezing all year round, and in 1983 a Russian research station recorded a low of just -89.2°C (-128.6°F). Even in summer, temperatures rarely

A large group of chinstrap penguins on an iceberg.

Arctic foxes frequently trail wandering polar bears across the pack ice in the hope of securing the remnants of their food.

exceed -20°C (-4°F) inland, and it is only along the coast that they might reach 0°C (32°F). This brutally cold weather makes the air extremely dry, and there is very little snowfall. Scientists based in the Antarctic fear the mighty storms that can rage here, with wind speeds hitting 300 km/h (186 mph). Low temperatures, powerful storms, dry air, high altitudes, and dark winters all conspire to make the Antarctic the most inhospitable place on

A leopard seal on the hunt for penguins.

Earth. In the many research stations, the scientists are the only human inhabitants, while the area's flora and fauna are concentrated on the Antarctic Peninsula – the king penguin and the smaller Adélie penguin being two of its best-known representatives. Streams of ice drain the inland areas of the Antarctic continent and feed the ice shelves that account for 40% of the nearly 18,000-km (11,200-mile) long coastline. The total shelf-ice area is estimated to be around 1.5 million sq. km (579,000 sq. miles), and the two largest ice shelves are the Ross ice shelf and the Ronne-Filchner ice shelf. Inland ice, glaciers, and ice streams all help to sustain these floating ice masses, continually moving ice to the seaward front of the shelf. Tabular icebergs are formed when the ice shelf becomes detached from the seabed. This reduction in the size of the ice shelf goes hand in hand with the break-up of ice shelves like the Larsen B ice shelf in the last five years. These spectacular events are a sign of the dramatic retreat of the glaciers, and scientists point to regional warming as the explanation. Over the last 50 years, average temperatures have increased by 2.5°C (36.5°F).

WALRUSES

The walrus is the second largest pinniped species, and the largest in the Arctic. Found in the waters of the eastern Canadian Arctic and northern Greenland, walruses live on the Arctic drift ice, escaping the pack ice in the summer by moving south. Male walruses grow up to 3.5 m

Life on the ice can get crowded.

The walruses' tusks are their most distinctive feature.

(11½ feet) long and weigh around 1,200 kg (2,646 lb), while the smaller females weigh in at up to 800 kg (1,764 lb). Both sexes have long tusks, which they use to pull themselves out of the water, defend against predators, and generally demonstrate their social standing. The animals have a 5–8-cm (2–3-inch) thick layer of fat beneath their skin that serves to protect them both from the cold and from injury.

These giant sea mammals are not fish eaters. Instead, they dive beneath the ocean surface for mussels, which they break off the seabed with their tusks (their upper canine teeth) and guzzle up through their bristles (which are thick enough to act like straws). Turning up their upper lip, they then close it over the mussel shell. Walruses also scour the sea floor for starfish, sea urchins, and worms.

POLAR BEARS

Polar bears are found in the Arctic. Along with the Kodiak bear, the polar bear is the largest land-based predator. The male has a body length of as much as 2.6 m (8½ feet), a shoulder height of up to 1.6 m (5¼ feet), and a weight of up to 800 kg (1,764 lb).

Unlike other bears, polar bears are serious carnivores, and animals such as seals and young walruses are the mainstay of their diet. The holes in the ice where the polar bear's prey come up for air provide the bears with their main hunting spots. Polar bears have an excellent sense of smell, and are able to detect seals that are still deep below the ice. Hunting aside, polar bears spend about two-thirds of their time resting and sleeping.

Polar bears are able swimmers.

The polar bear is a close relative of the brown bear. Its emergence along the Arctic coasts and edges of the drift ice is – in geological terms – relatively recent, dating back about 50,000 years. This capable swimmer's thick, white fur – from which water simply drips off – allows it to blend seamlessly into the polar landscape.

King of the Arctic: polar bears are at the top of the Arctic food chain, and seals (top) are their dinner of choice. Polar bear cubs are born in the winter. The mother gives birth in a snow den, and the cubs spend the first three months of their lives here before finally following their mother out on to the ice. They stay with their mothers for two years, during which time she patiently teaches them everything they need to know to survive (above).

Named after the male animal's trunk-like nose, the elephant seal is the world's largest pinniped species. There are two species – the northern elephant seal and the southern elephant seal – the former found along the west coast of North America, and the latter in the Sub-Antarctic, primarily on islands like South Georgia, the Kerguelen Islands, Heard Island, and Macquarie Island. The southern elephant seal population currently numbers around 750,000, of which more than half are found on South Georgia. The males grow to

Young elephant seals on South Georgia.

lengths of up to 5 m (16 feet) and weigh as much as 4 tonnes (4.4 short tons), making them the largest animals in the entire Antarctic. The females, by contrast, are significantly smaller and lighter. Essentially loners, elephants seals do nonetheless form large colonies during the mating season. There is approximately one male for every 10–20 females, and the latter become the objects of great rivalries.

Elephant seals and king penguins – seen here on the Atlantic island of South Georgia – live in peaceful harmony.

The wandering albatross, the largest of the albatross species, weighs up to 12 kg (26 lb) and has a wingspan of more than 3.5 m (11½ feet). There are many different species of this seabird, most of which are found on – or rather, above – the polar and subpolar seas of

Wandering albatross, Prion Island, South Georgia.

the southern hemisphere. They spend most of their lives in the air or hunting for food in the water below, only returning to land to breed. Despite their not inconsiderable weight, these birds are capable of flying long distances. Take-off and landing, however, are more complicated. They need a long run-up before taking flight, and their similarly long glide back to the ground sometimes ends in something of a bumpy landing. When they establish breeding colonies, albatrosses therefore always keep a stretch of land free of nests so that they can come and go easily.

Soaring above the ocean waves, the flight of the albatross is truly elegant. Albatrosses feed on octopuses, crabs, and fish near the surface.

Albatrosses have a complicated mating ritual. The two birds stick their heads out, extend their wings, rub their beaks on the sides of their bodies, and make a range of mating calls (top and middle). They are monogamous and mate with the same partner every year. Only when one of the pair dies does the surviving partner find a new mate. Both birds take turns at incubating the single egg in their nest (above).

TUNDRA AND TAIGA

North of the boreal coniferous forests of Eurasia and North America, the tundra is a region of steppes characterized by long, cold winters and short summers with little rainfall. Even in summer, the permafrost never completely thaws, so only plants and animals that can adapt to the region's barren soil and low temperatures survive. During the summer months, a wide variety of bird species can be found here. South of the tundra, the taiga is the world's largest continuous expanse of coniferous forest, interrupted only by the occasional huge swamps. Large parts of these woodlands have

A carpet of blooming flowers in Canada.

yet to be explored by man. As in the tundra, the ground here is permafrost and the climate typified by long, cold winters and short, cool summers. This, too, is an environment in which only the most hardy plants and animals can get by.

Tombstone Territorial Park is a protected area that spans the Ogilvie Mountains in Yukon, Canada. This permafrost region is home to caribou, moose, dall sheep, grizzly bears, brown bears, and numerous bird species.

NORTHERN ASIAN TUNDRA

Northern Asia is characterized by its polar climate and mostly tundra landscape.

Beyond the Arctic Circle, the area loosely termed northern Asia stretches from the Novaya Zemlya archipelago in the west to the Byrranga Mountains of northern Siberia and on to the Anadyr Range in the far east of the continent. The tundra is a generally narrow strip of land along the Siberian coast of the Arctic Ocean. Almost completely devoid of trees, this steppe-like landscape becomes forest tundra in the south – the terrain scattered with a few, small trees – before finally turning into the boreal coniferous forests of the taiga. The tundra climate is one of extremely cold, long winters and short, cool summers during which the sun never truly sets and the permafrost only thaws at the surface. The animals that live in this environment face a sparse choice of food. In the summer, grasses, berry-bearing bushes, mosses, and lichen are all that grow here, but they are enough to sustain musk oxen, reindeer, red deer, Arctic hares, and lemmings. In winter, the reindeer scrape the frozen ground with their hoofs and antlers to uncover the lichen beneath. The tundra's bird population includes snowy owls, red-breasted geese, and common guillemot.

Left: Forest tundra in Siberia. Forest tundra is found between areas of boreal coniferous forests and tundra proper, where there are no trees at all. Below, clockwise from bottom left: Snowfields and water in the tundra and mountains of Russia's Wrangel Island; mountain tundra in the Magadan area of eastern Siberia; mountains and clumps of grass on Wrangel Island; and the fall in the tundra near Provideniya, Russia.

NORTH AMERICAN TUNDRA

Vast expanses of inhospitable tundra are the dominant feature of the North American landscape beyond the Arctic timberline.

Permafrost and sparse vegetation are also the signature features of the tundra in the subpolar regions of North America. Covered by a layer of snow, the plants here are able to survive the Arctic winter. The snow along the Arctic coast begins to melt in May, and the temperature need only hit 0°C (32°F) for the plants to spring back into life. Having remained active under snow cover, they have already developed buds and leaves. Peat mosses are a significant feature of the landscape in the more moist areas, while lichen and shrubs – the latter bearing berries in the fall – thrive in the drier parts. The rocky southern slopes are bathed in warm sunlight by the low sun, turning them into veritable gardens of blossoming flowers. More than 100 different bird species breed in the Arctic Circle, including Brant geese, long-tailed ducks, and Arctic terns. Come April, caribou herds arrive on the tundra from the forests of Canada. There is also a significant growth in the population of small rodents like lemmings, voles, and blue hares, thus attracting skua birds and Arctic foxes. In the fall, however, most of the animals return to the south.

Caribou antlers on the tundra of Baffin Island, Canada.

In summer, the tundra becomes a sea of flowers.

Left: A grizzly bear prowls the autumnal tundra on the hunt for food. Berries, insects, birds, rodents, and larger animals such as caribou can all find their way on to the grizzly bear's menu.
Below: Fall in the North Klondike valley, part of Tombstone Territorial Park in Canada's Ogilvie Mountains.

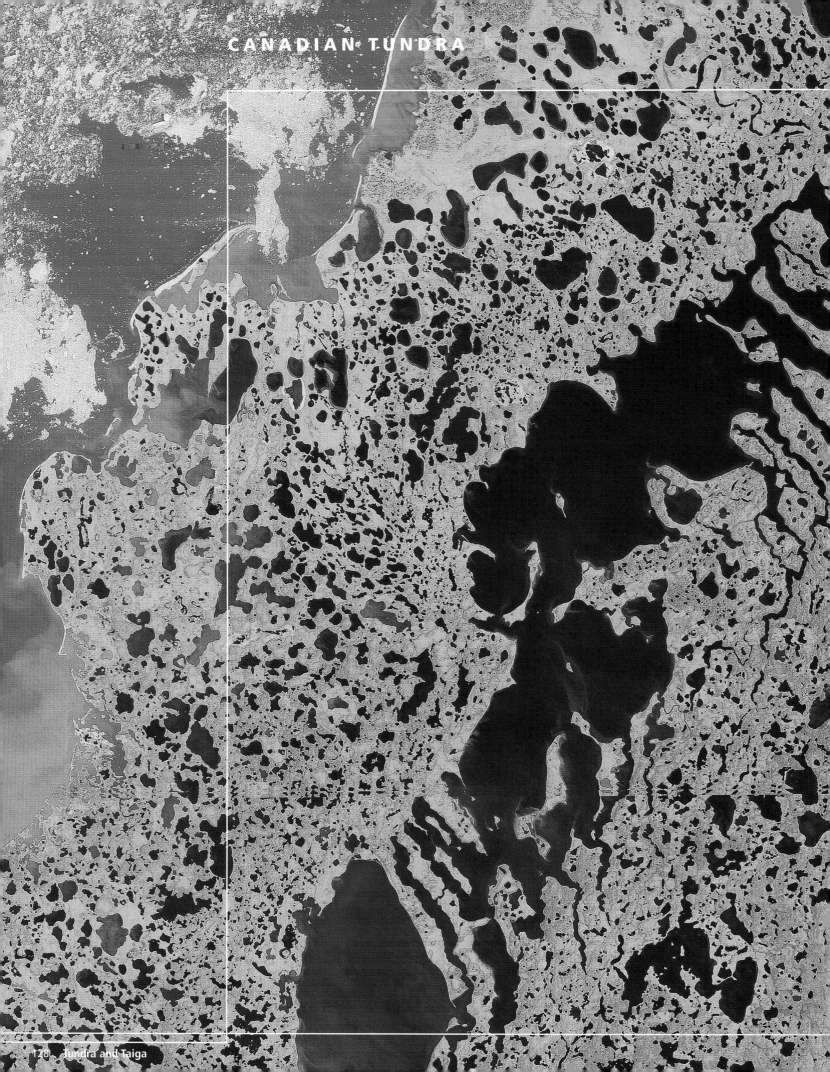

CANADIAN·TUNDRA

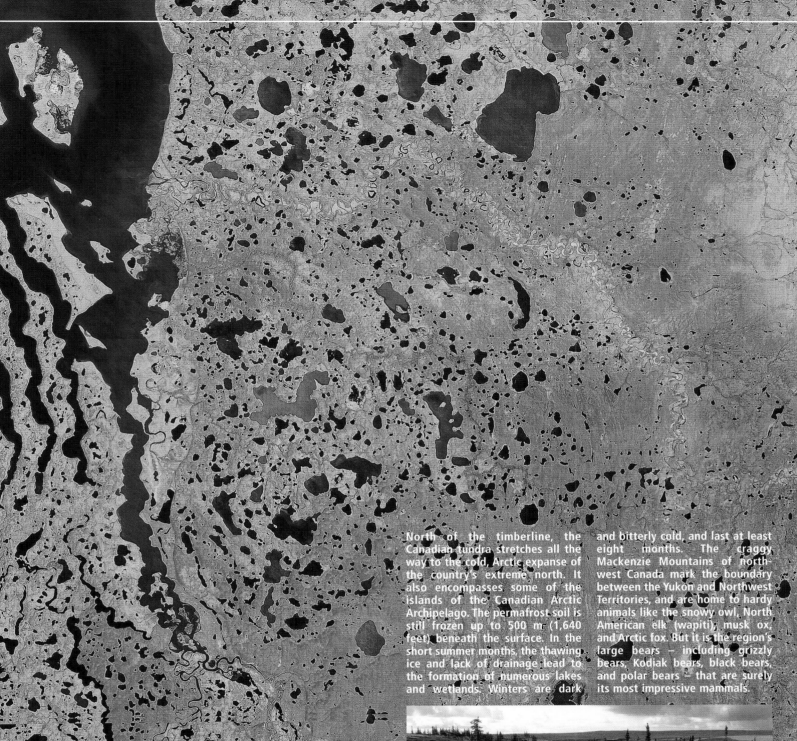

North of the timberline, the Canadian tundra stretches all the way to the cold, Arctic expanse of the country's extreme north. It also encompasses some of the islands of the Canadian Arctic Archipelago. The permafrost soil is still frozen up to 500 m (1,640 feet) beneath the surface. In the short summer months, the thawing ice and lack of drainage lead to the formation of numerous lakes and wetlands. Winters are dark and bitterly cold, and last at least eight months. The craggy Mackenzie Mountains of north-west Canada mark the boundary between the Yukon and Northwest Territories, and are home to hardy animals like the snowy owl, North American elk (wapiti), musk ox, and Arctic fox. But it is the region's large bears – including grizzly bears, Kodiak bears, black bears, and polar bears – that are surely its most impressive mammals.

Main image: North-east of the Mackenzie Delta, the Tuktoyaktuk Peninsula stretches into the Beaufort Sea for a distance of some 100 km (62 miles). Tuktoyaktuk, the only settlement, is visible in the bottom left of the image – surrounded by lakes and meandering rivers. The drift-ice fields that lie off the coast of the peninsula become a tightly packed belt of pack ice as you move north-west. Liverpool Bay – sticking finger-like in toward the south-west – separates the peninsula from the mainland. The Eskimo Lakes lie to the south.

The fall on the tundra of Canada's Northwest Territories.

MUSK OXEN

Musk oxen live in large, strictly hierarchical herds. Their long, thick coats make them ideally suited to the inhospitable tundra climate, and they survive on the region's sparse pickings of grasses, sedges, flowering plants, mosses, lichen, and shrub leaves. These are the largest

A musk ox and its magnificent mane.

animals in the tundra, the bulls growing up to 2.5 m (8 feet) tall and weighing as much as 400 kg (882 lb). During the short Arctic summer, musk oxen build up their reserves of fat to help get them through the deprivations of the coming winter.

Threatened by wolves or bears, musk oxen group together in a sort of living fortress. The eldest animals form a circle or semicircle around the young, turning their heads toward their adversaries to show their horns and horn bases (the thick bulges on their foreheads).

CARIBOU

The word "caribou" comes from the language of the Mi'kmaq Native North Americans. The caribou is the North American equivalent of the rather smaller European reindeer. There are two types of caribou: the barren ground caribou and the woodland caribou of western Canada,

Caribou on the autumnal tundra.

Part of a large caribou herd.

which are now extinct in most parts of the USA. Caribou live in herds, preferring wide, open terrain – especially that of the tundra. Here, they scrape the snow off the tangled bed of lichen with their hoofs. Shrubs, grasses, tree shoots, and the so-called "reindeer moss" are all staples of the caribou diet. Caribou and Eurasian reindeer are the only deer whose females have antlers, albeit smaller and less elaborate than those of the male animals. In winter, the herds migrate to warmer southern climes, returning north again in the spring. These migratory routes cover distances as great as 5,000 km (3,100 miles).

Caribou are herd animals, moving around in groups. Fall sees the male caribou compete for female mates. The females give birth to one or two young 240 days after mating.

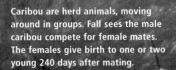

NORTHERN EUROPEAN, NORTHERN ASIAN, AND NORTH AMERICAN TAIGA

This boreal coniferous forest, or taiga, stretches from Scandinavia to Russia, Siberia, and all the way to North America – making it the largest uninterrupted expanse of coniferous woodlands on Earth.

EUROPE

Europe's boreal coniferous zone – or taiga – begins where the climate becomes too harsh for deciduous forests. Average temperatures in the taiga hover around just 5°C (41°F), and winter – which lasts for over six months – is particularly cold. The boreal zone takes in almost all of northern Russia and Scandinavia, from Norway to Sweden and Finland. The harsh climate and lack of nutrients in the soil mean that few species survive here. The floor of the boreal coniferous woodlands is covered in a thick layer of needles and twigs, which – thanks to the cold – takes a very long time to decompose. With the exception of the occasional birch or other small-leaved deciduous tree, lichen, pines, and larches dominate the woods, coniferous trees having the advantage of being better adapted to the cold. The animal population of the European taiga includes moose (European elk), wolves, lynx, bears, and marten. There are also considerable numbers of bird species, notably the crested tit, which is found only in coniferous woodlands.

NORTHERN ASIA

Taiga is Russian for "forest". The taiga of northern Asia stretches all the way from Siberia to China. Extensive parts of this woodland landscape have yet to be fully

Ferns and mosses in the taiga woodlands.

explored by mankind. The taiga terrain is mostly flat. It is dominated by coniferous forests, but there are also numerous marshes and peat moors. Like the tundra, the taiga is subject to long, cold winters and short, cool summers, so that only the hardiest plants and animals survive. Larches, stone pines, firs, and spruces are among the coniferous trees that grow here. Twinflowers are also typical of the Asian taiga (albeit now widely found in Scandinavia as well), while Siberian irises thrive in the marshes. The taiga is home to a much wider variety of animal species than the more northerly tundra, and brown bears, black bears, otters, lynx, sables, ermines, wolves, moose (European elk), wild boars, wolverines, Siberian weasels, squirrels, and countless bird species are all found here. The Siberian salamander is also relatively common, its habitat stretching from the Urals into Mongolia and as far as Hokkaido. The leopard and Siberian tiger populations are mostly concentrated along the Amur River.

Right: Taiga and marshlands on Canada's sparsely populated Labrador Peninsula.

Coniferous woodlands characterize the taiga landscape (left). The woodland contains grasses, mosses, lichen, and just two types of tree.

NORTH AMERICA

North of the 50th parallel, a large swathe of coniferous forest runs right across the vast North American land-mass, meeting the treeless tundra to the north, and mixed and deciduous woodlands to the south. The Russian word taiga may be correctly applied to these coniferous areas, whose cold, humid climate is typified by extremely

Squirrels are common in the woods.

long, hard winters and short summers. The Arctic Circle runs right through the middle of this zone, which provides a relatively uniform habitat for a number of plants and animals. Many of these animals, however, are only able to withstand the harsh, snowy winters by virtue of hibernation or migration to distant warmer climes. The North American forests exhibit a far wider variety of species than the European woodlands, and the continent has – if deciduous trees are included – some 130 different types of tree, including the ash, maples, elms, oaks, hickories, beeches, chestnuts, pines, Douglas firs, spruces, and cedars. The variety of animal species is also greater. One such inhabitant of the coniferous forests is the wood bison. Long believed to have become extinct, the wood bison came back on to the scene in 1957, and is now a well-established resident of the 45,000-sq. km (17,370-sq. mile) large Wood Buffalo National Park, Canada's largest protected reserve. Other animals found in the taiga of Canada and the northern extremes of the USA include the North American elk/wapiti (North America's second largest deer after the moose), the Canadian lynx (most prevalent in Alaska and Canada), the snowshoe hare, both the red and gray squirrel, and the grizzly, Kodiak, and black bears. The approximately 6,000-strong bison population is particularly notable.

Coniferous trees reflected in the surface of Lake Saimaa, Finland's largest lake.

In Alberta, Canada, coniferous woodlands are again the dominant feature of the landscape.

SIBERIAN TAIGA – THE WORLD'S LARGEST WOODED AREA

The taiga of central and eastern Siberia is the world's largest uninterrupted woodland area. The western Siberian lowlands in particular exhibit a distinct succession of vegetation zones, from tundra to taiga, forest steppe, and steppe.

The world's largest solid swathe of coniferous forests spans a 1,000-km (620-mile) wide and 4,800-km (3,000-mile) long expanse of northern Russia. This taiga terrain is characterized by its marshy or – for long periods – frozen ground, a sparse layer of plants, dwarf shrubs, and mosses the only covering. Most of the taiga is far from the ocean, and the climate is therefore continental. Harsh winters with heavy snowfall and dry, warm – or, in some parts of Siberia, even extremely hot – summers are the rule, with as much as 100°C (212°F) separating summer and winter temperatures. The vegetation period – during which the temperature rises above 10°C (50°F) – lasts just two to three months in the southern taiga, and is even shorter further north. Though there is little diversity in the region's flora and fauna, the number of plants and animals is very high. The woodlands are made up of spruces, pines, and larches, while animals capable of withstanding the cold are the taiga's most significant mammals. Many of its bird species spend the winters in warmer climes, other animals going

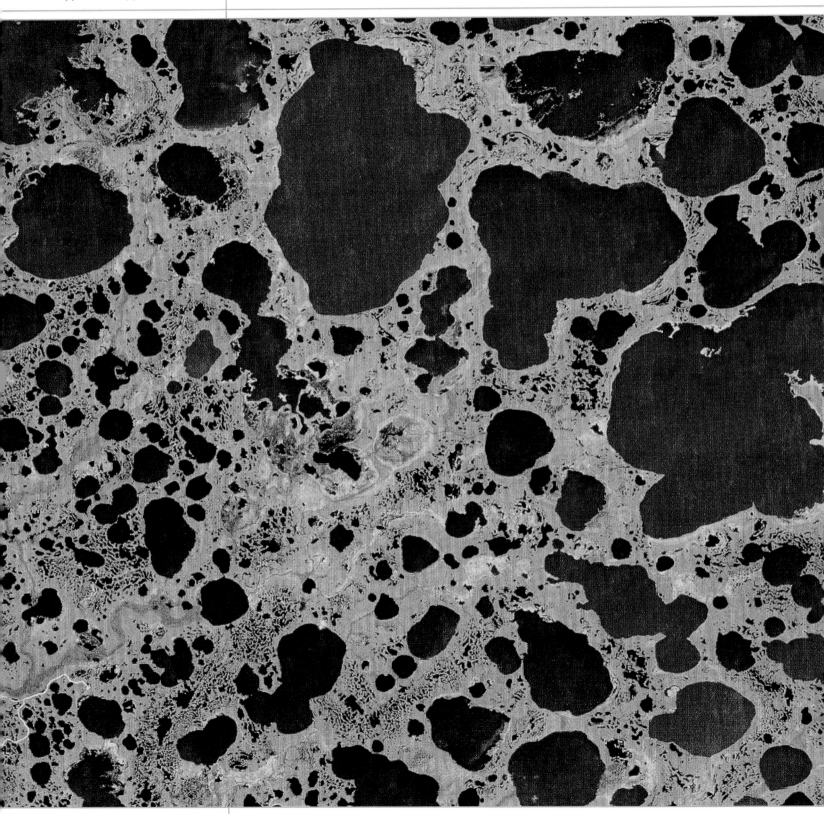

into hibernation for the colder months. Large parts of the taiga fall within the world's permafrost zone, an area covering approximately one-fifth of the planet within which the ground is permanently frozen for depths of up to 1,000 m (3,280 feet). Come summer, the top sections of earth thaw. Since there is no drainage, the formation of extensive marshlands is the result.

Left and satellite image, below: North of Surgut, boreal coniferous forests, moors, and lakes are the main features along the middle sections of the Ob River. Spruce, fir, larch, and birch are the dominant tree species. In summer, the backwaters and marshes become a breeding ground for mosquitoes. The lines drawn by the embankments and oil pipelines are visible signs of human intervention upon the natural world.

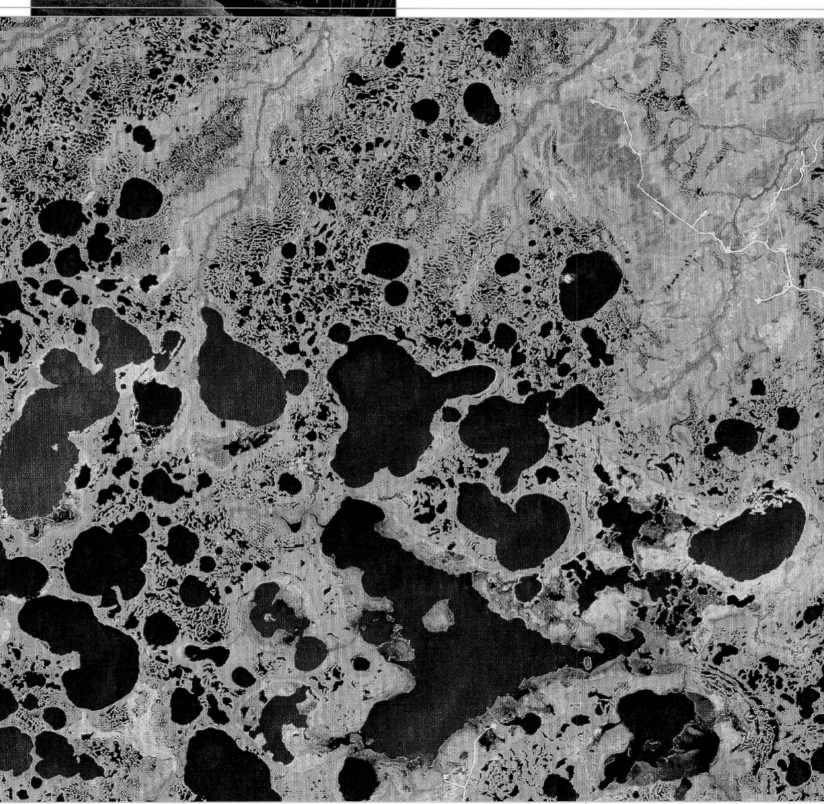

The forests along the Amur River and its tributaries, in the far east of Russia and adjacent parts of China and North Korea, are still home to a scattered population of some 450 wild Siberian (or Amur) tigers. Despite the tiger's protected status, hunting continues to

The tiger's long, thick coat protects it from the extreme cold.

place it at acute risk of extinction. It is the importance of the Siberian tiger to East Asian traditional medicine that constitutes the greatest threat.

The animal represents a highly lucrative kill for hunters, as there is hardly a part of its body that is not associated with some medicinal benefit. Its skin, bones, teeth, claws, blood, and even its gallstones and genitals are all considered to have medicinal value in the treatment of illnesses such as rheumatism, epilepsy, and skin and eye conditions. Some tiger-based products are said to stimulate intelligence, increase virility, and improve general well-being. Furthermore, it is not only in China, but also in the USA and Europe that tiger-based medicines command high prices. The animals' furs are also used to make high-end coats, which are exported at great profit. Up to 3-m (10-foot) long and weighing up to 300 kg (661 lb), tigers are solitary and primarily nocturnal creatures. They are the kings of an extensive territory, traversing 15–20 km (9–12 miles) every day on the hunt for animals like goral, wild boar, and red deer. The tigers must eat some 10 kg (22 lb) of meat every day if they are to survive the cold climate.

The Siberian tiger is the strongest and largest of the world's predatory cats. It is hunter and hunted – overcoming wild boar, deer, and cattle while at the same time being highly prized by hunters itself. Shy and nocturnal, Siberian tigers spend most of their time alone. Today, they are found in the mountains and birch forests of Jilin province, northeast China. The Siberian tiger's summer coat is, like those of its tropical cousins, short and smooth. In winter, however, this grows into a particularly thick and luxuriant fur.

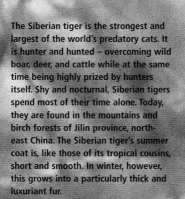

Tigers are loners, and will fight to defend their territory from other tigers.

A grizzly bear in the tundra.

A bear's fur shields it from the cold.

North America's large bears – including the grizzly, Kodiak, black, and even polar bear – are all brown bears belonging to the *Ursus* genus. Measuring up to 3.8 m (12½ feet), the Kodiak (or Alaskan grizzly) bear is found in Alaska and northwest Canada. The grizzly (or silvertip) bear, meanwhile, is now only found in Canada and the mountains of Montana. But it is the slightly smaller black (or baribal) bear that is the most common of North America's bears. Measuring approximately 2 m (6½ feet), the black bear feeds on a mostly vegetarian diet – just like the Kodiak and grizzly bears.

All brown bears prefer to occupy a fixed territory and the grizzly, which lives in the tundra and forests of northern USA – Alaska and the Yukon in Canada – is no exception. The size of its territory is determined by the food that is available, and can vary between 10 and 1,000 sq. km (4 and 386 sq. miles).

Brown bears catching salmon at Brook Falls in Katmai National Park on the Alaska Peninsula.

KAMCHATKA BEARS

The Kamchatka (or Siberian brown) bear is a subspecies of the brown bear that is native to the Kamchatka Peninsula of East Asian Russia. These bears have a body length of up to 2.7 m (9 feet), and weigh up to 600 kg (1,320 lb) – making them the second largest bear alive today after the Kodiak bear. The Kamchatka bear's fur varies between dark brown and black. An omnivore, the

Kamchatka bear feeds on the berries, roots, insects, birds, and fish it finds within its up to 2,000-sq. km (770-sq. mile) hunting ground. Along the coast, seals and other marine mammals are also among the Kamchatka bear's prey. Both the Siberian and North American brown bears hibernate for the winter. There is only a slight drop in the sleeping animals' body temperature during this period, but their heart and breathing rates both decline significantly.

MOOSE

Moose or elk, as they are known in Europe, are a type of deer found in the boreal coniferous forests of Europe, Asia, and North America. The moose is native to Alaska, Canada, and the Great Lakes region of the USA and is the world's largest deer. The male animals, also

Bulls test their strength.

called bulls or bucks, can be as tall as 2.3 m (7½ feet) at shoulder height, and weigh as much as 500 kg (1,100 lb). Their mighty, many-pronged antlers, which they shed in winter, are particularly impressive, and can measure up to 1.6 m (5¼ feet) across. The cow (female) is smaller than the male, and does not have antlers.

Moose are ruminants, and branches, deciduous leaves, grasses, and aquatic plants are the main components of their diet. They particularly like to graze alongside water, since this provides protection from insects.

Moose meet at special spots for the rutting season in the fall. Having mated, the cows go their own way, but the male animals only move on when all the females have been claimed. After an approximately eight-month pregnancy, the female gives birth to one or two calves. These stay with their mother until she sends them to fend for themselves shortly before giving birth to the next year's offspring. Active during the day, moose are loners. They reach maturity in 16 months, and can live for up to 27 years, although they rarely pass 15 in the wild.

A bull together with a cow and her calf is a rare sight indeed.

MIXED AND DECIDUOUS WOODLANDS

A brown bear cub in the forests of Bavaria, Germany.

Mixed and deciduous forests are almost entirely confined to the northern hemisphere. Europe's mixed forests stretch from Great Britain to France, central and eastern Europe, and as far as the Ural Mountains. In East Asia, they are found in Korea, Japan, and north-eastern China, while in North America they are found south of the Great Lakes all the way to the Atlantic coast and Gulf of Mexico. The signature feature of mixed and deciduous forests is that the deciduous trees shed their leaves in the fall, a characteristic that protects them from drying out during the cold months. Unlike the tropical rainforests, mixed and deciduous woodlands exhibit a relatively narrow diversity of species – a circumstance that is a legacy of the last ice age.

European beech trees dominate Bavaria's Spessart Nature Park. Noted for their smooth, gray bark, these magnificent trees can grow to heights of up to 40 m (131 feet). They are particularly highly prized as a valuable source of timber, and their triangular beechnuts are an important source of food for many woodland animals.

Mixed forests represent transition zones between boreal coniferous forests and deciduous woods. Characterized by their cooler climate, mixed forests are found from central Scandinavia to eastern Europe and the British Isles.

SCANDINAVIA

Beech, oak, chestnut, birch, elm, spruce, and pine trees are all found in the large forests of Norway and Denmark, but it is Sweden and Finland that boast some of the world's most extensive woodlands. Woods cover more than half of Sweden's surface area, and three-quarters of Finland's.

Finland is Europe's most densely forested country, and wide areas of green woodlands dominate an aerial view of the country's terrain. These are mostly areas of boreal coniferous forest (or taiga), but mixed forests – with both conifers and deciduous trees – become more common as you move south. Deer (including red deer), moose (European elks), foxes, raccoons, wild boars, badgers, martens, hares, hedgehogs, squirrels, and numerous insect and bird species are among the animal inhabitants of the Scandinavian forests, and strictly enforced conservation measures have in recent years also seen a recovery in the population of predators like the wolf, lynx, and brown bear, which can also be found in the French Pyrenees and in the Alps.

THE CENTRAL UPLANDS OF WESTERN AND CENTRAL EUROPE

Europe's central uplands run east from the Belgian and French Ardennes to central Germany and the Czech Republic, before finally coming to an end near the Carpathian Mountains of Slovakia. In Germany, woodland encompasses the Harz, Rhön, Thuringian Forest, Fichtel, Kyffhäuser, Westerwald, Weser, Spessart, Taunus, Hunsrück, and Bavarian Forest ranges. Up to about 700 m (2,300 feet), most of these extensive woodlands are deciduous. Beech is

Moss-covered trees in the Spessart region of Germany.

the dominant tree, but there are also pedunculate oaks, maples, rowans, birches, elms, and willows. Further up, around 700–800 m (2,300–2,600 feet) above sea level, there are also areas of natural mixed beech and spruce forests, although these are increasingly giving way to managed coniferous woodlands. In the Harz Mountains, northern Germany's highest mountain range, 80% of the trees are spruce, 12% beech, and the rest oak, rowan, and birch. The Eurasian lynx, capercaillie, wildcat, deer (including the red deer), raccoon dog, and raccoon are just a few of the animals to be found in many of the low mountain forests of western and central Europe. Some of these species were believed to have died out, but they have since been successfully reintroduced into the wild. The raccoon dog is now also widespread throughout northern and eastern Europe, thriving in moist forests with abundant undergrowth.

Beech and oak trees are typical of deciduous and mixed forests (left). At higher altitudes, where the air is cooler, deciduous trees give way to evergreen conifers, above all spruces and pines.

THE WOODLANDS OF EASTERN EUROPE

The beech forests of eastern Europe stretch all the way to the Baltic, thriving in the region's limestone earth. That said, the area's geology

An autumnal scene in the deciduous woodlands.

means that the eastern European continental beech forest beyond the Vistula River is now in decline. Only a narrow strip of deciduous oak woods remains, merging into a wide mixed wood area before then becoming a coniferous zone. Conifers cover most of the cold, northern part of the East European Plain in European Russia, while mixed and deciduous forests – including oak, beech, linden, ash, and maple trees – dominate further south. Poland's extensive woodlands, especially those in the east of the country, are even home to wolves, and Bialowieska Forest, near the border with Belarus, constitutes one of Europe's last remaining primeval forests. Yet these green woods are dying. According to a 2003 UN study, only eight in every 100 Polish trees are healthy. In many eastern European countries, up to 90% of the trees are sick. Romania, however, is an exception, its Carpathian forests lying far enough away from industrial conurbations to protect the woods from pollution.

THE ROMANIAN CARPATHIANS: EUROPE'S LARGEST SINGLE WOODED AREA

Europe's largest solid woodland area (left and main image) spans the Romanian section of the Carpathian Mountains, stretching from the country's northern border for a distance of some 300 km (186 miles) to both the south and west. These mountains mark the edge of Transylvania. The forests of the Romanian Carpathians are home to bears, wolves, lynx, Carpathian deer, and many other animals.

OAK AND BEECH TREES

THE MOST COMMON TREES OF EUROPE'S DECIDUOUS FORESTS

OAK TREES

There are more than 200 different species of the deciduous oak tree, but the three most prevalent species in central Europe are the Turkey oak, pedunculate oak, and sessile oak. The most common of all, found in almost every European region, is the pedunculate oak. These trees can be 20–40 m (66–131 feet) high, and their trunks have a diameter of up to 3 m (10 feet). Pedunculate oak trees can be 500–1,000 years old, and some

A passage runs through this ancient oak.

Europe's oldest pedunculate oak, the Grabeiche in Nöbdenitz, Thuringia, Germany.

are older still. Rich in starch, sugar, and protein, the acorn – the cylindrical, nut-like fruit of the oak tree – is an important food for numerous forest animals, especially rodents, wild boar, and deer.

The Sababurg primeval forest is a protected area in the German state of Hessen (left). With their thick trunks, the oak and red beech trees here are 200–600 years old.

BEECH TREES

A carpet of bluebells in the beech forests.

Autumnal leaves in the deciduous woods near Ashridge, England.

A winter's scene in the woods of Slovakia's Carpathians.

The beech is a deciduous tree that bears green leaves in summer and has a flat, gray bark. Beeches can grow to heights of up to 40 m (131 feet), and are found throughout central Europe. In fact, they originally constituted 40% of Europe's forests, but the long history of human settlement – and the associated exploitation of the woods for timber – has taken its toll on the continent's woodlands, and there are now hardly any virgin beech forests left. Europe's only true surviving primeval forests are those of the Eastern Carpathian Mountains. Stretching some 180 km (112 miles) along the Slovak–Ukrainian border, ten separate areas of protected woodlands were listed as a World Heritage Site in 1992. Beech trees grow best in places with mild winters and cool summers, and are not found in regions that experience harsh frosts and high levels of dryness. Their fruit, the beechnut, is an important food for wild animals.

Together with the aurochs, the wisent was once the dominant wild cattle of Europe's deciduous and mixed forests, and these two species could still be found in the woods of central Europe as recently as the early

A wisent with her calf.

Middle Ages. The wisent is closely related to the bison that roams the American steppes, but it has much less pronounced forequarters. The long, woolly hair on the wisent's head and the front part of its body provides excellent protection against the cold. The animals feed on grasses, lichen, mosses, leaves, and tree bark. They were all but extinct at the beginning of the 20th century, with only a few captive examples scattered across the world's zoos. Today, the population of wild wisent in Bialowieska National Park, along the Polish-Belarusian border, numbers some 300 animals.

Weighing in at up to a ton, wisents have a body length of up to 3.3 m (11 feet) and a shoulder height of up to 2 m (6½ feet) – making them Europe's largest and heaviest land-based mammals.

Though wisents live in herds, the bulls are often loners.

With a body length of 80–120 cm (31–47 inches) and a shoulder height of 50–70 cm (20–28 inches), the Eurasian lynx is Europe's largest predatory cat and its third largest predator after the bear and wolf. The lynx was once considered to have become extinct in western

A lynx pounces upon its prey.

Europe, but it was reintroduced into the wild in the 1950s, and is now found in the mountains of central Europe and in the Alps. The lynx's tufted ears, very short tail, and pronounced whiskers are the most distinctive features of its appearance. These are solitary animals, only pairing up for the mating season, which lasts from February to April. After a 70-day pregnancy, the female lynx gives birth to between two and five cubs, and these remain with their mother until the following spring.

A lynx with two of her cubs. The young animals are entirely dependent upon their mother for almost the entire first year of their lives. After that, they must fend for themselves.

The landscape of East Asia is essentially one of wooded steppes, the terrain somewhere between a mixed forest and unforested steppe in character. Deciduous woods and meadow steppes are the dominant features.

EASTERN CHINA

The extensive mixed forests of East Asia are home to a large number of endemic species, notably the Siberian tiger – the largest of the world's predatory cats – and the Chinese pangolin. Many of the region's animal species have only existed here since the latter part of the last ice age. On the border with Tibet, the forests that span the Meili mountain range are one example of eastern China's vast woodlands. The rare birds and animals that live here are not found anywhere else on Earth, and in spring and summer the meadows in the clearings come alive with flowers. In October, Miyaluo in Abi prefecture is famous for the spectacular golden yellows and deep reds of its deciduous trees. The rare flying dragon is another example of the forest's rich fauna. Mount Laoshan, whose eastern reaches meet the Yellow Sea, is one of China's most famous coastal mountain ranges. The summer flood season brings the waterfalls and streams to life, the woods turning to beautiful shades of red and brown come the fall.

JAPAN
HOKKAIDO

Visitors to Japan's legendary industrial cities and urban metropolises are probably unaware that mountains, hills, and woods cover two-thirds of the country's territory. This non-urbanized landscape boasts a rich and diverse flora and fauna. Hokkaido, Japan's sparsely populated second largest island, is

Hokkaido: the Asian Alaska.

frequently compared with Alaska for its vast natural landscape, with its virgin forests, magnificent snow-capped peaks, numerous mountain chains and volcanoes, clear lakes, hot springs, and large number of plant and animal species – many of them rare. Brown bears, red foxes, raccoon dogs, and sika deer are just some of the animals found in the woods of Hokkaido, and the graceful Manchurian crane is a common sight on the island's marshes. Hokkaido's long, harsh winters last from the beginning of December to the end of March, with temperatures frequently dropping as low as -40°C (-40°F). There follows a short spring, during which the island's lilac bushes and cherry and plum trees are all in full bloom. Summer is equally short, but it is warm – with average temperatures around 30°C (86°F) and humidity at 60–70%. The fall, which lasts about one and a half months, paints the mixed forests in an intense palette of seasonal hues. Hokkaido's cool climate and the absence of the summer rains seen elsewhere in Japan have contributed to its being dubbed *Hanataikriku* ("flower continent"), and nature lovers come from far and wide to admire its spectacular blooming plants.

Splendid natural forests in the Meili mountains of eastern China (far left), Miyalou (middle), and Jilin province (left). Below, left: Extensive woodlands and inland lakes are typical features of the landscape of Japan's Honshu island, and the autumnal hues of the deciduous woodlands around Lake Tsutanuma are truly magnificent.

JAPAN
HONSHU

Honshu is Japan's largest island, and the seventh largest island in the world overall. It is divided into several vegetation zones. Rice fields, woodlands, and mountains dominate the northern part of the island, while some of Japan's highest mountains – notably the world famous Mount Fuji – rise above central Honshu. Industrial facilities and a scattering of agricultural land characterize the densely populated coastal regions and the greater Tokyo area. There are many picturesque inland lakes, as well as both deciduous and mixed forests. The trees here are typical of a temperate climate zone, with pines,

Deciduous forest in Nikko National Park.

Yasunotaki waterfall during the fall.

oaks (including sawtooth oaks), willows, birches, beech trees, maples, and Japanese cypresses. There are also extensive mulberry and lacquer tree plantations – the former helping to rear silkworms and the latter providing the sap that is the basis of Japanese and Chinese lacquer art.

A red maple tree in Canada.

There are some 150 species of the deciduous maple. They are found throughout Europe, in North America, and in East Asia, and are most prevalent in low mountain ranges. The sycamore, which can grow to heights of up to 30 m (100 feet), is one of the largest maple species. The Norway maple (including the Crimson King) and field maple are examples of European maple species. The five-pointed maple leaf – its silhouette reminiscent of a human hand – is the national symbol of Canada. The maple gets its name from the shape of its leaves, acer being the Latin word for "pointed" or "sharp". The maple fruit has wings that allow the trees to distribute seeds over a wide area.

Autumnal maples in the north-east of Honshu, Japan. Many of the 150 maple species are native to America and Asia. Some are exclusive to the Japanese islands, notably the red snakebark maple found on Honshu and Shikoku.

The maple is the world's most common deciduous tree. It can grow both in isolation and in maple forests. In summer, maples bear green leaves, which take on their splendid signature hues in the fall. The aerodynamic shape of the falling maple seed lets it glide slowly down to the ground, thus maximizing the distance the wind can carry it. Rarely burned for fuel, maple wood is primarily used for furniture and construction. Sycamore wood is one of the most highly prized deciduous wood types on the planet, and the sycamore was crowned "Tree of the Year 2009" in Germany. In Canada and the eastern United States, the sugar maple is used to make sugar and syrup.

Maple trees in the imperial Japanese city of Kyoto.

Maple forests near Elliot Lake. The maple is the national tree of Canada, and its leaf adorns the Canadian flag.

Measuring 45–75 cm (18–30 inches), the snow monkey is the world's most northerly ape species. It is also known as the Japanese macaque, a reflection of the fact that it is only found on the Japanese islands of Honshu, Shikoku, and Kyushu, and a few of its smaller islands.

A curious Japanese macaque.

A macaque on Yakushima island.

Japanese macaques are at home in various forest environments, found in both mountainous northern woods and subtropical southern woodlands. The primate's most distinctive feature is a bald face, whose tone can be anything from pink to deep red. Though omnivores, these animals mostly feed on plants. Their exact diet varies according to the time of year. In winter, with up to 1.5 m (5 feet) of snow on the ground, Japanese macaques eat roots and bark, but in summer berries, nuts, and fruit are added to the menu. They live in largish groups of 30 to 60 animals, each group maintaining its own territory.

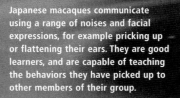

Japanese macaques communicate using a range of noises and facial expressions, for example pricking up or flattening their ears. They are good learners, and are capable of teaching the behaviors they have picked up to other members of their group.

Japanese macaques live in hierarchical social groups. They are famous for taking long baths in the hot thermal springs, allowing them to maintain their body temperature in the winter.

With up to eight layers, the deciduous forests of North America provide ample space for countless animals. Some of the most common deciduous trees include the hickory, tulip tree, maple, oak, linden, horse chestnut, and magnolia.

THE APPALACHIANS

The Appalachians are a range of low, wooded mountains that run for 2,400 km (1,500 miles) of North America's Atlantic coast – from the Canadian province of Québec all the way to the US state of Alabama. These mountains are the western part of a mountain chain that, before the formation of the Atlantic Ocean, reached as far as northern Scandinavia. Dating back more than 400 million years, the Appalachians are significantly older than the Himalayas, Alps, or Rocky Mountains. The Green Mountains, White Mountains, Catskill Mountains, Blue Ridge Mountains, and Cumberland Mountains are some of the main Appalachian mountain chains, their summits and valleys mostly covered by thick mixed and deciduous forests. The Appalachian forests stand out not only for their size, but also for their many fascinating animal species and tremendous plant diversity – there are more tree species in the southern part of this region alone than there are in the whole of Europe.

ROCKY MOUNTAINS

The Rocky Mountains run along the west coast of North America, from the Brooks Range in Alaska to the eastern Sierra Madre of Mexico, which is a distance of more than 4,300 km (2,700 miles). Volcanoes

Aspen and oak forest in Colorado.

and glaciers were responsible for the formation of this enormous mountain range, and 74 of the summits reach altitudes above 3,500 m (11,500 feet). Canyons, mountain lakes, corries, moraines, and high basins like the Colorado Plateau, which includes the Grand Canyon, are the components of a landscape characterized both by its great diversity and its stark contrasts. Thus the coniferous forests of the northern Rockies are set against temperate North American rainforests along the coast and lush tropical vegetation in the south. The Rocky Mountains mark a distinct climatic boundary and watershed, with moisture from the Pacific raining down on the western slopes while the east gets hardly any rain at all. The forests of the more northerly Rocky Mountains are much thicker than those of the south, and Douglas firs, Colorado spruce, and trembling aspen are among the trees found here. At higher altitudes, conifers like spruces, firs, and pines are more or less the only trees. Animal inhabitants of the Rocky Mountains include the puma, Canadian lynx, red fox, white-tailed deer, raccoon, and the rare bighorn sheep, for which the Rockies provide a vital last refuge.

Right: Come the fall, the aspen trees on Hart Mountain, Oregon, turn a vivid shade of orange.

The densely forested Great Smoky Mountains (left), part of the Appalachians, lie on the border between North Carolina and Tennessee.

NEW ENGLAND

The New England region of the northeastern United States encompasses the states of Connecticut, New Hampshire, Maine, Massachusetts, Rhode Island, and Vermont. This is the most European part of America, its landscape, climate,

Autumnal tones in eastern America.

and vegetation similar to those of northern and central Europe. Alongside some of the most significant places in the early history of the USA, New England also has fine coasts, beaches, and extensive forests. Maine, the largest New England state, is also the least populated. It has New England's richest forest, and Maine's Acadia National Park, boasting mixed woodlands, rivers, streams, lakes, cliffs, and mountains, is one of the most visited protected areas in the entire United States. This is truest during the so-called "Indian Summer", when visitors flock to see the deciduous trees turn yellow, red, and brown. New Hampshire is another popular destination for nature lovers. Although it has barely 20 km (12 miles) of coastline, this state does number some 1,300 lakes and wonderful waterfalls. Connecticut also has an abundance of historic places and cultural treasures, and its landscape is again characterized by the great diversity of its features, with lakes, rivers, mountain peaks, and forests. All in all, the view of the New England states is not one of a homogenous terrain, but rather an ever-changing vista of sea, mountains, woods, and meadows.

Bearfence Mountain in Shenandoah National Park, in the southern Appalachians.

Clouds descend upon the forests of the Great Smoky Mountains like a fine veil of smoke. At altitudes of 250–2,000 m (820–6,600 feet), the mountains are home to a wide variety of species.

The Appalachians are a forested, low mountain range in the eastern part of the North American continent. They stretch for more than 2,400 km (1,500 miles) from the Canadian province of Québec to the northern part of the US state of Alabama. Dating back some 400 million years, they are among the world's oldest mountains.

The vast expanses of thick mixed and deciduous woodlands that cover the many Appalachian mountain ridges and valleys are no less impressive, and are home to some of the most diverse ranges of flora and fauna on Earth. There are, for example, more species of tree in the Great Smoky Mountains National Park than there are in the whole of Europe. The variety of flowers is also tremendous, and in spring the forest floor is transformed into a resplendent fabric of azaleas, cornus, and laurels. The fall – during which this area is perhaps at its most spectacular – bathes the forest foliage in an intense spectrum of seasonal hues. The Appalachians are also home to 10% of the world's salamander species, which emerge from hiding come spring and the significant rainfall it brings. Healthy numbers of black bears and white-tailed deer are two examples of the larger animals found in the Appalachians. The Appalachian Trail, meanwhile, is one of the world's longest hikes, covering some 3,500 km (2,175 miles) from the south-eastern state of Georgia all the way up to Maine. Some of the old paths it incorporates were once used by the Cherokee Native North Americans, until they were forcibly resettled in 1838.

The forests of the Great Smoky Mountains National Park, in the North Carolina and Tennessee Appalachians, are among the world's oldest woodlands. They are also the largest primeval forest in the eastern USA.

PRAIRIES, STEPPES, AND SAVANNAS

Steppes are dry, treeless, grassy regions located in temperate latitudes – one such, the Eurasian Steppe, stretches from the Hungarian Puszta to Mongolia. In North America, this form of vegetation is

Camels grazing in the southern Gobi.

known as prairie and can be found on the Great Plains between the Rocky Mountains and the Great Lakes. Savannas are flat grasslands found in subtropical and tropical latitudes. This vegetation type covers around a sixth of the total mainland surface of our planet. In areas of high precipitation, savannas generally give way to tropical moist forests, in drier regions they become deserts or semi-arid grassland. Both types of grassland are characterized by sparse vegetation, as steppes and savannas generally lie in the continental interior and thus far from the oceans.

Tall, dry grass, dwarf shrubs, and thorny acacias are typical of the vegetation of the Serengeti, a savanna stretching some 30,000 sq. km (11,600 sq. miles) across northern Tanzania.

EURASIAN STEPPE –
THE WORLD'S LARGEST STEPPE REGION

The dry and treeless grassy landscape of the Eurasian Steppe covers a temperate zone stretching from the Black Sea to the Gobi Desert and from eastern Europe to deepest Mongolia.

The Eurasian Steppe is a vast landscape extending around 5,000 km (3,100 miles) from the Puszta in Hungary to the furthest reaches of Mongolia in Asia. The largest part of the Eurasian Steppe lies in Central Asia and only a small part is to be found in eastern continental Europe (in Russia, the Ukraine, and Hungary). Steppe areas are generally considered to be cheerless, barren, and bleak, with only a very few people – mainly nomads – braving such supposedly inhospitable regions. The steppes stretching across the Eurasian continent are surprisingly full of life, however, and more than 1,500 plant forms thrive here, as well as saiga antelope and Przewalski wild horses. Thought to be the ancestor of the domestic horse, these animals were once found throughout Europe but have since been forced back into the remotest corners of Eurasia. A small breeding population was reintroduced in Mongolia and there is now thought to be around 250 animals in the wild. Millions of birds also gather from time to time on these supposed "wastelands", as the grassy steppe landscape promises water and other nourishment.

The smaller, scattered trees of the Central Asian steppe gleam reddish-orange and yellow in the autumnal sun.

The broad, grassy steppe landscape adjoining the taiga in northern Mongolia provides sufficient food for the nomads' horses and cattle (left).

A typical draw-well on the Puszta.

Grass steppes of Mongolia.

The expanses of The Mongolian Steppe.

PUSZTA

The Puszta (meaning "plains") is an enclave of the Eurasian Steppe in the Hungarian lowlands that was created as man cleared forests and canalized rivers in order to gain pasture land. Cattle stocks in Hungary have since declined and extensive parts of the grassland have been turned over to agriculture. No more than about 400,000 ha (990,000 acres) of the Hungarian salt and grass steppes are still in existence.

MONGOLIAN STEPPES

Steppes are the predominant form of landscape in Mongolia, with alpine and shortgrass steppes making up around half of Mongolia's sovereign territory. This grassland still offers the (nomadic) farmers sufficient pasture for their cattle. Besides the grasses, the steppes also allow other plants to flourish, especially mosses and lichens as well as low shrubs. The majority of our cereal crops also originated on the steppes. While the grassland grows lush, only a few larger plants, such as trees, thrive in the dry climate. Small groves of trees are a rare sight in the Mongolian steppe landscape and are to be found only in perfect locations. Corsac foxes, urial sheep, bustards, and all kinds of rodents make the Mongolian steppes their home with ideal conditions.

The exact geographic demarcation of the Gobi Desert, an arid steppe region in Central Asia, is still disputed. It covers an area

The hilly steppe of the Gobi Desert.

Horses grazing on the steppes.

Nomads herd sheep and live in yurts.

reaching roughly from the Pamirs to the Great Khingan mountain range, bounded to the north by the Altay and Changai ranges and to the south by the Nanshan and Kunlun Shan mountains. It stretches for more than 2,000 km (1,250 miles) from west to east and some 8,000 km (5,000 miles) from north to south. The total area is more than 1 million sq. km (400,000 sq. miles), and on average it lies around 1,000 m (3,280 feet) above sea level. The climate is continental with cold winters (as low as -40°C/-40°F) and hot summers. Yearly precipitation is on average around 200 mm (8 inches). The wetter borderlands to the north and east are used to farm livestock. Nowhere on Earth is home to fewer people than the Gobi Desert, but camel caravans of Mongolian nomads have journeyed through the steppes for centuries.

A herd of camels migrates through a sea of wild flowers as the Gobi Desert comes into bloom.

THE DROMEDARY

The dromedary (from the Greek *dromas*, meaning "runner") grows to a height of around 2 m (6½ feet) at its shoulder and weighs up to 500 kg (1,100 lb). It has only one hump and is smaller in bulk than the Bactrian camel; it is also a more nimble mount. The animals generally have fur the shade of sand, a long neck, and keratinous footpads that protect them from burns as they come into contact with hot sand. Domesticated dromedaries are found not only in the desert regions of Asia and Africa, but also in Australia, where many specimens were introduced as pack and draft animals or as mounts in the 19th century.

THE BACTRIAN CAMEL

The two-humped or Bactrian camel remains an important means of transport in Mongolia, and there is still a residual population of wild animals in the Gobi Desert. This two-humped camel, the largest inhabitant of the Asian steppes, reaches a shoulder height of up to 2.3 m (7½ feet) and can weigh up to 500 kg (1,100 lb). It has been domesticated in areas such as the Hindu Kush because it can also be put to use as a draft animal in snow. Camels are ruminant herbivores and will eat even thorny and salty foods. They can survive for several days without water and when necessary can consume more than 100 litres (26 US gallons) in a short time.

Their shaggy coat protects them against the cold in winter; in summer it falls out in tufts, such that the camels (above) are almost bald.

Dromedaries (above) have shorter fur than Bactrian camels and can survive for longer without water.

Bactrian camels can carry loads of up to 450 kg (990 lb) and travel distances of 50 km (31 miles) a day. Their original native habitat was the steppes and the semi-deserts of Central Asia but now they are found only in south-western Mongolia (in the Gobi Desert) and in north-western China.

Chang Tang and Qiangtang, the two extensive steppe regions of the Tibetan Plateau, are lush grassland in the warm summer months but take on desert-like characteristics during the very dry, cold winters. Bounded by the Trans-Himalayas and the Kunlun Mountains, Chang Tang lies at an average of 4,500 m (14,750 feet) above sea level, making it the world's highest-lying steppe region. Although there is some vegetation, there is an area of around 1 million sq. km (400,000 sq. miles) where not a single tree is to be found. A wide variety of wildlife lives in the steppe region, however. Once found all over Tibet, animals such as the wild yak, Tibetan brown bear, Tibetan gazelle, and Tibetan antelope have since been driven back into this area. Animal stocks on the Tibetan steppes have increased significantly since 1983, when the Chinese government set up the Qiangtang Nature Reserve, the largest national park in Asia with an area of 298,000 sq. km (115,000 sq. miles).

A typical feature of the steppes: wide, treeless grassland.

The snowy, ice-capped tip of Shishapangma (8,013 m/26,289 feet) towers over the Tibetan steppes.

Horses on the way to Kailash near the Bayan Har Mountains in the Tibetan Plateau.

Wet savannas are found adjoining tropical rainforests at the equator; nearer the tropics they become dry savannas. This type of vegetation occurs primarily in Africa and Asia, but is also found in Australia and South America. Savannas are found in various forms, including dry

Im indischen Kaziranga-Nationalpark

savannas, in areas of northern, eastern, western, and central India. The yearly monsoon determines the extent of wet savannas: from June to September it rains so much that swollen rivers flood the surrounding areas, carrying with them fertile silt. Temperatures reach around 32°C (90°F) in summer and 10°C (50°) in winter. Flooded savannas typically feature evergreen grasses that can grow to a height of as much as 6 m (20 feet).

The savannas are usually bordered by hills of monsoon and moist deciduous forests, which need less water. Alluvial grassland covers 70% of the area of the Kaziranga National Park in north-eastern India. The park offers a protected refuge for animals such as the Asian elephant, the Indian rhino, the Bengal tiger, and the wild water buffalo.

Sambar im Kaziranga-Nationalpark

Nilgai antelope in Blackbuck National Park, Velavadar, India.

Wild water buffalo in search of food in Kaziranga National Park in Assam. Wild water buffalo are a highly endangered species, with remaining numbers estimated at between 200 and 4,000 specimens.

The Indian rhinoceros is the largest of the three Asian rhinos, measuring 1.8 m (6 feet) at the shoulder with a length of 3.7 m (12 feet) and a weight of up to 2.2 tonnes (2.4 short tons). On its nose it has a single horn that can grow to a length of up to 50 cm (20 inches).

Indian rhinos can be safely observed from the back of an elephant.

Indian rhinos prefer open, marshy territory, but many of them have been known to retreat into the forests to avoid man. Their original distribution area stretches from Pakistan west to Bangladesh and Assam; around 2,500 wild Indian rhinos now live in Bhutan, Nepal, and India, and more than 80% of these live in the Kaziranga National Park. Floodwater from the Brahmaputra covers this grassy landscape during the monsoon season, turning the region into an ideal habitat for the animals.

Several hundred rare Indian rhinos (large image) still live within the Chitwan National Park, the oldest national park in Nepal.

AUSTRALIA'S OUTBACK

Lying far from civilization, Australia's sparsely covered inland areas are called "the outback". The term can be applied

Dales Gorge in Karijini Park.

The "moonscape" of the outback.

to more than two-thirds of Australia's total area, including regions of the Northern Territory, Western Australia, Queensland, New South Wales, and South Australia. In large areas of the extremely dry outback in the west of the continent there can be no rainfall for years and temperatures often exceed 50°C (122°F) in summer. Karijini National Park in Western Australia encompasses some 620,000 ha (2,400 sq. miles) of steppe landscape, with spectacular rock formations and rivers that can quickly swell in the infrequent, but sometimes torrential, summer rainstorms. The park's famous waterfalls cascade into its gorges.

NEW ZEALAND'S HIGH COUNTRY

The Lindis Pass in Otaga, New Zealand lies on the main route to the Mackenzie Basin.

The elevated areas of vegetation in New Zealand known as "high country" are comparable to Australia's steppe-like outback, the Pampas in Argentina, or the Highveld in South Africa. The Mackenzie Basin and Central Otago on New Zealand's South Island, as well as parts of the North Island Volcanic Plateau, have all been described as high country. One common factor to all these expansive areas is the low rainfall resulting from the location of the plateaus in the rain shadows of the New Zealand Alps or its many volcanoes. They also all lie more than 600 m (1,970 feet) above sea level, have an extremely low population density, and enjoy a continental climate of hot summers and very cold winters. Livestock — usually sheep, but occasionally alpacas or deer — is often to be found grazing on the tussock grass of the steppes.

Spiky spinifex grass growing between bizarre-looking, red-brown termite mounds in Australia's outback.

The development of marsupials in Australia provides one of the best examples of evolution. Their origin goes back 150 million years to when Australia was isolated by the break-up of the Gondwana supercontinent: in contrast with Asia and South America, marsupials were able

Kangaroos have muscular hind legs and a strong tail.

to evolve without competition from higher mammals. The red and eastern grey kangaroos are the largest species of the marsupial class. The male red kangaroo can reach a height of 1.6 m (5¼ feet) and weigh up to 90 kg (200 lb). The females are around 25% smaller. The tail grows to a length of about 1 m (3 feet). The red kangaroo, which is particularly common in Australia's interior, has a reddish-brown coat.

Usually found in Australia's grassland, scrubland, and semi-deserts, the red kangaroo (*Macropus rufus*) sometimes lives in groups but often alone.

Australia's national animal, the large, flightless emu, lives in the dry, flat, lightly wooded bushland and semi-deserts of Western Australia. After years of hunting, which saw its complete extinction in Tasmania, the emu is now protected in game reserves. As Australia's

Australia's national animal: the emu.

largest bird and the world's largest flightless bird after the African ostrich, the emu can grow to a height of 1.9 m (6¼ feet) and weigh up to 45 kg (100 lb). The females are somewhat taller and heavier than the males, who are solely responsible for hatching and caring for the young. The emu's long, strong legs enable it to reach speeds of up to 60 km/h (37 mph).

The emu's feathers are grayish-brown and shaggy. After molting, they become darker and are gradually lightened by the sun's rays.

The emu's green eggs are incubated by the males while the female moves on. The 25-cm (10-inch) chicks are able to walk about five hours after they have hatched and after only a week they leave the nest with the male, with whom they maintain a very strong bond for around six months. The young chicks have characteristic striped plumage, which helps to provide camouflage. They keep this plumage for around three months (right).

THE SAHEL

The Sahel (Arabic for "bank") is an area crossing the entire African continent in a wide 300-km (186-mile) belt which stretches from Mauritania and Senegal on the Atlantic coast to Somalia on the Horn of Africa. It represents a gradual transition zone between the arid extremities of the Sahara to the

Goat herding in Mali.

north and the wet and dry tropical savannas of the south. The Sahel consists mostly of thornbush savanna with occasional grassland, areas also suitable for nomadic cattle farming. Irrigation has also proved possible in the regions surrounding the Niger, the Sénégal, and Lake Chad, further to the south. Large areas of the orig-

inal forestation and scrubland have been destroyed by extensive agriculture and cattle farming. Overgrazing has led to heavy soil erosion, and several million tons of dust from this region are displaced far and wide every year, even reaching as far as Europe.

The Cliffs of Bandiagara, a chain of sandstone peaks stretching for more than 200 km (125 miles) across Dogon country in southern Mali, rise from an escarpment 250 m (820 feet) above the surrounding plains. Riddled with caves, some of its cliffs can reach heights of 700 m (2,300 feet).

The East African state of Kenya includes several large areas of savanna, such as the 1,510-sq.-km (580-sq.-mile) Masai Mara National Reserve. The reserve is bounded to the east by the 390-sq.-km (150-sq.-mile) Amboseli National Park and to the south by the savanna of the Serengeti, which in Tanzania rises to heights of between 1,500 and 1,800 m (4,900 and 5,900 feet). The south-eastern parts of this extensive area of grassland consist of shortgrass steppes, and in the west there are areas of long grass interrupted by isolated gallery forests, dominated by the umbrella thorn acacias typically found in African savanna forests. With an area of around 14,750 sq. km (5,700 sq. miles), the eponymous national park at the heart of this area is richer in wildlife than almost any other on Earth. The Serengeti became legendary for the migration of immense herds of animals. As the rains dry up in the south in May and June and the grass plains have been heavily grazed, gazelles, wildebeest, zebras, lions, hyenas, leopards, and birds migrate north-west to the Masai Mara National Park, returning to the Serengeti in the fall.

High grass and thorny acacias are typical savanna vegetation.

Zebras in the Ngorongoro Crater on the edge of the Serengeti in Tanzania.

Sunset in Amboseli National Park in south-western Kenya, whose open grassland is home to countless species of big game.

The African elephant is the largest animal on Earth. Its ears and tusks are much larger than those of the Asian elephant and it also has two fingers on its trunk. Elephants cannot sweat and excess body heat is lost through the animals' ears, which explains their size. An elephant uses its trunk to tear off tree branches which it eats, including all the bark, leaves, and fruit. It can drink around 220 litres (58 US gallons) of liquid a day and regularly dowses itself with water. It gets rid of parasites by having extensive dust baths.

The tusks of a 50-year-old bull African elephant weigh around 50 kg (110 lb).

A herd of African elephants roams the
arid steppe in search of water. Elephants
live in herds of bulls and cows. The young
are suckled for up to three years.

With their long necks and their even longer legs, giraffes are able to reach the highest branches of the acacias on the savannas. Found only in Africa, though there are many subspecies, the giraffe is the world's tallest animal. Just like man, it has only seven neck vertebrae, although these are extremely elongated. It uses its 40-cm (16-inch) tongue to tear branches, leaves, and thorns from trees. Its area of distribution has shrunk considerably and larger

Inquisitive giraffes in Kenya.

A mother suckling its young.

herds are now only found in areas of central East Africa. Giraffes live in separated herds: females and young live in one group, and males in another. When fighting for dominance in the herd, they strike each other with their heads and necks. In order to drink, giraffes must spread their legs far apart. When threatened they will run away, cantering at speeds of 50 km/h (31 mph). They defend themselves against lions with fatally powerful kicks.

Giraffes on the Namibian savanna. The animals, which can be up to 6 m (20 feet) tall, are primarily yellowish-brown with brown spots of various sizes.

AFRICAN BUFFALO

Thanks to its powerful horns, the African buffalo (also called the Cape buffalo) was once one of the most frequently hunted animals in Africa. This easily irritated, mighty animal has turned the tables on many a big game hunter, however, as well as killing plenty of lions, its

African buffalo are considered aggressive.

only natural enemy (apart from man). Because it has poor eyesight, it often reacts unexpectedly to moving objects. African buffalo travel across the savanna in stately herds of 50 to 500 animals, grazing at night and at dawn. During the hot daylight hours they retire to a thicket or cool themselves in water or mud baths.

Enormous herds of African buffalo migrate across the African savannas, following the rhythm of the rainy and dry seasons.

THE LARGEST CATTLE OF THE AFRICAN SAVANNAS

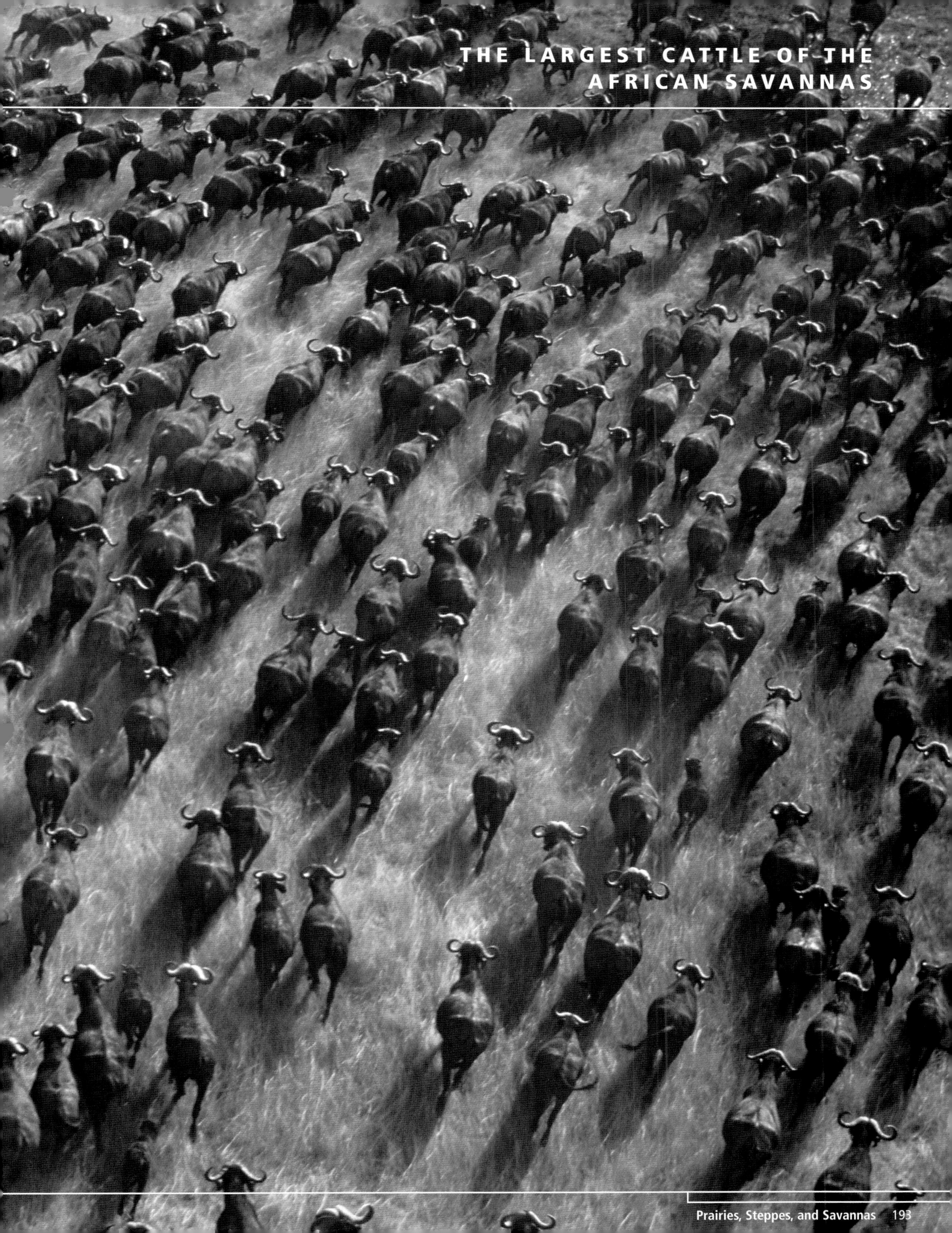

Wildebeest, which belong to the antelope family, feed on fresh short steppe grass and require a lot to drink. Twice a year they migrate across the savanna in herds of tens of thousands to search for water and fresh pastures, especially in the Serengeti. A herd can cover 1,600 km (1,000 miles) in a year. Weighing 200 kg (440 lb), a wildebeest measures about 2 m (6½ feet) from rump to snout, and stands about 1.3 m (4¼ feet) tall at the shoulder. The animals have short fur, a mane along their chest and another along the top of their neck, a tuft of hair on the end of their tail, and powerful horns, which the males use to settle territorial disputes.

A herd of wildebeest crossing the Mara, the only river in the Serengeti National Park which never dries up, assuring the survival of many animals.

Several species of zebra are to be found in sub-Saharan Africa, including the mountain zebra, the plains zebra, and Grevy's zebra. Zebras are equines; in other words, they are Africa's wild horses. They form mixed-species herds, often roaming the African wilderness with ostriches and wildebeest. The zebra's stripes are effective camouflage in the savanna – at any distance from the observer, the contours of the animal are broken up completely. Recent research suggests that a cooling circulation of air occurs between the white pelt and the black stripes. Zebras can reach speeds of up to 80 km/h (50 mph) when fleeing danger, often zig-zagging from side-to side.

The seasonal wildebeest migration between May and July sees herds of many thousands galloping in a cloud of dust that darkens the sky. A single zebra has strayed among the wildebeest here. The largest wildebeest migrations in southern Africa take place in the Makgadikgadi Pan in Botswana.

LIONS

With a length of 2.50 m (8 feet) and a height at the shoulder of about 1.20 m (4 feet), the lion is the largest land-based predator cat in continental Africa. The lion is the only cat species to live in a family pride, to which the females belong throughout their life. The pride, which includes the females and the young, is led by a single male lion. Young males are driven out of the pride at about the age of three; they then lead solitary lives or form a group with other bachelors until they manage to take over a pride led by an old, often toothless, lion. The females in a pride hunt together, while the male defends his family and guards his territory from rivals. The male's mighty mane protects him against the sweeping claws of opponents, but is primarily used to intimidate. Lionesses lurk or hunt in packs, and defeat even heavy prey. Only elephants and rhinos are safe from attack, or are only hunted by large packs. Lions can reach 20 years of age in the wild.

The lion's mane differs depending on the animal's age and subspecies. Some males have hardly any, but as a general rule it grows longer the further north the animal lives.

Lions are mighty hunters and require large amounts of fresh meat for themselves and their pride. A resting pride of lions is ignored by antelopes, zebras, and wildebeest, and no panic ensues even if the hunters begin to roam around. Only the chosen victim has anything to fear. Lions' prey includes zebras, wildebeest, antelopes, and buffalo, as well as hares, birds, and fish. Even carrion is acceptable, and lions often drive hyenas away from their prey.

CHEETAHS

As the fastest land mammal, a cheetah can not only cover short distances (up to 500 m/ 1,640 feet) at speeds approaching 120 km/h (75 mph), it can accelerate from resting to 100 km/h (62 mph) within five seconds. The cheetah's unbelievable speed is due less to its long legs than its extraordinarily efficient lungs. Even zigzagging gazelles are unable to escape cheetahs, who can compensate for rapid changes of direction with their long

A female cheetah with its young on the African savanna.

tails. They have usually caught their prey within 20 seconds, knocking it over with one blow of a paw and then killing it with a bite to the throat. They then bolt down their food before it is stolen by lions or hyenas. They usually prey on smaller ungulates, such as gazelles, which are much easier to overpower than the larger zebras or wildebeest. Cheetahs differ from other cats in that are sheathed and also blunted to give them better traction at speed.

Cheetahs live alone, as pairs, or in groups on their own territory in the African savanna. They sometimes hunt together.

SOUTH AFRICA'S SAVANNAS AND VELDS

NAMIBIA
(Etosha, Caprivi)

Namibia's largest national park, covering 23,000 sq. km (8,880 sq. miles) of the Kalahari Desert, is known as Etosha, which has several possible translations: "place of the great white expanses", "place of dry water", or (in the San language) "hopping from one foot to the other because of the hot ground". All of these descriptions are true of the Etosha Basin, a salt basin of 5,000 sq. km (1,900 sq. miles) in the middle of the national park. The remains of an ice age lake, this broad expanse of white clay and salt fills with water for just a few weeks every year, although there are usually a few nearby water-

Zebras and kudu at a waterhole in the Etosha National Park.

holes. These pools attract giant flocks of waterfowl, herds of zebras and antelopes, and the inevitable predators, such as lions, cheetahs, and hyenas. There is an astonishing variety of animal life in Etosha; almost all the large fauna to be found in southern Africa roam free here, including hippopotamuses, crocodiles, water-

Oryxes in the Kalahari Desert.

bucks, and buffalo. The 400-km-long (250-mile) Caprivi Strip, a stretch of land which extends into several adjacent countries, is mostly taken up with nature reserves. Caprivi is the only part of Namibia to lie completely within the tropics and the heavy precipitation in the rainy season between December and March, as well as the many rivers of all sizes, make it the wettest region in the country. The result of this is dense and lush green vegetation and large numbers of wild animals – there is a particularly large elephant population here. As there are no border fences, the animals can roam unimpeded, and may even wander into other nearby countries, such as Botswana and Zambia.

A wary herd of springboks grazing in the Etosha National Park in Namibia – ever ready to flee at speeds of up to 90 km/h (56 mph) at the first sign of danger.

SOUTH AFRICA AND BOTSWANA
(Kruger National Park, Karoo, Kgalagadi Transfrontier Park)

A number of regions of South Africa consist of extensive velds (prairies). One of the most famous is the Kruger National Park, the largest game reserve in the country. Located in the north-east, to the east of the Great Escarpment, this park of 20,000 sq. km (7,700 sq. miles) encloses savanna, scrubland, forests, and hills. Measuring about 350 km (220 miles) from north to south and about 60 km (37 miles) from east to west, the Kruger National Park is home to some 150 species of mammal, including the African "Big Five": elephants, lions, buffalo, rhinos, and leopards. About 500 species of birds and 100 different reptiles also live here. The

The scrub of the Kgalagadi Transfrontier National Park, South Africa/Botswana.

Karoo, a semi-desert of about 500,000 sq. km (193,000 sq. miles) surrounded by mountains lying north of the Great Escarpment, takes up about a third of South Africa's total territory. As little rain falls here, the area consists mainly of dry plains with sparse vegetation. The Karoo National Park is home to elands, zebras, and black rhino, as well as a

number of species of reptile, including the parrot-beaked Cape tortoise and the speckled Cape tortoise, the world's smallest land turtle with a shell length of only 5–10 cm (2–4 inches). North-eastern South Africa contains the southernmost reaches of the Kalahari Desert, and the Kgalagadi Transfrontier National Park, which stretches beyond the border into Botswana, is composed of scrub and grassland providing a home for many wild animals.

Buffalo in the Kruger National Park.

Calvania, Great Karoo, South Africa.

THE WHITE RHINOCEROS

African rhinos inhabit dry steppes, although their Asian cousins prefer damper habitats. The two species of rhino to be found in Africa have preferences for different kinds of food. The white rhino grazes mainly on grass. It lives a sociable life in

A white rhino with its young.

small mixed groups which keep to their own territory. It has excellent hearing and a good sense of smell, but does not see well. These colossal animals, which reach full size between seven and nine years old, measure 1.60–2 m (5¼–6½ feet) high at the shoulder and are 3–4 m (10–13 feet) in length. There are two subspecies: the northern white rhino is found in the Democratic Republic of the Congo and the southern white rhino is found in South Africa, Botswana, Namibia, Swaziland, Zimbabwe, Kenya, and Zambia. The northern white rhino is threatened with extinction and there are very few specimens left in the wild; numbers of the southern white rhino are estimated at about 14,500. The white rhino differs from the black rhino in having large, pointed ears, a wide flat mouth with no prehensile tip, and a marked hump at its neck.

A white rhino in the Kruger National Park, founded in 1898 and South Africa's largest game reserve. White rhinos prefer savanna with enough scrub and bushes to offer shade and cover.

THE BLACK RHINOCEROS

The black rhino is smaller than its cousin, standing 1.60 m (5¼ feet) at the shoulder and measuring 3.50 m (11½ feet) in length. It is a bold and solitary creature with darker skin and a

A female black rhino with its young.

finger-like protuberance on its upper lip, which it uses to grasp bark, leaves, saplings, and shoots of grass. It prefers savanna with thorn bushes, scrub, and trees as a habitat, never straying far from waterholes. The front horn of a black rhino can reach lengths of up to 1.30 m (4¼ feet) and the animal is to be found in Angola, Cameroon, Zimbabwe, Mozambique, Kenya, Namibia, Rwanda, Swaziland, South Africa, and Tanzania. Only about 4,000 specimens remain.

ELANDS

The eland, with its relatively straight, spiral horns, reaches lengths of 2–3 m (6½–10 feet), making it the world's largest species of antelope. Elands live in herds in the dry savanna and mountains of Africa. They are good runners (reaching 70 km/h, or 43 mph) and jumpers,

An eland with its elegant horns.

and live on foliage, grass, and roots, which they dig out with their hooves. They have adapted well to high temperatures: to avoid losing moisture through sweating, their body temperature rises by 7°C (12.6°F) during the dry season.

A fish eagle surveying a herd of elands on the banks of Lake Nzerakera in the Selous Game Reserve in Tanzania, Africa's largest monitored nature reserve.

Ostriches no longer use their wings to fly; they are used instead to maintain balance when running.

The African ostrich, the world's largest bird, is a flightless bird. The males can grow to a height of some 2.5 m (8 feet) and the females about 1.90 m (6¼ feet). They have a characteristically long, featherless neck and a small head in proportion to their body. Their wings are large for a flightless bird, but the animals are much too heavy – a cock bird can weigh up to 130 kg (290 lb) – to ever take off. Ostriches live in loose groups which, although constantly chang-ing, have a clear hierarchy. During the mating season the groups disband and sexually mature males gather a harem around them of a main mate and several spares. Before mating, the male scratches a nesting hole about 3 m (10 feet) across in the earth, and here the female lays her eggs. She incubates the eggs by day and the male takes care of the nightshift. Incubation takes 35–45 days. Survival rate is low with only one bird per nest reaching maturity.

Ostriches settle fights over dominance with threatening gestures.

GREAT PLAINS

With a length of more than 5,000 km (3,100 miles) and a width varying between 500 and 1,200 km (300 and 750 miles), the Great Plains lie to the west of the Interior Plains. They extend from the delta of the Mackenzie River on the Arctic coast to the Río Grande in central

Herds of bison on the Great Plains.

Texas, where they merge with the plains of the Gulf coast. The Great Plains have a total area of about 2 million sq. km (770,000 sq. miles) spread across ten US states and three Canadian provinces (known as the "prairie provinces"). Their average elevation in the east is only about 400 or 500 m (1,300–1,600 feet), but to the west, the Great Plains – now a series of plateaus riven by countless rivers – rise to heights of 1,600 m (5,250 feet) at the foot of the Rocky Mountains. The grassland on the eastern edge of the Great Plains is known as prairie, steppe-like regions mostly featuring grasses and wild flowers, with few trees.

Sundown behind a wheat field in the Great Plains of North America. The region is often called the "bread-basket" of the USA, as about half of all American wheat is grown on the Great Plains.

The plateaus of the Great Plains were once extensive areas of naturally occurring grassland. When the first white settlers took control of the lands, bringing cattle and horses, the area's appearance changed, losing its original character – giant fields where a monoculture of wheat is cultivated are now the most likely sight.

BISON

The bison, America's largest and most powerful animal, was carefully, systematically, and extremely cynically exterminated, down to a very few surviving examples: the white settlers were trying to remove the Native North Americans' means of subsistence. Around the year

Rivals fighting during the mating season.

1700, some 60 million of these wild cattle, which are closely related to the buffalo, would follow the same paths across this wide land from north to south; by 1885 no more than 90 specimens in the entire USA had survived the wholesale slaughter; protection and breeding of the bison began in the 20th century. The prairie bison, which lives on grasses and herbs, is like the forest bison descended from the European *Bison occidentalis* which came to America a million years ago. This mighty animal with its massive skull and powerful forequarters can reach a length of 3 m (10 feet) and weigh 1 tonne (1.1 short tons). The bison lives in segregated groups of bulls and cows, which come together only during the mating season. The cows give birth to a reddish-brown calf after a gestation period of nine months.

Main image: bison have pronounced forequarters, high withers and both males and females have short, pointed horns on their massive heads. Their fur, which is light or dark brown (or sometimes black), is noticeably longer at the front than at the back.

Although the bison was almost extinct, there are now more than 20,000 specimens.

The savannas of central Brazil, known as *cerrados*, are spread across ten states with a total area of 2 million sq. km (770,000 sq. miles), making up about a quarter of the total area of Brazil. The region is composed mainly of plateaus, some of which reach a height of 900 m (2,950 feet) above sea level. The *cerrados* have a dry climate with two seasons: a rainy period (October to April)

Clouds drifting across the *cerrado*.

and a dry period (May to September), during which there is a drought. The ground is dry but there is still moisture at a depth of about 2 m (6½ feet) below ground. Many of the plants have adapted to the conditions over time, and some species have roots 30 m (100 feet) long,

which reach down to the ground-water. Grasses and plants with roots nearer the surface soon dry out during the dry season. The trees on the *cerrados* grow to a height of about 10 m (33 feet) and are similar to those of the African wet savanna; some retain their foliage throughout the year, others shed at least some of their leaves during the dry period. The *cerrados* are also home to some 10,000 succulents, of which about half are

indigenous. The savanna fauna includes nearly 200 species of mammal, 800 birds, 180 reptiles, and more than 100 different amphibians. As agriculture on the plains is spreading by the day, the diversity of these ecosystems is under threat. The region now produces soya, beans, maize, and rice, and is responsible for a large percentage of the country's beef cattle production and cellulose pulp destined for the paper industry.

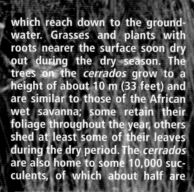

The Chapada dos Veadeiros plains in the state of Goiá are just part of the *cerrado*.

The grass of the *cerrados* desiccates completely during the dry season, only turning green when the rainy season comes.

PAMPAS

Argentina's extensive pampas stretch as far as southern Uruguay. They are largely treeless plains, rising gently from east to west and extending from the foothills of the Andes in the west to the Atlantic coast, and from the Gran Chaco region in the north down to the Patagonian Plateau in the south. As they cross different climatic and vegetation zones, it is possible to draw a distinction between the *pampa húmeda* to the east and the *pampa seca* in the west. The thorn bushes of the *pampa seca* grow in an arid climate, although there is tropical dry forest to the north. The *pampa húmeda* is pure grassland and covers 530,000 sq. km (205,000 sq. miles). The levels of rainfall decrease towards the east, and

Gauchos herding sheep on the Tierra del Fuego.

A storm brewing over the Argentine pampas.

droughts and floods become increasingly common; such conditions are ideal for the growth of natural grassland. The soils of the pampas are fine and loose, and retain water. There are no major rivers, the largest being the Río Carcarana in the north and the Río Salado to the south. Intensive farming of the pampas began in 1880, with arable land adjoining pasture for sheep and cattle. The pampas is now one of the largest agricultural areas in the southern hemisphere and Argentina's economic heartland; 60% of its cattle graze here. Many of its animal and plant species have been forced out – or wiped out – by humans. Parts have recently been turned over to vineyards.

The unusually uniform *pampa seca* in Patagonia in southern Argentina. It is much less densely populated than the fertile reaches of the *pampa húmeda*.

DESERTS

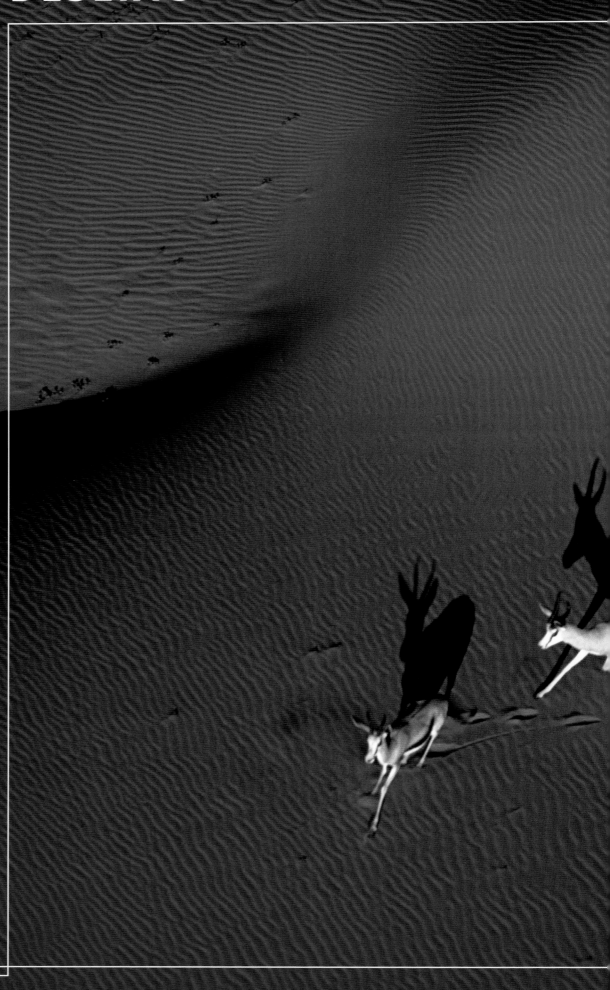

Some regions of the planet are so dry or cold that only desert plants can grow there, and no vegetation is able to take over the land. Dry and hot deserts are often found in subtropical areas of high pressure, on coastlines exposed to cold currents, and in enclosed mountain valleys. The annual precipitation in practically

The fight for survival in a barren area.

vegetation-free dry and core deserts amounts to less than 100 mm (4 inches).

THE WORLD'S LARGEST DESERTS

❶ **Sahara**	8.7 million sq. km
North Africa	(3.4 million sq. mi)
❷ **Gobi**	1.3 million sq. km
Central Asia	(500,000 sq. mi)
❸ **Kalahari**	1.0 million sq. km
South Africa	(380,000 sq. mi)
❹ **Rub al-Khali**	780,000 sq. km
Saudi Arabia	(300,000 sq. mi)
❺ **Patagonian**	
Desert	673,000 sq. km
South America	(260,000 sq. mi)
❻ **Great Basin**	540,000 sq. km
USA, Nevada	(208,000 sq. mi)
❼ **Atacama**	
Argentina,	400,000 sq. km
Chile, Peru	(155,000 sq. mi)
❽ **Chihuahua**	
Desert	363,000 sq. km
USA, Mexico	(140,000 sq. mi)
❾ **Great Sandy**	
Desert	360,000 sq. km
Western Australia	(139,000 sq. mi)
❿ **Gibson Desert**	330,000 sq. km
Western Australia	(127,000 sq. mi)
⓫ **Taklamakan**	
Desert	320,000 sq. km
China	(123,000 sq. mi)
⓬ **Sonora Desert**	320,000 sq. km
USA, Mexico	(123,000 sq. mi)
⓭ **Kyzl Kum**	300,000 sq. km
Central Asia	(116,000 sq. mi)
⓮ **Karakum Desert**	280,000 sq. km
Central Asia	(108,000 sq. mi)
⓯ **Great Victoria**	
Desert	274,000 sq. km
Australia	(106,000 sq. mi)
⓰ **Dasht-e Lut**	274,000 sq. km
Iran	(106,000 sq. mi)

Sand dunes that change in color
according to the humidity of the air
and the time of day are a feature of
the Namib-Naukluft National Park in
the Namib Desert in Namibia, the
oldest desert on earth (large image).

SAHARA –
THE WORLD'S LARGEST DESERT

The world's largest desert is not as inhospitable as one might think: some 200,000 sq. km (77,200 sq. miles) of it feature fertile oases, and plants and animals have adapted to the otherwise extremely harsh conditions.

The world's largest desert covers an area of some 8.7 million sq. km (3.4 million sq. miles). This vast plateau of sand and gravel, with its few oases, runs along an east-west axis for more than 6,000 km (3,700 miles) between the Atlantic and the Red Sea, and extends from north to south for more than 2,000 km (1,250 miles) to the Sudan. Only about 20% of the Sahara is sand desert, the rest is composed of scree or basins of stones, sometimes forming gravel plains (*serire*) or plateaus of bare stone (*hammadas*). At their edges, the basins form so-called wadis – river beds which contain water only after heavy rain. Large stretches of the northern Sahara, reaching as far as the Mediterranean coast, feature depressions covered with mighty seas of sand (*ergs*) or salt flats (*shatts*). These depressions continue toward the south to form the Ténéré, Libyan and Arabian Deserts. The central Sahara features inselbergs (or monadnocks) and plateaus such as the Tademait, Tassili, and Djado, which in turn are dominated by mountain ranges such as the Ahaggar, Tibesti, Aïr, Iforas, and Ennedi. The only constant body of

TIBESTI AND AHAGGAR: THE HIGHEST MOUNTAINS IN THE SAHARA

The Ahaggar Mountains, which cover some 300,000 sq. km (116,000 sq. miles), are the largest mountain chain in the central Sahara. The heart of this spectacular chain of peaks , which formed about 600 million years ago and has been shaped by volcanic activity ever since, is the bizarre basalt scenery of the Atakor massif, from which Mount Tahat rises to a height of 2,918 m (9,573 feet). To the north and east, the Ahaggar chain is surrounded by the Tassili uplands, which rose about 250 million years ago. The sandstone strata of these plains have been washed away by ancient rivers and eroded by wind and sand to form strange shapes – the extensive Tassili n'Ajjer, from which Mount Adrar reaches a height of 2,158 m (7,080 feet), is now a fantastic lunar landscape. The steep gorges and bizarre erosion formations of the Tibesti Mountains, which cover 100,000 sq. km (38,600 sq. miles) of the central Sahara, have created one of the continent's most striking landscapes, with jagged highlands jutting out like a spur from the surrounding plains. The base of the Tibesti Mountains is formed from strata of granite and slate which were folded up during the Quaternary and Tertiary periods. Volcanoes formed in the wake of this tectonic activity and the resulting petrified lava now forms the mountain peaks on this base.

The Ahaggar and Tibesti Mountains are characterized by the bizarre-looking formations of stone columns surrounded by dunes, which have arisen over time through the action of erosion and weathering (above).

water in the Sahara is the Nile. The world's largest desert has an extreme climate: daytime temperatures exceed 50°C (120°F), but during summer nights, it can drop to below freezing. Rainfall rarely occurs in the Sahara. Half of the desert receives less than 2.5 cm (1 inch) of rain per year, but when it rains after long dry periods it is torrential and can last for years.

Dunes as far as the eye can see: the Grand Erg Occidental or Great Western Sand Sea in the Sahara (left). Mighty sand dunes (main image) make up only a small proportion of the Sahara's landscape, which features a wide variety of relief forms.

SAHARA

Extensive, enclosed areas of dunes known as *ergs* make up about 20% of the Sahara's total surface area. One typical feature of *ergs* are large *draa* dunes, which occur only in the world's largest sandy regions. Such dunes can reach heights of 200 m (660 feet), with

Dunes in the Grand Erg Occidental.

exceptional cases even higher. The largest of these sand seas are the Grand Erg Oriental (Great Eastern Sand Sea), which stretches from north-eastern Algeria into Tunisia – its area of 600 x 200 km (370 x 125 miles) is a world record – and the Grand Erg Occidental (Great Western Sand Sea), which is also located in northern Algeria. There are no human settlements here, nor yet any roads through the endless dunes.

The satellite photo shows a section of
the Grand Erg Oriental in the Algerian
Sahara. There is a strikingly uniform
distribution of golden-yellow star dunes
formed by the interplay of sand and
wind. Star dunes have between three and
five arms radiating from the highest
point of the dune.

RUB' AL-KHALI

The 780,000 sq. km (301,000 sq. miles) of the world's largest sand desert are largely unexplored, usually being viewed only from satellite pictures, and the Rub' al-Khali remains one of the world's most remote areas. Incense caravans once made their way across the

Wahiba Sand Sea in Oman.

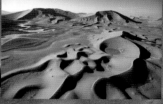

Dunes with deposits of clay and salt.

desert around the year 300, but as desertification continued, such trading journeys became impossible and the once wealthy ancient city of Ubar in modern Oman sank beneath the sands.

Oil has made a number of Arab countries very rich. Drill holes can be seen between the dunes of the Arabian Desert.

"EMPTY QUARTER"

The first successful crossing of the desert was achieved by Bertram Thomas, a Briton. The Rub' al-Khali, literally the "empty quarter", consists largely of sand dunes – no less than 500,000 sq. km (193,000 sq. miles) of them. The temperatures in this tropical desert (where high pressure systems break up clouds and no precipitation falls) fluctuate wildly, ranging from 0°C at night to 60°C during the day. Incredibly, despite such conditions, spiders, rodents, and a few plants still manage to survive here.

Cross or star dunes can reach heights of 300 m (990 feet).

The Rub' al-Khali, the Taklamakan, and the Gobi are some of world's most famous deserts, but many of the world's largest deserts are to be found on the Asian continent.

SYRIAN DESERT
260,000 sq. km (100,000 sq. miles)

The Syrian Desert is a chalk plateau of steppes and desert lying in the north of the Arabian Peninsula. It covers northern Saudi Arabia, north-eastern Jordan, south-eastern Syria, from which it takes its name, and western Iraq. This arid area is bordered to the north by the plains of the Fertile Crescent, to the north-east by the Euphrates, and to the south-east by the Hauran volcanic massif. Great pipelines connecting the oil fields of Saudi Arabia and Iraq with the Mediterranean run through the Syrian Desert, and the old caravan routes through the steppes and dunes are now scattered with the ruins of ancient cities, built near the old oases, such as 1st-century BC Tudmur. As the Syrian Desert receives an annual average of only 130 mm (5 inches) of precipitation, the areas which have been cultivated for agriculture have to be intensively irrigated. The main crops are cotton, wheat, barley, olives, rice, sugar beet, millet, and tobacco.

NEGEV DESERT
12,000 sq. km (4,600 sq. miles)

Some 60% of the total surface area of Israel is taken up with the Negev Desert, part of the band of deserts which stretches from the Atlantic to India. The northern and western reaches of the desert are monotonous, dusty plains, whereas the south is characterized by mountains and erosion craters. After heavy rain, the wadis turn into raging rivers and the desert briefly blooms.

There are many isolated mushroom rocks in the Negev Desert.

RUB' AL-KHALI
780,000 sq. km (300,000 sq. miles)

The Rub' al-Khali ("Empty Quarter") or Great Arabian Desert is the world's largest contiguous area of sand and covers a third of the Arabian Peninsula, from Najd in Saudi Arabia to the north down to Hadhramaut in Yemen to the south and the United Arab Emirates to the east. The main desert, which is 1,500 km (900 miles) wide, is covered in dunes 300 m (990 feet) high. The extremely arid climate, with only 50 mm (2 inches) of rain per year, creates only very few oases, such as the great Liwa Oasis in the north, to the south of Abu Dhabi.

NEFUD DESERT
104,000 sq. km (40,000 sq. miles)

The red sands of the Nefud Desert in Saudi Arabia are subject to strong winds that blow up suddenly, forming dunes up to 180 m (590 feet) high. The sandstone cliffs have been partially eroded to form bizarre shapes. In some oases it is even possible to cultivate fruit, vegetables, and cereals. The "Little Nefud" merges with the Rub' al-Khali to the south-east.

A camel train passes the mountains of the Nefud Desert in Saudi Arabia.

KARAKUM
280,000 sq. km (108,000 sq. miles)

The Karakum ("black sand") Desert combines with the adjacent Kyzyl Kum ("red sand") Desert to make up much of the Turan Plain in Central Asia. The Karakum lies almost completely within Turkmenistan, with a small section in Uzbek territory. The desert's continental location makes it particularly dry and the scenery ranges from clay desert through chalk plateaus to sandy desert. Instead of the high dunes found in other deserts, the sand forms low waves here; however, the sand is not actually black.

AD-DAHNA
104,000 sq. km (40,000 sq. miles)

The Ad-Dahna Desert is a bow-shaped corridor of sand and gravel approximately 1,300 km (800 miles) long and approaching 50 km. It connects Saudi Arabia's two great deserts, the Rub' al-Khali to the south and the Nefud in the north. The high iron oxide content of the sand makes the dunes of the Ad-Dahna seem reddish, sometimes even taking on shades of deep scarlet. Important transport routes connecting Kuwait with Riyadh and Riyadh with Al-Hasa run through the desert.

KYZYL KUM
300,000 sq. km (116,000 sq. miles)

The Kyzyl Kum, a desert of sand, gravel, and scree shared between Turkmenistan, Uzbekistan, and Kazakhstan, lies between the Amudarja River to the south-west and the Syrdarja to the north. It consists of a wide plain which falls away to the north-west and several isolated mountain peaks reaching heights of up to 922 m (3,025 feet). The heart of the Kyzyl Kum conceals the granite Muruntau massif, where gold is mined.

Foxtail lilies blooming in the Kyzyl Kum Desert of Uzbekistan (left).

The Wadi Rum, the largest dry river bed in Jordan, is about 100 km (62 miles) long and 60 km (37 miles) wide. This dry valley is flanked by steep cliffs and mountains of sandstone and granite.

LUT
274,000 sq. km (106,000 sq. miles)

Lying to the south of the Zagros Mountains, the Dasht-e Lut, Iran's largest desert, borders the Kavir, the second largest desert in the country, to the north. There are several extremely high dunes in the Lut, on a par with those in the ergs of the Sahara. With temperatures of 70.7°C regularly recorded, the Lut Desert is the hottest place on Earth. No traces of human habitation or fossils have ever been found here, and the desert remains uninhabited.

The sand dunes of the Lut Desert reach heights exceeding 300 m (990 feet).

THAR
260,000 sq. km (100,000 sq. miles)

Two-thirds of the Thar, a desert region in Upper India, lie within Rajasthan, with the rest in Haryana, the Punjab, and Gujarat. It consists of a mixture of wandering and static dunes, cliffs, and salt basins. The climate features extremes of temperature ranging from 0°C (32°F) in winter to 50°C (120°F) in summer. The annual rain levels average less than 150 mm (6 inches) in the west and 350 mm (14 inches) in the east.

A camel caravan on the crest of a dune in the Thar sandy desert in India.

TAKLAMAKAN
320,000 sq. km (124,000 sq. miles)

The world's second largest sandy desert is the Taklamakan Desert in Central Asia. It stretches from Xinjiang in China across the Tarim Basin to Route 218 (east of this road it is known as the Lop Desert). The Taklamakan consists largely of dunes more than 100 m (330 feet) high which wander considerably, due to the high winds. The Taklamakan is considered extremely arid, with less than 30 mm (1¼ inches) of precipitation each year.

The undulating dune landscape of the Taklamakan Desert in China.

GOBI

1.3 million sq. km (502,000 sq. miles)

The Gobi, a steppe desert lying mostly in Mongolia in Central Asia, is bounded by mountains: to the east and south-east there is the Greater Khingan, to the south the Altunshan and Nanshan, to the west the Beishan, and to the north the

A camel in the Khongryn dunes of Mongolia's Gobi National Park.

The fertile Crescent Moon oasis.

The "Flaming Cliffs" of Bayanzag glow red and yellow at dawn.

Khangai and Yablonovy ranges. Large areas of the desert are covered with gravel and loess, but there are also cliffs and even lakes; the Gobi is a true sandy desert only in one section to the south-west which makes up about 3% of its total surface area. The average elevation of the Gobi is some 900 m (2,950 feet) in the east and 1,500 m (4,900 feet) in the west. The average rainfall is less than 200 mm (8 inches), but more rain falls at the edges of the desert, where some expanses have even been exploited for agriculture. There is a continental climate with very cold winters and hot summers, and cold sand- and even snow-storms are not unknown in spring.

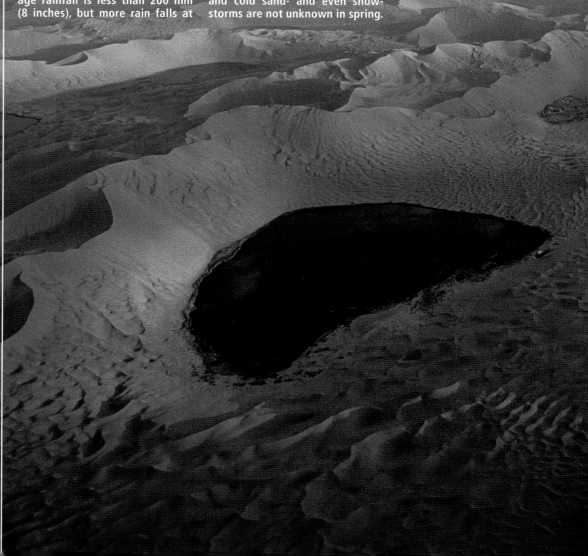

A bird's-eye view of the dunes and lakes of the Badain Jaran sandy desert, which forms the south-western part of the Gobi steppes.

Australia is the world's driest continent, with about two-thirds of its area covered in desert or semi-desert, and with many astonishing geological formations.

GREAT SANDY DESERT

388,000 sq. km (150,000 sq. miles)

The Great Sandy Desert is located in Western Australia's Canning Basin in the north-west of the continent, a depression between the Pilbara and Kimberley Mountains. Only a few Aboriginal tribes inhabit this desert with its numerous salt lakes. The areas around the coast and the Kimberley Mountains average approximately 300 mm (12 inches) of rainfall a year, although this tends to fall at irregular intervals, and the rest of the desert averages 250 mm (10 inches), which for a desert is quite a lot. The great heat causes much evaporation, however – temperatures in summer average 38°C (100°F) and never fall below 25°C (77°F), even during the winter. Very little grass can grow under such circumstances, and yet the area is the preferred habitat of the Alexandra parakeet, a species of parrot that has adapted to life in dry climates.

GREAT VICTORIA DESERT

274,000 sq. km (106,000 sq. miles)

The Great Victoria Desert, a semi-desert in southern Australia, is shared between the states of South and Western Australia. Many of its sand dunes, which average only 15 m (49 feet) in height, are secured by the grass growing on them, although there are some wandering dunes as well. Between the dunes there is grassland and salt lakes. One peculiarity of the Great Victoria Desert is the crescent-shaped dunes which form on the lee side of lakes from deposits on the lake beds. Average temperatures vary between 18°C and 40°C (64°F and 104°F) and there are occasional frosts in winter. Some areas of the desert are wet enough that mulga (a species of acacia endemic to Australia) can grow. Reptiles such as geckos and monitor lizards roam the desert.

GIBSON DESERT

330,000 sq. km (127,000 sq. miles)

The Gibson Desert in Western Australia lies south of the Great Sandy Desert and north of the Great Victoria Desert on the Tropic of Capricorn. In geographical terms, the Gibson Desert is part of Australia's Western Plateau and consists of large expanses of undulating sand, dune fields, low cliffs – the highest point is barely 500 m (1,640 feet) above sea level – and regions of extensive laterite formations. The middle of the Gibson Desert is marked by a number of salt lakes. A few roads lead through the desert, but the only settlement of any note is Warburton on the edge of the arid zone. The Gibson's climate is dry and hot, with annual precipitation between 200 and 250 mm (8–10 inches) and an extremely high rate of evaporation. Temperatures range from 40°C (104°F) in the summer months to 18°C (65°C) in the winter, sometimes even dropping as low as 6°C (43°F). Wildlife includes red kangaroo, emu, the endangered Greater Bilby, lizards, and reptiles.

Few grasses are able to survive in Western Australia's Great Sandy Desert. Places of growth are often determined by the presence of sand dunes and salt lakes.

The dry grass covering the Gibson Desert beside the Kintore Range in Western Australia.

TANAMI DESERT
180,000 sq. km (70,000 sq. miles)

The Tanami Desert, lying east of the Great Sandy Desert and north-west of Alice Springs in the Northern Territory, is the northernmost desert in Australia. More precipitation falls this far north than anywhere else in the continent, and the Tanami Desert receives an annual average of 400 mm (16 inches). The great heat (daily temperatures in summer average 38°C/ 100°F, dropping to 25°C/77°F in winter with the occasional night frost) causes considerable evaporation and very little vegetation is able to flourish. Punctuated by low chains of hills, the vast red sandy plains of the Tanami Desert are crossed by the popular, but extremely long (1,000-km/ 620-mile) Tanami Track, the shortest route from Kimberley to the middle of Australia. This natural track is a navigable, dirt road but is often flooded and impassable during the summer rainy season. Four-wheel drive vehicles are recommended.

SIMPSON DESERT
250,000 sq. km (97,000 sq. miles)

The Simpson Desert also lies within the Northern Territory. It is bounded to the west by the Finke River and the Mabel Range, to the north by the Adam Range, to the east by the Georgina and Diamantina Rivers, and to the south by Lake Eyre. There is a large artesian basin beneath the desert, which is threatening to dry up as, in recent years, it has been comprehensively drained by man. The interior of the Simpson Desert features extensive wandering dunes and the edges are marked by bare rock formations. The region is largely uninhabited and has been protected as nature reserves, including the Simpson Desert National Park and the Witjira National Park. Compared to other Australian deserts, very little rain falls in the Simpson Desert (less than 150 mm/6 inches annually) and so the little scrub that grows is confined to the edges; as you progress further into the heart of the desert, the bushes gives way to spinifex, a species of tussock grass.

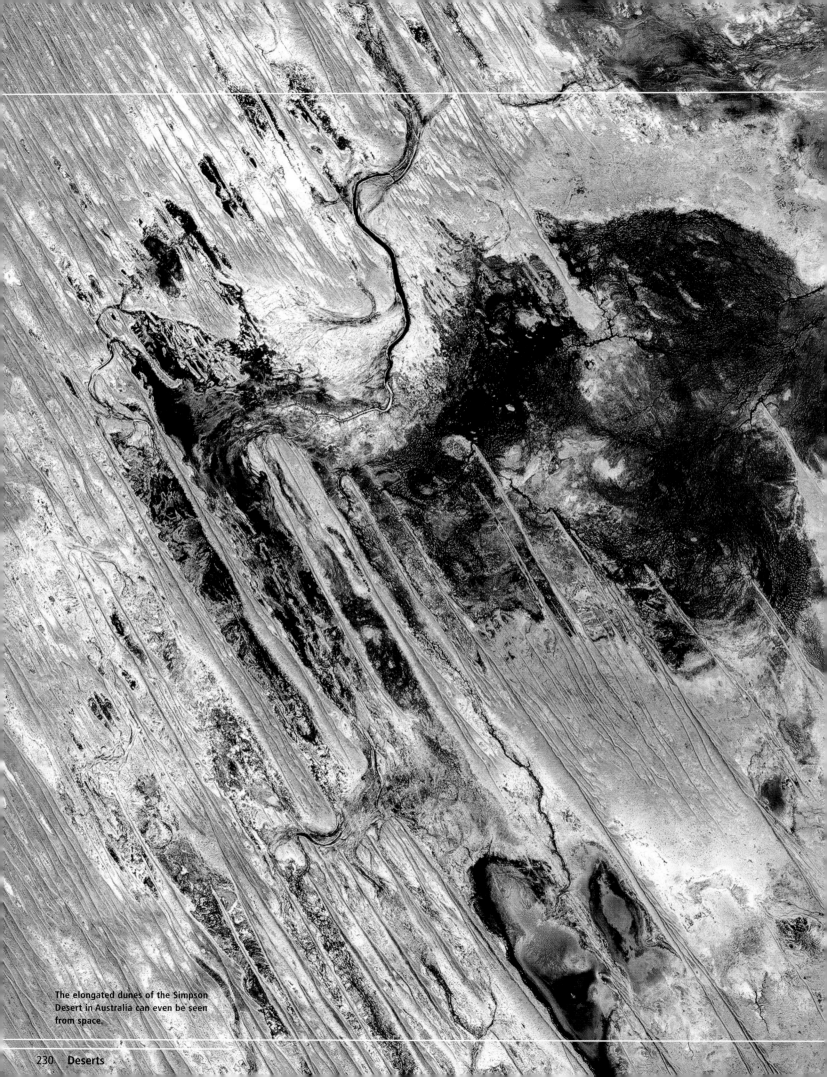

The elongated dunes of the Simpson
Desert in Australia can even be seen
from space.

SIMPSON DESERT
THE WORLD'S LONGEST SAND DUNES

THE WORLD'S LONGEST SAND DUNES

The world's longest sand dunes are a particular feature of the Simpson Desert.

Red dunes and spinifex.

A typical feature of the Simpson Desert is the elongated, parallel dunes which, though only 3–30 m (10–100 feet) high, can reach lengths of 300 km (190 miles). Nappanerica, the best-known, is 40 m (131 feet) high and is also known as "Big Red". The dunes are evidence of the region's most recent geological past: back in the days when the temperate zones were undergoing the change from a cold to a warm phase and parts of Central Europe were glaciated, a series of dry and wet periods alternated here, and the enormous Lake Dieri was created during a wet phase. When this lake dried up at the high point of the last period of cold, it left behind sandbars, dunes, and marine and alluvial sediment. The wind moved the sand to create the characteristic elongated dunes that can be seen today. Their sparse vegetation has fixed them in place and they are indicative of the prevailing north-south winds.

SIMPSON DESERT
250,000 sq. km (97,000 sq. miles)

The climate in the Simpson Desert is marked by hot summers of 38–40°C (100–104°F) and warm winters between 18°C and 24°C (64°F and 75°F). Night frosts are often likely. The average precipitation never rises above 120 mm (5 inches) per year and is very unreliable – after many years of drought, short but violent rainstorms can sometimes occur. The troughs then carry the water away to closed depressions, which can cause devastating floods. The end result is salt flats, salt lakes, and dried-up river valleys. However, the desert hosts more than 150 bird species, 17 small mammal species, four types of frog and 54 reptile species.

The Sahara is the world's largest desert and thus the largest in Africa, but there are plenty of other extensive deserts and semi-deserts on this continent.

ARABIAN DESERT
220,000 sq. km (85,000 sq. miles)

The Arabian Desert, a dry, hilly region in eastern Egypt, should not be confused with the Rub' al-Khali, the Great Arabian Desert. The Arabian Desert, which shares with the Nubian Desert the distinction of being the easternmost section of the African Sahara, extends from the Mediterranean in the north to the Nubian Desert in the south, and from the Nile in the west to the Red Sea and the Gulf of Suez in the east. The steep cliffs of the Nile valley give way to a jagged upland plateau further east before the terrain climbs to form sheer volcanic mountains at the Red Sea which then drop away abruptly as they reach the water.

Here you will find Hurghada, Egypt's largest tourist resort on the Red Sea – the desert begins where the town ends. The highest point of the Arabian Desert is Jebel Shayib al-Banat at 2,187 m (7,175 feet) above sea level. The desert experiences intermittent rainfall and there is a network of wadis (the dry beds of seasonal rivers). The desert, which is more or

NAMIB
50,000 sq. km (19,000 sq. miles)

This dry desert, whose name means "empty area", covers an area of the Atlantic coast of West Africa, lying within Namibia and Angola, which is about 1,800 km

Oryx in the sand dunes of the Namib.

(1,100 miles) long and between 80 and 130 km (50 and 80 miles) wide. It is bordered by the Great Escarpment. The Kaokoveld in northern Namibia consists of a series of inselbergs (or monadnocks) which reach their highest point at the Brandberg (2,579 m/8,461 feet). The extreme aridity is caused by the nearby Benguela Current, which creates large amounts of fog. Large areas of the north of the desert, which merges with the Kalahari, consist of scree and gravel and are almost entirely devoid of vegetation. The middle sections feature many wide dunes which can reach heights of up to 300 m (990 feet) and change coloration depending on the time of day and their moisture content. At 80 million years old, the Namib is the world's oldest desert and one of the most inhospitable regions on Earth: daytime temperatures can exceed 50°C (120°F) before dropping to below freezing at night. Droughts can last for years and the Namib is plagued by sandstorms. The only source of moisture for plants and animals are the coastal fogs. Welwitschia, one of the world's oldest plants, has adapted well to this environment.

Surrounded by giant dunes, the Sossusvlei salt and clay pan retains water into the spring.

less cut off from the rest of Egypt, is rich in natural resources such as oil (which is extracted on land and in the Gulf of Suez) as well as phosphorite, nitrates, uranium, and gold. Most of the inhabitants of the Arabian Desert live in fishing villages or in oil industry communities on the Red Sea. The tourist trade is also important for the local population.

Surrounded by dunes and cliffs, many typical jagged granite and basalt formations are to be found in the Arabian Desert near the Egyptian city of Hurghada on the Red Sea (left).

KALAHARI
1,000,000 sq. km (386,000 sq. miles)

The enclosed, arid basin of the Kalahari is made up of broad plateaus which together form the largest unbroken expanse of sand in the world, although not technically a desert. The large dune fields, typically found in the west of the desert, have existed since the ice age. The only high points in this seemingly endless flat dry savanna, at 900 m (2,950 feet) above sea level, are a few rocky hills. The Kalahari also has several salt pans, remnants of ice age lakes, including the Makgadikgadi Pan and the Etosha Pan, two of the world's largest. The swamps

Fossil dunes in the Kalahari.

The Kalahari: an undulating sea of dunes.

of the Okavango Basin lie to the north. In contrast to the Namib, the dunes of the Kalahari form long narrow ribs which run parallel to each other. These are "fossil" dunes – their bases turned to stone long ago and they cannot move. In the troughs between the dunes there is water near the surface, and this underground network of channels is connected to the inland Okavango delta. When there is a surfeit of water in the delta, the excess flows to the furthest reaches of the channel network, and when it dries up, the water flows back. This process ensures relatively high fertility for the Kalahari, and giraffes, oryxes, zebras, and springboks all find enough to eat in its valleys.

The Namib Desert is famed for its unusual coloration and exceptionally high dunes. Many of the dunes here are among the world's tallest. One of the most impressive is "Dune 7", which rises to a height of 350 m (1,150 feet) – making it the world's highest sand dune. The

The myriad hues...

...of the Namib-Naukluft National Park.

coloration of the dunes in the Namib can take on the most varied and intense shades, depending on the position of the sun and the moisture content of the air and sand.

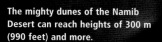

The mighty dunes of the Namib Desert can reach heights of 300 m (990 feet) and more.

The hot Namib Desert lies directly
adjacent to the cold Atlantic Ocean;
this satellite image even shows the
undulating crests of the dunes.

NAMIB DESERT

The waves of the Atlantic wash up against waves of sand.

The giant Central Namib Desert in south Namibia is relatively unexplored and yet it has been placed under strict protection as a nature reserve. Tourists are allowed only to enter the edge of the area, visiting the dunes surrounding the Sossusvlei salt and clay pan, the equally majestic dunes further south in the private Namib Rand Nature Reserve, and Walvis Bay, a unique network of lagoons on the coast near Sand-wich Harbour. It is thought to be the world's oldest desert, having existed for over 55 million years.

SECHURA DESERT

Crescent-shaped sickle dunes in the Sechura Desert.

The Sechura Desert on the Pacific coast of Peru, just south of the Piura Region is thought to be one of the world's driest deserts, despite its location near the ocean and its moderate temperatures, which lie between 24°C and 38°C (75°F and 100°F) in summer and 16°C and 24°C (60°F and 75°F) in winter. The Sechura consists of rock, scree, and sand, with low mountain ranges and salt flats. Sickle dunes are often found here, with a concave lee side (i.e. the "opening" of the sickle points in the direction of the wind).

QUIVER TREES

Aloe dichotoma, the quiver tree, is extremely picturesque. It is first mentioned as the "kookerboom" in a report of 1685 made by Simon van der Stel, the governor of the Cape Colony, in which he recounts how the bushmen would make arrow quivers from the branches

Succulent fingers of blossom.

and bark of the tree. The quiver tree's long history in Africa is proved by rock art in which its characteristic appearance is unmistakable. The plant is endemic to South Africa but has learnt Namibian survival tricks: the sponge-like trunk and branches store water which tide the tree over during the dry months. Its bark is paper-thin but its dark-green leaves, which grow yellow with age, are succulent. When the yellow blossom of the aloe plant appears in June and July, the treetops are surrounded by a crown of bees and birds, and even baboons are tempted to climb the trees. Quiver trees prefer rocky soils and usually stand alone – the wood of quiver trees at Keetmanshoop in southern Namibia is an exceptional case. Sociable weaver birds often build nests at the tops of quiver trees, making them look like haystacks.

Thanks to their ability to store water, the massive trunk and characteristic branches of the quiver tree are able to survive the long dry seasons.

WELWITSCHIA

This confused tangle of dying leaves and fresh shoots was first found in the desert and identified as a new species by the Austrian botanist Friedrich Welwitsch in 1859. Scientists soon began to suspect that it was a survivor from a wetter period of the Namib's history and that what had once been a tree had shrunk down to its present size in the face of growing aridity. Named *Welwitschia mirabilis* after the person who discovered it, the plant had developed a most unusual method of maintaining its moisture content. Growing in areas of the Namib Desert near the coast, it has an extensive root system lying close to the surface. As banks of fog move in from the coast, the moisture condenses on the plant's foliage, dropping to the ground before being sucked up by the roots. Fog moisture is exploited by several other plants and even animals: the Tenebrio beetle stands on its head as the fog approaches, guiding the moisture down its shell carapace into its mouth. The oryx takes a similar approach, standing on top of a dune and licking the condensed moisture from its nostrils. Clouds of Atlantic fog can drift as much as 100 km (62 miles) inland and on some days, the dunes of the Sossusvlei are swathed in mist.

The *Welwitschia mirabilis* is a symbol of the perseverance, determination, and resourcefulness that plants need in order to survive in arid Namibia.

NORTH AND CENTRAL AMERICA

The area from Texas to the mountains of southern California, from Oregon to Mexico, is covered with deserts and semi-deserts, with a huge variety of plant life.

GREAT BASIN
540,000 sq. km (208,000 sq. miles)

The Great Basin is an extensive, enclosed desert plateau composed of about 100 sub-basins. It is bounded by the Columbia Plateau to the north, the Mojave Desert to the south, the Sierra Nevada to the west, and the Wasatch Range, an arm of the Rocky Mountains, to the east. The largest section of the Great Basin lies in the US state of Nevada, but smaller sections are to be found in Oregon, Idaho, Utah, Arizona, and California. Small but steep mountain chains cross the basin from north to south, and one of its highest points is a 3,677-m (12,064-foot) peak located in the Humboldt Range. The Great Basin is characterized by steppes, stones, sand desert, dried-up river beds, canyons, salt lakes, salt pans, and lakes of various sizes, such as Lake Utah and the Great Salt Lake. Great Basin National Park is famed for its ancient pines, which are the oldest living things on Earth. The park has little rainfall during the year, with most falling as winter snow or summer thunderstorms.

DEATH VALLEY
8,500 sq. km (3,280 sq. miles)

Named for its supposedly inhospitable climate, Death Valley, a depression in the Great Basin surrounded by several mountain ranges, reaches its lowest point at Badwater, a brackish pond 86 m (282 feet) below sea level, which makes it the lowest place in North America. Although Death Valley is only a few hours' drive from the Pacific Ocean, it is one of the driest places on Earth: the highest temperature recorded here is 56.7°C (134°F). One special feature of Death Valley is the Artist's Palette, a rock formation on the slopes of the Black Mountains. The oxidation of various metals in the rocks has left a spectacular blaze of various hues: the red is probably from iron, the green from copper.

Dunes (top right) and rocks (right) at the Artist's Palette in Death Valley.

MOJAVE DESERT
40,000 sq. km (15,400 sq. miles)

The Mojave Desert, which is shared between the US states of California, Utah, Nevada, and Arizona, is an enclosed desert basin flanked by a series of mountain ranges. Garlock and the San Andreas Fault lie to the west of the desert. The most famous water source in the Mojave is the river of the same name, which flows only intermittently and eventually peters out in the Mojave Depression. The desert conceals a number of "ghost towns" which grew up during a period of silver mining and the construction of Route 66. Many reptiles, such as the desert tortoise and the rattlesnake, have made their home in the wilderness. The endemic Joshua tree is also a frequent sight.

Antelope Valley (top right) and evening primroses in the southern Mojave (right).

Only thin scrub grows in dried-up High Rock Lake in the sparsely populated Great Basin, Nevada, with its desert steppes and elongated valleys.

SONORAN DESERT
320,000 sq. km (124,000 sq. miles)

The broad valleys and parallel mountain chains beside the north Pacific coastal plain in the Mexican state of Sonora were created in the middle and late Tertiary period. The Sonoran Desert begins in the north of this dry landscape and extends as far as California and south-eastern Arizona. To the north, it borders the Mojave and, to the east, the Chihuahua Desert. The Sonoran Desert is one of the world's most diverse desert regions, with a host of different species: many reptiles and birds make their home here, as well as a range of cactus species, which are best viewed at the Organ Pipe Cactus National Monument in the northern part of the desert. The organ pipe cactus pictured here is endemic to the United States.

The Organ Pipe Cactus National Monument in the northern Sonoran Desert.

CHIHUAHUA DESERT
363,000 sq. km (140,000 sq. miles)

The Chihuahua Desert covers an area which extends from southern New Mexico and west Texas in the US to the Mexican states of Chihuahua and Coahuila. The desert basin is punctuated with a few smaller mountain ranges such as the Sierra del Carmen, where it is considerably cooler and moister than in the desert, allowing coniferous forests to grow. The Chihuahua Desert has typical desert vegetation, including agave, cactus, peyote, and grassland. The most striking section of the desert is the dunes of the White Sands National Monument, which are made of crystals of white gypsum. The gypsum is deposited by rainfall in the surrounding mountains which is then sluiced into Lake Lucero; from here there is nowhere for the water to go and it evaporates during the summer, leaving crystals of gypsum, which the wind fashions into dunes.

Prickly pears lend a bit of variation to the Chihuahua Desert in Mexico.

JOSHUA TREES AND SAGUARO CACTUSES

JOSHUA TREES – THE WORLD'S LARGEST AGAVE PLANTS

Joshua trees, or palm tree yuccas, stand out like silent sentries against the usually clear skies of the Joshua Tree National Park to the east of Palm Springs. These cactus-like plants are closely related to yuccas and can grow to heights

A Joshua tree in bloom, Mojave Desert.

of 12 m (39 feet) during their 900-year lifespan. The plants are an important part of the ecosystem in the Mojave, providing many desert animals with sustenance and shade. The tree's fibers can be used to make string and ropes.

The Joshua Tree National Park in southern California is named after the eponymous tree which grows throughout the park.

244 Deserts

SAGUAROS – THE WORLD'S LARGEST CACTUS

The two sections of the Saguaro National Park in southern Arizona are divided between the Tucson Mountains and the Sonoran Desert. Within the park there is an especially densely packed and beautiful collection of Saguaro cactuses. *Carnegiea gigantea*, the plant's botanical name, remembers Andrew Carnegie, the American industrialist and philanthropist. These enormous succulents can reach heights of 15 m (49 feet) and although they have an average lifespan of 85 years, some specimens have lived for 200 years. A fully grown saguaros can weigh up to 15 tonnes (16½ short tons). Each of the long-stemmed blossoms is pollinated by bats, humming birds or woodpeckers, and blooms for a

Saguaro National Park in the south-western United States takes its name from the saguaro or candelabra cactus.

single day in May, just before the rainy season. The fruit, which is red both inside and out, grows to a length of between 6 and 9 cm (2½ and 3½ inches), although the saguaros grows extremely slowly, only 4 cm (1½ inches) per year. The greatest danger to the cactuses is represented by black-tailed jackrabbits, bush rats, and moun-

The flowers, up to 12 cm (4¾ inches) long.

tain sheep, for whom they provide a tasty snack. Woodpeckers build their nests in the trunks of the cactus, and larger birds such as falcons roost in the upper branches. The tasty flesh of the fruits is dried and eaten by the Papago Indians. The cactus grows very slowly and from seed only. Its growth rate depends on the level of rainfall.

The Joshua tree was named by the Mormons, who were reminded of the prophet's outstretched arms by its branches.

The Atacama and Sechura
Deserts on the Pacific coast of
South America were created by
the Humboldt Current, whose
cold water rarely evaporates,
meaning that rain therefore
rarely falls on the coast.

SECHURA DESERT
180,000 sq. km (70,000 sq. miles)

The Sechura Desert runs along the
northern Pacific coast of Peru, where
the ocean waves break directly onto
the sand of the desert. It runs inland
for about 100 km (62 miles) to the
low foothills of the Andes. At its
northern end near the city of Piura,
the arid scenery of the desert gives
way to the equatorial dry forests of
the Tumbes Piura. The Sechura Desert
suffers relatively minor variations in
temperature near the Pacific, with
warm summers (December to March)
and cool winters (June to September),
but is nonetheless one of the world's
driest places, along with the adjacent
Atacama Desert. Humans have lived
in the Sechura Desert for millennia,
especially on the banks of the many
short rivers which cross it, and
modern Peru's largest cities, such as
Piura and Chiclayo, are now located
here. The expanses of the Sechura
Desert are famed for their easily
identifiable sickle dunes. This desert is
one of the few that receives most of
its precipitation in the form of fog.

ATACAMA DESERT
140,000 sq. km (54,000 sq. miles)

The Atacama Desert, South America's largest desert, is composed of
a series of enclosed basins in
northern Chile along the arid west
coast of the continent. Beginning

The Atacama Desert, Chile.

Salar de Atacama – Chile's largest salt lake.

at 600 m (1,970 feet) above sea
level, the Atacama forms a series
of rising steps between the coastal
cordilleras and the Andes. The Valle
de la Luna ("moon valley"), where
erosion has formed thousands of
so-called "earth pyramids" from
the various rocks of the *cordilleras*;
their coloration varies with their
mineral composition. Large tracts
of the Atacama are covered with
salt flats: extreme aridity – the
Atacama is thought to be the
world's driest place – and sharp
drops in temperature (from
30°C/86°F during the day to
-15°C/5°F at night) prevent vegetation from taking root. The El Tatio
geyser field in the Atacama Desert
lies to the north of San Pedro. The
"smoking grandfather" is among
the world's highest-lying geyser
fields and is fed from the nearby
Cerros del Tatio volcano.

At 4,320 m (14,173 feet), El Tatio has
one of the highest elevations of any
geyser field on Earth.

Dunes in the Sechura Desert (far left) and the stormy Pacific coast (left) of Peru's Paracas National Reserve on the Paracas Peninsula, much of which is desert.

TEMPERATE RAINFORESTS

Rainforests are classified as areas that receive at least 2,000 mm (79 inches) of rainfall every year. In the temperate climate zones, only forests on the slopes of coastal mountains fall into this category. There are sizeable temperate rainforests in North and South America, Australia and Tasmania, New Zealand,

Ferns and evergreen southern beech trees in Victoria, Australia.

Anatolia, and Georgia. In North America, extensive areas of temperate rainforest run along the Pacific from the Alaskan coast to Canada and northern California. Smaller temperate rainforests are found in Norway, South Africa, and East Asia. Commercial forestry, however, means that many of these forests are under threat, because of the great demand for the best examples of their highly prized trees.

The Australian state of Victoria also has extensive temperate rainforests. Eucalyptus is the dominant tree, including Victorian ash (*Eucalyptus regnans*). Victorian ash trees generally reach heights of up to 80 m (262 feet), with some even rising above 100 m (328 feet).

CHINA

The temperate rainforests of southern China gradually merge into areas of tropical rainforest. Bamboo woods are a particularly characteristic feature of the temperate rainforests, Shunan Bamboo Forest in the west of the country being the world's largest example. It is home not only to the endangered giant panda, but also to the red panda and monal. As well as bamboo, the forest flora includes azaleas, orchids, and peach trees.

KOREA

With the exception of its mountainous areas, the Korean Peninsula enjoys an essentially temperate climate. Its lush rainforests are home to a wide range of endemic plant and animal species, and the Korean fir (*Abies koreana*) – once found only in Korea – has even found its way to European gardens. Bamboo, laurel, and evergreen oak all grow along the southern coast and on the offshore islands of Jeju-do and Ulleungdo. Bears, tigers, and leopards, however, are examples of once common predators that have all but disappeared thanks to forestry and illegal hunting.

JAPAN

The Taiheiyo forests are the remaining sections of temperate rainforest along the Pacific coast of the islands of Shikoku,

Japan's Yakushima cedar forest.

Kyushu, and Honshu in southwestern Japan. The forest is made up of evergreens at lower altitudes, with deciduous trees at higher altitudes. Evergreen oak, Japanese chinquapin, and Japanese beech are the most widespread tree species to be found here.

Just off the southern tip of Kyushu, the island of Yakushima is the location of a dense primeval forest. Its ancient Japanese cedars (*Cryptomeria japonica*) are conifers belonging to the cypress family. They can reach heights of up to 40 m (131 feet), their roots visible above ground at the bottom of their trunks (main image). The Jomon Cedar is the forest's most famous cryptomeria. It is estimated to be some 3,000 years old, and its trunk has a circumference of 16 m (52 feet).

THE WORLD'S LARGEST BAMBOO FOREST

At altitudes of 600–1,000 m (1,970–3,280 feet), Shunan Bamboo Forest lies in the eastern foothills of the Himalayas, in the Sichuan province of western China. This hilly forest spans some 120 sq. km (46 sq. miles), and contains 60 different bamboo species. It looks like a giant expanse of green water, and is often called "the Bamboo Sea". The forest is home to the giant panda. Feeding exclusively on the forest's bamboo plants, the giant panda has long been an endangered species.

Giant bamboo (*Dendrocalamus giganteus*) is the world's largest bamboo species. The plant's stalks can measure 20–30 cm (8–12 inches) across, and it can grow to heights of up to 4 m (13 feet), shooting up at a rate of 70 cm (28 inches) a day during the growing season. Like other

The bamboo plant's leaves grow from the knots along its stalk.

bamboo species, giant bamboo rarely blooms, flowering only once every 40 years or so. All bamboo plants of the same species flower at the same time all over the world. Afterward, they die, but new clumps of bamboo grow from their seeds. Giant bamboo was originally found in Burma (Myanmar) northern India, the Chinese province of Yunnan, and Thailand. It was introduced to other tropical regions – including East Africa, Madagascar, and East Asia – during the colonial period, and can also be admired in many of the world's botanic gardens.

The bamboo forests in the southern part of China's Sichuan province contain dozens of bamboo species, including *Dendrocalamus giganteus*. Bamboos can grow to great heights in an astonishingly short period.

The endangered giant panda can be found in several of the national parks in China's Sichuan province. There are estimated to be under 2,500 pandas in the wild. They grow to around 1.6 m (5¼ feet) and weigh 80–120 kg (175–265 lb).

A giant panda feeding in Sichuan.

Wolong Nature Reserve, Sichuan.

The panda's natural habitat lies at altitudes of 1,800–3,800 m (5,900–12,500 feet). Here, the animal's thick fur provides superb protection against cold, rain, and snow. In the wild, pandas live for about 20 years, and – with the exception of the mating season during April and May – spend most of their time alone. Panda cubs are born in late summer. They spend the first 18 months of their lives with their mother, reaching maturity at about 4–6 years of age. When large swathes of bamboo died off in 1975, 140 giant pandas died of starvation. Since then, the population of wild pandas within protected areas has recovered.

Giant pandas feed exclusively on bamboo, especially its shoots and leaves. Since these have little nutritional value, the animals must devour 10–40 kg (22–88 lb) of the plant every day. As a result, they spend 10–12 hours a day eating.

TASMANIA

Mount Anne in Tasmania, Australia.

Tasmania's temperate climate provides perfect conditions for its flourishing rainforests. Some of the eucalyptus trees in the Styx Valley reach heights of more than 95 m (312 feet) and are over 400 years old. However, only about a quarter of Tasmania's former forests have survived, and a third of these are under threat. Animals found in the Tasmanian rainforest include the Tasmanian pygmy possum, quoll, and Tasmanian devil – Tasmania's national animal.

NEW ZEALAND

National parks, primeval forests, and protected areas account for more than 2% of New Zealand's surface area. They feature a wide variety of unspoiled natural vegetation. The coast of the country's South Island, for example, is covered by thick rainforests that exhibit a large number of native plants. There are over 700 endemic species in Fiordland National Park alone, notably the famous tree ferns. The Tuatapere Hump Ridge Track leads hikers through both the park's rainforest and subalpine vegetation.

A stream splashes down between the ferns and other trees in the dense rainforest traversed by New Zealand's Hump Ridge Track.

SOUTHERN AUSTRALIA

Rainforest in Yarra Ranges National Park, Victoria.

Tree ferns and eucalyptus trees.

Giant eucalyptus in Great Otway National Park, Victoria.

The temperate climate of southern Australia has allowed a unique flora and fauna to develop. Yarra Ranges National Park, in the state of Victoria, is home to more than 40 different species of mammal and 120 species of bird. The park also has some very old trees, including tree ferns and magnificent giant eucalyptuses. These are some of the world's tallest deciduous trees, and they can be as much as 400 years old. The sparse eucalyptus forests of Great Otway National Park, also in Victoria, are home to koalas.

Cyatheales (tree ferns) have grown on Earth for millions of years, making them the real dinosaurs of the plant world. They are mostly found in tropical and subtropical regions, although some species – notably those of the *Dicksonia* genus – also thrive in the temperate rainforests of Australia, Tasmania, and New Zealand. They have stems rather than trunks, formed not of wood but of roots and old leaf bases. Aside from the crowning leaf fronds, there are not usually any further branches. *Dicksonia* tree ferns can grow to some 5 m (16 feet) in height – sometimes even more – and can live for up to 200 years. The fronds can grow up to as much as 1 m (3 feet) in length, spanning out from the middle of the plant like an umbrella in a typical fern manner.

Frond of *Dicksonia antarctica*.

Branchless tree fern stems.

Giant *Dicksonia antarctica* (or Tasmanian tree fern) in the dense rainforests of Westland/Tai Poutini National Park on New Zealand's South Island. Their stems are formed of intertwined roots, through which the plants get their water.

NORTH AMERICAN
PACIFIC COAST

Conifers dominate the temperate rainforests along the Pacific coast of North America, from California to Alaska. California is also home to *Sequoia sempervirens* (the coast redwood), the

Redwood National Park, California.

world's tallest tree species – numerous examples of which can be seen in the state's Redwood National Park. The greatest concentration of these giant trees south of San Francisco, meanwhile, is found in Big Basin Redwoods State Park in the Santa Cruz Mountains, also in California. In the state of Washington, mild temperatures and plentiful rainfall sustain the lush, green rainforest of Olympic National Park, with its hemlock trees, western red cedars, ferns, lichen, and mosses. The forest is also home to cougars, mule deer, black bears, bobcats, coyotes, and some 300 species of bird.

Olympic National Park, Washington.

Moss-covered trees in the rainforest of Olympic National Park.

SOUTH AMERICAN PACIFIC COAST

The temperate cloud forests of southern Chile and Argentina are considered to have the greatest diversity of all the world's forests. The southern hemisphere's last surviving temperate rainforest is home to a wide range of trees, including some ancient Patagonian cypresses. Related to the Californian *Sequoia sempervirens*, the Patagonian cypress or alerce (*Fitzroya cupressoides*) is an evergreen whose treetop grows to a point, rather like a pyramid. It can grow to 50 m (164 feet) high, and its trunk can measure up to 5 m (16 feet) in diameter. They

Densely packed Patagonian cypress trees in the North Patagonian rainforest.

grow slowly, and can reach a great age. Some of the trees in Los Alerces National Park, near Esquel, Argentina, and Alerce Andino National Park, near Puerto Varas in southern Chile, are believed to date as far back as 3,500 years.

Surrounded by coast redwoods, water cascades down Berry Creek Falls in Big Basin Redwoods State Park, the oldest state park in California.

SEQUOIAS

Evergreen sequoias, or California redwoods, are the largest trees on earth by volume: reaching a height of 90 m (300 feet), their trunks can grow to a diameter of more than 12 m (40 feet) at the base. Some specimens are more than 2,500 years old and the lower branches of these older trees can be more than 50 m (160 feet) from the ground. The redwood was originally to be found on the western slopes of the Californian Sierra Nevada at elevations between 1,350–2,500 m (4,400 and 8,200 feet), although it has now spread worldwide, including to Europe. The redwood forests in the USA have been felled to a mere 10 percent of their original size.

Giant redwood trees in Yosemite National Park in California can reach heights of 90 m (300 feet).

GENERAL SHERMAN

Between 1,900 and 2,500 years old, the General Sherman Tree in Sequoia National Park, California, is 83.8 m (275 feet) tall and 8.25 m (27 feet) in diameter. It is the largest tree in the world by volume (1,487 cu m/ 52,500 cu feet).

GENERAL GRANT

The second-largest tree, General Grant in Grant Grove in the Kings Canyon National Park, California, is between 1,500 and 1,900 years old, 81 m (266 feet) tall, 9 m (29 feet) across, and has a volume of 1,320 cu m (46,600 cu feet).

THE LARGEST TREES ON EARTH

THE THICKEST TRUNK

In the village churchyard at Santa Maria El Tule in the Mexican state of Oaxaca, there is a 2,000-year-old Mexican swamp cypress called "El Arbol de Tule" standing at 41 m (140 feet). The circumference of the tree trunk at ground level is no less than 46 m (152 feet). It takes at least 30 people to touch hands around the base of the tree, and more than 500 people can stand in its shade. Tree surgeons were able to cut over 10 tons of dead wood from the "Tule Tree" in 1996. According to legend, it was planted by one of the Aztec priests who served their wind god Ehecatl.

THE OLDEST TREES

The bristlecone pine is one of the easiest trees on earth to date; its rings are very distinct and easy to read, even though there can be as many as 4,000 of them. The bristlecone easily outstrips any other species and grows at elevations above 3,000 m (10,000 feet) in Bristlecone Forest on California's White Mountains. Named, appropriately, after the oldest person in the Bible, Methuselah is a venerable old bristlecone pine that was dated at 4,784 years in 2010 and continues to thrive in the inhospitably dry high mountain climate.

TROPICAL RAINFORESTS AND MONSOON FORESTS

Tropical rainforests are exclusiv[e] to perpetually humid climat[e] zones. Found in South America[,] Central America, Africa, south[-] ern Asia, and Australia, the[y] experience an average annua[l] rainfall of 2,000–4,000 mm

The red-eyed tree frog is native to the rainforests of Central America.

(79–157 inches). Temperature[s] are fairly constant throughou[t] the year, with daily highs aroun[d] 24–31°C (75–88°F). Tropica[l] rainforests are characterized [by] their multilayered compositio[n] from the forest floor through the understory layer, which rise[s] up to 5 m (16 feet) above th[e] ground, all the way up to th[e] thick canopy at heights of 40 [m] (131 feet). A few giant trees ris[e] even higher still (the emergen[t] layer). In monsoon forests, [by] contrast, the trees are short[er] and the understory layer mo[re] pronounced. The range [of] species found in monsoo[n] forests is markedly smaller tha[n] that of the tropical rainforests. Together with coral reef[s,] tropical rainforests exhibit th[e] world's densest concentratio[n] of different plant and anim[al] species. Most of the animals [in] the tropical rainforests a[re] arthropods, but there are als[o] mammals such as elephants an[d] tigers, large reptiles such a[s] crocodiles, small reptiles an[d] amphibians, primates such a[s] orangutans and gorillas, an[d] countless vividly feathered bir[ds.] There are also large numbers [of] fish in the rivers that run throug[h] the rainforests.

The word "jungle" comes from *janga[l,]* the Hindi term for forest. It usually refers to a wild tropical primeval forest or Asian rainforest like this on[e] in Borneo. These depend upon a con[-] sistently hot climate with regular, heavy rainfall.

AMAZON BASIN

The Amazon Basin encompasses parts of Brazil, French Guiana, Suriname, Venezuela, Guyana, Colombia, Peru, Ecuador, and Bolivia. Spanning approximately 7 million sq. km (2.7 million sq. miles), the Amazon rainforest is the world's largest block of uninterrupted forest.

Sandoval Lake in Peru.

The Amazon Basin is traversed by the huge river system of the Amazon and its numerous tributaries, ten of which are – like the Amazon itself – among the world's 25 greatest rivers by volume of water. The region's tropical rainforests also stand out for their tremendous diversity of species. Although the exact number of animal species is difficult to estimate, scientists believe they have only discovered a fraction of the total figure, which may lie between five and ten million.

This aerial image reveals how the Amazon snakes through the thick, tropical rainforest of Brazil.

Tropical Rainforests and Monsoon Forests

Southern Asia exhibits a particularly high concentration of developed rainforests and monsoon forests. The 4–5-month dry period is a signature feature of the regional climate.

WESTERN INDIA
Western Ghats

The Western Ghats mountain range stretches along the edge of the Deccan Plateau for some 1,600 km (1,000 miles), separating it from the coastal plain on the Arabian Sea. The mountains mark a watershed, taking the brunt of the annual monsoon rainfall. Originally, rainforest covered almost all of this 160,000-sq.-km (61,800-sq. mile) area. Today,

Clouds above the Western Ghats.

only a 12,000-sq.-km (4,600-sq.-mile) section remains in its untouched, natural state, protected by several national parks. The Western Ghats range is home to what is considered to be one of the world's most diverse plant and animal populations, and many species are exclusive to the region. The area's geology is also diverse. Generally speaking, the north is markedly drier than the south. The mountains may be divided into four ecoregions, with sections of deciduous forests at lower altitudes and cooler, moist areas of montane rainforest in both the north and south. The southern montane rainforests are home to the greatest concentration of species anywhere in India, with 80% of the Western Ghats' flowering plants found here. Endemic species constitute 35% of the plants, 42% of the fish, 48% of the reptiles, and 75% of the amphibians.

SOUTH-WESTERN INDIA
Malabar Coast

Famed for its pepper, the Malabar Coast on the Arabian Sea stretches from Mangalore, in the state of Karnataka, all the way down to the southern tip of the Indian subcontinent – a distance of some 650 km (400 miles). To the east lie the Western Ghats, with the many lagoons and waterways of the so-called "backwaters" running parallel to the coastline. The humid climate provides ideal conditions for bamboo, kapoks, and highly prized trees such as teak and sandalwood. It also supports many palms, including coconut, areca palm, and oil palm – all of which are commercially cultivated. Tea and coffee plantations, as well as numerous herbs – including cinnamon, tamarind, ginger, and pepper – also thrive extremely well in this climate. Large areas of the densely populated Malabar Coast's natural rainforest and tropical moist forest have, however, given way to human settlements.

The "backwaters", a complex network of waterways, lie along the central section of the Malabar Coast. They have served as transport arteries and trade routes for centuries. This image (left) was taken on the rainforest-lined coast near Mobor, in the Indian state of Goa.

SRI LANKA

The island of Sri Lanka, off the southern tip of India, is famous for the large number of plant and animal species found on its relatively small landmass. Yet this natural treasure is under threat. According to one environmental organization, only 1.5% of the original forest remains, the rest having been cleared. The Sinharaja Forest Reserve, in the south-west, is Sri Lanka's most important area of tropical rainforest and one of the oldest reserves in southern Asia. It was declared a national park in 1978, and is also inscribed on the UNESCO World Heritage list. Spanning nearly 9,000 ha (22,000 acres), the forest gets up to 5,000 mm (197 inches) of rainfall every year. It has more than 200 tree species and many endemic animals. A startling 95% of the park's birds are native to Sri Lanka, and the proportion of endemic species among its mammals and butterflies is also well over 50%.

Left: The spectacular Devon Falls in the Sri Lankan rainforest.

ANDAMAN ISLANDS

Located in the Bay of Bengal, the 204 islands of India's Andaman archipelago are still largely covered by untouched tropical rainforest. The islands' climate is hot and humid, with temperatures

Unspoilt nature. Middle Andaman Island.

ranging from 18–34°C (64–93°F) and up to 150 days of rain a year. The gentle breeze makes the high atmospheric humidity (66–85%) bearable. There are flourishing mangroves along the coast, although some were destroyed by the devastating tsunami of December 2004.

LODOICEA MALDIVICA: THE PALMS WITH THE LARGEST SEEDS

The Seychelles palm – otherwise known as Coco de Mer – is exclusive to the islands of Curieuse and Praslin, in the Seychelles in the Indian Ocean. The palm's staminate inflorescence can measure up to 2 m (6½ feet), and its green, heart-shaped fruit develops about six or seven years after pollination. This fruit contains a seed that weighs up to 25 kg (55 lb).

Male Coco de Mer inflorescence.

CORYPHA: THE PALMS WITH THE LARGEST INFLORESCENCE

Inflorescence of a talipot palm, one of the six subspecies of *Corypha*.

RAFFIA: THE PALMS WITH THE LONGEST LEAVES

Raffia palms in Tortuguero National Park, on the Caribbean coast of Costa Rica.

This genus of palm is most common in Africa and Madagascar, with a further variety found in Central and South America. Its leaves can be up to 25 m (82 feet) in length, and its stems as high as 16 m (52 feet). One species of raffia native to South Africa and Mozambique has a palm frond that grows straight up into the air.

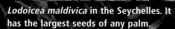

Lodoicea maldivica in the Seychelles. It has the largest seeds of any palm.

Female Coco de Mer seed.

Corypha umbraculifera, or the talipot palm, is a fan palm found in Southeast Asia and northern Australia. It grows to heights of up to 50 m (164 feet), and has the largest inflorescence of any plant in the world, bearing some ten million flowers every time it blooms. It is also the source of sago, which is used as a thickening agent.

THE WORLD'S LARGEST LEAVES, INFLORESCENCE, AND SEEDS

The word "palm" comes from the Latin word *palma*, which loosely translates as "flat hand" – a reference to the similarity of the plant's leaves

Palm trees near Hilo on the Hamakua coast of Big Island, Hawaii.

to an outstretched hand. Palm stems, which do not usually have branches, grow to heights of 0.25–60 m (1–197 feet). They are topped by a bundle of fan or feather-like leaves, interspersed by blossoms on tightly packed inflorescences. There are some 2,600 different species of palm throughout the tropics, subtropics, and oceanic islands. They are useful, cultivated plants – about 100 palm species bear edible fruits (notably that of the date palm), while others produce edible seeds (including coconuts). Sago is extracted from the stems of some palm species, and palm juice is the basis of palm sugar, palm wine, palm honey, and numerous drinks. In many places, palm wood is also used as a building material and to make furniture.

Palm trees in the tropical rainforest near Soufrière, on the south-west coast of St Lucia.

Together with forests in Thailand and Laos, India's Ganges Basin forms part of the world's largest belt of monsoon forest. The Ganges delta is a labyrinth of waterways, swamps, lakes, and

A great hornbill in Thailand.

alluvial islands. It takes in the Sundarbans, the world's largest mangrove forests. Monsoon forests typically occur in regions that have particularly distinct dry and rainy seasons. They usually have two tree layers: an upper layer of deciduous trees such as teak and ebony, and a lower layer containing evergreen plants such as bamboo. Monsoon forests have a thinner canopy than tropical rainforests, and the greater amount of sunlight shining through the trees leads to a lush and diverse forest undergrowth. There are still monsoon forests on the Indochinese Peninsula and Malay Archipelago, as well as in northern Australia, eastern Brazil, and East Africa. Many of these forests are, however, threatened by the demand for firewood and agricultural land.

Khao Sok National Park in the Thai province of Surat Thani is characterized by evergreen monsoon forests in the north (main image) and tropical rainforests in the south.

Lush rainforest in Kachin, Burma (Myanmar).

Grasslands leading to the forests of Thailand's Khao Yai National Park.

Nam Tok Haeo Suwat waterfall in Khao Yai National Park.

Tat Kuang Si waterfall near Luang Prabang, Laos.

The Asian elephant (*Elephas maximus*) is the world's second largest land animal after the African elephant. It is primarily distinguished from its African cousin by its smaller ears and the fact that it only has one – not two – "fingers" at the end of its trunk.

Asian elephants consume around 150 kg (330 lb) of grasses, leaves, branches, and tree bark every day.

While elephant cows and their young live in familial herds, elephant bulls are essentially solitary animals. Only in their youth do the male animals form their own groups, which in turn temporarily attach themselves to a herd for the mating season. The Asian elephant's natural habitat once spanned both tropical rain-forest and open grassland, but the animals are now only found in the densest forests. The Asian elephant is a highly endangered species, and there are now thought to be just 35,000–55,000 remaining in the wild. Of these, some 40% are found on the Indian sub-continent, a further 40% on mainland Southeast Asia, and the rest on Sri Lanka and the other Southeast Asian islands.

Elephant cow and its offspring.

A bull shows its magnificent tusks.

Asian elephants are smaller than their African brethren. They are no more than 3 m (10 feet) tall at shoulder height, and their body measures a maximum of 6 m (20 feet). Elephant cows weigh in at around 2.7 tonnes (3 short tons), but bulls can weigh more than 5 tonnes (5.5 short tons).

SUNDARBANS

The Sundarbans ("beautiful forests") are the largest mangrove forests in the world, covering an area of 6,000 sq. km (2,400 sq. mi). They lie at the deltas of four great rivers, which flood seasonally and

Watercourses, islands, and mangrove forests are typical features of the Sundarbans.

carry away precipitation from the southern slopes of the Himalayas. Large portions of the Sundarbans, which are a UNESCO World Heritage Site, are also part of a national park straddling the border of India and Bangladesh. Countless birds, fish, deer, crocodiles, pythons, and wild pigs live in the mangrove forests, and the Sundarbans are also the last refuge of the Bengal tiger, which has become a symbol of the extinction of species in the area. The matted roots that enable the mangroves to stand on hard, sandy, or loose soil are a typical feature of the forest. As the muddy ground is completely deprived of oxygen below a depth of a few millimeters, special growths called pneumatophores are interwoven between the roots, enabling the trees to breathe.

MANGROVES – A STRANGE SPECIES OF TREE BETWEEN THE LAND AND THE SEA

Mangrove forests on the island of Bornea, Malaysia.

Red mangroves (*Rhizophora mangle*) in the salt waters of the Everglades National Park in the US state of Florida.

Mangrove forests are found in tidal areas on tropical coastlines and consist of salt-tolerant trees and shrubs of various species that have adapted to the living conditions in brackish river estuaries: some store salt in their cells and others store water to dilute the salt concentrations. Excess salt is excreted through special glands, and leaves that accumulate too much salt are shed. Mangrove forests are among the most productive and diverse ecosystems on earth, along with coral reefs and tropical rainforests. Reptiles, mammals, and birds live in the canopies of mangrove forests, and countless fish, mussels, and shrimp survive in the waters around their roots.

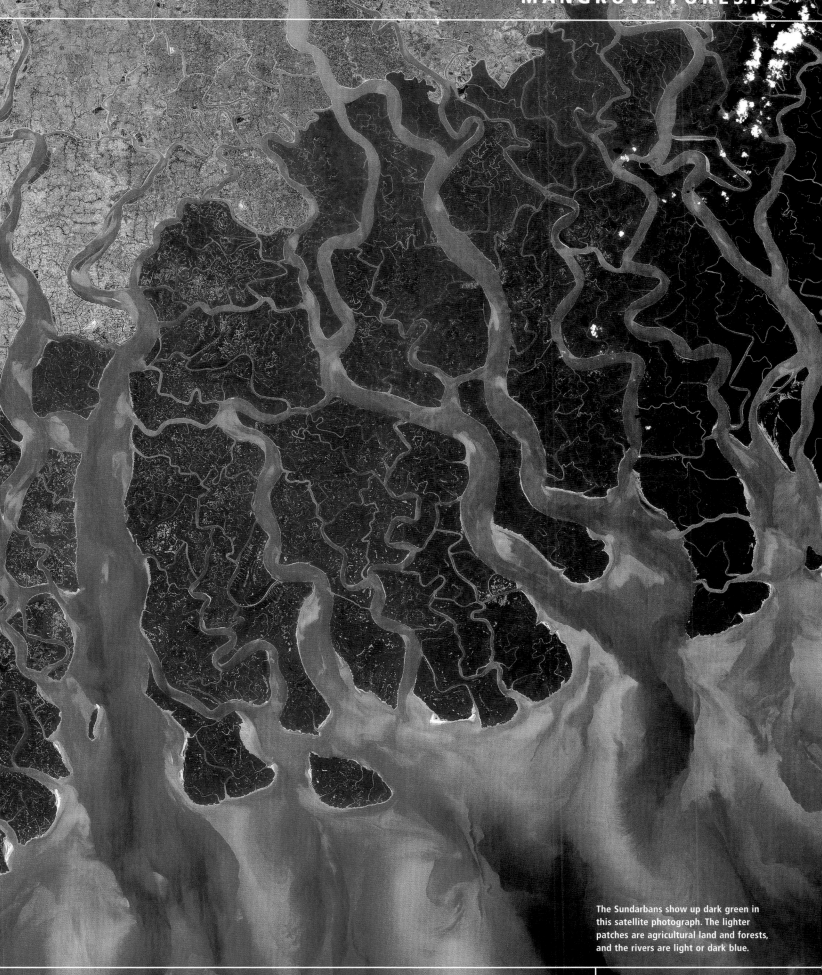

The Sundarbans show up dark green in
this satellite photograph. The lighter
patches are agricultural land and forests,
and the rivers are light or dark blue.

THE BENGAL TIGER

The endangered Bengal tiger (*Panthera tigris tigris*) is the second largest animal of its species after the Siberian tiger. Once found across Asia, it now survives only in India, Bangladesh, Bhutan, Nepal, and Burma (Myanmar). The largest Bengal tiger population is

Tiger in an Indian national park.

A tiger creeps up on its prey.

that located in the Sundarbans mangrove forests.

With its orangey-yellow fur, brown stripes, and powerful body, this majestic predatory cat prowls the jungle with supple grace. Bengal tigers grow to a length of 1.9–2.8 m (6¼–9¼ feet) and weigh 180–260 kg (400–570 lb). Their canine teeth can grow to a length of 6 cm (2½ inches), and their claws can be as long as 10 cm (4 inches). They feed on some 9 kg (20 lb) of meat a day.

Tigers are endangered because of the increasing encroachment upon their natural habitat. The Bengal tiger, however, is the most common member of its species, its population numbering around 3,000–5,000 animals.

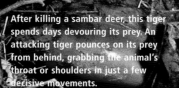

After killing a sambar deer, this tiger spends days devouring its prey. An attacking tiger pounces on its prey from behind, grabbing the animal's throat or shoulders in just a few decisive movements.

The Southeast Asian climate has both perpetually humid and semi-humid zones, and the landscape includes cloud and tropical montane rainforests, subtropical rainforests, monsoon forests, and tropical lowland rainforests.

MALAY PENINSULA

Sometimes known as the Golden Peninsula, the Malay Peninsula is a narrow swathe of land extending from the bottom of the Southeast Asian mainland. Its territory is shared between the states of Burma (Myanmar), Thailand, and Malaysia. It is characterized by its diverse landscapes and ecosystems, from lowland plains to mountainous regions, lakes, beeches, and rainforests, the latter being typical of areas near the equator. The vast, untamed tropical rainforests of Taman Negara National Park, in the northern part of the Malaysian section of the peninsula, date back some 130 million years — making them the oldest forests on Earth. While the effects of the ice ages, climate change, and variation in sea levels have transformed other parts of the world, conditions on the Malay Peninsula have remained fairly constant, and the region's flora and fauna has evolved almost undisturbed. The Taman Negara rainforest, for example, is home to Asian elephants, black leopards, Malayan tapirs, wild boars, apes,

SUMATRA

The tropical rainforests on the Indonesian island of Sumatra are a world famous refuge for some of the most rare and endangered species on Earth. Now national parks, the island's last surviving primeval forest areas are home to the Sumatran tiger, Malayan tapir, hornbill, great argus pheasant, Sumatran elephant, white-handed gibbon, crab-eating macaque, and Sumatran orangutan. With its 176 mammal species, 194 reptile species, 62 amphibian species, and 320 bird species, Sumatra boasts the most diverse wildlife of all the Indonesian islands. Sumatra's flora is similarly rich, including *Rafflesia*, titan arum (the plant with the world's largest inflorescence), as well as numerous endemic orchids, ferns, and mosses. The abundant tropical rainforests of Sumatra were inscribed on the UNESCO World Heritage list in 2004.

BORNEO

The Indonesian island of Borneo is the world's third largest island. With its primeval rainforests, mangroves, orangutans, and many endemic plants, the island still has numerous pockets of untouched natural beauty. Borneo is home to over 220 different species of mammal, including gibbons, the Sumatran rhinoceros, sun bears, clouded leopards, and long-nosed monkeys. The hornbill is just one of the island's 622 bird species, and there are also 400 reptile and amphibian species — notably the kapuas mud snake, the only snake capable of changing its appearance like a chameleon. This fantastic wildlife shares a tropical rainforest habitat that is itself made up of some 15,000 different vascular plants. Borneo also has the world's greatest concentration of orchid species. Yet here as elsewhere, deforestation and the use of land for agriculture threaten to destroy the superb flora and fauna.

Borneo's Danum Valley Conservation Area.

The Kinabatangan River, Malaysian Borneo.

and some endangered species such as the Malayan tiger and Sumatran rhinoceros. There are also some 1,000 different types of butterfly and over 600 bird species. The abundance and diversity of nature is outstanding, making it one of the world's richest and most complex ecosystems. The climate here is tropical all year round, the atmospheric humidity particularly high.

Left: A thick veil of dawn cloud shrouds the rainforest of northern Malaysia.

LESSER SUNDA ISLANDS

The Lesser Sunda Islands include Bali, Lombok, Sumbawa, Flores, Timor, Sumba, and a host of smaller islands. Part of the Indonesian archipelago, they lie just to the east of Java. The Wallace Line – an imaginary line that marks the boundary between the ecoregions of Asia and Australia – runs between Bali and Lombok. Monsoon forests once spanned large areas of the Lesser Sunda Islands, but the advance of agriculture has severely encroached upon the former woodlands. In southern and western Bali, sections of the island's original forests are now protected by the Bali Barat National Park, which was established in 1984. Some parts of the forest on both Bali and Lombok have remained relatively untouched by human intervention, and have instead developed naturally. There can be few more interesting places for nature lovers to visit than the mountains, forests, rivers, and coastlines of these two islands.

PHILIPPINES

The Philippines lie in the western Pacific Ocean. They include over 7,000 islands, which together constitute one of the world's most diverse ecosystems. There are some 14,000 different plant species, and over 5,000 different animal species – including water buffalo, parrots, dolphins, crocodiles, snakes, tarsiers, turtles, lizards, and Philippine ducks – the latter endemic to the region. The island of Bohol is famous for its Chocolate Hills, a landscape of 1,268 conical hills. Reaching heights of 40–120 m (131–394 feet), these natural limestone formations are the result of the falling sea level, volcanic activity, and erosion. The deforestation of the landscape over the last few centuries has given rise to the spread of the extremely hardy grasses that give the Chocolate Hills their name – they turn chocolate brown in the dry season.

Left: Rainforest along the banks of the Loboc River, Bohol, Philippines.

View of the Philippine island of Palawan.

The Chocolate Hills, Bohol, Philippines.

These reddish-brown primates belong to the anthropoid suborder. There are now only two species of orangutan left, both found in the tropical rainforests of the Southeast Asian islands of Sumatra and Borneo. Fossil evidence, however, proves that orangutans were once also common in southern China, Vietnam, and Java. Whether sitting on or hanging from the forest branches, orangutans are superbly adapted to life in the treetops. When it comes to

Male Bornean orangutan.

A baby on board...

...but no less agile.

feeding, for example, they use their powerful arms to bend or break even the thicker branches in order to get to the fruit that — together with leaves — is the mainstay of their diet.

Orangutans have long, reddish-brown or dark brown hair, very long arms, and relatively short legs. They spend their days swinging through the treetops. Standing up, the largest orangutans can be nearly 2 m (6½ feet) tall.

THE KOMODO DRAGON

The Komodo dragon, the world's largest lizard species, is found exclusively on the Indonesian islands of Komodo, Rinca, Gili Motang, and Flores, where it lives in the forests and bushland. Although they can grow to be as long as 3 m (10 feet), most of the Komodo dragons living in the wild are significantly smaller, measuring closer

Komodo dragon on Komodo Island.

to about 1.8 m (6 feet) on average. On an empty stomach, Komodo dragons rarely weigh more than 50 kg (110 lb), but their ability to consume large amounts of food in a short period means that they can quickly eat as much as 100 kg (220 lb). Considered to be one of the most intelligent reptile species, Komodo dragons are extremely supple and possessed of some acute senses. Though

A group of Komodo dragons share their prey, which can even include deer and buffalo.

they mainly feed on the carcasses of dead animals, Komodo dragons also eat some of their prey alive — from small reptiles, birds, and rodents, right up to fully grown deer and wild boars. They will swallow the smaller animals in one go.

Komodo dragons are active during
the day, generally spending the
night in their burrows. Despite their
size, Komodo dragons are fast runners
and able swimmers. They can also
climb trees.

TITAN ARUM

Apart from the specimens grown in botanical gardens, the titan arum (*Amorphophallus titanum*) is to be found only on the island of Sumatra. Botanists consider its single inflorescence the largest of any plant in the world, and the record is held by the Wilhelmina titan arum in Stuttgart Zoological Gardens, which in 2005 was measured as having a height of 2.94 m (10 feet) and a circumference of 1.5 m (5 feet). The titan arum

A rare sight: a magnificent titan arum in full bloom.

blooms only very infrequently, usually every nine to 12 years. Its smell of rotting flesh has earned it the nickname "carrion flower" in Indonesia.

RAFFLESIA

The bloom of *Rafflesia arnoldii* is the largest in the plant kingdom with a diameter of up to 1 m (3 feet) and a weight that can approach 11 kg (25 pounds). Rafflesia is a parasite and lives entirely within its host plant, extending only its flower to lie on the forest floor. Like the titan arum, it imitates the appearance and smell of carrion to attract insects for its pollination. *Rafflesia arnoldii* is found in Sarawak in Malaysia and Kalimantan Barat in Indonesia, as well as on the island of Sumatra.

NEW GUINEA

Australia, New Zealand, and other island states of Oceania still have vast expanses of tropical rainforest and monsoon forest.

Tropical rainforest dominates the island landscape of New Guinea. This is the second largest island on Earth after Greenland, and – with some 20,000 different plant species – it is also one of the world's ten most ecologically diverse regions. The high proportion of endemic species (those not found anywhere else on the planet) is particularly striking, standing at around 55%. The tremendous number of species can be explained both by the island's geographic diversity, and by the fact that its large areas of uninterrupted plant cover – forest alone accounts for some 75% of New Guinea's surface area – have remained largely untouched by human intervention. The island's fauna is also impressive, with 400–600 species of bird, over 400 amphibian and butterfly species, 180 mammal species, and numerous spiders, reptiles, and insects. There are also more than 1,000 different species of fish in the island's lagoons, lakes, and rivers.

In the eastern part of the island, forest clearing has taken a heavy toll on Papua New Guinea's rainforests, but this is still the world's third largest rainforest.

Lorentz National Park lies on the western side of the island. Covering an area of 23,555 sq. km (9,100 sq. miles), it is the most extensive national park in Southeast Asia. It is also unique in the range of terrain it covers. Stretching from equatorial glaciers to the tropical sea, the park takes in lowland and montane rainforests, subalpine vegetation, swamp forest, and mangroves.

Left: Waterfall in the highlands of Papua New Guinea. With its primeval forests, the country is a tropical paradise, and its rainforests are the third largest on Earth. Below: Thick tropical rainforest spans Cape Tribulation, a headland on the coast of Queensland, Australia.

AUSTRALIA'S NORTHERN PACIFIC COAST

The Atherton Tablelands in Queensland are the largest solid block of rainforest on the northern Pacific coast. Spanning an area of 800 sq. km (310 sq. miles), the Atherton Tablelands take in 11 different types of forest, of which liana forests – with their many tree ferns and epiphytes – are the most prevalent. Queensland's Daintree National Park reaches all the way to the Great Barrier Reef. There are 13 different types of rainforest in this park alone. The area, which makes up 0.2% of Australia's total landmass, is home to 30% of the country's mammal species, 65% of its bat and butterfly species, and 20% of its bird species. Also in Queensland, the Cape Tribulation headland is where the tropical rainforest meets the Great Barrier Reef. With its tropical climate, this untouched natural landscape provides ideal conditions for a fantastic range of plants and animals, and more than 3,500 different plant species thrive in this, the most diverse part of the continent. The local wildlife is equally multifarious, in particular the many reptile species. There are approximately 7,480 sq. km (2,890 sq. miles) of tropical rainforest on the Cape York Peninsula, as well areas of savanna, heath, and mangrove forest. The area has 3,300 different species of plant and is home to 700 animal species.

Wet Tropics of Queensland (top); and Millaa Millaa Falls in the Atherton Tablelands (above).

The flightless southern cassowary is the third largest bird on Earth after the African ostrich and the emu. Weighing up to 70 kg (154 pounds), cassowaries measure up to 1.5 m (5 feet) in length and are around 90 cm (35 inches) tall at shoulder height. This ratite

Only the cassowary bears this unique "helmet".

bird hides away in the forests of New Guinea and Australia, its casque, like a helmet, protecting its head in the thicket. The southern cassowary is now an endangered species. Its natural habitat is disappearing, and it is threatened by vehicle traffic and hunted for its decorative feathers.

Southern cassowaries are solitary animals that generally stick to the same area. The exception to this is during the breeding season (right), when the female abandons its large, light green eggs immediately after laying them. The male then incubates the eggs — between three and eight in total — until they hatch, and spends the next nine months or so looking after the light brown, striped chicks. Southern cassowaries mostly feed on fruit, mushrooms, insects, small mammals and birds, and bird eggs.

A southern cassowary explores a cornfield in the Australian state of Queensland. Its real natural habitat, however, is in the understory of the region's dense rainforests.

Evergreen rainforest now covers less than 10% of the African continent on either side of the equator. Numerous areas of savanna now interrupt the region's once closed belt of green forest.

WEST AFRICA

West Africa, with its semi-humid, tropical climate, still has large expanses of thriving rainforest. The forests of Côte d'Ivoire (the Ivory Coast), for example, boast orchids, epiphytes, baobab trees, and a diverse variety of wildlife. The country gets its name from the valuable tusks of the African elephant, and it is poachers hunting for elephant ivory that are to blame for the decline in the animals' population – a fall so dramatic that the only surviving elephants today are those in the protected reserves. The Côte d'Ivoire rainforest is also home to hippopotamuses, primates (including the now endangered chimpanzee), rodents, pangolins, predatory cats such as lions and leopards, crocodiles, snakes, and countless birds. There are large forests within the territory of Ghana (formerly the Gold Coast). Here, too, the plant and animal life is tremendous, despite being only half as rich as it was 50 years ago – a development that is the result of forest clearing in order to meet the export demand for fine woods like mahogany and walnut.

CONGO BASIN

The Congo Basin region accounts for the largest proportion of Africa's tropical rainforest. Spanning the central part of the continent, it is the world's second largest solid block of rainforest after the Amazon Basin. Despite their proximity to the densely populated west coast, these still intact rainforests have remained largely uncharted. This makes them a sort of wildlife repository – a place where species long extinct elsewhere are still alive. Both the gorilla and the rarer mountain gorilla are found here, as well as chimpanzees and bonobos, forest elephants and buffalo, bongo antelopes, and okapis. The region's biodiversity is truly remarkable, its forests home to over 400 mammal species, more than 1,000 bird species, and an estimated 10,000 or more plant species. Much of the forest wildlife is found in the upper layers of the rainforest, whose inhabitants have established well-traversed passages through the tree

Nouabalé-Ndoki National Park, Congo.

branches. Researchers have yet to study many of these species, and others are probably still to be discovered. Even on the forest floor, some animals have only recently come to naturalists' attention.

This aerial image shows the swampy forest clearing of Mbeli Bai in Nouabalé-Ndoki National Park, in the Congo Basin.

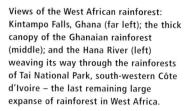

Views of the West African rainforest: Kintampo Falls, Ghana (far left); the thick canopy of the Ghanaian rainforest (middle); and the Hana River (left) weaving its way through the rainforests of Tai National Park, south-western Côte d'Ivoire – the last remaining large expanse of rainforest in West Africa.

MADAGASCAR

Madagascar broke off from the African continent 130 million years ago, drifting far into the Indian Ocean to become the world's fourth largest island. Some 400 km (250 miles) off the East African coast, Madagascar's isolation has turned it into something of a Noah's ark, preserving animal and plant species that have long since died out on the African mainland. However, this unique natural paradise is now threatened by slash and burn agriculture. Because Madagascar did not rise out of the sea like a volcanic island, its plants and animals were spared the challenge of establishing themselves here from scratch. Instead, most of Madagascar's species already existed in the region when it became an island.

Montagne d'Ambre National Park.

They survived because conditions – notably the lack of competition from more highly developed species – were more conducive to their survival than those faced by their mainland counterparts. Madagascar's only animal colonists were those few creatures capable of swimming or flying across the Mozambique Channel, but it is the island's reptiles and amphibians that are its true original inhabitants. Around 80% of Madagascar's flora (including 86% of its flowering plants) and many of its animal species are endemic, found only in this part of the world. Furthermore, roughly two-thirds of the world's chameleon species are exclusive to Madagascar, including the giant Madagascar chameleon. Experts believe there to be many as yet undiscovered plants and animals on the still uncharted Masoala Peninsula.

Views of the protected rainforests of Madagascar (left): forest covers the Ambatotsondrona in Marojejy National Park (top); and giant trees in Andringitra National Park (bottom).

The dark gray forest elephant is the third largest land animal on Earth. It is markedly smaller than its African cousin, and also has much smaller ears. The forest elephant's key distinguishing features are its gentle saunter, mighty body, arched back sloping down toward the rear, and trunk, whose two "fingers" allow the elephant to reach its food – including leaves, grass, branches, tree bark, roots, and fruit – with ease. Forest elephants spend up to 16 hours a day feeding, consuming some 100–150 kg (220–330 lb) of food. They are found in the equatorial rainforests and swamps of central and West Africa, and are a relatively common sight in the Congo Basin region. Yet hunting and the destruction of the tropical primeval forests have placed the forest elephant at acute risk of extinction. Female forest elephants and their young form stable familial herds, the adults usually sisters or other close relatives. The herd's matriarchal leader determines when the animals eat, drink, bathe, or sleep. The bulls, by contrast, prefer to live either in much less tightly knit groups of other bachelors or in solitude, only briefly attaching themselves to a herd when a cow is ready to mate. While different groups of African elephant cows and young bulls have been known to form super-herds, the forest elephant has never displayed this behavior.

Forest elephants are found either alone or in small herds.

Elephants drink 80 l (21 US gallons) of water a day. Though they cannot jump across water, they are competent swimmers, happily letting the water carry them long distances along the lakes and rivers – without getting tired.

GORILLAS

MOUNTAIN GORILLAS

The gorilla's natural habitat once stretched all the way from the coast of Equatorial Guinea to East Africa. Today, the gorilla population is divided into two species (eastern and western), and lowland and mountain gorillas are subspecies of these. The latter is found exclusively in the Virunga volcanic mountains along the borders of Uganda, Rwanda, and the Democratic Republic of the Congo (DRC). There are believed to be just

A silverback throws its weight around.

Gorilla in Virunga National Park, DRC.

400–700 mountain gorillas left. These plant-eating primates live in familial groups that are made up of a fully grown silverback male, about four females capable of bearing young, and their offspring. Mountain gorillas spend most of their time at ground level, rarely climbing into the trees.

Despite appearances, gorillas are essentially peaceful beasts and rarely aggressive. Their diet is vegetarian.

LOWLAND GORILLAS

Lowland gorillas are divided into eastern and western subspecies. Eastern lowland gorillas are, at heights of up to 1.7 m (5½ feet), the world's largest primates. They live in the hills and lowlands on the eastern edge of the Congo Basin. Western lowland gorillas, meanwhile, are the most common gorillas. They are found along the coast of the Gulf of Guinea, between the mouths of the Niger and Congo Rivers. Like their mountain counterparts, low-

Western lowland gorillas in Nouabalé-Ndoki National Park, Congo.

land gorillas are active during the day, spending the nights in the leafy nests they build in the trees or on the ground. Thanks to their size and intelligence, these peaceful nomads need fear no enemies. They are, however, threatened by the activities of humans. For though the gorillas' remaining natural habitats enjoy protected status, these forest areas are still being cleared to provide firewood, timber, and to create agricultural land. Many gorillas have also fallen victim to poachers, who are able to sell the primates' meat, hands, feet, skin, and skulls, all of which are highly prized. The latter are used as trophies.

BAOBABS

The baobab or monkey bread tree is one of the most typical trees of tropical Africa. It has a short but very thick trunk, and a broad overarching crown whose branches, when bare, look like roots – giving rise to the legend that the gods, angered by the sins of mankind, had torn the baobab out of the ground and replanted it upside down. Baobabs are deciduous trees, sprouting leaves just before the rainy season. They are found across sub-Saharan Africa, and there are also endemic baobab species on the island of

Baobabs on the island of Madagascar.

The tree's trunk is often extremely thick.

A South African baobab.

Madagascar. During the rainy season, the tree can store up to 140,000 l (36,700 US gallons) of water in its trunk, creating a valuable source of water for both man and animals during the dry months. The baobab's hardy trunk can even survive fire, sustaining hardly any damage.

The Avenue of the Baobabs, near Morondava on the western coast of Madagascar, is formed of *Adansonia grandidieri* trees, a species of baobab.

THE WORLD'S LARGEST BAOBAB

The Big Baobab, near Tzaneen, South Africa, reaches a height of 22 m (72 feet) and has a circumference of some 47 m (154 feet) – making it the world's largest monkey bread tree. The tree is estimated to be around 6,000 years old. In 1993, the owners of the land on which the tree is situated hollowed out its trunk and set up a bar inside. Nevertheless, it still blooms every spring.

PARSON'S CHAMELEON AND GIANT MADAGASCAR CHAMELEON

Two-thirds of the world's chameleon species, including both the Parson's chameleon and the giant Madagascar chameleon, are endemic to the forests and savannas of Madagascar. The latter can be as much as 68 cm (27 inches) long, and both have magnificent, casqued heads. Male Parson's chameleons also have two scaly, shovel-like appendages at the end of their snouts. The males are generally turquoise, the females more green. Some also have a yellow spot around the middle of their bodies. As for the giant Madagascar chameleon, the males are distinguished by their slightly dirty-looking brownish-gray camouflage, while the females' skin appears in brighter, mostly green shades, with white spots along the sides. Since chameleons mostly feed on insects, locals see them as extremely useful fly catchers.

A female giant Madagascar chameleon.

Found only in the rainforests of Madagascar, Parson's chameleons can grow to lengths of up to 60 cm (24 inches). Up in the trees, they hunt for insects, small birds, and small mammals, whipping out their muscular, sticky tongues to catch their prey. The chameleon's tongue is as much as twice the length of its scaly body.

CENTRAL AMERICA

Tropical rainforests are concentrated in Central America. The North American climate, meanwhile, sustains temperate rainforests.

There are still large expanses of rainforest in several Central American countries, notably Costa Rica, Honduras, Panama, and Nicaragua. Thick rainforests typify the hilly landscape of the Panamanian province of Darién, although forest clearing continues to threaten the region's diverse range of species. North-west of Panama, Costa Rica (literally "Rich Coast") owes its name to its breathtaking natural treasures. This border region between North and South America is still home to animals hailing from both continents, including rare species such as the capuchin monkey and jaguar. Fifty years ago, the forests of Costa Rica had been almost completely cleared, but efforts to restore them are now beginning to pay off. The tropical rainforests of Nicaragua exhibit a particularly great diversity of species, and the country also boasts mangrove swamps. There are still areas of uncharted primeval forest in Honduras, providing a refuge for countless plant and animal species.

Costa Rica has some simply breathtaking landscapes, with sights such as the Arenal volcano (far left) and plants such as this bromeliad (left). The cloud forests and rainforests of eastern Panama stand out for their biodiversity (middle). Dense rainforest covers many of the mountains on St Lucia, an island in the Lesser Antilles. The twin Pitons (below, inset) rise to altitudes of nearly 800 m (2,600 feet).

CARIBBEAN ISLANDS

Cuba's national parks were set up to protect the country's ecosystems. They include the Alejandro de Humboldt National Park, with its dry forests, rainforests, and mangroves. Jamaica's Cockpit Country – noted for its particularly great biodiversity – is another lush, green forest landscape. The area serves as a last refuge for species driven out of the rest of the island by human activity, and is home to numerous snakes, butterflies, parrots, and frogs. Rainforest still covers about half of the island of Hispaniola, whose terrain is divided between Haiti and the Dominican Republic. The part of the island belonging to the latter state boasts an especially high number of animal species, including hummingbirds, land turtles, sea turtles, flamingos, and herons. In Puerto Rico, waterfalls, ferns, orchids, palms, and other tropical vegetation, as well as countless bird species, characterize the splendid El Yunque rainforest. The forest is home to the brightly feathered Puerto Rican parrot and coqui tree frog, the country's national mascot. Dominica, with its tropical flora and fauna, is considered to have the best-preserved natural landscape of all the Lesser Antilles islands, and the central part of the island, in particular, is covered by dense rainforests. Guadeloupe National Park, located on the island of the same name, also has tropical rainforests, including mahogany trees. Parrots, parakeets, bats, Guadeloupe raccoons, mongooses, and endangered agoutis are just a few examples of the park's wildlife. The extensive rainforests of Trinidad and Tobago are home to beautiful waterfalls, and the islands also boast a diverse plant and animal life as well as vast swamplands. On St Lucia, rivers flow through the volcanic highlands, a rainforest-covered landscape filled with bougainvilleas, hibiscuses, wild orchids, and roses. At higher altitudes in particular, this original vegetation continues to flourish.

The tropical rainforests of Panama's Darién National Park reach right into the mountains. Covering some 5,790 sq. km (2,235 sq. miles), this is the largest national park in Central America.

JAGUARS

Jaguars can grow to a length of 1.5 m (5 feet). They are the world's third largest feline after the tiger and lion, and the largest big cat of the Americas. The jaguar's yellow fur and black spots resemble the African and Asian leopard, but the jaguar's spots are bigger and its tail somewhat shorter.

The rainforests of South and Central America, in particular

Jaguars are extremely heavily built.

The jaguar is a solitary beast.

the Amazon region, are the jaguar's preferred natural habitat. Jaguars feed on animals including agoutis, peccaries, and deer, stalking their prey before delivering a fatal strike of their paw or biting into the animal's skull – the cat's substantial head and powerful jaw muscles working like a nutcracker, which can even crunch through the shell of a turtle. No other big cat overcomes its prey in this manner.

A jaguar takes a drink of water. Given the opportunity, jaguars will also catch fish and even small caimans.

Although they live on different continents, jaguars and leopards are close relatives. Both belong to the genus *panthera*, and both are susceptible to melanism, which can turn their fur black. Black jaguars are, like black leopards, known as black panthers. Though their fur appears to be completely black, closer examination in good light reveals that their spotted pattern is still intact. The spots on jaguars form rosettes of different sizes, which act as unique fingerprints. As a result camera traps can be used to estimate their numbers in the wild in a particular area.

THE BEE HUMMINGBIRD

The minute bee hummingbird (*Mellisuga helenae*), which is also known as *zunzuncitos*, belongs to the hummingbird family. It is the world's smallest bird, the female measuring just 7 cm (2¾ inches) from the tip of its beak to the end of its tail, and the male an even more diminutive 6.3 cm (2½ inches). These tiny birds weigh around just 2 g (0.07 oz).

Bee hummingbirds are endemic to the Caribbean island of Cuba, where they are found in

Perched on the end of a pencil, the bee hummingbird's tiny size is obvious.

three distant woodland areas. The female bird builds its nest out of plant fibers, the male playing almost no part in incubating. The chicks hatch after about two weeks, and are able to fly three weeks after that. Bee hummingbirds feed on nectar and the small insects that they find in the flowers.

A female bee hummingbird sitting in its nest on the island of Cuba. The female bird breeds two or three times a year. Each time, two eggs are hatched.

These tiny featherweights have beautiful feathers. Flapping their wings at a rate of 80 beats per second, they hover in front of the flowers from which they garner the nectar that is their primary food. The birds use their tongues and thin beaks to suck the nectar out of the flowers. Their tongues are twice as long as their beaks.

SOUTH AMERICA

Most of the world's tropical rainforests are in South America, and this is also the location of the world's largest block of rainforest, the Amazon Basin.

ORINOCO LOWLANDS

The landscape of Venezuela can be divided into three main areas: the Andes Mountains, Guiana Highlands, and Orinoco lowlands. The vast Llanos (plains) is one of most beautiful parts of Venezuela, characterized by lush, fertile grassland and home to an incredible number of animal species.

The Orinoco and other rivers and channels snake through the varied scenery toward the Atlantic Ocean. But it is tropical rainforest – complete with palms, fruit trees, orchids, bromeliads, tree ferns, and rivers filled with mangrove vegetation – that accounts for the majority of the landscape. Jaguars, cougars, ocelots, raccoons, giant otters, howler and capuchin monkeys, as well as capybaras are just a few examples of the Orinoco lowlands' wildlife. There are large numbers of amphibians, reptiles, and fish, and the region is also well-known as a paradise for birds, with hummingbirds, parrots, cormorants, toucans, kingfishers, and birds of paradise numbered among its many feathered inhabitants.

THE GUIANA HIGHLANDS

Bordered by the Atlantic Ocean, the Amazon, and Orinoco lowlands, the rugged mountain landscape of the Guiana Highlands spans a huge 1.5 million-sq.-km (579,000-sq.-mile) area from eastern Colombia to southern Venezuela, northern Brazil, Guyana, Suriname, and all the way to French Guiana. These highlands are an ancient geological

Epiphytes on a tree in Venezuela.

formation. Made mostly of granite rock, they also include the magnificent flat-topped mountains known as tepuis. The tepuis tower over the Gran Sabana, a flat, sandstone plateau that rises more than 1,000 m (3,280 feet) above sea level. Thanks to their isolation from the rainforests, the high mountain plateaus have fostered an endemic flora and fauna. Raging waterfalls cascade down some of the mountains into the tropical rainforest below. One of them, Salto Angel, is – at a height of 979 m (3,212 feet) – the world's highest waterfall. The region's highest mountain, meanwhile, is the Pico da Neblina, which rises 2,994 m (9,823 feet) above sea level. To the east, tropical rainforests cover the lower mountains. The forests boast an astonishing variety of plants and animals, with a particularly high number of bird species. Savannas and grasslands dominate the landscape further west, and cocoa, rice, sugarcane, cotton, and other produce are all cultivated here.

Giant tree ferns (*Dicksonia sellowiana*) are part of the diverse vegetation of Brazil's dense Atlantic Forest.

Tropical rainforest trees reflected in a tranquil lagoon of Venezuela's Orinoco delta (left).

BRAZIL'S ATLANTIC FOREST

The Atlantic Forest (Mata Atlântica) once stretched for nearly 3,000 km (1,900 miles) along the Atlantic coast of Brazil. Today, in a world shaped by man's cultivation of the landscape, only small pockets of the former forests remain. Yet despite their reduced size, these forests still exhibit a rich variety of plants and animals, many of them endemic. Because Brazil's largest cities fall within the Atlantic Forest area, the region's rainforests are some of the most endangered woodlands in the world. Though UNESCO has declared the Atlantic Forest a biosphere reserve and made some parts of the area a

Begonias, including climbing begonias, thrive in the Brazilian rainforest.

World Heritage Site, this has failed to prevent illegal forest clearing. From the Cananéia coastal plain to the 1,400-m (4,600-foot) high Serra Paranapiacaba, the Atlantic Forest's scenery is characterized by a great diversity of terrain, from saltwater lagoons, shifting dunes, sandy beaches, and mangroves to pastures, and arable land. It is one of the most ecologically valuable portions of land in South America. Ferns, orchids, begonias, and bromeliads grow both on and in the rainforest trees, and these plants are in turn home to the forest's tree frogs. Other examples of the Atlantic Forest wildlife include the lowland tapir, neotropical river otter, and harpy eagle.

Moss and lichen cover many trees in the rainforest.

Flamingo flowers bring a vivid splash of red to the rainforest.

THE GREEN ANACONDA

It is hard to appreciate the green anaconda's true size without having seen one of these giant snakes in real life. These Peruvian Matses hunters show off their prize: an anaconda measuring 5.5 m (18 feet).

The green anaconda (*Eunectes murinus*) is primarily found in the Amazon and Orinoco rainforests. It grows to lengths of up to 9 m (29 feet), and can weigh approximately 150 kg (330 lb). Although the Asian reticulated python can equal its length, this much thinner snake is no match for the green anaconda's bulk. This makes the green anaconda the world's largest snake. Two rows of large, dark, oval spots run the length of the snake's muscular body. While its body is yellowish-to grayish-brown, the snake's

The green anaconda's skin provides superb camouflage.

belly is a pale yellowish shade. Starting behind its eyes, two black lines lead down to the snake's throat. Anacondas are slow and rather sluggish on land, but they are excellent swimmers, keeping their nostrils tightly closed as they cut through the water. Land-based animals are the anaconda's preferred food, and the snake catches its prey on land before dragging it beneath the water's surface and strangling it with its body. Female anacondas give birth to litters of more than 30 live young, each newborn snake measuring some 70 cm (28 inches).

Hiding among the branches, a green anaconda lies in wait for its prey. The snake suffocates capybaras, tapirs, and even caimans by wrapping its body around them.

MOUNTAINS AND HIGHLANDS

The majestic beauty of mountains has always been captivating. Many peoples still regard such unattainable summits as the seats of their gods or the homes of spirits. The peaks more than 8,000 m (26,000 feet) in the Karakoram and the Himalayas, the highest mountain ranges on Earth, remained unclimbed until well into the 20th century. Maurice Herzog and Louis Lachenal were the first to reach the summit of Annapurna I in 1950, and three years later, Edmund Hillary and Tenzing Norgay conquered Mount Everest, the "Throne of the Gods" and the world's highest mountain. Just like the European Alps, the Rocky Mountains in the USA, and the Andes in South America, these mountains in

Dusk over Mount Everest.

Asia had arisen over long periods from folds in the Earth caused by the constant movement of the continental plates. As these float together, landmasses are constricted, folded, and piled up to form mountain ranges. This constant tectonic movement means that the Earth's summits are continually rising by a few millimeters every year. Almost every landmass has a mountain range of superlatives.

THE WORLD'S HIGHEST MOUNTAIN RANGES
Height above sea level

❶ **Himalaya**, Asia
Mount Everest
    8,850 m (29,035 feet)
❷ **Karakoram**, Asia
K2   8,611 m (25,341 feet)
❸ **Kunlun Mountains**, Asia
Ulugh Muztagh
    7,724 m (25,341 feet)
❹ **Pamir Mountains**, Asia
Kongur Tagh
    7,719 m (25,325 feet)
❺ **Hindu Kush**, Asia
Tirich Mir
    7,707 m (25,285 feet)
❻ **Tian Shan**, Asia
Jengish Chokusu
    7,439 m (24,406 feet)
❼ **Trans-Himalayas**, Asia
Norin Kang
    7,206 m (23,642 feet)
❽ **Andes**, South America
Aconcagua
    6,963 m (22,845 feet)

❾ **Alaska Range**, North America
Mount McKinley
    6,194 m (20,322 feet)
❿ **Saint Elias Mountains**,
North America
Mount Logan   5,959 m (19,551 feet)
⓫ **Kilimanjaro**, Africa
Kibo   5,895 m (19,340 feet)
⓬ **Sierra Nevada de Santa Marta**,
South America
Pico Cristóbal Colón
    5,775 m (18,947 feet)
⓭ **Caucasus Mountains**, Europe
Mount Elbrus   5,642 m (18,510 feet)
⓮ **Sierra Madre Oriental**,
Central America
Pico de Orizaba
    5,636 m (18,491 feet)
⓯ **Mount Kenya**, Africa
Batian   5,199 m (17,057 feet)
⓰ **Ellsworth Mountains**, Antarctica
Mount Vinson
    4,892 m (16,050 feet)

Snow-capped Mount McKinley
reflected in Wonder Lake in Denali
National Park. At 6,194 m (20,322
feet), Mount McKinley in the Alaska
Range is the highest mountain in
continental North America.

HIMALAYAS

The satellite image shows only a
small part of the Himalayas. Seen
from the south, the mountain chain
looks like a gigantic arch, with the
world's highest summits concentrated
toward the middle. Because of their
enormous mass, the Himalayas
function as a vegetation and climatic
divide between north and south.

The satellite image shows a section of the world's highest mountain range, the Himalayas in Tibet and Nepal, where a horseshoe-shaped chain of 7,000 and 8,000-m (23,000–26,250-foot) peaks enclose numerous almost snow-free valleys, all of which lie in the Nepalese Sagarmatha National Park. The world's most famous peaks over 8,000 m (26,000 feet) are to be found here, including Cho Oyu (8,201 m/26,906 feet), Mount Everest (8,850 m/29,035 feet), Lhotse (8,516 m/27,940 feet), and Makalu (8,463 m/27,766 feet). It is difficult to miss the great tongues of the glaciers protruding down into the valleys; the glacier rivers percolate into the Dudh Kosi, which

The north face of Mount Everest.

A satellite image of Mount Everest. The summit is more or less in the middle of the image.

flows south toward the Sun Kosi and the sources of the Brahmaputra, Ganges, and Indus, the greatest rivers in Asia. Several of the 19 rivers draining the Himalaya system to the south follow deep rift valleys with sheer sides up to 5 km (3 miles) deep.

THE FIRST ASCENT

Several groups from a British expedition attempted to scale the world's highest mountain, the "Throne of the Gods", in the spring of 1953. Edmund Hillary, a mountaineer and apiarist from New Zealand, and Tenzing Norgay, his Nepalese Sherpa, were the first two-man team to reach the summit of Mount Everest on 29 May, after a previous team had been obliged to turn back just 100 m (328 feet) short of their goal. Many hundreds of climbers have conquered the mountain since Hillary and Norgay's first ascent, although more than 200 have died, either on the way up or the way down.

Tenzing Norgay and Edmund Hillary drinking tea on the Western Cwm after their conquest of Mount Everest in May 1953 (top). This was to be the beginning of a life-long friendship.

Named after Sir George Everest, a British surveyor, Mount Everest is known as Sagarmatha ("Goddess of the Sky") in Nepalese, and Qomolangma ("Goddess of the Earth") in Tibetan. Standing some 8,850 m (29,035 feet) above sea level in the Khumbu Himal in Nepal on the Tibetan border, it is the world's highest mountain. It forms part of the Sagarmatha National Park on the Nepalese side, and its northern slopes are part of the Qomolangma National Nature Reserve. Like the rest of the Himalayas, Mount Everest was created by plate tectonic forces released as the Indian and Eurasian Plates collided. The

THE WORLD'S HIGHEST
MOUNTAIN

smaller Indian Plate continues to slide beneath the Eurasian by about 3 cm (1¼ inch) every year and Mount Everest is thus still growing, although by only a small amount a year.

Such great altitudes mean that the air pressure on Mount Everest is only a third of normal pressure at sea level. Despite the wild variations of temperature and very strong winds, the local population regard the eternal snows of the steep Himalayan slopes as the home of the gods. Mountaineers have been testing their mettle on peaks above 8,000 m (26,000 feet) since the turn of the 20th century, and after

Edmund Hillary and Tenzing Norgay's first ascent in 1953 Reinhold Messner and Peter Habeler were the first to reach the summit without supplemental oxygen in 1978. The quickest ascent was achieved by Sherpa Pemba Dorjie, who took little more than eight hours to reach the summit from base camp. The oldest climber to reach the top was Min Bahadur Sherchan, a 76-year-old Nepalese, in 2008. Mount Everest tourism has taken off since the 1980s, and such great demand and the refuse it brings to the mountain has caused environmental problems. Twelve people overtaken by

sudden changes in conditions never returned from the mountain during the 1996 season – thin air, icy cold, and unpredictable weather remain a mortal danger to mountaineers, even though climbing equipment has improved considerably over the last few decades. Mount Everest nonetheless continues to attract scores of people who wish to stand on the world's highest summit.

The Chinese north face of Mount Everest. The goal of all the ascents is the summit plateau just 2 m (3 feet) square.

K2, Karakoram   8,611 m (28,250 feet)

Kangchenjunga, Himalayas   8,586 m (28,170 feet)

Lhotse, Himalayas   8,516 m (27,940 feet)

Dhaulagiri, Himalayas   8,167 m (26,795 feet)

Makalu, Himalayas   8,463 m (27, 766 feet)

Manaslu, Himalayas   8,163 m (26,781 feet)

Cho Oyu, Himalayas   8,201 m (26,900 feet)

Nanga Parbat, Himalayas   8,126 m (26,660 feet)

Annapurna I, Himalayas   8,091 m (26,545 feet)

THE 14 HIGHEST MOUNTAINS ON EARTH

All the world's peaks reaching a height of over 8,000 m (26,000 feet) are in Asia: nine are to be found in the Himalayas and five in neighboring Karakoram. The mountains are distributed between China (including Tibet), India, Nepal, and Pakistan. Five of the mountains are exclusively in one country, the other nine divide their territory between two different nations. The first 8,000-m (26,000-feet) peak to be conquered was Annapurna in 1950, and three years later the first men stood on Everest, the highest mountain on earth. More than 4,100 mountaineers have reached the summit since then, and an ascent of Mount Everest is the greatest ambition of almost every climber.

Everest, Nuptse, and surrounding peaks.

THE 14 SUMMITS OVER 8,000 M (26,000 FEET)
(with date of first ascent)

❶ Mount Everest   8,850 m
Nepal, China   (29,029 feet)
Hillary, Norgay   1953

❷ K2   8,611 m
Pakistan   (28,250 feet)
Compagnoni, Lacedelli   1954

❸ Kangchenjunga   8,586 m
Nepal, India   (28,170 feet)
Band, Brown   1955

❹ Lhotse   8,516 m
Nepal   (27,940 feet)
Luchsinger, Reiss   1956

❺ Makalu   8,463 m
Nepal   (27,766 feet)
Terray, Couzy   1955

❻ Cho Oyu   8,201 m
Nepal   (26,900 feet)
Tichy, Jöchler, P. Dawa Lama   1954

❼ Dhaulagiri   8,167 m
Nepal   (26,795 feet)
Diemberger, Na. Dorje, Forrer,
Schelbert, Diener, Ny. Dorje   1960

❽ Mansalu   8,163 m
Nepal   (26,781 feet)
Norbu, Imanishi   1956

❾ Nanga Parbat   8,126 m
Pakistan   (26,660 feet)
Buhl   1953

❿ Annapurna I   8,091 m
Nepal   (26,545 feet)
Lachenal, Herzog   1950

**⓫ Gasherbrum I
(Hidden Peak)**   8,068 m
Pakistan, China   (26,470 feet)
Schoening, Kauffman   1958

⓬ Broad Peak   8,047 m
Pakistan, China   (26,400 feet)
Buhl, Diemberger, Schmuck,
Wintersteller   1957

⓭ Gasherbrum II   8,035 m
Pakistan, China   (26,362 feet)
Moravec, Larch, Willenpart   1956

⓮ Shisha Pangma   8,013 m
China   (26,289 feet)
Chin. Exped. Hsu Ching   1964

Mount Everest towers over the other 8,000-m (26,000-ft) peaks. The damp air above its pyramidal peak condenses to a white cloud and climbers use the appearance of this "cloud trail" to estimate the wind speed (large image).

Gasherbrum I, Karakoram   8,068 m (26,470 feet)

Gasherbrum II, Karakoram   8,035 m (26,362 feet)

Broad Peak, Karakoram   8,047 m (26,400 feet)

Shisha Pangma, Himalayas   8,013 m (26,289 feet)

Lupins in the Torres del Paine National Park in southern Chile.

Known in Spanish as the Cordillera de los Andes, the Andes are the world's longest mountain range, running the length of the entire Pacific coast of continental South America. Several "sub-cordilleras" run parallel to one another for much of this distance. The range reaches a width of more than 700 km (435 miles) where the Peruvian, Bolivian, and Chilean borders meet.

The granite towers of the Fitz Roy massif rise to a height of more than 3,000 m (9,800 feet) above the Patagonian plains in the Los Glaciares National Park. Cerro Fitz Roy, the highest peak, is 3,375 m (11,073 feet) high and is considered one of the world's most difficult climbs (large image). At 5,897 m (19,347 feet), Cocopaxi (right) in Ecuador is one of the world's highest active volcanoes.

The Andes stretch more than 7,500 km (4,700 miles) from the Caribbean Sea in the north to Cape Horn at the tip of South America, where the chain breaks up into countless little islands. The Southern Andes consist of a narrow mountain chain reaching heights approaching 1,500 m (4,900 feet) in Tierra del Fuego, but further to the north, the summits vary between 3,000 and 5,000 m (9,800 and 16,400 feet), and central Chile

and western Argentina boast peaks of more than 5,000 m (16,400 feet), including Aconcagua (6,963 m/ 22,845 feet), the highest mountain in the Andes and, indeed, the whole continent of South America. Above the 27th parallel south, the chain broadens out into the Central Andes, and the East and West Cordilleras run either side of the salt flats and lakes – such as Poopó and Lake Titicaca – of the Altiplano.

The two chains converge again north of Lake Titicaca and by the North Peruvian Gap on the 5th parallel south the peaks are beginning to flatten and narrow. This marks the start of the Northern Andes, which divide into two chains in northern Ecuador and include the extinct volcano of Chimborazo, at 6,310 m (20,702 feet) the country's highest point. The Cordillera de Mérida, foothills of the Cordillera Oriental,

reach as far north as Venezuela. The mighty peaks of the Cordillera de los Andes and their great length from north to south down the continent of South America make the mountain chain the world's largest climatic divide. The prevailing *passat* winds bring the eastern foothills of the Andes plenty of precipitation, although large portions of the western slopes of the chain are characterized by aridity.

The collision of the Afro-Arabian and Eurasian Plates 35 million years ago has given rise to a whole series of mountains.

CAUCASUS MOUNTAINS
Mount Elbrus (western peak)
5,642 m (18,510 feet)

The Caucasus Mountains are a 1,100-km (680-mile) Eurasian mountain range located between the Black and Caspian Seas on territory belonging to Russia, Georgia, Armenia, Azerbaijan, and Turkey. The chain includes the Greater and Lesser Caucasus Mountains. The highest point – and Russia's highest mountain – is the summit of Mount Elbrus in the Greater Caucasus Mountains. Whether this mountain or Mont Blanc is the highest in Europe depends on the location of the border between Asia and Europe: some consider the Caucasus to mark the border, others place it at the Kuma-Manych Depression to the north. More and more climbers regard Mount Elbrus as Europe's highest mountain and thus one of the Seven Summits (the highest on all seven continents). The twin summits of Mount Elbrus, an inactive volcano, lie 1,500 m (4,900 feet) apart. More than 70 glaciers flow from Mount Elbrus into the valley, forming a sheet of ice with an area of 145 sq. km (56 sq. miles).

Mont Blanc and its eponymous massif, reflected in the waters of Lac des Chéserys at dawn.

ALPS
Mont Blanc   4,807 m (15,771 ft)

The slopes of Mont Blanc (Monte Bianco in Italian), the highest mountain in the Alps, are divided between France and Italy, and this granite monolith has two distinct sides: to the north it is rounded and almost entirely glaciated, to the south it presents a massive expanse of rock with vertiginously steep walls. The first ascent of Mont Blanc, completed in 1786 by two Frenchmen named Jacques Balmat and Michel-Gabriel Paccard, marked the beginning of Alpine mountain climbing.

SIERRA NEVADA
Mulhacén   3,482 m (11,424 feet)

Mulhacén is the highest point of the Sierra Nevada ("Snow-capped Mountains") in the provinces of Granada and Almería in the Spanish region of Andalusia. It is the highest peak in Europe beyond the Alps and the Caucasus, and the entire chain is usually capped with snow from November to May and skiing is available at several high-level resorts. The mountains were created as the African continental plate slipped beneath the Eurasian Plate. Proximity to the Mediterranean provides a mild climate in spring and summer, with long days of abundant sunshine.

PYRENEES
Pico de Aneto 3,404 m (11,168 feet)

The Pyrenees mountain range runs between the Atlantic and the Mediterranean, separating the Iberian Peninsula from the rest of Europe. The Franco-Spanish border follows the course of the mountains. The tiny state of Andorra lies in the eastern Pyrenees. Created during the Tertiary, the chain has some 200 peaks more than 3,000 m (9,800 feet), and its highest point is marked by the Pico de Aneto, Spain's third highest mountain, which forms the southern section of the Maladeta Massif ("damned mountains" in Spanish).

MOUNT ETNA
Summit   3,323 m (10,902 feet)

Sicily's Mount Etna is around 600,000 years old and both the highest and the most active volcano in Europe. It has four summit craters – one main crater and three others, created in 1911, 1968, and 1979 respectively – and approximately 400 vents on the slopes of its conical peak. The sheer number of eruptions places Etna at the top of the list of the world's most active volcanoes. It lies on the Messina Fault, a large region of significant tectonic movement, the cause of both Etna's volcanism and local earthquake activity.

A majestic panorama: the view from the 5,642-m (18,510-foot) summit of Mount Elbrus in the Caucasus Mountains (left).

RILA
Musala **2,925 m (9,596 feet)**

Musala is Bulgaria's highest peak and the highest point on the entire Balkan Peninsula. The Bulgarians named the mountain after their divinity Tangra, but the Ottoman Turks changed this to Musala ("praise of god") in the 15th century; between 1949 and 1962 it was known as "Stalin". The first recorded ascent of the mountain was achieved by King Philip II of Macedonia (382–336 BC), the father of Alexander the Great. The summit now boasts a weather station and a laboratory conducting cosmic ray research.

MOUNT OLYMPUS
Mytikas **2,917 m (9,570 feet)**

Mount Olympus in Macedonia is part of Greece's highest mountain chain, of which Mytikas is the tallest peak. The highest chapel in the Balkans is located on Profitis Ilias, a nearby summit. Its particular geological formations and unique flora and fauna (including a number of endangered species) caused UNESCO to inscribe the peaks as a biosphere reserve in 1981. Mount Olympus plays a major role in Greek mythology as the seat and assembly of Zeus, Poseidon, Hades, and the other gods known as the Twelve Olympians.

PIRIN MOUNTAINS
Vihren **2,914 m (9,560 feet)**

The Pirin Mountains run for 40 km (25 miles) on a north-west/south-east axis through south-western Bulgaria, with Vihren as their highest point. The range is also the country's largest national park, with an area of 265 sq. km (102 sq. miles), and has been inscribed as a UNESCO World Natural Heritage Site. The mountains are named after Perun, the supreme god in Slavic mythology. Vihren is noted for the whiteness of its rocks and the steepness of its slopes. The 400-m (1,300-foot) north face of the summit was first climbed by a German team in 1934.

APENNINES
Corno Grande **2,912 m (9,554 feet)**

The much-climbed Corno Grande ("great horn"), an impressive peak in the heart of the Gran Sasso d'Italia in the Abruzzo Mountains, is the highest point of the 1,500-km (930-mile) Apennines range, which crosses Italy from the north-west to the south-east. The three highest points of its extended summit – known as the Occidentale, Centrale, and Orientale respectively – together form a corrie containing the Calderone, Europe's southernmost glacier and the only ice field in the Apennines, though it is expected to disappear within a few decades.

ALPS

Europe's central mountain range, the Alps, cover an area of some 220,000 sq. km (84,900 sq. miles). The chain of fold mountains stretches for some 1,200 km (750 miles) and varies in width between 150 and 250 km (90 and 150 miles).

The range is divided into the Eastern Alps and the higher Western Alps by two transverse valleys originating in Lake

Mount Blanc, the highest mountain in the Alps

Constance to the north and Lake Como to the south. The Passo dei Giovi near Genoa is considered the starting point of the Apennines, and the Alps reach as far as Lake Geneva to the north before descending to the Rhône valley in the west. They extend as far as the Danube near Vienna to the north-east and as far as the Po valley to the south. Germany, Monaco, France, Italy, Liechtenstein, Austria, and Slovenia all have territory in the Alps, but most of the nearly 100 peaks above 4,000 m (13,100 feet) are to be found in Switzerland. Mont Blanc, the highest peak, is divided between Italy and France. The range forms the principal watershed between the North Sea, the Mediterranean, and the Black Sea, and the climatic divide between both western and south-eastern Europe and central and southern Europe.

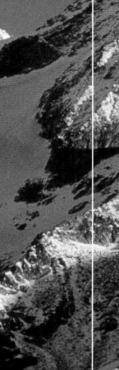

THE HIGHEST PEAKS IN THE ALPS

❶ **Mont Blanc**, France/Italy
4,807 m (15,771 feet)

❷ **Dufourspitze (Monte Rosa)**
Switzerland/Italy
4,637 m (15,213 feet)

❸ **Nordend**, Switzerland/Italy
4,609 m 4,609 m (15,122 feet)

❹ **Zumsteinspitze**,
Switzerland/Italy
4,563 m (14,970 feet)

❺ **Signalkuppe (Punta Gnifetti)**
Switzerland/Italy
4,556 m (14,948 feet)

❻ **Dom**, Switzerland
4,545 m (14,911 feet)

❼ **Lyskamm**, Switzerland/Italy
4,527 m (14,852 feet)

❽ **Weisshorn**, Switzerland
4,505 m (14,780 feet)

❾ **Täschhorn**, Switzerland
4,490 m (14,731 feet)

❿ **Matterhorn**, Switzerland/Italy
4,478 m (14,692 feet)

⓫ **Mont Maudit**, France/Italy
4,465 m (14,649 feet)

⓬ **Parrotspitze**, Switzerland/Italy
4,436 m (14,554 feet)

MONTE ROSA – THE MIGHTIEST MOUNTAIN MASSIF IN THE ALPS

Monte Rosa is an extended, highly glaciated massif in the Pennine Alps on the Italian-Swiss border. Named after the Swiss general Guillaume-Henri Dufour, the Dufourspitze, the highest peak at 4,637 m (15,213 feet), is also the highest peak in Switzerland and the second highest in the Alps. The loftiest nearby peaks are the Nordend (4,609 m/15,122 feet), the Zumsteinspitze (4,563m/ 14,970 feet), the Signalkuppe (4,556 m/14,948 feet), and the Parrotspitze (4,436 m/14,554 feet). The chain has more peaks above 4,500 m (14,750 feet) than the Mont Blanc Massif. The northern slopes are covered with several glaciers that eventually combine to form the Gorner Glacier, the second largest contiguous glacier in the Alps after the Aletsch Glacier.

The majestic Dufourspitze.

The Monte Rosa Massif and Gorner Glacier.

The Täschhorn (4,490 m/14,731 feet).

The Matterhorn (4,478 m/14,692 feet).

The Weisshorn (4,505 m/14,780 feet) in the Pennine Alps has a strikingly regular pyramidal shape. John Tyndall, Johann Joseph Brennen, and Ulrich Wenger were the first to climb the mountain in 1861.

At 8,850 m (29,035 feet), Mount Everest reigns supreme over the Himalayas in Asia, but the continent has plenty of other mighty mountain chains and summits to offer.

KARAKORAM

K2   **8,611 m (28,251 feet)**

The mountains of Karakoram in Central Asia can boast not only the world's second highest peak, but also a further three summits more than 8,000 m (26,000 feet): Gasherbrum I (8,068 m/26,470 feet), Broad Peak (8,047 m/26,401 feet), and Gasherbrum II (8,035 m/26,362 feet). Nowhere else on Earth is there such a concentration of eight-thousanders in such a small area as at Karakoram, and some of the largest glaciers outside the polar regions (including Alaska and Patagonia) are to be found here too, including the Biafo and Hispar Glaciers. K2, otherwise known as Lamba Pahar, on the Sino-Pakistani border is part of the Baltoro Muztagh subrange and is considered a far more challenging climb than Mount Everest. K2 was assigned its name by Thomas George Montgomerie of the Royal Engineers, who surveyed the Karakoram summits, assigning each a number. Seen from the west, Masherbrum (K1) was the first discernible peak, K2 the next, and so on – the numbers are unrelated to the heights of the mountains.

PAMIR MOUNTAINS

Kongur Tagh   7,719 m (25,325 feet)

Lying within Kyrgyzstan, China, Afghanistan, and Tajikistan, the Pamir fold mountain range links several of the major Asiatic chains: Tian Shan, Karakoram, Kunlun Mountains, and the Hindu Kush. The highlands of Tibet lie to the east. The Pamir's highest peak is Kongur Tagh

The eternal ice of the Pamir Mountains.

in China; due to its remote location, it was discovered only in 1900. The ascent is considered particularly challenging, not least because of the inhospitable weather conditions, and the summit was not reached until a British expedition's ascent in 1981.

HINDU KUSH

Tirich Mir   7,707 m (25,285 feet)

The geology of the Hindu Kush range is of relatively recent origin, arising as the Indian Plate pushed against the Central Asian mainland. The range is still growing. Its largest portion lies in Afghanistan, but the eastern section with the highest peaks lies in Pakistan. The main range, on the

The glaciers of Tirich Mir.

Afghan-Pakistani border, is a chain similar to the Himalayas, with several peaks above 7,000 m (23,000 feet). The ridges of Tirich Mir, the highest peak, extend in all directions.

K2 (left) – the world's second highest mountain – and Broad Peak (right) are just two of Karakoram's peaks higher than 8,000 m (26,000 feet).

KUNLUN MOUNTAINS
Ulugh Muztagh   7,724 m (25,341 feet)

The Kunlun Mountains in China run east from Karakoram, forming the

The awe-inspiring Kunlun Mountains.

border with the Tibetan Highlands for 2,500 km (1,550 miles), and boast more than 200 peaks above 6,000 m (20,000 ft); the highest point is the summit of Ulugh Muztagh. In 2001, an earthquake in the southern Kunlun Mountains tore a 400-km (250-mile) gash in the Earth's surface, the longest rift ever to appear through tectonic activity. Featuring in Taoist mythology, the Kunlun are associated with the martial arts.

TIAN SHAN
Jengish Chokusu   7,439 m (24,406 feet)

The Tian Shan ("heavenly mountains") range lies within the sovereign territory of China, Kazakhstan, Kyrgyzstan, and Tajikistan, and divides the Central Asian plains of Turkestan into a northern and a southern section. The heavily glaciated Jengish Chokusu, the highest peak in the range and indeed in all

The Tian Shan Massif in Turkestan.

Kyrgyzstan, is usually referred to as the world's northernmost seven-thousander, although it is geographically more exact for this title to fall to the 7,010-m (22,999-foot) Khan Tengri, which is also part of the Tian Shan range.

The summits of the Tian Shan range in the Central Asian highlands of Turkestan lie shrouded in clouds and fog.

Besides the world's highest mountains (those with summits higher than 8,000 m/26,000 feet), continental Asia boasts a whole series of other impressive high mountains.

TRANS-HIMALAYAS
Norin Kang   7,206 m (23,642 feet)

The Trans-Himalayas, a mountain system consisting of several ranges in southern Tibet, run on an east–west axis more or less parallel to the Himalayas for a distance of 1,600 km (1,000 miles). The range's name comes from its location: viewed from India, it is beyond (*trans*) the Himalayas. The chain was once also known as the Hedin Range, commemorating Sven Hedin, who discovered it. The highest point of the western section of the range (Gangdisê Shan) is to be found at the summit of Loinbo Kangri (7,095 m/23,278 feet) and the eastern section (called the Nyainqêntanglha Mountains) culminates in Norin Kang (7,206 m/23,642 feet). While the northern slopes of the Trans-Himalayas are particularly arid, with many desert and semi-desert features, the southern slopes are heavily glaciated. The Indus and its greatest tributary, the Sutlej, both rise in the Trans-Himalayas, fed by glacial streams.

ASSAM-BURMA RANGE
Hkakabo Razi   5,881 m (19,295 feet)

Hkakabo Razi is the tallest peak in Burma (Myanmar) and all Southeast Asia. It is located on the Chinese border with Kachin state, part of Burma. The territory is renowned for the extraordinary diversity of its plant and animal life and was protected as the Hkakabo Razi National Park in 1998. The mountain itself is covered in rainforest to an elevation of 2,700 m (8,860 feet), and above this there is a band of deciduous forest. Coniferous forest predominates above 3,400 m (11,150 feet), but beyond 4,500 m (14,750 feet) Hkakakbo Razi is covered in snow and ice all year round. Takashi Ozaki from Japan and Nyama Gyaltsen from Burma completed the first successful ascent on 15 September 1996. The late date of the conquest of Hkakabo Razi is a result of foreigners being banned from entering the area until 1993.

ANATOLIAN HIGHLANDS
Mount Ararat   5,165 m (16,946 feet)

The Armenian or Anatolian Highlands are located at the eastern end of the Caucasus on Turkish, Georgian, and Armenian territory, and the range's highest peak is also the highest point

Mount Ararat is Turkey's highest mountain.

in Turkey: last erupting in 1840, Mount Ararat is an extinct volcano with heavily glaciated upper reaches. The Turkish authorities have allowed foreigners to attempt the climb to the summit only since 2001, on payment of a fee.

ALBORZ
Mount Damavand   5,670 m (18,602 feet)

Lying in northern Iran between the Caspian Sea and the Persian highlands, the Alborz Mountains have an average height of some 2,000 m (6,600 feet). The range represents the vegetation and climatic divide between the wetter coastal landscape of the north and the land-locked and desert-like arid highlands of the south. Mount Damavand ("frosty mountain") is Iran's tallest peak and the highest point in the entire Near East; besides Kilimanjaro, it is one of the world's tallest free-standing mountains, and its 5,670-m (18,602-foot) glaciated volcanic cone towers over all the surrounding peaks. It very occasionally emits a puff of smoke. Although the volcano is officially extinct, the hot springs on its slopes suggest activity within the mountain's interior. The summit was first reached by W. Taylor Thomson of Great Britain.

KAMCHATKA
Klyuchevskaya Sopka   4,750 m (15,584 feet)

The Kamchatka Peninsula, lying on Russia's East Asian extreme, contains a volcanic region that was declared a UNESCO World Heritage Site in 1996. Klyuchevskaya Sopka is a heavily glaciated peak about 8,000 years old, lying on the Pacific Ocean Ring of Fire. It is the largest active stratovolcano (composite or conical volcano) and the highest active volcano in Asia. This

Klyuchevskaya Sopka, Kamchatka.

steep mountain arose on the slopes of a previous volcano, hence its great height, and has 27 subcraters.

Aerial view of the heavily glaciated and snow-capped Nyainqêntanglha Mountains in the Tibetan Trans-Himalayas.

ZAGROS MOUNTAINS
Zard-Kuh   4,548 m (14,921 feet)

The Zagros Mountains are the highest in Iran, although smaller sections of the range also lie within Iraqi territory. The chain runs for about 1,500 km (900 miles) from Kurdistan province to the Strait of Hormuz, where western Asia and the Arabian Peninsula lie just 50 km (31 miles) apart. The mountain's geology is of relatively recent origin and the chain represents a continuation of a line running through the Pyrenees, the Alps, the Balkans, and the Alborz Mountains in Turkey. The Hindu Kush, Karakoram, and the Himalayas continue this line into East Asia. Exceeding 3,000 m (9,800 feet) and always covered in snow, a great proportion of the highest peaks in the Zagros Mountains are to be found near the city of Isfahan, and Zard-Kuh (Yellow Mountain), the highest of all, is no exception. Many of Iran's great rivers rise on this mountain near the city of Kuhrang.

CROCKER RANGE
Mount Kinabalu   4,095 m (13,435 feet)

Mount Kinabalu is Malaysia's highest mountain. A relatively recent geological arrival, this largely granite peak

Mount Kinabalu, Malaysia's highest mountain.

towers over the other mountains on the island of Borneo and dominates the Malaysian state of Sabah. The summit is located about 90 km (56 miles) from Kota Kinabalu, the state capital. Mount Kinabalu is still growing by 5 mm (¼ inch) every year and its flora is so diverse that there are nearly as many plant species growing on its slopes as in all Europe.

Towering above the eponymous national park, the steep slopes of Mount Kinabalu afford a fascinating panorama of the diverse natural habitats in the surrounding hills and valleys.

DHAULAGIRI
South face
4,000 m (13,123 feet)

Dhaulagiri ("white mountain") is part of the eastern section of the Dhaulagiri Himal Massif in north-western Nepal. At 8,167 m (26,795 feet), it is the world's seventh highest mountain and lies separated from another giant peak, Annapurna I (8,091 m/26,545 feet), by the Kali Gandaki river valley, whose walls can reach as much as 5,600 m (18,370 feet), making it the world's deepest valley. The mighty south face of Dhaulagiri rises to a sheer

The south face of Dhaulagiri.

height of 4,000 m (13,123 feet), and the west face is not much below this.

Dhaulagiri was first surveyed in 1809 and the resulting figure of 8,190 m (26,870 feet – it is now known to be 8,167 m/26,795 feet) made it briefly the world's highest mountain, although still higher peaks were soon discovered. The image shows the view of Dhaulagiri from Poon Hill.

NANGA PARBAT
Rupal Slope   4,600 m (15,090 feet)

At 8,126 m (26,660 feet), Nanga Parbat is the world's ninth highest mountain and the loftiest peak in the Western Himalayas. It is located in the area of Kashmir controlled by Pakistan. Its southern face, the 4,600-m (15,090-foot) Rupal Slope, is the highest cliff in the world. Composed of granite and gneiss, the mountain towers some 7,000 m (23,000 feet) above the Indus valley, 25 km (16 miles) away. Nanga Parbat has been called the "Killer Mountain" – more than 30 German climbers died during the first attempts on the summit. An Austro-German expedition finally made it to the top in 1953.

Dawn over Diamir ("King of the Mountains"), the Rupal Slope of Nanga Parbat.

The Trango Towers are part of the Baltoro Muztagh in the middle of northern Pakistan's Karakoram Range. Lying to the north of the Baltoro Glacier (754 sq. km/291 sq. miles), one of the largest glaciers in the world outside the polar regions, these sheer, almost vertical granite spires are more than 6,000 m (19,700 ft) high. The absolute height of the spires, however, is dwarfed by the surrounding four peaks above 8,000 m (26,000 feet). These are K2 (8,611 m/28,251 feet), Gasherbrum I/Hidden Peak (8,068 m/26,470 feet), Broad Peak (8,047 m/26,401 feet), and Gasherbrum II (8,035 m/26,362 feet). Great Trango Tower is the highest peak of the group at 6,287 m (20,627 feet), although this majestic massif has a total of four summits: the main peak, plus the south (6,250 m/20,505 feet), east (6,231 m/20,443 feet), and west (6,223 m/20,417 feet) summits. The east face, one of the world's greatest vertical drops is more or less sheer and 1,600 m (5,250 feet) high.

The Trango Towers seen from Baltoro.

Great Trango Tower.

The east face of Great Trango Towers: vertical granite, 1,600 m (5,250 feet) high.

Clouds cling to the summits of the
Trango Towers. Great Trango Tower can
be seen in the left foreground. Partially
lit by sunlight here, the summit of Trango
(or the Nameless) Tower, rises to a height
of 6,251 m (20,509 feet). Trango Monk
can be made out in shadow to the far
right. These extreme granite cliffs are
among the most difficult climbs above
5,000 m (16,400 feet).

Lying at an average of 4,000 m (13,100 ft) above sea level, the Tibetan Highlands are the world's highest plateau. They were created about 50 million years ago when the Indian Plate encountered continental Asia, lifting the Tibetan Highlands and folding up the

Himalayan peaks.

mountains of the Himalayas. Officially known as the Qinghai-Tibetan Plateau, it includes the entire Tibet Autonomous Region of the People's Republic of China, as well as the Himalayas and Karakoram among others. The highlands are bounded by the deserts of the Qaidam and Tarim Basins to the north and the mountains of the Pamir, Karakoram, and Himalayas ranges to the south and west. The plateau is composed of peaks in the order of 6,000–8,000 m (19,700–26,000 ft), as well as salt lakes, broad steppes, deserts, and thick forest. These have become the natural habitats of numerous animal species, including the Saiga antelope, the Asiatic black bear, and the yak, as well as such rarities as the kiang (Tibetan wild ass).

Many Tibetans and Mongolians continue to pursue a life of nomadic pastoralism in the Tibetan Highlands. During the summer months they make extensive use of the wide, rugged upland valleys as pasture for their sheep, goats, and yaks. The cool highland climate's considerable temperature variations – with an average of 8°C (46.4°F) in the south and south-east, 0°C (32°F) or less in the north – have not prevented the cultivation of some types of cereals, but only in limited areas. The north and west are largely uninhabitable.

Lake Pekhu-Tso in the Tibetan Highlands. Shisha Pangma, the least of the summits above 8,000 m (26,000 feet), is not far away.

YAKS

Endangered wild yaks live on the slopes of Mount Everest in Nepal's Sagarmatha National Park.

Weighing up to 1,000 kg (2,200 lb), the wild yak (*Bos mutus*) can reach a length of 3.25 m (11 feet) and a height of 2 m (6½ feet) at the shoulder. This species of cattle is excellently suited to the extremely cold and barren upland plains of Central Asia. Wild yaks live at elevations between 4,000 and 6,000 m (13,100 and 19,700 feet). The species is endangered, with perhaps only 10,000 animals still living in China, India, Nepal, and Bhutan, and these are different from the smaller domestic yak (*Bos grunniens*), which is far more widespread. Domesticated yaks provide milk and can be used as mounts or draft animals. Their pelts are used to make clothes and their dung can be burned as fuel for cooking and warmth.

Yaks eat grasses, herbs, and lichens.

Thanks to their long, matted coats, yaks can endure extreme cold approaching -40°C (-40°F). This hardy and undemanding species has been domesticated since the Neolithic period, and it is estimated there are now some 12 million tame yaks.

Australia boasts many smaller mountain ranges and inselbergs such as Uluru. The east is dominated by the Great Dividing Range.

SUDIRMAN RANGE
Puncak Jaya   4,884 m (16,024 ft)

The Sudirman Range, a subrange of the Maoke Mountains, lies in West Papua, the western part of the island of New Guinea that belongs to Indonesia. The range includes Puncak Jaya ("Victory Peak"), sometimes known as Carstensz Pyramid, the highest peak in Oceania and thus the highest point between the Himalayas and the Andes. It was first named after the Dutch sailor and explorer Jan Carstensz, who was the first to record the mountain in 1623. Grasberg Mine, the world's largest gold mine, has grown up in the shadow of Puncak Jaya. Whether the mountain should be Australia and Oceania's representative for the Seven Summits (the highest mountains on the respective continents) is still disputed – politically, it is part of Indonesia, and thus Asia, but it is also part of the Australian continental landmass and thus separate from Eurasia. Most experts agree that Puncak Jaya is Oceania's highest peak and thus one of the Seven

NEW ZEALAND ALPS
**Mount Cook (Aoraki)
3,764 m (12,316 feet)**

Mount Cook (Aoraki, in Maori), New Zealand's highest peak, lies in the New Zealand Alps on South Island and forms the focal point of Mount Cook National Park, which can boast two superlatives – it has the country's tallest mountain and also the largest glacier. The Tasman Glacier is 27 km (16½ miles) long, 4 km (2½ miles) wide, and 600 m (1,970 feet) thick. Aoraki lost 10 m (33 feet) of its height in 1991, when a mass of ice and moraine fell from the summit into the valley below.

MOUNT RUAPEHU
2,797 m (9,177 ft)

Mount Ruapehu in Tongariro National Park is New Zealand's highest volcano and the highest point on North Island. Its summit conceals a crater lake warmed by volcanic gases. The crater is nonetheless glaciated, and the slopes of Ruapehu are covered with seven smaller glaciers. The most recent flare-up of this still-active volcano took place without any warning in September 2007. The eruption severely injured one hiker and the ensuing smoke cloud reached a height of 5,000 m (16,400 feet).

EMPEROR RANGE
Mount Balbi   2,715 m (8,907 feet)

The various volcanoes of the Emperor Range on Bougainville, one of Papua New Guinea's Solomon Islands, include Mount Balbi, the island's highest peak. Mount Balbi is a Holocene stratovolcano with five craters that run along a ridge to the north of the summit, one of which contains a crater lake. Despite the numerous fumaroles near the craters, Mount Balbi has not erupted in recorded history and is considered extinct. Of Bouganville's two other large volcanoes – Mount Takuan and Mount Bagana – only the latter is historically active.

MOUNT TARANAKI
2, 518 m (8,261 feet)

Mount Taranaki – "bald mountain" in the Maori language – is a lone volcano with a symmetrical cone in the west of New Zealand's North Island. It is a relatively recent geological arrival and is thought to have become active only 135,000 years ago. The last major eruption took place in the 16th century and the mountain is regarded as extinct. Below the snow and ice of the summit, the cone of the mountain is covered with dense rainforest. A German geologist named Ernst Dieffenbach was the first to reach the summit in 1839.

Summits – the highest mountains on each of the world's seven continents. It is one of the most challenging climbs among them, although it is comparatively lowly, and technically far more demanding than Mount Everest or Mount McKinley, although the altitudes and temperatures of the latter two make them a far more arduous ascent.

The jagged summit of Puncak Jaya in New Guinea is the highest peak in Oceania (left). Mount Cook (3,754 m/ 12,316 feet), New Zealand's highest peak, towers over dense forests on the shores of Lake Pukaki (below).

MEYER RANGE
Mount Taron 2,400 m (7,874 feet)

The Hans Meyer Range is located in the southern part of the island of New Ireland, which is part of the Bismarck Archipelago of Papua New Guinea. It is named after the German explorer and zoologist Hans Heinrich Josef Meyer (1858–1929), who was also the first to climb Kilimanjaro. At 2,400 m (7,874 feet), Mount Taron is the tallest peak in the range and the highest point on New Ireland. The island's last remaining rainforests are to be found in the valleys of the Hans Meyer Range.

MOUNT POPOMANASEU
2,335 m (7,661 feet)

Majestic Mount Popomanaseu is the highest peak of the volcanic Kavo Range, which runs across the main island of Guadalcanal in the Pacific Republic of the Solomon Islands. The island is mountainous and forested but has an extensive coastal plain. Mount Makarakomburu, initially measured at 2,447 m (8,028 ft), was long thought to be the highest mountain in the Solomon Islands, but the survey proved inaccurate (it is in fact 2,310 m/7,579 feet), making Mount Popomanaseu, further to the east, more than 20 m (66 feet) taller.

MOUNT OROHENA
2,241 m (7,352 feet)

Mount Orohena, an extinct volcano which is the highest mountain in French Polynesia, is to be found on the South Pacific island of Tahiti. Geographically part of the Society Islands, the landscape of Tahiti's twin islands is dominated by several steep peaks. Mount Orohena lies on Tahiti Nui (Great Tahiti), whilst the highest point on Tahiti Iti (Little Tahiti) is Mount Ronui (1,322 m/4,337 feet). Running water has carved out deep valleys at several locations as it cascades down the mountain sides, and these are flanked by steep ridges.

GREAT DIVIDING RANGE
Mount Kosciuszko
2,228 m (7,310 feet)

The Great Dividing Range, Australia's largest mountain chain, culminates in Mount Kosciuszko, the highest point of continental Australia. The range runs the length of the east coast from the northern tip of Queensland through New South Wales to Victoria. Mount Kosciuszko and the surrounding Snowy Mountains lie in New South Wales' largest national park, the Kosciuszko National Park (6,900 sq. km/2,664 sq. miles). The Alpine climate resulting from the extreme altitude here is unusual for Australia.

EL CAPITAN

El Capitan is a 914-m (2,998-foot) monolith in Yosemite National Park in the US state of California. Its summit lies 2,307 m (7,569 feet) above sea level. With an area of some 1,300 ha (5 sq. miles), it is one

El Capitan, shaped by glaciers.

of the world's largest free-standing granite monoliths and almost twice as high as the Rock of Gibraltar. Its steep walls with few rills make El Capitan a paradise for free climbers – its "Nose", which sticks out over the valley floor, is a particularly popular sporting challenge.

The Mercedes River and El Capitan in the evening sun.

MOUNT AUGUSTUS
THE WORLD'S LARGEST MONOLITH

Mount Augustus in Western Australia is the world's largest monolith. It is 7 km (4½ miles) long and 3 km (2 miles) wide, and its summit rises to a height of 1,105 m (3,625 feet) above sea level and 600 m (1,969 feet) above the surrounding desert. Its volume is two and a half times that of Uluru (which in any case is not a true monolith as it is not formed from a single piece of rock). Now lying at the heart of the eponymous national park, Mount Augustus was named after Sir Augustus Charles Gregory, the brother of Francis Gregory, who first reached the summit on 3 June 1858.

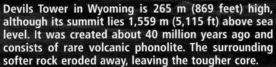

Mount Augustus in Australia is about 1,000 million years old.

DEVILS TOWER

Devils Tower in Wyoming is 265 m (869 feet) high, although its summit lies 1,559 m (5,115 ft) above sea level. It was created about 40 million years ago and consists of rare volcanic phonolite. The surrounding softer rock eroded away, leaving the tougher core.

STONE MOUNTAIN

Stone Mountain near Atlanta, Georgia, is the world's largest granite monadnock and the second largest monolith after Mount Augustus. It is famed for the carvings of three distinguished American citizens on the north face, forming the world's largest relief.

Devils Tower, the first National Monument in the United States.

Stone Mountain near Atlanta has a park named after it.

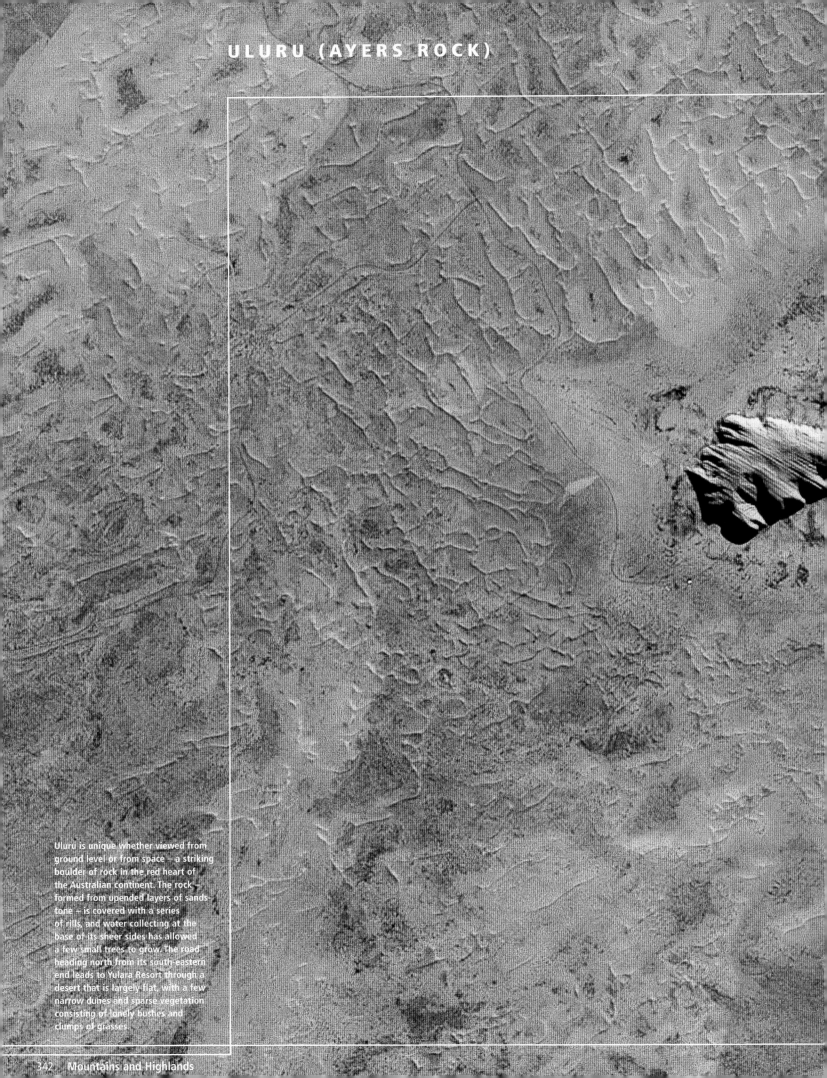

ULURU (AYERS ROCK)

Uluru is unique whether viewed from
ground level or from space – a striking
boulder of rock in the red heart of
the Australian continent. The rock –
formed from upended layers of sandstone – is covered with a series
of rills, and water collecting at the
base of its sheer sides has allowed
a few small trees to grow. The road
heading north from its south-eastern
end leads to Yulara Resort through a
desert that is largely flat, with a few
narrow dunes and sparse vegetation
consisting of lonely bushes and
clumps of grasses.

The "red heart of Australia" lies in the middle of an extensive dry savanna, the Uluru-Kata Tjuta National Park. As the name suggests, it contains one of Australia's emblems, Uluru ("seat of the ancestors"), one of the world's largest inselbergs. The Aborigines, Australia's original inhabitants, consider the mountain sacred, and so instead of climbing it, visitors undertake the 9.4-km (5¾-mile) "Base Walk" around it. Lying like a beached whale, the massif is 3.5 km (2¼ miles) long and 2.4 km (1½ miles) wide. It rises 348 m (1,142 feet) above the surrounding plains, but extends for

An aerial view of Uluru and its surroundings in the Uluru-Kata Tjuta National Park.

William Gosse, who "discovered" Uluru in 1873, named it Ayers Rock after the Australian prime minister.

nearly ten times that distance underneath the ground. When sunlight strikes it, its high iron content makes it take on a variety of shades: deep purple, rust, pink, brown, dark blue, even silvery after rainfall — an eternally fascinating spectacle. Its creation some 570 million years ago is closely connected with that of Kata Tjuta, a group of 36 inselbergs. The extremely resilient rocks of these formations weathered only slowly in comparison with the surrounding strata, leaving them sticking out of the ground as mighty, fossilized evidence of the great antiquity of the Earth.

AFRICA

The world's second largest continent lies on average 650 m (2,130 feet) above sea level, but there are numerous high mountain chains, including Kibo, the highest summit, and Mount Cameroon, the highest active volcano.

KILIMANJARO
Kibo   5,895 m (19,340 feet)

Kilimanjaro in north-eastern Tanzania is the highest massif in Africa, and Kibo, one of its volcanic cones, is the continent's highest peak, and thus one of the Seven Summits. Kilimanjaro is often called the highest mountain in Africa, but this is topo-graphically incorrect, as the name refers to the entire massif. Kilimanjaro was created volcanically: the African and East African Plates have been drifting apart here for millions of years, forming the East African Rift. The mountain is located about 340 km (210 miles) south of the equator near the Tanzanian border with Kenya. Although this is a hot, tropical region, the mountain is Africa's third most glaciated peak after the Rwenzori Mountains and Mount Kenya. Kibo's ice cap lost 75% of its original surface area between 1912 and 1989, and had reduced further to around 2.5 sq. km (1 sq. mile) by 2003. Kilimanjaro's two other volcanic peaks are Mawenzi and Shira, which are extinct.

MOUNT KENYA
Batian   5,199 m (17,057 feet)

Batian, the continent's second highest mountain, is one of the summits of Mount Kenya which lies in the heart of Mount Kenya National Park to the north-east of Nairobi, the Kenyan capital. As with many of the Seven Second Summits, the second highest peaks of each continent, the climb is more difficult than the ascent of the Kibo, which is highest mouniutain in Africa.

Above 4,300 m (14,100 feet) there are only glaciers, lakes, and snowfields.

ATLAS MOUNTAINS
Toubkal   4,167 m (13,671 feet)

The Atlas Mountains in north-west Africa represent a striking dividing line between the moist climate of the furthest reaches of northern West Africa and the extreme aridity of the Sahara. Located in the south of Morocco, Toubkal, the highest peak in the "High Atlas" section of the range is also the highest in the country. The steep sides of the mountain dominate the similar peaks clustered around it and the surrounding countryside. Extensive snowfields are still to be found on the upper slopes, even late in summer.

RWENZORI RANGE
Margherita Peak
**   5,109 m (16,762 feet)**

The mountains of the Rwenzori Range in East Africa are often referred to as the "Mountains of the Moon". The border between the Democratic Republic of the Congo and Uganda runs across the highest peak in the massif: Mount Stanley's Margherita Peak. Despite its location in a hot tropical region, it is glaciated above 4,500 m (14,750 feet).

Wind lifts the banks of clouds shrouding the Rwenzori ("rainmaker") Range.

MOUNT CAMEROON
**   4,095 m (13,435 feet)**

Mount Cameroon (also known as Fako), West Africa's highest peak, is located in the south-western province of Cameroon on the Gulf of Guinea. The flanks of this active volcano are covered in dense unspoilt forest, although savanna and alpine meadows predominate on the upper slopes. Only lichen can grow at the summit, which is occasionally dusted with snow. The mountain's south-western slopes receive 11,000 mm (433 inches) of precipitation a year, making it one of the world's rainiest places.

ETHIOPIAN HIGHLANDS
Ras Dashen   4,620 m (15,157 ft)

Ras Dashen, a group of nine rocky peaks, is the highest mountain in the Ethiopian Highlands and the highest point of Ethiopia. Located right in the heart of the Simien Mountains, Ras Dashen is largely composed of volcanic basalt and is the only mountain in Ethiopia to be covered in snow during the winter months. The conditions at the summit are quite hospitable, and there are high altitude pastures.

Ras Dashen was first climbed by Europeans in 1841.

PICO DEL TEIDE
**   3,718 m (12,198 feet)**

Despite its location off the coast of Morocco, the volcanic island of Tenerife is politically part of Spain. Pico del Teide, the highest peak of the Canary Islands, is also the highest point on Spanish soil; as the world's third highest island volcano, it has become synonymous with Tenerife. Rising from the gigantic Las Cañadas caldera (a volcanic crater basin), its slopes are sparsely vegetated and in winter covered with snow. Some 20,000 ha (77 sq. miles) of the area around the base of the mountain were declared a national park in 1954.

Kilimanjaro, Africa's highest mountain, is surrounded by its eponymous national park in north-eastern Tanzania (left).

DRAKENSBERG
Thabana Ntlenyana
3,482 m (11,424 feet)

The Drakensberg ("Dragon Mountains") is the highest mountain range in southern Africa. Thabana Ntlenyana ("beautiful little mountain") lies in the kingdom of Lesotho, where the chain is known as the Maloti Mountains. The range was created by volcanic activity about 180 million years ago during the Jurassic period. Sedimentary strata were flooded with layers of basalt, and these now remain as high mountains.

Clouds create stunning contrasts of light and shade on the Drakensberg.

TIBESTI MOUNTAINS
Emi Koussi   3,415 m (11,204 feet)

The volcanic Tibesti Mountains in Chad are the highest range in the Sahara. The mountains are riddled with steep cliffs in places and are among the most isolated regions on Earth. Emi Koussi, the highest peak, is also an active volcano. Its extremely remote location meant that no volcanic activity was recorded until the 1970s, when a satellite happened to take pictures of an eruption.

Trou au Natron, a giant caldera in the Tibesti Mountains.

AHAGGAR MOUNTAINS
Tahat   2,918 m (9,573 feet)

The Ahaggar (Hoggar) Mountains, a series of volcanic peaks in southern Algeria, are famed for their bizarre rock formations, with domes, spires, and features resembling fortifications. Mount Tahat, the highest point of the highest mountain range in the Sahara is also the highest peak in Algeria. The region is principally inhabited by Tuaregs, and the largest populated oasis in the Ahaggar region is to be found at Tamanrasset.

The Ahaggar Mountains look most mysterious at dusk.

The satellite image shows a section of the Ethiopian Highlands north of Addis Ababa. The 4,154-m (13,629-foot) peak of Choke Terara can be made out in the top left-hand corner of the image, surrounded by a star-shaped cluster of radiating valleys. The country's largest river, the Blue Nile, and its tributaries have carved their mark deeply into these bare highlands. Crossing a large drainage basin, the Nile's largest tributaries flow from the east and south. Descending from the north, the Blue Nile flows around Choke Terara before turning north-west at the bottom of the image. The slopes of the majestic mountain have been cultivated for agriculture.

The Ethiopian Highlands are a chain of peaks running across central and northern Ethiopia whose north-eastern extremities extend into northern Eritrea. The highlands merge into the Nubian Desert to the north-west and in the south-east they are bounded by the East African Rift Valley. To the south-west and west they join the many valleys of the Blue and White Niles. The highlands are divided into a series of smaller upland areas reaching heights of up to 3,000 m (9,800 feet), with several peaks above 4,000 m (13,100 feet), including Talo (4,413 m/14,478 feet), Guma Terara (4,231 m/13,881 feet), and Guge (4,203 m/13,789 feet). At 4,620 m (15,157 feet), Ras Dashen is the tallest peak of all. The highest-lying regions are blanketed in snow for several months a year, which often results in the Blue Nile, which rises to the west of the highlands at Lake Tana, being unable to take any more meltwater and bursting its banks.

The highlands are about 1,000 km (620 miles) long and some 500 km (300 miles) wide, a size roughly corresponding to that of the Alps. The Ethiopian Highlands feature dry, moist, and thorn savanna, especially in the north and east. The plateaus, grassland, and tropical rainforest found in the middle of the highlands gradually fall away as the terrain descends to the west.

Enigmatic and almost surreal: Ethiopia's rugged highlands.

The scenery of western North America is punctuated by a series of large, extended mountain chains such as the Pacific Mountain System – with its main range, the Rocky Mountains – and the Appalachians.

ALASKA RANGE
Mount McKinley
6,194 m (20,322 feet)

The Alaska Range, the southernmost chain of the Western Cordillera in Alaska, describes an arc from the Alaska Peninsula in the south-west, where it adjoins the Chigmit Mountains in the Aleutian Chain, to the area around the border with Yukon in Canada to the east. Here it merges with the Wrangell Mountains, part of the Saint Elias Range in the Coast Mountains. The mountain range forms the continental watershed between the Bering Sea to the north-west and the Gulf of Alaska to the south. Mount McKinley, named after William McKinley, the 25th president of the United States, is the highest peak of the Alaska Range and the highest point in North America. It is thus one of the Seven Summits. The official Alaskan name, Denali ("the High One"), is also widely used and the national park surrounding the mighty mountain was founded in 1917 with this name. It is home to a wide range of flora and fauna.

EASTERN SIERRA MADRE
Pico de Orizaba
5,636 m (18,491 feet)

Pico de Orizaba (or Citlaltépetl, meaning "star mountain"), a volcano and Mexico's highest mountain, is located in the Eastern Sierra Madre mountain range on the border between the states of Veracruz and Puebla in north-eastern Mexico. The most recent eruption was in 1687. After a long period of dormancy some fumaroles have recently appeared, which may presage a renewed period of activity.

SIERRA NEVADA
Mount Whitney
4,418 m (14,495 feet)

Much of the Sierra Nevada lies in California in the USA, with a smaller portion lying in Nevada. Mount Whitney, the highest mountain in the chain and in all of the USA beyond Alaska, was named after Josiah Whitney, a geologist. Three local fishermen completed the first ascent in 1873, and the ease of the climb has since made it very popular with mountaineers. Today it offers climbs and trails to suit most levels of technical ability.

ROCKY MOUNTAINS
Mount Elbert
4,399 m (14,432 feet)

The Rocky Mountains, an extensive range of fold mountains in the west of North America, form just one part of the American Cordillera, which run from Tierra del Fuego to Alaska. Running from Mexico through the continental United States to Canada and Alaska, the Rocky Mountains' highest peak is Colorado's easily climbed and thus very popular Mount Elbert, which is also the second highest point on the North American mainland.

CASCADE RANGE
Mount Rainier
4,395 m (14,419 feet)

The Cascade Range runs parallel to North America's west coast, from British Columbia to northern California. It is of volcanic origin and forms part of the Pacific Ring of Fire. The best-known and most active peak in the chain is Mount St. Helens, but the Cascade's highest peak is Mount Rainier, a stratovolcano near Seattle in Washington state, which is a good 2,500 m (8,200 feet) taller than its nearest competitors. It lies in Mount Rainier National Park.

Rising majestically over the other peaks in the Alaska Range, Mount McKinley – otherwise known as Denali – is North America's highest mountain (left). Below: Mount Rainier in the Cascade Range reflected in the waters of Tipsoo Lake by the light of a magnificent sunset.

SOUTHERN SIERRA MADRE
Teotepec   3.703 m (12,149 feet)

The mountains of the Southern Sierra Madre in the south of Mexico run for more than 1,000 km (620 miles) from south of Michoacán in a line heading east through Guerrero to the Tehuantepec Isthmus east of Oaxaca. This region of the Sierra Madre is known for the diversity of its flora and fauna and the unique number of endemic species. The highest peak in the range is Cerro Teotepec in the middle of the Mexican state of Guerrero.

WESTERN SIERRA MADRE
Nevado de Colima
4,330 m (14,206 feet)

Colima, Mexico's most active volcano, lies in the Western Sierra Madre, which straddles western Mexico and the south-western reaches of the United States. It has erupted more than 40 times since 1576, most recently in November 2000. Colima has two summits, the extinct Nevado de Colima and the decidedly active Volcán de Colima (3,860 m/12,664 feet), which the UN has listed as one of the world's 16 most dangerous volcanoes.

MOUNT SHISHALDIN
2,857 m (9,373 feet)

Mount Shishaldin on Unimak Island is one of the most active volcanoes in the Aleutian Arc, with at least 27 recorded eruptions since 1775, the last one being in 1999 since when it maintained seismic activity. A small crater at the summit of the symmetrical cone of this stratovolcano produces a constant plume of smoke and occasionally throws out some ash. Larger ash clouds sometimes limit visibility for pilots on this busy air route between Asia and America. The mountain is covered with snow and ice.

COLORADO PLATEAU, COLUMBIA PLATEAU, AND THE GREAT BASIN

The Western Cordillera in the USA enclose a complex system of basins divided into three main regions: the Colorado Plateau, the Columbia Plateau, and the Great Basin. The Colorado Plateau in the north is bounded by the Cascade Range to the west and the Rocky Mountains to the east. To the south it merges with the Great Basin, an arid, desert-like high plain about the size of Spain. The Great Basin extends from the Sierra Nevada and the Cascade Range in the west to the Wasatch Range in the east. To the south, the Basin merges with the Mojave Desert. As the Columbia Plateau and the Great Basin are contiguous, they are often regarded as a single region. The Colorado Plateau lies to the east of the Great Basin, bounded by the Wasatch Range and the Rocky Mountains.

The image shows three of the buttes (from left: West Mitten, East Mitten, and Merrick) in Monument Valley in the Colorado Plateau. The plain with its characteristic mesas and buttes, composed of various hard varieties of sandstone and limestone, lies between Arizona and Utah at an elevation of about 1,900 m (6,200 feet). The buttes can reach heights of up to 300 m (990 feet) and their reddish coloration is due to iron oxide in the stone.

COLORADO PLATEAU

Sparse desert vegetation with buttes on the horizon.

This high plain across Arizona, Utah, Colorado, and New Mexico rises from some 1,500 m (4,900 feet) to 3,300 m (10,800 feet) above sea level. The Colorado River cuts across the plateau, forming the 446-km (277-mile) Grand Canyon, reaching depths of up to 1,800 m (5,900 feet) and varying between 6 and 29 km (4 and 18 miles) wide.

COLUMBIA PLATEAU

The strata of the Columbia Plateau represent a cross-section of the Earth's history.

GREAT BASIN

The Great Salt Lake, which gave its name to Salt Lake City, is completely flat.

This plain is mainly confined to the states of Oregon and Idaho, although its foothills reach as far as Washington state. It was created from large amounts of low-density lava produced by volcanic activity during the late Miocene and early Pliocene periods. The plateau is crossed by the Columbia River.

This dry and desert-like basin lies mainly in the state of Nevada, although small sections reach as far as California, Oregon, Idaho, and Utah. The Great Basin can climb to elevations of up to 1,500 m (4,900 feet) to the north, but to the south it falls below sea level, reaching its deepest point at Badwater Basin in Death Valley (-86 m/-282 feet).

COUGARS

The cougar (*Puma concolor*) is a member of the Felinae, the small cat family, although it is still North America's largest cat. Weighing up to 50–60 kg (110–130 lb), it can grow to a length of 1.3 m (4¼ feet) and reach a height of 65 cm (26 inches) at the shoulder. Its

Pumas are good climbers.

black-tipped, 80-cm (31-inch) tail is particularly striking. Oddly, a cougar is unable to roar, and instead howls loudly. Cougars live as strict loners in a variety of habitats and can be found in semi-deserts, rainforest, lowlands, and mountains from Canada to southern Argentina. The cougar, which can reach an age of 20 in the wild, was once widespread across the USA but the population has now shrunk to an estimated 50,000, and is found in sparsely populated areas and national parks. Cougars were thought to be extinct on the East Coast, although recent evidence suggests they may be returning.

The cougar, which is also known as the puma, mountain lion, catamount, or panther, has a distinctive reddish-brown or silvery-gray coat. Its head looks disproportionately small for such a big cat and its muzzle has a characteristic white patch ringed with a black line that runs from the corners of its mouth to its pink nose.

ANDES
Aconcagua   6,963 m (22,845 feet)

At 6,963 m (22,845 feet), the "stone guardian" – for such is the literal meaning of Ackon Cauak, the Quechua name from which Aconcagua is derived – is not only Argentina's highest mountain, but also the highest peak in the Andes. Lying in the Parque Provincial Aconcagua, the mountain attracts thousands of climbers every year, as its north route is considered an easy climb. The first ascent in modern times

was achieved by Matthias Zurbriggen of Switzerland on 18 January 1897, but it must be assumed that the original Native American population climbed the mountain they considered holy at a much earlier date, because in 1982 the 550-year-old mummy of a seven-year-old Inca boy was discovered in a ritual grave at an elevation of 5,200 m (17,000 feet). The southerly routes are more difficult.

Dry steppes near the city of Mendoza, with Aconcagua in the background.

SOUTH AMERICA'S HIGHEST MOUNTAINS

GUIANA HIGHLANDS
Pico da Neblina
2,994 m (9,823 feet)

The Pico da Neblina ("foggy tip") is both the highest mountain in Brazil and the highest point in South America beyond the Andes. It is one of the tepuis of the Guiana Highlands, whose endemic plant and animal species and characteristic mighty plateaus are the backdrop for some of the world's highest waterfalls, such as the Salto Angel, which plummets thousands of feet down the rock into the rainforest below.

BRAZILIAN HIGHLANDS
Pico da Bandeira
2,892 m (9,488 feet)

The Brazilian Highlands on the eastern shores of continental South America run parallel to Brazil's Atlantic coast. Pico da Bandeira, Brazil's third-highest mountain, forms the highest point of the massif. As it is located in a densely populated area (in contrast to Pico da Neblina) and is easy to reach, the country's best-documented mountain has become extremely popular with mountaineers.

SIERRAS DE CÓRDOBA
Cerro Champaqui
2,880 m (9,449 feet)

The Sierras de Córdoba, a range of mountains in the west of the central Argentinian province of Córdoba, are one of Argentina's most popular tourist destinations, attracting three million visitors every year. The Sierras de Córdoba are essentially made up of three distinct mountain chains, all running north–south: the Sierra Chica, the Sierra Grande, and the Sierra de los Comechingones, which also boasts the highest peak, Cerro Champaqui.

Glaciers of lengths up to 10 km (6 miles) run down the slopes of Aconcagua, the highest mountain outside Asia.

The Altiplano is an arid upland plain of some 170,000 sq. km (65,600 sq. miles) in the Central Andes, formed where the East and West Cordilleras diverge. Lake Titicaca, at 893 cu. km (214 cu. miles) South America's largest lake by volume and the largest mountain lake in the world, lies to the north of the Altiplano. Several high peaks, such as the Parinacota volcano, break up the plateau's average elevation of 3,600 m (11,800 feet), and the Altiplano's climate is cold and semi-arid to arid; evaporation far exceeds precipitation, with the result that the region suffers low humidity. Large areas of the Altiplano exhibit all the characteristics of Puna grassland, a kind of mountain prairie with a changeable, moist climate. Sparse clumps of *ichu* grass are ubiquitous.

Parinacota, a 6,342-m (20,807-foot) volcano on the Chilean-Bolivian border, and Lake Chungará, one of the world's highest lakes.

Patches of snow in a valley in the Atacama Desert in Chile, south-west of the Altiplano.

A group of succulents on the Isla del Pescado in Bolivia's Salar de Uyuni, the world's largest salt lake.

The llama (*Lama glama*), the guanaco (*Lama guanicoe*), the alpaca (*Vicugna pacos*), and the vicuña (*Vicugna vicugna*) together form the South American camelid family and are easily identified by their lack of humps. Of these, the largest animals in the Andes, only the guanaco and the vicuña are still found in the wild; the llama and alpaca, domesticated descendants of the guanaco, are used as a pack animal or food (llama) or as a source of wool (alpaca). Weighing up to 100–120 kg (220–265 lb), the guanaco can reach a length of 120–220 cm (47–87 inches) and a height of 120 cm (47 inches) at the shoulder. The coat is light brown with a white belly and a black head. They are found at elevations up to 4,000 m (13,100 feet). The vicuña is smaller and slighter (length 160 cm/63 inches, shoulder height 95 cm/37 inches, weight up to 50 kg/110 lb), with a fine, very dense coat. Its coat is lighter, with a black face, and it lives at elevations of 3,700 to 5,500 m (12,100 to 18,000 feet). The llama is slightly larger than the guanaco (shoulder height up to 130 cm/51 inches, weight up to 150 kg/330 lb) with a variable coat (white, brown, black, or piebald). Weighing only up to 65 kg (140 lb), the alpaca is a little smaller than the llama but has a similarly variegated coat.

The alpaca is a good source of wool.

The llama is a reliable pack animal.

The vicuña, smallest New World camelid.

Living in family groups consisting of a male, a female, and a litter of young, the guanaco is found everywhere from dry mountains and plains to sea level. It is thus far more widespread than the vicuña, which prefers higher elevations. All of the South American camelids will resort to spitting if they feel threatened.

The Andean condor (*Vultur gryphus*), a member of the New World vulture family, is the world's largest vulture. With a body length of 110 cm (43 inches) and weighing 12–15 kg (26–33 lb), the bird's wingspan is often considerably in excess of 3 m (10 feet), making it one of the world's largest wingspans and enabling it to climb to altitudes of 7,000 m (23,000 feet). The Andean condor has the characteristic bald head and neck surrounded by a white collar found in the vulture family, and the male's head bears a fleshy comb. The female lacks this and is also smaller. The upper plumage of both sexes is predominantly black with a few white feathers. An endangered species, the Andean condor lives to an age of about 40 in the wild but can reach an astonishing 85 years in captivity. Its range stretches along the Andes from Venezuela to Patagonia. The bird prefers mountainous regions where it can exploit differences in rising thermals for gliding. Andean condors often cover short stretches on foot. They spend most of the day resting and grooming one another, which serves to strengthen pairs and group bonds. Once airborne, the condors soar and wheel, held aloft on the thermal currents.

The gigantic wingspan of the Andean condor enables it to reach altitudes in excess of 7,000 m (23,000 feet) and the highest peaks of the Andes. It uses rising thermal currents from the mountains.

TEPUIS:
THE WORLD'S HIGHEST PLATEAUS

Tepuis are mesas found in Venezuela, Guyana, and Brazil. Composed largely of sandstone, they can reach heights of up to 3,000 m (9,800 feet) and their summits are almost always only accessible by air, due to the cracks and rills in their almost vertical walls.

Mount Roraima, a tepui in Venezuela.

Tropical vegetation grows close to the rocky cliffs of the tepuis. Evolutionary exchange can only occur from the tepui down, not in the other direction, and this has allowed many of the isolated plateaus to evolve endemic flora and fauna.

Frequently situated in isolated and inaccessible locations, there are a number of tepuis that man has never set foot on. In the language of the indigenous people, tepui means "house of the gods". These mesas are remnants of a giant sandstone plateau that once spread out from the Amazon Basin and the Orinoco between the Atlantic coast and the Rio Negro. Erosion has worn away the plain over millions of years, leaving the tepui inselbergs. The Gran Sabana in south-eastern Venezuela boasts no less than 115 such tepuis, rising to heights of up to 1,000 m (3,280 feet) above the rainforest. Dense, impenetrable forest and jagged cliffs alternate on the mountains' giant plateau summits, and erosion and weathering have created bizarre rock formations and networks of caves. The elevation of the tepui plateaus isolates them from the rainforest completely, leading to the evolution of endemic flora and fauna.

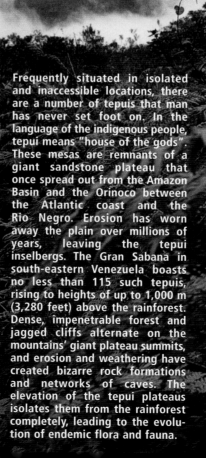

The tepuis rise up out of the Canaima National Park, a reminder of the Earth's distant geological past.

A view of Mount Roraima in the Gran Sabana, on whose plateau countless endemic species have survived.

Salto Angel, which falls from the Auyan Tepui in Venezuela, is the world's highest free-falling waterfall (979 m/3,212 feet).

ANTARCTICA

The Ellsworth Mountains on the western edge of the Ronne ice shelf in West Antarctica are the highest chain on the continent of Antarctica. They also contain Mount Vinson in the Sentinel Range, the continent's highest peak and thus one of the Seven Summits.

The Transantarctic Mountains, which run for some 3,500 km (2,175 miles) across the entire continent, are the world's fifth longest mountain range. Their highest peak is Mount Kirkpatrick.

Branscombe Glacier, Mount Vinson.

ANTARCTICA'S HIGHEST MOUNTAINS

1. **Ellsworth Mountains,** Sentinel Range, Mount Vinson 4,892 m (16,050 feet)
2. **Sentinel Range,** Mount Tyree 4,852 m (15,919 feet)
3. **Sentinel Range,** Mount Shinn 4,666 m (15,308 feet)
4. **Queen Elizabeth Range,** Mount Markham 4,602 m (15,098 feet)
5. **Sentinel Range,** Mount Epperly 4,600 m (15,092 feet)
6. **Sentinel Range,** Mount Gardner 4,587 m (15,049 feet)
7. **Transantarctic,** Mount Kirkpatrick 4,528 m (14,856 feet)
8. **Whitmore Mountains,** Mount Rutford 4,477 m (14,688 feet
9. **Sentinel Range,** Mount Craddock 4,368 m (14,331 feet)
10. **Transantarctic Mountains,** Mount Bell 4,305 m (14,124 feet)

ELLSWORTH MOUNTAINS – ANTARCTICA'S HIGHEST RANGE

The continental ice sheet is occasionally interrupted by mountain peaks.

The Ellsworth Mountains lie on the western side of the continent, between the Filcher-Ronne Ice Shelf and the Bellinghausen Sea to the south of the Antarctic Peninsula. The northernmost and largest section of the chain is known as the Sentinel Range, and here Mount Vinson, the highest mountain in Antarctica, is to be found immediately adjacent to the Minnesota Glacier and the Heritage Range. The chain was named after American scientist Lincoln Ellsworth, who was the first to discover it as he flew over it in 1935.

TRANSANTARCTIC MOUNTAINS –
ANTARCTICA'S LONGEST MOUNTAIN CHAIN

The Transantarctic Mountains were formed about 65 million years ago.

This highly glaciated chain of mountains stretches the length of the entire continent of Antarctica (more than 3,000 km/1,900 miles) in a series of ranges extending from the coast of Victorialand south to the Weddell Sea. The highest point is the summit of Mount Kirkpatrick (4,528 m/ 14,856 feet). Most of the chain is covered in a thick layer of ice interrupted only by the mountain summits. One peculiarity is the occasional dry valley – ice and snow-free stretches of land where no precipitation falls.

Mount Vinson was discovered by the US Air Force in 1957 and named after Senator Carl Vinson, who had promoted the exploration of Antarctica.

VOLCANOES

A large part of the Earth's crust consists of molten lava that has risen to the surface from the bowels of the Earth to cool and form volcanic rock. Such volcanic activity is confined almost exclusively to the edges of tectonic plates, and of the world's 500 to 600 volcanoes, some 80% are located on converging (and 15% on diverging) plate boundaries. Accounting for the further 5%, so-called "hot-spot" volcanoes are formed above a particularly hot area of the Earth's mantle, which always erupts at the same point as the tectonic plate moves above it. New volcanoes form as the old ones move away. Some of the world's most famous volcanoes are of this type, including the 2,400-km (1,500-mile) long chain of the Hawaiian Islands, all of which arose over a fixed hot spot above which the Pacific Plate has moved. These fire-breathing cones can be subdivided according to their magma output: multi-vent volcanoes, such as Mount Etna on Sicily, erupt from a number of different craters (fissures) and the resulting lava flows only slowly downhill. Volcanic pipes, such as Vesuvius, near Naples, are different in that they have a duct-like channel to their magma chamber; during an eruption, volumes of lava are explosively expelled and a caldera (a basin-like depression) may form as a result.

Volcanoes are also classified according to their shape: strato-volcanoes, such as Mount Fuji in Japan, are cone-shaped, but there are also shield volcanoes (such as Mauna Loa on Hawaii), lava domes, plateau volcanoes (where lava of a thinner consistency forces its way to the surface through fissures), cinder cones (which are somewhat smaller and usually feature a characteristic symmetrical cone, such as that of Stromboli in Italy), maars, created by an explosion without lava and usually leaving a funnel- or dish-shaped crater, such as in the Eifel in Germany, and calderas, basin-shaped depressions such as the Caldera de Taburiente on La Palma.

THE WORLD'S HIGHEST VOLCANOES

1 Ojos del Salado Argentina/Chile	6,887 m (22,595 feet)	
2 Monte Pissis Argentina	6,795 m (22,293 feet)	
3 Cerro Bonete Chico Argentina/Chile	6,759 m (22,175 feet)	
4 Llullaillaco Argentina/Chile	6,739 m (22,110 feet)	
5 Tupungato Chile	6,550 m (21,490 feet)	
6 Sajama Bolivia	6,542 m (21,463 feet)	
7 Illimani Bolivia	6,462 m (21,201 feet)	
8 Coropuna Peru	6,425 m (21,079 feet)	
9 Parinacota Chile/Bolivia	6,342 m (20,807 feet)	
10 Ampato Peru	6,288 m (20,630 feet)	
11 Pomerape Chile/Bolivia	6,288 m (20,630 feet)	
12 Chimborazo Ecuador	6,267 m (20,561 feet)	
13 Guallatiri Chile	6,071 m (19,918 feet)	
14 Acotango Chile	6,052 m (19,856 feet)	
15 Acamarachi Chile	6,046 m (19,836 feet)	
16 Hualca Hualca Peru	6,025 m (19,767 feet)	
17 Cotopaxi Ecuador	5,897 m (19,347 feet)	
18 Kibo (Kilimanjaro) Tanzania	5,895 m (19,340 feet)	
19 Ka-er-daxi (Kunlun) China	5,810 m (19,062 feet)	
20 Pico de Orizaba Mexico	5,636 m (18,490 feet)	

Tungurahua in Ecuador, a 5,016-m
(16,457-foot) stratovolcano (large
image), has undergone repeated phases
of great activity, such as that between
1916 and 1925. It became active again
in 1999 and a particularly powerful
eruption took place in 2006, resulting in
a pyroclastic flow (a fast-moving current
of fluidized hot gas, ash, and rock).
The resulting column of ash rose 12 km
(7 miles) into the air.

Ojos del Salado in the Atacama Desert between Argentina and Chile is both South America's second highest mountain and the world's highest volcano. Some 20th-century surveys even placed it higher than Aconcagua, making it South America's highest mountain, but more modern, GPS-based measurements have since refuted this. A 1994 survey of Monte Pissis found it to be 6,882 m (22,579 feet) high, relegating Ojos del Salado to third place, but this too proved to be inaccurate. It has since been established beyond doubt that at 6,887 m (22,595 feet), Ojos del Salado is about 100 m (328 feet) higher than Monte Pissis. As there is no record of explosive eruptions, Ojos del Salado is assumed to be extinct, but there have been many reports of gaseous activities: steam and sulfurous clouds were expelled from the crater in 1937 and 1956, and once again as recently as 14 November 1994. A Chilean citizen driving a modified all-terrain four-wheel-drive vehicle reached an altitude of 6,688 m (21,942 feet) on Ojos del Salado, setting a world record for the greatest height achieved using such a mode of transport.

Ojos del Salado, the world's highest volcano and South America's second highest peak, at dusk.

A view over the Puna de Atacama from the summit of Monte Pissis, Argentina's third highest peak and the third highest volcano on Earth. Ojos del Salado and Cerro Nacimiento are visible in the foreground.

In contrast to regular volcanoes, supervolcanoes do not form a cone such as those of Mount Etna or Mount Fuji. Pressure in the volcanic system builds up deep beneath the crust until a mighty eruption brings magma to the surface, and after erupting a giant funnel is created when the Earth collapses in on the empty magma chamber. Such eruptions are sometimes heralded by increased seismic activity, variations in the level of the volcano floor, and the formation of vents in the area. Such eruptions can have devastating global repercussions – material is catapulted high into the atmosphere by the explosion, falling to Earth in a radius of more than 200 km (125 miles), the sun is obscured, and the surface temperature of the Earth is reduced, leading to a "volcanic winter" that can last for several decades. Science has recorded only a couple of such eruptions, and their severity is measured on the VEI, the Volcano Explosivity Index; supervolcano eruptions reach an 8 on the scale.

LA GARITA CALDERA
Colorado, USA

The greatest known eruption in world history took place some 27 million years ago on the site of the present-day La Garita Caldera in south-western Colorado (above: tuff formations). Some 5,000 cu. km (1,200 cu. miles) of volcanic ash and rock were hurled into the atmosphere, leaving a geologically homogeneous caldera measuring 35 x 75 km (22 x 47 miles). The main explosion was followed by seven further large eruptions.

YELLOWSTONE
Wyoming, USA

Yellowstone is considered the most dangerous supervolcano of them all, erupting violently every 700,000 to 900,000 years. The last such eruption released 1,000 cu. km (240 cu. miles) of ash and volcanic material, resulting in a global volcanic winter. The activity of the Yellowstone volcano is due to a hot spot beneath it, feeding a magma chamber 8,000 m (26,000 feet) below the surface. Palpable and visible evidence of increased seismic activity is to be found in local earthquakes and geysers, while variations in pressure in the magma chamber result in changes in the shape of the caldera: fissures form at the edges and gas and lava are expelled. Recurrent periods of "thermal unrest" have been recorded in recent decades, although such activity seems to have quietened of late.

Deposits of sulfur and other minerals at the edges of the Grand Prismatic Pool. There is plenty of evidence to suggest that the Yellowstone National Park is sitting on a powder keg.

THE WORLD'S MOST DANGEROUS VOLCANOES

LAKE TOBA
Sumatra, Indonesia

Lake Toba (above) on Sumatra, the world's largest volcanic lake with an area of 1,146 sq. km (442 sq. miles), is evidence of the most violent volcanic eruption of the last 500,000 years. Scoring 8 on the Volcano Explosivity Index (VEI), the eruption caused the world's atmosphere to cool by up to 17°C (63°F) and ushered in the 1,000 coldest years of the Würm glacial period. The eruption released an estimated 2,800 cu. km (670 cu. miles) of volcanic material into the atmosphere, spreading ash across the entire world at altitudes approaching 50 km (31 miles) and introducing a so-called volcanic winter. The island of Samosir lies in the middle of the lake.

LAKE TAUPO
North Island, New Zealand

A mighty volcanic eruption shook the North Island of New Zealand about 22,600 years ago, releasing 1,170 cu. km (280 cu. miles) of ash and volcanic rock into the world's atmosphere. Taupo has erupted 28 times since, but none of these approached the magnitude of the first. With an area of 616 sq. km (238 sq. miles) and a depth of 186 m (610 feet), Lake Taupo is New Zealand's largest lake.

EUROPE

Volcanic activity is most common on the periphery of Europe. Iceland has some 30 active volcanoes, but the continent's highest peak is to be found further to the east, at Mount Elbrus in the Caucasus.

MOUNT ELBRUS
Russia   5,642 m (18,510 feet)

Lying in the Caucasus Mountains between the Caspian and Black Seas, Mount Elbrus is Russia's highest point, and also Europe's, if the Caucasus are considered part of that continent. With its two peaks – a western (5,642 m/18,510 feet) and an eastern summit (5,621 m/18,442 feet) – the mountain is a currently dormant, heavily glaciated stratovolcano created in a giant caldera during the Holocene. The eastern summit is topped with a 250-m (820-foot) wide volcanic crater. Mount Elbrus last erupted about 2,000 years ago and although silence has reigned since then, there are faint signs of volcanic activity, such as the presence of hot springs. Renewed activity brings with it the danger that any swift thawing of the gigantic icecap would release meltwater and lahars (mudflows), which would bury the surrounding area. The slopes of Mount Elbrus are covered with extensive glaciers and snowfields that only partially thaw in spring.

MOUNT KAZBEK
Georgia   5,047 m (16,558 feet)

The highest points in the Caucasus, a bridge of land between the Black and Caspian Seas, are to be found in the Central Caucasus between Mount Elbrus and Mount Kazbek, where there are no less than 15 peaks higher than 4,800 m (15,750 feet). Located not far from the Georgian Military Road, Mount Kazbek is 5,047 m (16,558 feet) high and thus Georgia's third highest mountain and the eighth highest peak in the Caucasus. Considered an extinct stratovolcano, it was first climbed in 1868.

MOUNT ARAGATS
Armenia   4,095 m (13,435 feet)

Located about 40 km (25 miles) north-west of Yerevan, the Armenian capital, in Aragatsotn province, Mount Aragats, a free-standing, extinct stratovolcano with four summits surrounding a volcanic crater, is the highest peak in Armenia. Created during the Pliocene or Pleistocene, it is now covered by glaciers; the many fissures on the slopes of Mount Aragats were once outlets for streams of lava that would flow down into the valley after eruptions.

KABARGIN OTH GROUP
Georgia   3,650 m (11,975 feet)

The Caucasus Mountains, which run for around 1,100 km (680 miles) across Russian, Georgian, Armenian, Azerbaijani, and Turkish territory between the Black and Caspian Seas, also include the volcanoes of the Kabargin Oth Group. Consisting of around a dozen cinder cones and lava domes, they are located on Georgian soil near the Russian border south-west of Mount Kazbek, a steep-sloped dormant stratovolcano in the Greater Caucasus.

Mount Kazbek, with Tsminda Sameba pilgrimage church.

Mount Aragats is Armenia's highest peak.

The snow-covered slopes of Mount Elbrus in the Caucasus betray no evidence of the hot springs to be found here.

GHEGAMA MOUNTAINS
Armenia   3,597 m (11,801 feet)

Created during the Holocene, the Ghegama Mountains, a volcano field located between Yerevan and Lake Sevan in western Central Armenia, has covered an area measuring 65 x 35 km (40 x 21½ miles) with its lava flows, and its highest peak (Ghegam Ridge) now reaches 3,597 m (11,801 feet). Lava from the central and eastern volcanoes once flowed into Lake Sevan. The most recent activity of the Ghegama Mountains, about 2,000 years ago, created a number of further cinder cones and lava flows, but the chain is now considered extinct.

DAR-ALAGES
Armenia   3,329 m (10,922 feet)

Sometimes known as the Daly-Tapa Group, the Dar-Alages Group in the western foothills of the Vardenis chain is a row of six cinder and lava cones dating back to the Pleistocene and the Holocene. In the distant past (most recently between 3,000 and 4,000 years ago), gigantic streams of lava resulting from eruptions of the Vaiyots-Sar lava dome would block the Arpah River and flow for some 10 km (6 miles) further west. The Dar-Alages lie south of Lake Sevan, which is situated at a high altitude.

MOUNT ETNA
Italy   3,323 m (10,902 feet)

Created about 600,000 years ago, Mount Etna in north-eastern Sicily is Europe's highest active volcano. Its central cone is 300 m (990 feet) high, but besides its four summit craters there are more than 300 lateral or parasitic craters. Mount Etna erupts explosively almost every year and the sheer number of its recorded eruptions places it at the top of the list of the world's most active volcanoes. Lava is usually ejected not from the summit craters but from the slopes of the mountain's secondary craters.

The snow-capped summit of Mount Etna on Sicily. Several of the four summit craters can be seen clearly here.

MOUNT ETNA

Taormina and the Ionic Sea. Mount Etna can be seen in the background about 40 km (25 miles) away (right).

Located on the Italian island of Sicily, Mount Etna is 3,323 m (10,902 feet) high and the highest active volcano in continental Europe. It was created about 600,000 years ago on the western side of a large area of volcanic activity known as the Messina Fault, at a point where a sea sound penetrated

A plume of smoke above Mount Etna.

Mount Etna erupted in 2002.

deep into the island's interior. It is difficult to estimate the current height of the volcano as this varies according to the cinder cones created and destroyed by its regular eruptions. The base of Mount Etna covers an enormous area of some 1,250 sq. km (483 sq. miles) with a circumference of some 250 km (155 miles).

The column of smoke rising from the snow-capped summit of Mount Etna is a reminder of the volcano's continual activity. The Nebrodi Mountains can be seen to the north-west of the volcano and the Peloritani to the north-east. The almost barren slopes of the volcano offer a marked contrast to the fertile plains of Catania, and the many secondary craters on the slopes of the main summit are a typical feature of Mount Etna. The caldera to the east of the snowfields is the crater of Trifoglietto, Etna's predecessor, and a number of lava beds can be made out as dark brown areas to the west and north.

The Canaries, the Cape Verde Islands, the Azores, and the Madeira archipelago are all part of a region known as Macaronesia and all of these islands were created as a result of volcanic activity.

TENERIFE
Pico del Teide   3,718 m (12,198 feet)

The Canary Islands are politically part of Spain, although they lie between 100 and 500 km (60 and 300 miles) out in the Atlantic Ocean to the west of Morocco. They are all of volcanic origin and Tenerife, the largest island, with an area of 2,034 sq. km (785 sq. miles), was created some five million to seven million years ago, although the volcanic mound rising at its hub is a little more recent. The Las Cañadas caldera contains the Pico del Teide volcano, which at 3,718 m (12,198 feet) is Spain's highest mountain. The last major eruption of Pico del Teide was a good 200,000 years ago, but traces of it can still be seen right across the island, in deposits from the gigantic cloud of ash, avalanches of mud, and pumice stone that was catapulted across the island. The island remains geologically active, but the eruptions of the last few millennia have been smaller and more localized; lava last flowed from the north-western slopes of the mountain in 1909.

FOGO
Pico do Fogo   2,829 m (9,281 feet)

Fogo, one of the "under the wind" (*sotavento*) Cape Verde Islands, is a symmetrical volcanic cone with a giant caldera containing the mighty summit of Pico do Fogo, not only the archipelago's highest peak and only active volcano, but also the highest active volcano in the Atlantic. One eruption in 1680 was so violent and lit up the mountain for so long that sailors were able to use it as a beacon for navigation.

The summit of Pico do Fogo rising up from the caldera of the island of Fogo.

JAN MAYEN
Beerenberg   2,277 m (7,470 feet)

Located on the Norwegian island of Jan Mayen, north-east of Iceland in the Greenland Sea, Beerenberg is the world's northernmost active volcano. This stratovolcano is located on a tectonic fault known as the Jan Mayen Fracture Zone, which connects two sections of the Mid-Atlantic Ridge. Heavily glaciated, Beerenberg was thought to have become extinct after a major eruption in 1818, but in 1970 it unexpectedly resumed activity and the most recent lava flow was recorded in the years 1984 and 1985.

LA PALMA
Roque de los Muchachos
2,426 m (7,959 feet)

La Palma is one of the newest of the Canary Islands. The Caldera de Taburiente is the world's largest collapsed caldera, with a diameter of 9 km (5½ miles), a circumference of 28 km (17 miles), and a distance of 2 km (1¼ miles) from crater lip to caldera floor. Roque de los Muchachos, one of the summits on the lip of the crater, is the island's highest peak.

Roque de los Muchachos on La Palma, swathed in cloud.

SÃO TOMÉ AND PRÍNCIPE
Pico de São Tomé   2,024 m (6,640 feet)

São Tomé and Príncipe, lying 200 km (125 miles) off the African coast, is the second smallest African state after the Seychelles. Composed of a chain of extinct volcanoes, its highest point is to be found at the summit of Pico de São Tomé in the eponymous island's Obo National Park. São Tomé is a gigantic stratovolcano on the Cameroon line, a rift zone stretching south-west out into the Atlantic from Cameroon. The base of the mountain lies more than 3,000 m (9,800 feet) beneath the ocean surface.

PICO
Ponto do Pico 2,351 m (7,713 feet)

Pico, the second largest island in the Azores with an area of 442 sq. km (171 sq. miles), is named after the volcano of Ponta do Pico, Portugal's highest peak with a height of 2,351 m (7,713 feet). It last erupted in 1718. It is currently thought to be dormant, although geological activity still persists. Despite the threat posed to the islanders by the volcano, they use its lava to build houses and protective walls against the ocean winds.

Clouds gathering around Pico herald a change in the weather.

GRAN CANARIA
Pico de las Nieves   1,949 m (6,394 feet)

Only about 5% of the submerged volcanic mountain range whose highest peaks form the Canary Islands is visible above water. One such peak is the almost circular island of Gran Canaria, the third largest island in the archipelago – after Fuerteventura and Tenerife – with an area of 1,560 sq. km (602 sq. miles). Gran Canaria's highest peak is the long since extinct volcano of Pico de las Nieves in the island's interior.

Pico de Las Nieves in the sparsely populated interior of the island of Gran Canaria (right).

The summit of Pico del Tiede, which remains covered in snow until late spring, forms a majestic backdrop for the spectacular Roques de García, stone pillars carved out by erosion (left). The Guanches, the original people inhabiting the Canaries, called Tenerife "the Mountain of Snows" in tribute to the dormant volcano that still dominates the island.

MADEIRA
Pico Ruivo   1,862 m (6,109 feet)

Forming a chain with the extinct volcanoes of Pico do Arieiro, Pico das Torres, and Pico Grande, the summit of Pico Ruivo is the highest peak on the Portuguese island of Madeira. Erosion has shaped the volcano's jagged lava beds into a number of interesting formations. The island represents just the tip of a series of volcanoes that now lie underwater at depths of up to 4,000 m (13,100 feet).

Pico do Arieiro at dusk, looking toward Pico Ruivo and Pico das Torres.

EL HIERRO
Malpaso   1,501 m (4,925 feet)

With an area of barely 270 sq. km (104 sq. miles), El Hierro is the smallest of the principal Canary Islands; only about 1.2 million years old, it is also the newest. The island's highest peak is Malpaso at 1,501 m (4,925 feet), and the volumes of lava to be found in the south and west of the island stem from eruptions dating back to the first millennium. The only recorded volcanic eruption on El Hierro was that of Lomo Negro in 1793

A landscape of lava on El Hierro, much of which has never been properly explored.

BASSE-TERRE
La Soufrière   1,467 m (4,813 feet)

The active volcano of La Soufrière (French for "the sulfur outlet") on Basse-Terre, one of the two main islands of the French Overseas Department of Guadeloupe, is the highest peak in the Lesser Antilles, an extended string of volcanic islands in the Caribbean. The population of the entire island was evacuated as a precaution before Soufrière's last eruption in 1977, but no damage ensued. Analysis of local geology reveals that the last great eruption of magma occurred in about the year 1440.

ICELAND

Lying in the northern Atlantic south of the Arctic Circle, Iceland is the second largest island in Europe and the world's largest volcanic island, with an area of 103,000 sq. km (39,768 sq. miles). The island was formed volcanically and some 30 of its 130 volcanoes are still active – in 2010, the explosive eruption of Eyjafjalla-

Kerlingarfjöll in the highlands of Iceland.

jökull threw volcanic ash into the atmosphere, severely disrupting air travel across Europe. Geysers and fumaroles (fissures from which gases escape to the Earth's surface) are clues to the continuing volcanic activity, which is especially prevalent on the western half of the island. This tectonic history and current volcanic activity makes Iceland one of the most interesting regions on Earth for geologists.

ICELAND'S HIGHEST VOLCANOES

❶	Oraefajökull (Hvannadalshnúkur)	
		2,110 m (6,923 feet)
❷	Bárdarbunga	2,000 m (6,562 feet)
❸	Kverkfjöll	1,920 m (6,299 feet)
❹	Hofsjökull	1,782 m (5,846 feet)
❺	Esjufjöll	1,760 m (5,774 feet)
❻	Grimsvötn	1,725 m (5,659 feet)
❼	Herdubreid	1,682 m (5,518 feet)
❽	Eyjafjallajökull	
		1,666 m (5,465 feet)
❾	Askja	1,516 m (4,974 feet)
❿	Katla	1,512 m (4,961 feet)
⓫	Hekla	1,491 m (4,892 feet)

Hvannadalshnúkur on the rim of the Öræfajökull volcano.

Hofsjökull in the western Highlands of Iceland.

THE WORLD'S LARGEST VOLCANIC ISLAND

SURTSEY – THE MOST RECENT VOLCANIC ISLAND

The 1.4 sq. km (½ sq. mile) island of Surtsey unexpectedly surfaced in the Atlantic about 30 km (19 miles) off the Icelandic coast after an underwater volcanic eruption on 14 November 1963. The ensuing plume of smoke from the eruption rose more than 3 km (2 miles) into the air. The action of waves, wind, and rain are gradually eroding the island and it has already lost half of its original volume.

The area surrounding the 818-m (2,684-foot) high volcano of Krafla is one of the most tectonically unstable zones on the island. After almost 2,000 years of inactivity, the volcano smothered the region in a thick layer of ash and lava at the turn of the 18th century before coming to life again in 1975. Its bubbling and steaming sulfurous springs are the most obvious signs of volcanic activity on Iceland.

The Kverkfjöll range is of volcanic origin.

Hekla is one of the three most active volcanoes on Iceland.

Much of the landscape of Asia, and many of the mountain chains and islands of the Pacific coast were created by plate tectonics: the subduction of the Pacific and Philippine Plates by the Eurasian Plate has led to considerable volcanic activity.

KA-ER-DAXI (KUNLUN)
China   5,810 m (19,062 feet)

The Kunlun Volcanic Group in the north-western Tibetan Highlands is part of the Kunlun Mountains, which extend for 3,000 km (1,900 miles) with peaks reaching heights of more than 7,000 m (23,000 feet). Ashi Shan, also known as Ka-er-daxi ("volcano"), at the western end of the group is 5,810 m (19,062 feet) high and both the most recent and the highest volcano in Asia. It is composed of approximately 70 well-preserved pyroclastic cones (consisting of various rock types ejected from the volcano) surrounding Aqqikkol Hu and Wuluke Lakes. The main pipe erupted most recently on 27 May 1951. The high concentration of volcanic cones in the area is explained by local plate tectonic activity; volcanoes are formed at such "weak spots" on the Earth's crust, and the Kunlun Mountains represent the point where the Indian subcontinent and the Eurasian Plate converged in the late Triassic (about 200 million years ago).

MOUNT DAMAVAND
Iran   5,670 m (18,602 feet)

Mount Damavand, (Persian for "frosty mountain") is a dormant volcanic cone whose highest crater nonetheless contains fissures emitting sulfurous gases. Lying 5,670 m (18,602 feet) above sea level, it is the highest mountain in the Alborz range, the tallest peak in Iran, and the highest point in the entire Near East. Along with Kilimanjaro, it is one of the world's highest free-standing mountains. From the base to the summit its height (4,700 m/ 15,420 feet) is considerably greater than that of Mount Everest.

KLYUCHEVSKAYA SOPKA
Russia   4,750 m (15,584 feet)

Located in the far east of Russia, Klyuchevskaya Sopka is the highest peak in Kamchatka. The volcano consists of a conical stump with a central crater, as well as some 70 subcraters and cones on its slopes. The volcano, which has erupted over 50 times since 1700, trails a characteristic plume of smoke from its summit. A station has been established at the foot of the mountain to monitor the peninsula's volcanic activity, which continues to be significant with ash and lava eruptions.

MOUNT ARARAT
Turkey   5,165 m (16,946 feet)

Mount Ararat, Turkey's highest peak, towers over the Anatolian Plains near the borders with Armenia and Iran. Despite its Kurdish name, Çiyayê Agirî, which means "fiery mountain", Mount Ararat is considered dormant and the most recent eruption took place in 1840. Mount Ararat, the holy mountain where Noah is said to have landed with his ark, has been open to climbers since 2001, subject to the payment of certain fees.

MOUNT KAMEN
Russia   4,585 m (15,043 feet)

The Klyuchevskoy Group on Russia's Kamchatka Peninsula contains both active and dormant volcanoes. Mount Kamen, one of the most beautiful and easily reached volcanoes in Kamchatka, is one of the inactive ones, with no recorded eruptions in the last 3,000 years. The Klyuchevskoy Nature Park is often referred to as the "land of fire and ice" – it contains not only several active volcanoes, but also the peninsula's largest glaciers, which cover a total of some 270 sq. km (104 sq. miles).

SABALAN
Iran   4,811 m (15,784 feet)

Sabalan, a dormant stratovolcano in north-western Iran, is the second highest volcano in the country after Mount Damavand. The crater lake at its summit is frozen for much of the year, thawing only occasionally at the end of July or the beginning of August. Glaciers have formed at elevations above 4,000 m (13,100 feet). The mountain's andesite rock is between 1.4 and 5.6 million years old and the most recent eruption of Sabalan took place less than 10,000 years ago, during the Holocene.

MOUNT SÜPHAN
Turkey   4,058 m (13,314 feet)

Mount Süphan (Turkish: Süphan Daği) lies on the banks of Lake Van in Eastern Anatolia in Bitlis province. The 4,058-m (13,314-foot), perennially snow-covered summit of this extinct volcano is a prized climb among mountaineers for the breathtaking panorama it affords of the eastern Taurus Mountains and the Euphrates River. It is popular for heli-skiing, where skiers are dropped on to its slopes from helicopters. Mount Ararat on the Armenian border is the only peak higher than Mount Süphan within 200 km (125 miles).

Mount Ararat has become one of the most famous mountains in the world thanks to the Bible, in which Noah and his ark come to rest in the mountain chain of the same name. Turkey's highest peak (5,165 m/16,946 feet) is a dormant volcano with a magnificent setting in the Armenian Highlands.

Yurts beside Lake Karakul in Xinjiang province in the furthest western reaches of China (left). The summit of the Kunlun Mountains can be seen in the background.

TAFTAN
Iran   **4,050m (13,287 feet)**

The north-eastern edge of the Arabian Plate is located on a largely convergent plate boundary. The subduction of the oceanic plates led to the creation of the now dormant volcanoes of Bazman and Taftan. The latter, a heavily eroded stratovolcano in south-eastern Iran, last ejected large plumes of smoke in 1909; lava flow was reported from Taftan in 1993, but this is assumed to have been nothing more than a stream of molten sulfur. The mountain can be climbed, though fierce winds make the ascent hazardous.

USHKOVSKY
Russia   **3,943 m (12,936 feet)**

Once known as Plosky Sopki (flat hill) due to its appearance, the Ushkovsky massif is located at the north-western end of the Klyuchevskoy Group in the middle of the Kamchatka Peninsula. It consists of a row of several volcanoes and while not as active as the other peaks in the Klyuchevskoy Group, the Ushkovsky stratovolcano (which gives its name to the group) was recently discovered by scientists to have new craters on its summit, as well as signs of fresh eruptions from secondary craters. The craters are filled with ice.

MOUNT ERCIYES
Turkey   **3,917 m (12,845 feet)**

At 3,917 m (12,845 feet), the dormant volcano of Erciyes Daği (Mount Erciyes) is Turkey's fifth highest peak. The mountain has also become the symbol of the city of Kayseri, about 25 km (15½ miles) away. The infamous and globally unique "moon landscape" surrounding the town of Göreme, which consists of tuff formations shaped like rocky domes (and romantically named "fairy chimneys" by the local people), is the result of lava flow after eruptions of Mount Erciyes. Its slopes are also home to a ski resort.

Klyuchevskaya Sopka, Kamchatka.   Mount Damavand, Turkey's highest mountain.   Mount Erciyes, Turkey.

The Indonesian island chain is a hotbed of tectonic instability with some 70 active volcanoes. The islands of Japan are formed entirely from the highest points of an underwater chain of volcanoes, and there are even a few active peaks among the many extinct ones.

MOUNT FUJI
Japan   3,776 m (12,388 feet)

Mount Fuji, Japan's highest peak, is revered as the seat of the gods because of its symmetrical shape. It lies above the triple junction of the Amurian, Okhotsk, and Philippine Sea Plates and is just one of the stratovolcanoes along the Pacific Ring of Fire. Mount Fuji is considered active, but the risk of an eruption is thought to be low. The last eruption in 1707 resulted in the formation of a secondary crater halfway up its slopes.

Mount Fuji, Japan's highest peak and its national symbol (right).

RINJANI
Indonesia   3,726 m (12,224 feet)

Mount Rinjani, an active stratovolcano on the island of Lombok, is Indonesia's second highest volcano. Rinjani's caldera, which measures 6 x 8.5 km (4 x 5¼ miles), contains a 230-m (744-foot) deep crater lake and several hot springs. Eruptions between 1994 and 1996 created a small new lava cone in the middle of the caldera whose lava flowed into the lake. Rinjani last erupted in May 2009, spreading ash and smoke up to 8 km (5 miles) into the atmosphere.

SAHAND
Iran   3,707 m (12,162 feet)

Sahand is an extinct stratovolcano located near the city of Tabriz in north-western Iran. The peak is covered in snow during winter and the resulting meltwater feeds the valley drainage systems in spring. It is not known for sure when Sahand last erupted, but the volcano is already heavily eroded and some of the lava fields are estimated to be about a million years old. The mountain is famed for the diversity of its plant and animal life. It has also become a popular winter sports venue.

MOUNT KERINCI
Indonesia   3,805 m (12,484 feet)

The volcanoes on the island of Sumatra form one of Indonesia's largest volcanic chains and include Gunung Kerinci, which at 3,805 m (12,484 feet) is Indonesia's highest peak, towering over the surrounding tea fields on the Kayu Aro plateau by up to 3,000 m (9,800 feet). Mount Kerinci's eruptions have followed a centuries-old pattern of constant but gentle activity interspersed with occasional sudden explosions. Heightened volcanic activity accompanied by eruptions, earthquakes, and increased ash output were last recorded for Mount Kerinci in 1998, when, after several years of dormancy, several eruptions brought a shower of ash down on the village of Palempok, and in 1999, which saw ash fall on the entire surrounding area, accompanied by constant earth tremors (low, frequent earthquakes) and some consequent changes in the topography of the summit. The volcano erupted most recently in 2009, and even today the column of smoke rising from the crater of Kerinci can reach heights of up to a 1 km (½ mile).

A fumarole (steam fissure) is constantly at work on the active volcano of Mount Kerinci in the Barisan Mountains on Sumatra (left).

Rinjani crater lake after rainfall.

Semeru in the Bromo Tengger Semeru National Park, Java.

TOLBACHIK
Russia   3,682 m (12,080 feet)

Lying on the Kamchatka Peninsula in Russia, the basalt Tolbachik volcano is actually two peaks: Plosky ("flat") Tolbachik, a shield volcano, and Ostry ("sharp") Tolbachik, a stratovolcano. The caldera at the summit of Plosky Tolbachik was created about 6,500 years ago when a large section of rock broke away from the southern side of Ostry Tolbachik. An eruption that created several new cinder cones in 1975 proved to be the largest eruption ever recorded in Kamchatka, when measured by volume of lava expelled.

SEMERU
Indonesia   3,675 m (12,057 feet)

The Semeru volcano on the Indonesian island of Java erupted in February 2007, when a violent explosion was followed by the ejection of a column of ash covering the densely populated eastern side of Java. Debris and stones rained down on the city of Lumajang, but no one was injured and the accompanying heavy rain soon washed away the layer of ash. The population is inured to occasional ash falls, as 3,675-m (12,057-foot) high Semeru is one of Indonesia's most active volcanoes and has been almost continuously erupting since 1967.

ICHINSKY
Russia   3,621 m (11,880 feet)

Known locally as Ichinskaya Sopka, Ichinsky is yet another Kamchatka stratovolcano and the highest peak in the Sredinny Range running down the middle of the peninsula. With a volume of some 450 cu. km (108 cu. miles), it is also one of the largest mountains on the peninsula. From the summit's ice cap several glaciers run down into the valley and the slopes beneath the caldera feature several lava domes. The most violent eruption took place about 6,500 years ago, producing lava streams up to 15 km (9 miles) long. Plumes of smoke are often seen rising from the caldera.

KAMCHATKA

Russia's Kamchatka Peninsula is a 1,200-km (745-mile) long spit of land between the Bering Sea and the Sea of Okhotsk; 450 km (280 miles) across at its widest point, it is one of the world's major volcanic regions. On a geological timescale, the peninsula is still very recent: the

Karymsky, a volcano in Kamchatka, spitting out ash and smoke.

wide subduction zone slowly pushing the peninsula up as the Pacific Plate slips under the Eurasian Plate has existed for only about two million years. Kamchatka's spine is formed by a chain of mountains running up its western side and culminating in Ichinsky at 3,621 m (11,880 feet). There is a parallel eastern range in the central area of the peninsula, surrounded by 160 volcanoes. The highest of the 29 active volcanoes is Klyuchevskaya Sopka (4,750 m/ 15,584 feet). On average, six of Kamchatka's volcanoes erupt each year. The Volcanoes of Kamchatka were given the status of a UNESCO World Heritage Site in 1996.

KAMCHATKA'S HIGHEST VOLCANOES

❶ Klyuchevskaya Sopka
    4,750 m (15,584 feet)
❷ Mount Kamen
    4,585 m (15,043 feet)
❸ Ushkovsky
    3,943 m (12,936 feet)
❹ Tolbachik 3,682 m (12,080 feet)
❺ Ichinsky   3,621 m (11,880 feet)
❻ Kronotsky
    3,528 m (11,575 feet)
❼ Koryak   3,456 m (11,339 feet)
❽ Gamchen   2,576 m (8,451 feet)

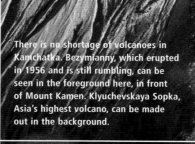

There is no shortage of volcanoes in Kamchatka. Bezymianny, which erupted in 1956 and is still rumbling, can be seen in the foreground here, in front of Mount Kamen. Klyuchevskaya Sopka, Asia's highest volcano, can be made out in the background.

Tolbachik, 3,682 m (12,080 feet)

Kronotsky, 3,528 m (11,575 feet)

Koryak, 3,456 m (11,339 feet)

Gamchen, 2,576 m (8,451 feet)

NEW ZEALAND

Mount Ruapehu 2,797 m (9,177 feet)
Mount Taranaki 2,518 m (8,261 feet)
Mount Ngauruhoe
2,291 m (7,516 feet)
Mount Tongariro
1,968 m (6,456 feet)

Mount Taranaki (or Mount Egmont) on New Zealand's North Island is a dormant volcano, the last major eruption occurring in 1655. This isolated, snow-covered volcanic cone is to be found on an almost circular peninsula with an area of about 60 sq. km (23 sq. miles), which has been slowly built up by lava deposits. Three further volcanic craters rising up in the middle of the North Island form the volcanic complex of Tongariro: the extremely active Mount Ruapehu (the North Island's highest peak), Mount Ngauruhoe, which last erupted in 1975, and Mount Tongariro, which is now extinct. Much of the mountain

Mount Taranaki, New Zealand.

Mount Ngauruhoe, a stratovolcano.

NEW GUINEA

Mount Giluwe   4,368 m (14,331 feet)
Mount Hagen   3,778 m (12,395 feet)
Doma Peaks   3,568 m (11,706 feet)
Crater Mountain 3,233 m (10,607 feet)

Mount Giluwe's double summit is Papua New Guinea's second highest peak after Mount Wilhelm (4,509 m/ 14,793 feet), and is the highest volcano in the entire Australia/ Oceania area. Mount Hagen, the country's second highest volcano, lies 35 km (21½ miles) to the north-west. The upper slopes of both of these stratovolcanoes are heavily glaciated, and both have been

The mountains of Papua New Guinea.

substantially eroded over the course of the millennia. Doma Peaks and Crater Mountain, New Guinea's smaller volcanoes, are similarly considered extinct.

complex is glaciated and riven by steep canyons. The area features many bizarre rock formations.

Australia is an even and homogeneous country with large open spaces and few variations in elevation. Oceania's highest mountains and volcanoes are to be found on the islands, especially New Zealand and Papua New Guinea: at 4,368 m

Volcanoes on North Island, New Zealand.

(14,331 feet), Mount Giluwe on Papua New Guinea is Oceania's highest volcano, just beating Mount Hagen (3,778 m/12,395 feet) into second place. Papua New Guinea's sovereign territory includes a range of islands with an impressive mixture of active and extinct volcanoes, and New Zealand's North Island is similarly rich in volcanic activity.

BOUGAINVILLE

Balbi	2,715 m (8,907 feet)
Takuan	2,210 m (7,251 feet)
Tore	2,200 m (7,218 feet)
Loloru	1,887 m (6,191 feet)
Bagana	1,730 m (5,676 feet)

Of the many volcanoes found on Bougainville, an island belonging to Papua New Guinea, the highest is Mount Balbi, whose five craters are considered active, although there have been no eruptions in recorded history. The most active volcano on the island is Bagana, which is also one of the world's most active volcanoes.

NEW BRITAIN

Ulawun	2,334 m (7,657 feet)
Bamus	2,248 m (7,375 feet)

The rumbling activity of Ulawun, a volcano on Papua New Guinea's island of New Britain, has been under constant surveillance since an eruption in 2000 in an attempt to warn locals of any future large explosions. Ulawun and Bamus are the highest peaks in the Bismarck Group in the New Britain subduction zone.

HEARD ISLAND

Big Ben (Mawson Peak)	
	2,745 m (9,007 feet)

Mawson Peak, the snow-capped highest point of the Big Ben stratovolcano towers over the eastern end of uninhabited Heard Island. Big Ben, whose crater is 70 m (230 feet) deep, is one of just two active volcanoes on Australian territory – the other is the McDonald Island volcano. Big Ben last erupted in 2008.

Bagana volcano, Bougainville.

The coast of New Britain in silhouette.

When Ruapehu on New Zealand erupts – as most recently occurred in 2007 – the crater lake just beneath its summit drains down its western slopes in an avalanche of mud and moraine. Such an avalanche destroyed a railway bridge in 1953, causing a train crash that claimed 151 lives.

The Pacific Ocean is flanked by a 32,500-km (20,195-mile) Ring of Fire. Consisting largely of volcanic island chains and volcanic mountain ranges, it runs from the Antarctic Peninsula through Tierra del Fuego to the volcanic ranges of the South and Central American Cordilleras. The arc of the Aleutian Islands, adjoining the volcanoes of Alaska, marks the northern boundary of the Pacific Plate, which then continues into Siberia's Kamchatka Peninsula and the Kuril Islands, where it is subducted beneath the Eurasian Plate. The Ring continues in a chain of islands running south from Japan and Taiwan to the Mariana Islands. This point marks the Pacific Plate's convergence with the smaller Philippines Plate, which in turn borders on three further plates and is responsible for the considerable volcanic activity in Indonesia and the Philippines. The Ring is closed by the volcanic

Chimborazo, Ecuador.

ranges of the Indo-Australian Plate, which run through Melanesia and Fiji toward New Zealand and several of the sub-Antarctic islands.

Main image: Volcanic Mount Mayon and peaceful paddy fields, Luzon island, the Philippines.

KAMCHATKA

The active Karymsky volcano.

The Kamchatka Peninsula in the furthest eastern reaches of Russia is the world's most active volcanic region: 29 of the peninsula's 160 volcanoes erupt regularly. The peninsula's highest peak is the volcanic Klyuchevskaya Sopka, at 4,750 m (15,584 feet).

KURIL ISLANDS

The volcanoes of the Kurils.

The Kurils, a group of more than 30 islands lying between Kamchatka and Japan, boast more than 100 volcanoes of which no less than 39 are still active. Sarychev, on the Kuril island of Matua, erupted in June 2009, sending clouds of ash over 1,000 km (620 miles) into the Pacific.

JAPAN

Sakurajima volcano, Kyushu province.

Some 40 of the 240 volcanoes scattered across the islands of Japan are still active. At 3,776 m (12,388 feet), Mount Fuji on the main island of Honshu is the country's highest peak and is still considered active even though the last eruption was at the turn of the 18th century.

PHILIPPINES

Mount Mayon, spitting lava.

Philippines consist entirely of volcanic peaks jutting out of the ocean The highest is Mount Apo (2,954 m/ 9,692 feet) on the Mind-anao island. One of the most violent eruptions of the 20th century occurred at Mount Pinatubo on Luzon in 1991.

MELANESIA

Mount Tavurvur, New Britain.

The islands of Melanesia, lying in the South Pacific to the north-east of Australia, are of volcanic origin. Of their many volcanoes, Mounts Yasur and Manaro, which last erupted in 2005, are considered to be the most dangerous.

NEW ZEALAND POLYNESIA

The active Ruapehu, New Zealand.

The islands of Polynesia were also created by volcanic activity and represent the tips of volcanic peaks rising some 4,000 m (13,100 feet) from the bed of the Pacific Ocean. The highest volcano in the archipelago is Ruapehu on the North Island of New Zealand.

NORTHERN ANDES

The snow-capped peak of Cotopaxi, Ecuador.

About 30 of Ecuador's volcanoes are active, including Cotopaxi, the world's highest active volcano (5,897 m/19,347 feet). Pichincha still represents a danger to Quito, the capital, and Tungurahua claimed many lives in 2006.

CASCADE RANGE

Mount Adams, Washington state.

Crater Lake National Park.

CENTRAL AMERICA

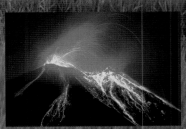

Arenal, Costa Rica, erupts regularly.

Poás volcano, Costa Rica.

ALEUTIAN ISLANDS ALASKA

Mount Shishaldin, Aleutian Islands.

Mount Veniaminof in Alaska is still active.

CENTRAL AND SOUTHERN ANDES

Smoke escaping from Sabancaya, Peru.

There are some 80 volcanoes in the Aleutian Island chain between North America and Asia, and some of these, such as Mount Cleveland on Chuginadak Island, are still active. There are also active volcanoes spread across mainland Alaska, including Mount Katnai, which suffered the region's most violent eruption in 1912.

The Cascade Range runs parallel to the west coast of North America from British Columbia through the US states of Washington and Oregon to northern California. The range's highest peak is Mount Rainier (4,395 m/14,419 feet) near Seattle, but the best-known volcano – and also the most active – is Mount St Helens (2,549 m/8,363 feet), which lost its summit in a spectacular eruption in 1980.

Costa Rica boasts a string of volcanoes, of which some – including Turrialba, Irazu (the highest volcano in the country at 3,432 m/11,260 feet), Barva, Poás, and Arenal – are active; the latter erupted in 1968 after a long period of inactivity, killing about 80 people, and has been active ever since. The Central American chain of volcanoes continues in a northerly direction.

Ojos del Salado (6,887 m/22,595 feet), the world's highest volcano, lies in Argentina, and many more active volcanoes are to be found in Peru, including Ubinas (5,672 m/18,609 feet), which erupted in 2006 after lying dormant since 1956.

All of the Hawaiian Islands were created volcanically, and if the areas beneath the sea's surface are included, the shield volcanoes of Hawaii are the world's highest volcanoes – the islands lie in waters up to 4,500 m (14,750 feet) deep. Loihi, the most recent volcanic addition, is still beneath the surface, at a depth of 969 m (3,179 feet); if its eruptions are as frequent as those of Mauna Loa, it should reach the surface in a few tens of thousands of years.

MAUNA KEA
Big Island   4,205 m (13,796 feet)

The summit of Mauna Kea.

Measured from its base to its summit, Mauna Kea has a total height of well over 9,000 m (29,500 feet), making it the world's highest mountain. In contrast with nearby Mauna Loa, it is inactive and is considered dormant.

Molten lava from Kilauea flowing into the sea: this means Pele, the volcano goddess, is angry, according to local belief. Some of the white-hot lava flows through lava tunnels.

MAUNA LOA
Big Island   4,170 m (13,679 feet)

The Mauna Loa stratovolcano is the second highest peak in the Hawaiian archipelago. It lies above a hot spot and last erupted in 1984. Although there is no lava flowing from it at the moment, it is still considered an active volcano.

Mauna Loa on Hawaii, one of the world's largest active volcanoes.

HALEAKALA
Maui Island   3,055 m (10,023 feet)

Haleakala, which takes up more than two-thirds of Maui's surface area, is the only volcano in Hawaii, apart from those on Big Island, to be active in the last 600 years. With a diameter of 34 km (21 miles), its crater is one of the world's largest.

Haleakala ("House of the Sun") last erupted in 1790.

HUALALAI
Big Island   2,521 m (8,271 feet)

Hualalai is considered a dormant volcano, although it erupted several times at the end of the 18th and the beginning of the 19th centuries. Keahole-Kona airport was built on one of the lava beds from this period.

The shield volcano Hualalai is one of five volcanoes on Hawaii.

AFRICA

The East African Rift, whose plate boundaries have given rise to a number of volcanoes, is the principal feature of a tectonically active landscape that runs right across continental Africa.

KIBO (KILIMANJARO)
Tanzania   5,895 m (19,340 feet)

Towering 5,895 m (19,340 feet) above sea level, Kibo ("the bright one" in Swahili) in Tanzania is the highest volcano and indeed the highest peak in Africa. It is one of the world's Seven Summits, the highest peaks on the seven continents. Located at the edge of the East African Rift, Kibo's highest point, known as Uhuru ("freedom"), stands out over the other summits of the Kilimanjaro massif, in itself the highest mountain range on the continent. Lying approximately 340 km (210 miles) south of the equator, Kibo is the highest of the three volcanoes in the Kilimanjaro massif and is connected to Mawenzi (5,148 m/ 16,890 feet), which lies about 10 km (6 miles) to the west, by a rocky saddle that has an average height of about 4,300 m (14,100 feet). Shira (3,962 m/ 12,999 feet) lies still further to the west, about 15 km (9 miles) from Kibo. Despite their active fumaroles, all three of the Kilimanjaro volcanoes have long since been declared dormant.

BATIAN (MOUNT KENYA)
Kenya   5,199 m (17,057 feet)

Batian is a dormant volcano located in the middle of the country about 140 km (87 miles) north-east of Nairobi, the Kenyan capital, and 15 km (9 miles) south of the equator. With a height of 5,199 m (17,057 feet) it is the second highest mountain in continental Africa and the highest point of the Mount Kenya massif. In 1997, it was inscribed as a UNESCO World Heritage Site.

A giant groundsel (*Dendrosenecio johnstonii*); Mount Kenya behind.

MOUNT KARISIMBI
Rwanda   4,507 m (14,787 feet)

The highest point in the East African state of Rwanda is to be found at the summit of Mount Karisimbi, one of eight dormant volcanoes in the Virunga Mountains, yet another section of the East African Rift. The mountain's name is derived from *isimbi*, meaning "little white shell", and is presumably a reference to the mantle of snow that sometimes covers the mountain. The Karisoke Research Center, where Dian Fossey used to observe mountain gorillas, a species now found only in this area, is located between Mount Karisimbi and the nearby peak of Mount Bisoke.

MAWENZI (KILIMANJARO)
Tanzania   5,148 m (16,890 feet)

Mawenzi ("the dark one" in the language of the Chagga people of the area), the second highest peak in Tanzania's Kilimanjaro massif after Kibo, is located approximately 340 km (210 miles) south of the equator. The heavily eroded summit area of this extinct volcano is not glaciated, instead being covered with scree and abrupt, rugged cliffs.

Mawenzi has been a UNESCO World Heritage Site since 1987.

MOUNT ELGON
Uganda   4,321 m (14,177 feet)

Mount Elgon, an extinct volcano with a massive crater (12 km/7 miles in diameter), is located on the border between Uganda and Kenya. After Kilimanjaro, Mount Kenya, and the Ruwenzori Mountains, Mount Elgon is the fourth highest mountain massif in East Africa and the oldest volcano on the Great Rift Valley, having been created during the Miocene (between 5.3 and 23 million years ago). Mount Elgon has not erupted for the last three million years, and existing moraine and crater lakes are proof that the mountain was once glaciated.

MOUNT MERU
Tanzania   4,562 m (14,967 feet)

Volcanic Mount Meru, Tanzania's second highest mountain, is located in the Arusha National Park in the north of the country, 65 km (40 miles) south-west of the Kilimanjaro massif. Mount Meru was once considerably higher, but its summit was annihilated in a prehistoric eruption. A smaller ash cone was created in this large crater during eruptions in 1880, but Mount Meru has not been active since 1910.

Mount Meru, with the Momela Lakes in the foreground.

MOUNT MUHABURA
Rwanda   4,127 m (13,540 feet)

Mount Muhabura is an extinct strato-volcano located at the eastern end of the Virunga Mountains on the border between Rwanda and Kenya. The crater lake that lies at its summit is only some 40 m (131 feet) across and the mountain is connected to nearby Gahinga, another dormant volcano, by a narrow saddle. It is not known when Mount Muhabura last erupted, but extensive lava fields were left behind.

The symmetrical cone of Mount Muhabura looms large from a verdant landscape (right).

Kibo is the highest mountain in the Kilimanjaro massif. Its peak is still covered with ice and snow, though the extent of this covering is shrinking visibly.

MOUNT CAMEROON
Cameroon   4,095 m (13,435 feet)

Mount Cameroon, also known as Fako and as Mongo ma Ndemi ("mountain of greatness"), is the highest peak in West Africa. This active volcano in south-western Cameroon lies over a hot spot, a fixed hot area of the Earth's mantle, from which molten magma rises up and is ejected as lava during volcanic eruptions. Mount Cameroon and all the other active volcanoes in Cameroon lie along the track of such a hot spot in the Atlantic.

The summit of Mount Cameroon: small spurs of rock surrounded by fields of ash.

MOUNT BISOKE
**Democratic Republic of the
Congo/Rwanda   3,711 m (12,175 feet)**

The symmetrical volcanic cone of Mount Bisoke lies at the north-eastern extremity of a row of stratovolcanoes at the southern end of the Virunga Mountains on the border between the Democratic Republic of the Congo and Rwanda. The crater lake at the summit is 450 m (1,475 feet) across. The last recorded eruption in 1957 created two small cones on the northern slopes of the volcano, about 11 km (6½ miles) from the summit.

The volcanoes of Mount Bisoke and Mount Karasimbi are connected by a saddle.

MOUNT SABINYO
**Rwanda/Democratic Republic
of the Congo/Uganda
                    3,634 m (11,923 feet)**

Mount Sabinyo, a long since extinct stratovolcano at the eastern end of the Virunga Mountains in the Great Rift Valley, lies where the borders of Rwanda, Uganda, and the Democratic Republic of the Congo converge. A group of endangered mountain gorillas lives on the slopes of Mount Sabinyo, spread between Rwanda's Volcanoes National Park, Uganda's Mgahinga Gorilla National Park, and the DRC's Virunga National Park.

The volcanic massif of Kilimanjaro is the highest mountain on
the African continent. It is composed of three volcanic summits:
Shira (3,962 m/12,999 feet),

Kibo, the highest peak in the massif.

Mawensi (5,148 m/16,890 feet),
and Kibo, whose highest point is
known as Uhuru. Reaching a
height of 5,895 m (19,340 feet), it
is the only peak to have a rater,
which measures nearly 2 km
(1¼ miles) across and in whose
depths there is still volcanic
activity. Steep glaciers cover the
slopes leading down from the
frozen summit to an elevation
of around 4,300 m (14,100 feet).
Kilimanjaro was classified as a
national park in 1971 and a UN-
ESCO World Heritage site in 1987.

A bird's-eye view of the summit of Kilimanjaro.

The caldera on the snow-capped summit of Kilimanjaro.

Tipped with snow, the 5,895-m (19,340-foot) summit of Kilimanjaro rises up between the rivers of the East African savanna, which appears light brown in this image. The circular caldera is clearly visible, as is the belt of green rain and cloud forest surrounding the volcano. Subjected to heavy agricultural use, the region directly below this forested area is slowly eating into the rainforest.

MOUNT NYIRAGONGO
Democratic Republic of the Congo   3,470 m (11,385 feet)

Located near the city of Goma in the east of The Democratic Republic of the Congo, Mount Nyiragongo, another of the eight Virunga volcanoes, is one of Africa's most famous peaks. A mighty eruption began on 17 January 2002, emitting lava that instead of rolling sluggishly downhill like other lava, flowed as fast as water; for those in its way, this often meant that there was no escape. Half a million people had to be evacuated as the lava flowed as far as the built-up area of Goma. Nyiragongo's crater is now about 1 km (½ mile) across and contains a sea of lava, the world's largest, lying about 600 m (1,970 feet) below the lip of the crater.

One of Nyiragongo's frequent eruptions.

Nyiragongo's crater lake.

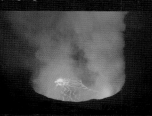
Nyiragongo's sea of lava.

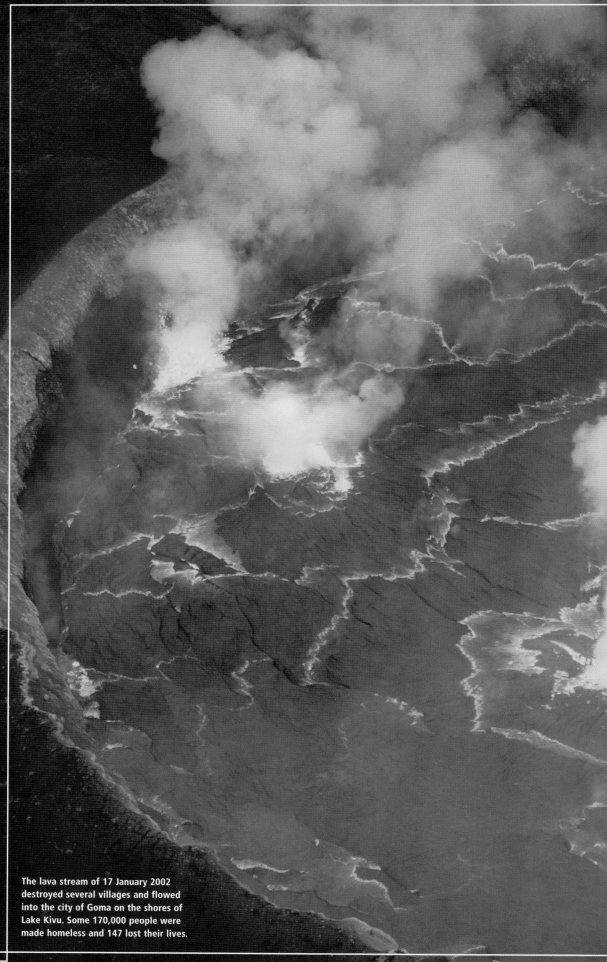
The lava stream of 17 January 2002 destroyed several villages and flowed into the city of Goma on the shores of Lake Kivu. Some 170,000 people were made homeless and 147 lost their lives.

VIRUNGA VOLCANOES

The eight volcanoes making up the Virunga Mountains lie on the Rwandan, Ugandan, and Congolese borders between Lakes Edward and Kivu. Mounts Nyiragongo and Nyamuragira (3,063 m/10,049 feet) lie entirely on Congolese territory. The chain's central group is formed by Mounts Karisimbi (4,507 m/ 14,787 feet), Mikeno (4,437 m/ 14,557 feet), and Bisoke (3,711 m/

Mount Kimanura, erupting.

A colorized satellite photo of the Virunga volcanoes in East Africa.

12,175 feet). Further east lie Mounts Sabinyo (3,634 m/11,923 feet), Gahinga (3,474 m/11,398 feet), and Muhabura (4,127 m/ 13,540 feet). The tropical rainforests on the slopes of the Virunga volcanoes are home to rare mountain gorillas, protected in three national parks.

RÉUNION

Piton des Neiges
3,069 m (10,069 feet)
Piton de la Fournaise
2,632 m (8,635 feet)

Réunion is an overseas department of France located in the Indian Ocean. Piton des Neiges ("Snow Mountain") is the highest point of the island, which was created about two million years ago over a hot spot. One slope of the volcano features a gully about 250 m (820 feet) deep, known as the Trou de Fer (the Iron Hole). Gigantic magma chambers deep within the volcano must have collapsed at some point to form what are now large calderas, knows as "cirques" for their rounded form. In contrast to Piton des Neiges, which became extinct about 12,000 years ago,

The Piton des Neiges stratovolcano.

Piton de la Fournaise is a shield volcano.

Piton de la Fournaise ("Furnace Peak") is much younger, having formed about 380,000 years ago, and is still very active: its main crater collapsed in a violent eruption in 2007.

MADAGASCAR

Ankaizina 2,878 m (9,442 feet)
Ankaratra 2,644 m (8,674 feet)
Itasy 1,800 m (5,905 feet)

The island of Madagascar off the east cost of Mozambique was also created over a hot spot in the Earth's mantle and the volcanoes of Ankaizina, Ankaratra, and Itasy provide the highest points on the island. Ankaizina, a dormant volcano in northern Madagascar, is a cinder cone but features

regular lava flows and several crater lakes. Located in the middle of the island, Ankaratra is now dormant but once ejected the

Fertile fields with Itasy in the background.

wide streams of lava and basalt boulders that cover the broad Ankaratra Plateau (2,300–2,700 m/ 7,550–8,850 feet). This is the most active region of the island and there are regular earthquakes just 20 m (66 feet) beneath the surface. Also located in the middle of the island, Itasy features "hornitos" (low volcanic mounds) and lava flows. Many kinds of geothermal activity can be observed on the shores of Lake Itasy, including hot springs, geysers, and fumaroles.

THE COMOROS

Mount Karthala 2,361 m (7,746 feet)
La Grille 1,087 m (3,566 feet)

The volcano of Mount Karthala towers over the southern end of Grande Comore, the largest of the Comoros, an archipelago lying to the east of Mozambique. La Grille, a considerably smaller volcano, marks the northern end. Mount Karthala has the world's largest active elliptical crater, measuring 4 x 3 km (2½ x 2 miles). It has erupted about 20 times since 1857, including annual eruptions between 2005 and 2007.

Mount Karthala on Grande Comore.

An eruption of the Piton de la Fournaise shield volcano on Réunion, one of the world's most active volcanoes; it has erupted more than 160 times since the 17th century.

As part of the Pacific Ring of Fire, western North America is continually shaken by natural forces in the Earth's interior, as was amply demonstrated by the eruption of Mount St. Helens in 1980.

MOUNT BONA
USA/Alaska   5,005 m (16,420 feet)

The Mount Bona stratovolcano is part of the Saint Elias Mountains in eastern Alaska. Forming the highest section of the Coast Mountains in North America, they run for about 400 km (250 miles) from south-eastern Alaska across Yukon in Canada to the north-western tip of British Columbia. The range represents the watershed between the Yukon River and the Pacific Ocean. The glaciers of the Saint Elias Mountains have a total length of 380 km (236 miles), making them the world's largest contiguous ice field beyond the polar ice caps. At 5,005 m (16,420 feet) Mount Bona is the fifth highest peak in the United States and the highest volcano in North America (not counting the three Mexican volcanoes of Pico de Orizaba, Popocatépetl, and Iztaccíhuatl). As with nearby Mount Churchill, to which it is connected by a saddle, almost the entire surface of Mount Bona is heavily glaciated. The Klutlan Glacier runs for no less than 64 km

MOUNT BLACKBURN
USA/Alaska   4,996 m (16,390 feet)

At 4,996 m (16,390 feet), Mount Blackburn is the highest peak in Alaska's Wrangell Mountains, the second highest volcano in America, and the sixth highest peak in the United States. This heavily eroded stratovolcano is almost entirely covered with ice fields, which feed glaciers such as the Nabesna and the Kuskulana. The mountain was named after Senator Joseph Blackburn from Kentucky.

Looking across the Nabesna Glacier to the mountains in the distance.

MOUNT SANFORD
USA/Alaska   4,949 m (16,237 feet)

The Mount Sanford shield volcano in the Wrangell Mountains is the second highest peak in the chain and boasts one of North America's steepest cliffs: its 1.6-km (1-mile) long southern face is a sheer drop of 2,400 m (7,874 feet), which makes it one of North America's steepest gradients. The volcano last erupted some 320,000 years ago.

Mount Sanford in the Wrangell Mountains.

MOUNT CHURCHILL
USA/Alaska   4,766 m (15,636 feet)

Mount Churchill is best known as the source of the White River Ash, an ash deposit of some 540,000 sq. km (208,500 sq. miles) resulting from two of the most violent volcanic eruptions of the last 2,000 years. The strata in the northern "lobe" date back to an eruption that took place some 1,900 years ago, and those in the eastern "lobe" were deposited about 1,250 years ago, when strong winds blew ash over these extensive areas, leaving a layer more than 60 cm (24 inches) deep in places.

(40 miles), reaching as far as Yukon in Canada, and the Russell Glacier to the north of the chain is of similar dimensions. The volcano was first named in 1897, when Luigi Amadeo from Savoy sighted it during the first ascent of Mount Elias and called it after his ship, the *Bona*. The mountain is still climbed today, with expeditions led by professional guides.

Like the rest of the Elias mountain range, the Mount Bona stratovolcano is heavily glaciated, with fields of ice stretching for great distances down into the valleys (left).

MOUNT RAINIER
USA/Washington
4,395 m (14,419 feet)

The stratovolcano of Mount Rainier, the highest peak in the Cascade Range, which lie south-east of Seattle in Washington state, is surrounded by its eponymous national park. The slopes of the mountain are glaciated above 1,800 m (5,900 feet) but no ice can form on the lip of the crater due to the heat emanating from this active volcano. The last documented eruptions of Mount Rainier took place between 1820 and 1854, but eyewitnesses have suggested that several more took place in the late 19th century.

MOUNT SHASTA
USA/California
4,317 m (14,163 feet)

Mount Shasta, located in northern California, is also part of the Cascade Range. Although still volcanically active, its last eruption took place in 1786. The glaciated summit of Mount Shasta is partly covered by the Whitney Glacier, California's largest ice field. The mountaineer Robert Webb set a world record here in 1998 when he ascended to the summit no less than six times within a 24-hour period, climbing a total of 11,500 m (37,730 feet).

MOUNT WRANGELL
USA/Alaska   4,317 m (14,163 feet)

Mount Wrangell and its eponymous mountain chain lie in south-eastern Alaska on the Canadian border and in the Yukon. Mount Wrangell is the only volcano in the Wrangell volcanic field that has erupted in recorded history, although these were generally small effusions of smoke and ash. The geothermal heat emitted by the mountain has risen sharply since the 1950s, suggesting a future eruption may be likely.

Glenn Highway affords a good view of Mount Wrangell (left).

MOUNT ADAMS
USA/Washington   3,743 m (12,281 feet)

Mount Adams, a stratovolcano in the Cascade Range, is the second highest peak in the Pacific north-western United States after Mount Rainier. Volcanic activity started in this area about 940,000 years ago, since which time Mount Adams has erupted more than 20 times, most recently about 1,000 years ago. The slopes reveal six lava fields, the largest of which was created 4,000 to 7,000 years ago and extended some 10 km (6 miles). The base covers an area of 650 sq. km (251 sq. miles) and the entire mountain has a volume of 350 cu. km (84 cu. miles).

MOUNT HOOD
USA/Oregon   3,425 m (11,237 feet)

The majestic summit of Mount Hood, the highest point in Oregon and the fourth highest peak in the Cascade Range, is located 70 km (43 miles) east of Portland, Oregon. It is considered a potentially active volcano, although no large-scale activity has been recorded since 1820; the last small eruption occurred in 1965. Its glaciers, which could turn into lahars (mudflows) during an eruption, present a constant danger.

Mount Hood reflected in the waters of Trillium Lake at dawn (left).

MOUNT SPURR
USA/Alaska   3,374 m (11,070 feet)

Mount Spurr, a stratovolcano in the Tordrillo Mountains, a subrange of the Alaska Mountains, was created at an elevation of 3,000 m (9,800 feet) in the caldera of an older volcano. Besides its main summit it has a second vent, known as Crater Peak. The main crater has not been active for some 10,000 years, but the secondary vent erupted in 1953 and again in 1992. Ash rained down as far away as Anchorage, 130 km (81 miles) away. The slopes of the mountain are covered in andesite lava fields (flows less readily than balsatic lava).

Mexico's highest peaks lie along the Cordillera Volcánica, whose continuous tectonic movement is the cause of the region's numerous earthquakes and volcanic activity.

PICO DE ORIZABA
Mexico   5,636 m (18,491 feet)

Also known as Citlaltépetl ("star mountain" in the Náhuatl language), Pico de Orizaba is Mexico's highest volcano, as well as being the highest peak in the country. Located in the Cordillera Volcánica between the Mexican states of Veracruz and Puebla, this stratovolcano is one of three volcanoes in Mexico whose summits are perpetually cloaked in ice and snow (the other two are Popocatépetl and Iztaccíhuatl). Although the mountain lies 110 km (68 miles) inland, it can seen from as far away as the Gulf of Mexico. Pico de Orizaba suffered a violent eruption in 1566, but the most recent activity occurred almost 300 years later, in 1846. The volcano has been dormant since then, but an increasing number of fumaroles have been sighted above the crater and this may indicate that a period of renewed activity is imminent, posing a threat to the nearby city of Orizaba, which was damaged in an earthquake in 1973, the worst ever to occur in Veracruz.

POPOCATÉPETL
Mexico   5,462 m (17,920 feet)

Popocatépetl ("smoking mountain" in Náhuatl), Mexico's second highest peak, is one of a pair of volcanoes in the middle of the country, the other being Iztaccíhuatl, its sister peak. Popocatépetl erupted most recently in December 1994, after 50 years of inactivity, and by 2000 a 5-km-high (3-mile) cloud of ash had formed over the crater. The volcano projected a giant cloud of ash and smoke into the atmosphere in December 2007, but the anticipated violent eruption did not occur.

IZTACCÍHUATL
Mexico   5,286 m (17,343 feet)

Volcanic Iztaccíhuatl ("white lady" in Náhuatl), the third highest peak in Mexico, lies about 70 km (43 miles) from Mexico City and on clear days can just be made out from the capital. The mountain's three summits are reminiscent of the head, breasts, and feet of a sleeping woman, and so Mexicans christened it *Mujer dormida* ("sleeping woman"). In contrast to Popocatépetl, Iztaccíhuatl is extinct and has lost much of its characteristic volcanic shape to erosion.

NEVADO DE TOLUCA
Mexico   4,690 m (15,387 feet)

Nevado de Toluca, a stratovolcano located near the city of Toluca in central Mexico, has a 1.5-km-wide (1-mile) caldera at its summit, which is open to the west, and there are two crater lakes at an elevation of about 4,200 m (13,800 feet). The most recent eruption of Nevado de Toluca took place about 10,500 years ago, raining sand and stones onto an area 80 km (50 miles) away where Mexico City now stands. An eruption of similar violence today would threaten the lives of 30 million people.

Popocatépetl, one of central Mexico's twin volcanoes.

One of Nevado de Toluca's two crater lakes.

The crater of Pico de Orizaba (Citlaltépetl), Mexico's highest peak, is about 400 m (1,300 feet) across. The north-western slopes are glaciated above 4,400 m (14,400 feet).

LA MALINCHE
Mexico   4,462 m (14,639 feet)

Also known as Malintzin or the Tlaxcaltec name Matlalcuéyetl, La Malinche is a long-since defunct volcano located in the Parque Nacional Malintzin. This national park covers more than 45,000 ha (111,000 acres) of the south-eastern portion of the Mexican state of Tlaxcala, which lies almost completely surrounded by the state of Puebla in the heart of Mexico. The volcano was named after the historic character Doña Marina – "La Malinche" – the Náhua interpreter and later the mistress of Hernán Cortés, the Spanish conquistador.

COLIMA
Mexico   4,330 m (14,206 feet)

Lying on the border between the states of Colima and Jalisco, Colima is actually two mountains: the older, dormant Nevado de Colima and the more recent Volcán de Colima or Volcán de Fuego, currently the most active volcano in Mexico and in North America, with more than 40 eruptions recorded since 1576. The worst of these took place in 1913, but both 1991 and 2005 witnessed gigantic effusions of ash. The UN regards Colima as one of the world's most dangerous volcanoes.

COFRE DE PEROTE
Mexico   4,282 m (14,049 feet)

Also known as Nauhcampatépetl, (meaning "Mountain of Four Sides" in Náhuatl), the extinct shield volcano of Cofre de Perote is a peak in the Sierra Madre Oriental located on the border between the plateau of the Mexican state of Puebla and the coastal region of Veracruz. The curved dome of Cofre de Perote is vastly different in appearance from the Pico de Orizaba stratovolcano to the south. The summit of Cofre de Perote, which is actually composed of two peaks, is covered with telecommunications pylons.

The slopes of Popocatépetl afford an excellent view of Iztaccíhuatl, the nearest volcano. The hill separating them is the site of one of the many monasteries founded in the region by the Spanish conquistadors.

Volcán de Colima's more recent and more active side.

CASCADE RANGE

The Cascade Range extends for some 1,100 km (680 miles) from British Columbia in Canada in the north down to California in the south, passing through the US states of Washington and Oregon. Its numerous peaks over 3,000 m (9,800 feet) in height are all extinct volcanoes;

Mount St Helens, Washington.

many of these are glaciated, and there are still some signs of volcanic activity. The highest peaks are the summits of Mount Rainier, Mount Shasta, and Mount Adams.

THE HIGHEST VOLCANOES IN THE CASCADE RANGE

❶ Mount Rainier	4,395 m	(14,419 feet)
❷ Mount Shasta	4,317 m	(14,163 feet)
❸ Mount Adams	3,743 m	(12,280 feet)
❹ Mount Hood	3,425 m	(11,237 feet)
❺ Mount Baker	3,285 m	(10,778 feet)
❻ Glacier Peak	3,213 m	(10,541 feet)
❼ Mount Jefferson	3,199 m	(10,495 feet)
❽ Lassen Peak	3,189 m	(10,463 feet)
❾ Mount St Helens	2,549 m	(8,363 feet)

Glaciated Mount Rainier shows some signs of activity.

Mount Adams, a stratovolcano in the Cascades.

Mount Hood, lying beside Trillium Lake, is still potentially active.

Lassen Peak, the world's largest lava dome, above Manzanita Lake.

The snow-capped peak of Mount Shasta bursting through the surrounding cloud layer over northern California. This active stratovolcano is the second highest peak in the Cascade Range.

The tectonic movement of the Andes is far from complete, and slips of the continental plates are accompanied by earthquakes and volcanic eruptions.

MONTE PISSIS
Argentina   6,795 m (22,293 feet)

Lying between the provinces of La Rioja and Catamarca in Argentina, Monte or Cerro Pissis is the third highest peak in continental America and the world's second highest volcano after Ojos del Salado, which is also in the Andes. A GPS survey in 1994 recorded the height of Monte Pissis as 6,882 m (22,579 feet) and suggested that it surpassed Ojos del Salado, but later observations refuted this finding. Towering over the Puna de Atacama plateau, the extinct volcano of Monte Pissis has no less than five main summits and it seems reasonable to assume that the mountain is the most heavily glaciated in the Puna de Atacama, with ice fields including the Pissis Glaicer covering its eastern flank. The slopes most exposed to the constant strong winds are covered with many interesting ice formations; however, the Monte Pissis can muster only a paltry showing of plant and animal life – straggly clumps of grass and a few crickets on the lower slopes.

CERRO BONETE CHICO
Argentina/Chile   6,759 m (22,175 feet)

Cerro Bonete Chico ("Little Bonete"), lying in the Sierra del Veladero in the High Cordillera of the Andes on the border between Argentina and Chile, is South America's fourth highest peak. Cerro Bonete Grande ("Great Bonete"), on the southern slopes of Monte Pissis, is in fact 800 m (2,600 feet) lower than its "little" sister, but its conical shape is maintained across its entire height, whereas Cerro Bonete Chico has only a little cone at its summit.

LLULLAILLACO
Argentina/Chile   6,739 m (22,110 feet)

Situated on the border between Argentina and Chile, Llullaillaco is one of the world's highest volcanoes, and the archeological finds unearthed on its summit are the highest-lying ever discovered. The top of the mountain is usually covered with snow, but Llullaillaco is nonetheless the world's highest unglaciated peak. This now extinct volcano last erupted in 1877, making it the highest volcano that has erupted in recorded history.

TUPUNGATO
Argentina/Chile   6,550 m (21,490 feet)

Although Tupungato, a stratovolcano located on the Chilean-Argentine border about 50 km (31 miles) south of Aconcagua, is one of the tallest peaks in the Andes with a height of 6,550 m (21,490 feet), it is rarely climbed – Aconcagua, the highest mountain in the Andes (and in all South America) is just too close by. A plane that crashed on Tupungato in 1947 remained lost for no less than 50 years, and traces of the wreckage were not found by climbers until 2000.

NEVADO SAJAMA
Bolivia   6,542 m (21,463 feet)

Situated in its eponymous national park on the border between Chile and Bolivia, Nevado Sajama is Bolivia's highest peak. It is located on a plateau in the Altiplano high plains at an elevation of about 4,200 m (13,800 feet), which makes the mountain seem somewhat lower than it actually is. This symmetrical and even-looking stratovolcano has been extinct for at least 25,000 years and its ice-cap obscures any signs of a crater.

Nevado Sajama's snow-white cap towers over the Altiplano (above).

The Cerro Pissis in north-western Argentina is the highest peak in a volcanic massif with five main summits (left).

ILLIMANI
Bolivia   6,462 m (21,201 feet)

With its four summits above 6,000 m (20,000 feet), Illimani is Bolivia's second highest peak and the highest point in the Cordillera Real. Pico del Indio (also known as Pico Sur) is the highest at 6,462 m (21,201 feet). One legend has it that another mountain called Mururata tried to grow larger than Illimani, who then knocked off the newcomer's snow-covered head. This landed 200 km (125 miles) to the west in the form of Sajama.

The snow-capped peaks of the Altiplano in Bolivia (left).

COROPUNA
Peru   6,425 m (21,079 feet)

At 6,425 m (21,079 feet), Coropuna is Peru's highest volcano and its third highest peak overall. Lying approximately 110 km (68 miles) from the Pacific coast, this heavily glaciated shield volcano was created as part of the Cordillera Volcánica in the south of the country between one and three million years ago and was last active in the Holocene period. Coropuna has displayed no signs of life during recorded history and is considered to be dormant, with only a few thermal springs near the volcano suggesting any activity.

There are many volcanoes in the Andes, including one of the world's highest active peaks, Guallatiri in Chile.

PARINACOTA
Chile/Bolivia 6,342 m (20,807 feet)

Situated in the Lauca National Park in the West Cordillera of the Central Andes on the border between Chile and Bolivia, Parinacota forms part of the Atacama Desert and, together with Pomerape, which lies slightly to the north-east, is also part of the Nevados de Payachata complex of volcanoes. Parinacota is extremely popular with climbers and mountaineers, both for its height of 6,342 m (20,807 feet) and the breathtaking scenery, which can be appreciated from its lower slopes as well. In contrast with most of the volcanoes of northern Chile, which are climbed along scree paths, glaciated Parinacota must be approached with an ice axe and crampons. From the summit itself there is a magnificent view of Cordillera Real in Bolivia. The crater on Parinacota's summit is about 700 m (2,300 feet) across and 240 m (790 feet) deep. Fumaroles above the crater hint at volcanic activity within, but the most recent eruption took place a good 500 or 600 years ago.

CHIMBORAZO
Ecuador 6,310 m (20,702 feet)

Chimborazo, an extinct shield volcano located in the West Cordillera of the Andes, is Ecuador's highest peak, and before the Himalayas were surveyed in 1856 it was also thought to be the highest mountain in the world. However, it was later established that it is not even the highest mountain in the Andes. The volcano, which now features a number of icy craters and 16 glaciers, last erupted in about AD 500 or 600.

Chimborazo, seen from Pulingui San Pablo, Ecuador (right).

AMPATO
Peru 6,310 m (20,702 feet)

Rising about 100 km (62 miles) northwest of Arequipa in the Andes of southern Peru, Ampato is part of a 20-km-long (12-mile) chain made up of three large stratovolcanoes: to the north there is the extinct Nevado Hualca Hualca (6,025 m/19,767 feet), in the middle, active Sabancaya (5,976 m/ 19,606 feet), and to the south, dormant Ampato. The discovery of a mummified girl on the summit in 1995 confirmed the suspicions of archeologists and anthropologists that around 500 years ago, the Inca had made human sacrifices here to their gods to ensure rain and thus good harvests.

POMERAPE
Chile/Bolivia 6,288 m (20,630 feet)

Created during the Pleistocene, Pomerape is a conical volcano located in what is now the Lauca National Park in the Atacama Desert on the border between Chile and Bolivia. Together with Parinacota, it forms the Nevados de Payachata ("twins") volcano complex. Both mountains are easily accessible and relatively easy climbs, making them very popular with mountaineers. Lago Chungará, one of the highest-lying lakes in the world, lies nearby at an elevation of 4,520 m (14,829 feet). The surrounding Lauca National Park is home to flamingos, vicuñas, alpacas, and even Andean condors.

From Lago Chungará there is a magnificent view of the glaciated peak of Parinacota volcano as it towers over the Atacama Desert.

Llamas grazing beside Lago Chungará in Chile's Lauca National Park.

GUALLATIRI
Chile   6,071 m (19,918 feet)

Rising majestically above the Lauca National Park in northern Chile, not far from the Bolivian border, Guallatiri is one of the most active volcanoes to be found in the Andes. At 6,071 m (19,918 feet), with a summit perennially cloaked in ice and snow, it is also one of the world's highest active volcanoes – this symmetrical stratovolcano last exploded as recently as 1960. Extensive areas of the northern and western slopes of the volcano are covered in ancient or more recent lava beds, while the active vent of the mountain is to be found on its southern face.

ACOTANGO
Chile   6, 052 m (19,856 feet)

Acotango is a stratovolcano located on the Chilean-Bolivian border and, along with Humarata and Capurata, part of the Nevados de Quimsachata ("three brothers") volcano group. Although heavily eroded, Acotango is the highest peak in the group and is still considered active, although its most violent volcanic period was probably 10,000 years ago. Acotango is thought to have been created during the Holocene. A glacier on the southern face of the volcano could present a danger during any eruption, as meltwater would cause flooding and mudflows.

ACAMARACHI
Chile   6,046 m (19,836 feet)

Also known as Cerro Pili, Acamarachi is a stratovolcano located on the Puna de Atacama plateau in northern Chile. Its crater contains a lake which, though only about 10 m (33 feet) across, is the second highest lake in South America and the second highest crater lake in the world (after the one in the Ojos del Salado crater). The volcano's slopes reach an angle of 45 degrees in many places and there is a lava dome located on Acamarachi's northern face. Discoveries of metal and fabrics suggest that the Inca considered the volcano to be a holy place.

HUALCA HUALCA
Peru   6,025 m (19,767 feet)

Hualca Hualca is not the tallest of the Ampato group peaks in the southern Peruvian Alps – Ampato is approximately 300 m (990 feet) higher – but of the three volcanoes it has the greatest bulk. The entire volcano group is situated in the Cañón del Colca, one of the world's deepest valleys. Hualca Hualca possesses a large, uneven platform summit with a number of peaks, including an imposing rocky column at the top of which has been found an altar together with traces of sacrifices made by the Cabana Indians; the tribe considered the mountain sacred to their gods.

ANDES

The illustration shows a section of
the Central Andes' West Cordillera on
the border between Chile and Bolivia.
Almost all of these stratovolcano
summits are covered with snow,
revealing the north-south axis of the
Cordillera. The bright white areas are
salt lakes (*salare*), evidence of the
region's extreme aridity. The largest
salt lake is the Salar de Ascotán in
the left half of the image. The
5,000–6,000-m (16,400–19,700-foot)
peaks fall away in the upper right of
the image to the Altiplano. This
almost uninhabited steppe region is
known as the Gran Pampa Pelada.

A salt-lake, known as a *salar*, in the Atacama Desert, with a chain of snow-capped volcanoes in the background.

ANTARCTICA

East of the Transantarctic Mountains, a fold belt formed 450 million years ago at the edge of the Antarctic Plate, is a region of volcanoes and seismic activity extending all the way from

A plume of smoke escapes Mount Erebus.

Ellsworth Land to the Scotia Arc. This rugged chain reached its highest points in Mounts Kirkpatrick (4,528 m/14,856 feet) and Markham (4,602 m/15,098 feet) beside the Ross Sea before falling away sharply to the coastline. Mount Erebus (3,794 m/ 12,448 feet), the highest still active volcano on this cold continent, is situated on an island in the Ross ice shelf where the Transantarctic Mountains enter Victorialand.

THE HIGHEST VOLCANOES IN ANTARCTICA

❶	Mount Erebus	3,794 m (12,448 feet)
❷	Mount Frakes	3,654 m (11,988 feet)
❸	Toney Mountain	3,595 m (11,795 feet)
❹	Mount Berlin	3,478 m (11,411 feet)
❺	Mount Takahe	3,460 m (11,352 feet)
❻	Mount Siple	3,396 m (11,142 feet)
❼	Royal Society Volcano	3,000 m (9,843 feet)
❽	Mount Andrus	2,978 m (9,770 feet)
❾	Mount Melbourne	2,732 m (8,963 feet)
❿	Mount Morning	2,723 m (8,934 feet)

Steam rising from a column of ice above the "Sauna Cave", 3,550 m (11,700 feet) above sea level on Mount Erebus. The heat of the magma within the volcano melts snow and ice beneath the ice columns to form tunnels and caves. As the air temperature is usually below −30°C (−22°F), the steam freezes to form towers of ice.

Mount Erebus, the world's southernmost active volcano, casts a long shadow across the Ross Sea.

The Greek island of Santorini in the Aegean Sea was the setting for a devastating volcanic eruption in 1630 BC. The most recent calculations suggest that the eruption would have reached a seven on the Volcanic Explosivity Index, which runs from zero to eight; an explosion of such intensity would be expected to occur only once in 1,000 years.

THE GREATEST VOLCANIC ERUPTIONS IN HISTORY

THE GREATEST VOLCANIC ERUPTIONS OF THE PRE-CHRISTIAN ERA:

1. **La Garita Caldera** — 27 million years ago
   Colorado, USA
2. **Bruneau-Jarbidge** — 11 million years ago
   Idaho, USA
3. **Yellowstone** — 2.2 million years ago
   Wyoming, USA
4. **Yellowstone** — 1.2 million years ago
   Wyoming, USA
5. **Valle Grande** — 1.1 million years ago
   New Mexico, USA
6. **Long Valley Caldera** — 760,000 years ago
   California, USA
7. **Yellowstone** — 640,000 years ago
   Wyoming, USA
8. **Mount Aso** — 30,000–80,000 years ago
   Kyushu, Japan
9. **Lake Toba** — 75,000 years ago
   Sumatra, Indonesia
10. **Campi Flegrei** — 35,000 years ago
    Campania, Italy
11. **Lake Taupo** — 22,600 years ago
    North Island, New Zealand
12. **Aira Caldera** — 22,000 years ago
    Kyushu, Japan
13. **Kurile Lake** — c.5700
    Kamchatka, Russia
14. **Mount Mazama** — c.4900
    Oregon, USA
15. **Kikai Caldera** — c.4300
    Ryukyu Islands, Japan
16. **Santorini** — c.1630 (BC)
    Cyclades, Greece

THE GREATEST VOLCANIC ERUPTIONS OF THE CHRISTIAN ERA:

1. **Ambrym** — (AD) 50
   Vanuatu
2. **Vesuvius** — 79
   Campania, Italy
3. **Lake Taupo** — 181
   North Island, New Zealand
4. **Eldgjá** — 936
   Iceland
5. **Baitoushan/Paektusan** — 1050
   China/Korea
6. **Etna** — 1169
   Sicily, Italy
7. **Kuwae** — 1453
   Vanuatu
8. **Vesuvius** — 1631
   Campania, Italy
9. **Etna** — 1669
   Sicily, Italy
10. **Lanzarote** — 1730–1736
    Canary Islands, Atlantic
11. **Laki/Lakagígar** — 1783–1784
    Iceland
12. **Tambora** — 1815
    Sumbawa, Indonesia
13. **Krakatoa** — 1883
    Indonesia
14. **Santa Maria** — 1902
    Guatemala
15. **Mount St Helens** — 1980
    Oregon, USA
16. **Montserrat** — 2005
    Caribbean

The effects of tectonic forces are felt most intensely at the edges of plates, where they also distort the Earth's crust the most violently. Volcanoes can destroy entire islands and choke whole landscapes with lava, fire, ash, and smoke. Huge

Crater Lake in volcanic Mount Mazama, Oregon.

eruptions which took place more than 100,000 years ago formed vast volcanic landscapes whose dimensions can only really be appreciated from satellite photographs. Some mountains which are known to be volcanic are active, while many are dormant – at least for the time being. The majority of the most active volcanoes – cracks and vents along mid-ocean ridges – lie beneath the surface of the sea and have not even been named yet, although gas and lava constantly flow from them.

VOLCANIC ERUPTIONS

People have settled near volcanoes since time immemorial. The inhabitants of such towns and villages are aware of the danger, but of course are hoping that the volcano on their doorstep is not going to erupt; however, a calm façade is often deceptive. Even volcanoes which have not erupted for a thousand years can explode at a moment's notice. There are about 550 active volcanoes on the Earth's surface, of which the most famous are Mounts Vesuvius and Etna in Italy, Pinatubo in the Philippines and Mount St Helens in the USA, all of whose eruptions have laid waste to whole landscapes and claimed many lives.

THE GREATEST VOLCANIC ERUPTIONS OF RECENT TIMES

❶ **Santa Maria** 1902
Guatemala
❷ **Mount Pelée** 1902
Martinique
❸ **Novarupta** 1912
Alaska Peninsula
❹ **Kelud** 1919
Java, Indonesia
❺ **Gunung Agung** 1963
Bali, Indonesia
❻ **Surtsey** 1963
Iceland
❼ **Eldfell** 1973
Iceland
❽ **Mount Nyiragongo** 1977
Zaire
❾ **Mount St Helens** 1980
Oregon, USA
❿ **Nevado del Ruiz** 1985
Colombia
⓫ **Mount Pinatubo** 1991
Philippines
⓬ **Cerro Hudson** 1991
Chile
⓭ **Montserrat** 1997/2005
Caribbean
⓮ **Tungurahua** 2000–2006
Ecuador

Vesuvius 1944

Gunung Agung 1963

Mount St Helens 1980

Mount Pinatubo 1991

Montserrat 2005

Mount Pinatubo on the Philippines island of Luzon erupted in June 1991. After 600 years of peace it once again began to emit a cloud of ash and gas with repercussions felt across the whole world. The eruption claimed some 1,000 lives.

VALLEYS AND CANYONS

Valleys are, as a rule, long depressions in the landscape which have been formed in rock either by the erosive power of rivers and weathering or through the creation of fissures on fault lines. A distinction is drawn between three valley types: tapering, V- and U-shaped

One of Europe's longest gorges: Samariá Gorge on the Greek island of Crete, which is 16 km (10 miles) long.

valleys, with their narrow valley floors; rift valleys, which cut through mountain ranges; and dry valleys, which flood only after heavy rainfall. Gorges and canyons are usually narrow valleys, and a canyon can be defined as a deep, narrow valley cut into more or less horizontal rock strata with graduated valley sides.

Large image: a boat crossing the green waters of Lake Powell in Glen Canyon in Arizona, USA, surrounded by striking red-and-white rock formations.

THE WORLD'S DEEPEST VALLEYS AND CANYONS

1 Kali Gandaki Gorge
Nepal   5,600 m (18,400 feet)

2 Yarlung Zangbo Grand Canyon
China/Tibet   5,382 m (17,657 feet)

3 Hutiao Xia (Tiger Leaping Gorge)
China   3,900 m (12,795 feet)

4 Cañón del Colca
Peru   3,269 m (10,725 feet)

5 Hells Canyon
USA   2,438 m (7,999 feet)

6 Great Gorge
USA   2,400 m (7,900 feet)

7 Barranca del Cobre
Mexico   1,870 m (6,135 feet)

8 Grand Canyon
USA   1,800 m (5,900 feet)

9 Tara Gorge
Montenegro   1,300 m (4,270 feet)

10 Yangtze Gorges
China   1,200 m (4,000 feet)

11 Yosemite Valley
USA   1,200 m (4,000 feet)

12 Vikos Gorge
Greece   1,000 m (3,280 feet)

13 Marble Canyon
USA   1,000 m (3,280 feet)

14 Blyde River Canyon
South Africa   800 m (2,600 feet)

15 Zion Canyon
USA   800 m (2,600 feet)

16 Grand Canyon du Verdon
France   700 m (2,300 feet)

17 Dead Horse Point
USA   600 m (1,970 feet)

18 Black Canyon
USA   555 m (1,821 feet)

KALI GANDAKI GORGE/
YARLUNG ZANGBO GRAND CANYON

The deepest valleys are to be found near the world's highest mountains, in Nepal and Tibet.

KALI GANDAKI GORGE
Nepal   **5,600m (18,400 feet)**

The Kali Gandaki Gorge, which runs between the 8,000-m-plus (26,250-foot) peaks of Dhaulagiri to the west and Annapurna to the east in the Himalayas of Nepal, is the deepest gorge in the world. In the section between the two mountains, the river runs between 1,300 and 2,600 m (4,300–8,550 feet) above sea level but some 5,500–6,800 m (18,000–22,300 feet) lower than the respective summits. The gorge stretches south from the village of Kegbeni, reaching its deepest point at Lete before broadening as it continues to the town of Beni. The gorge, which lies within the Annapurna Conservation Area, has been used as a trade route for centuries. More recently it has become a popular trekking trail which is part of the Annapurna Round Trek. The Gandaki River is older than the Himalayas themselves, and when tectonic activity forged the mountains millions of years ago, the river found a new course through the mountain landscape.

YARLUNG ZANGBO GRAND CANYON
China/Tibet   **5,382 m (17,657 feet)**

Rising at Mount Kailash, the Yarlung Zangbo River flows east for some 1,700 km (1,050 miles), drain-

The upper reaches of the Brahmaputra.

ing a region of the northern Himalayas before reaching this narrow gorge near Pe in Tibet. The Yarlung Zangbo Grand Canyon carves an arc around the 7,775-m (25,509-foot) peak of Namcha Barwa in the eastern Himalayas, and the river follows a precipitous descent through the gorge: from the beginning to the end of the valley it drops some 3,000 m (9,800 feet) to just 300 (990 feet) above sea level. After leaving the valley, the river eventually reaches Arunachal Pradesh in India, where it is renamed the Brahmaputra. In April 1994, a Chinese news agency declared the Yarlung Zangbo Grand Canyon, which had just been surveyed for the first time, to be the world's deepest river valley, deeper even than the Kali Gandaki Gorge in Nepal. It is certainly one of the world's most spectacular, if also most inaccessible, gorges, and its unique animal and plant life is still to be properly researched.

A hiker views the summit of Gyala Peri from the Yarlung Zangbo Grand Canyon.

The Kali Gandaki has cut a channel between the summits of Dhaulagiri (8,167 m/26,795 feet) and Annapurna I (8,091 m/26,545 feet).

HUTIAO XIA
China   3,900 m (12,795 m)

Hutiao Xia (Tiger Leaping Gorge), which the Yangtze River has carved for more than 15 km (9 miles) through south-western China, is only 30 m (100 feet) wide at its narrowest point. The name is derived from a legend which recounts how a tiger jumped across here when pursued by hunters. The river runs between Jade Dragon Snow Mountain (5,596 m/18,360 feet) and Haba Xueshan (5,396 m/ 17,703 feet) as it crashes down a series of rapids flanked by 2,000-m (6,600-foot) high cliffs, dropping 170 m (558 feet) as it travels 15 km (9 miles). Four canoeists who set off to negotiate the valley in 1980 were never seen again, and even though an expedition successfully negotiated it in 1986, the gorge is considered impassable.

White water in the Hutiao Xia.

The rugged peaks of Yunnan province can reach heights of 2,000 m (6,600 feet). The Yangtze River has carved its way between them, creating the Hutiao Xia, one the world's longest, deepest, and narrowest gorges.

COLORADO RIVER CANYONS –
THE WORLD'S LARGEST VALLEY COMPLEX

The world's largest valley complex by area is located on the Colorado Plateau in the south-western United States. The erosive power of a number of watercourses, but principally the Colorado River, has hollowed out a giant system of canyons.

BLACK CANYON OF THE GUNNISON
555 m (1,821 feet)

The Colorado Plateau covers an impressive area of 112,000 sq. km (43,000 sq. miles), which is distributed between the US states of Arizona, Utah, Colorado, and New Mexico. Mountain rivers have etched impressive valleys into the highlands, and the unique landscape of the Black Canyon of the Gunnison is the work of the Gunnison River, a tributary of the Colorado River, as it wore down the hard local gneiss. The canyon is so narrow that only very little sunlight can penetrate through to the valley floor, making its rocky walls appear particularly dark and bringing the canyon its name. The vertical drop reaches 555 m (1,821 feet) at Chasm Overlook and the canyon edges lie 345 m (1,132 feet) apart. The Gunnison River drops 18 m per km (95 feet per mile) and in one particularly vertiginous section drops at a rate of no less than 50 m per km (264 feet per mile), roaring at great speed through the canyon.

CANYONLANDS DEAD HORSE POINT
600 m (1,970 feet)

The Colorado and Green Rivers have carved deep gullies in the Canyonlands Plateau in Utah. This delightful area, which was declared a national park in 1964, is divided into four

sections, each with its own signature rock formations: the "Island in the Sky" to the north, "The Needles" to the south-east, "The Maze" to the west, and the little "Horseshoe Canyon" to the west.

The Green River winds its way through the rugged plateau.

GLEN CANYON LAKE POWELL
170 m (560 feet)

Lake Powell, which was created on the Utah-Arizona border when the progress of the Colorado River was blocked by the Glen Canyon Dam, is the United States' second largest manmade reservoir after Lake Mead in Nevada. The Colorado River was dammed on the east side of the Grand Canyon in the 1960s and this had been extended to include Lake Powell by 1980. The lake's 33 billion cubic meters (1,170 billion cu. feet) of water has flooded a total of 96 canyons and its coastline of 3,153 km (1,959 miles) is longer than that of the entire western seaboard of the United States. Rainbow Bridge, the world's largest natural stone bridge with a span of 82 m (269 feet) and a height of 88 m (289 feet), is located in a nearby canyon.

The last rays of the setting sun play across a bend in Glen Canyon.

No other canyon in North America offers such a heady mix of narrow entrances, steep walls, and vertiginously deep gorges as the Black Canyon of the Gunnison in Colorado.

MARBLE CANYON
HORSESHOE BEND
1,000 m (3,280 feet)

Marble Canyon in northern Arizona marks the beginning of the Grand Canyon. The largest dam ever built on the river was to be constructed here at the confluence of the Colorado and Little Colorado Rivers, but opposition led to the project's abandonment in 1968. A little further away, downstream from Glen Canyon and about 6 km (4 miles) south of the city of Page, is a spectacular bend in the Colorado River named Horseshoe Bend.

The Colorado River flowing through Marble Canyon (above) and the view from the sandstone cliffs of Horseshoe Bend (left).

GRAND CANYON
1,800 m (5,900 feet)

The Colorado River's most famous canyon is without doubt the Grand Canyon in northern Arizona. Over the course of millions of years, the river has cut a spectacular deep rift valley through the Colorado Plateau, exposing red sedimentary rock and strata of granite in its lowest reaches. The upper levels of the canyon are stepped, reflecting the differential resistance of the strata of sandstone and limestone. Reaching a length of approximately 446 km (277 miles), a depth of some 1,800 m (5,900 feet), and a width that varies between 6 and 29 km (4 to 18 miles), the Grand Canyon is not only a breathtaking sight but also a fascinating lesson in geological history. The surrounding hills feature dry forest and the plateau itself is covered with steppe vegetation.

The gorges of the Grand Canyon seen from the South Rim.

The deepest valley in the Alps is located in the Provence region of France in the far south-west of the range, an area which feels a lot closer to the sea than the mountains. The Grand Canyon du Verdon is about 25 km (15 miles) long and

The Grand Canyon du Verdon in Provence.

reaches depths of up to 700 m (2,300 feet). Its steep rocky cliffs and turquoise waters have made it one of Europe's most famous natural tourist attractions. The limestone plateaus through which the Verdon has cut a path are marine deposits laid down between 80 and 200 million years ago.

West of Castellane, the little Verdon River flows between towering rocky cliffs which at certain points at their bases are barely 6 m (20 feet) apart.

THE THREE GORGES OF THE YANGTZE RIVER

Boats negotiating Xiling Gorge.

Dawn over Wu Gorge.

The Yangtze twists and turns through the 44-km-long (27-mile) Wu Gorge on the border of Sichuan and Hubei provinces in Central China.

Several other rivers flow into the Yangtze in the Sichuan Basin, broadening it and increasing its flow until it breaks out of the Daba Mountains into the famous Sanxia, or Three Gorges – Qutang, Wu, and Xiling. These three river valleys have an aggregate length of 204 km (127 miles) and a drop of 120 m (394 feet). The surrounding cliffs can reach heights of between 500 and 1,000 m (1,640–3,280 feet). The shortest and narrowest of the three gorges is the Qutang, with its particularly charming scenery. Wu Gorge ("Witch Gorge") is 44 km (27 miles) long and is lined by the "Twelve Sisters"; legend has it that the goddess Jao Ji and her eleven sisters defeated an evil river dragon and were subsequently turned to stone so that they could guide ships down the river. The longest of the Three Gorges is Xiling at 66 km (41 miles), although at its narrowest point it is only 80 m (260 feet) wide. The controversial Three Gorges dam, completed in 2006, is one of the world's largest.

At 8 km (5 miles), Qutang is the shortest
and the narrowest of the three Yangtze
River Gorges, and is also considered the
most beautiful, not least because of its
steep and extremely high cliffs.

KINGS CANYON
Australia

Kings Canyon is located in the Watarrka National Park in the Northern Territory, and its 300-m-deep (990-foot) red, yellow, and white sandstone cliffs look like they have been carved with a knife. Erosion has created rounded rock formations at other locations, however, and the "Lost City", a collection of sandstone domes which resemble derelict houses, is not far away on the plateau.

The canyon floor contains a water hole known as the "Garden of Eden", named because so many rare, sub-tropical plants grow in its vicinity.

PURNULULU CANYONS
Australia

The Purnululu National Park rises to a height of more than 200 m (660 feet) above the surrounding plains. The entire area is crisscrossed with deep canyons, some of which have extremely steep sides; Echidna Chasm, Cathedral Gorge, and Piccaninny Gorge are among the most spectacular.

The beehive-like formations of the Bungle Bungle Range at Piccaninny Creek in Western Australia were a well-kept secret between scientists and the local population until the 1980s; the area has been a national park since 1987.

Blyde River Canyon forms part of the transition zone between the Lowveld, the South African lowlands, and the Highveld, which lies about 1,000 m (3,300 feet) higher. The transformation is particularly dramatic here, with the cliffs of the Drakensberg rising almost vertically from the plains below.

Green vegetation and red sandstone: Blyde River Canyon in the northern reaches of the Drakensberg, South Africa.

BLYDE RIVER CANYON

The Drakensberg is a mountain chain rising a few hundred kilometers east of Johannesburg and extending from Lesotho to Limpopo province. The Blyde River Canyon is a broad and wide red sandstone gorge in the chain's northern reaches, beginning at Bourke's Luck Potholes and continuing for about 26 km (16 miles). Its sheer sides present a vertical drop of up to 800 m (2,600 feet) down to the River Blyde below, which flows along the valley bottom past mighty, free-standing rock formations. The most spectacular of these are the three *rondavels* ("round huts"), almost perfectly circular rock formations with pointed spires, which closely resemble the huts of the local population.

FISH RIVER CANYON

At 650 km (404 miles) in length, the Fish River, which has been known to dry up completely, is the longest river in Namibia and one of the country's eight watery zones. It rises in the Naukluft Mountains and flows into the Oranje River south-west of Ai-Ais. The lower reaches of the river flow between

Erosion features in Fish River Canyon.

the 550-m-high (1,800-foot) walls of the Fish-River Canyon for some 150 km (90 miles). The canyon is the second largest in the world after the Grand Canyon and was created during a particularly wet period some 500 million years ago. The canyon is not just a result of erosion, however – movements of the Earth's crust have created a fault in the valley floor.

GRAND CANYON
BARRANCA DEL COBRE

GRAND CANYON
USA   1,800 m (5,900 feet)

In 1540, the Spaniard López de Cárdenas became the first European to glimpse the magnificent panorama of the Grand Canyon, but the area was not properly surveyed until the

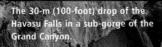

The 30-m (100-foot) drop of the Havasu Falls in a sub-gorge of the Grand Canyon.

mid-19th century and its geological history has still not been properly researched. It is assumed that the river began to find a route through the rocky plateau about six million years ago, creating, over the course of time, the unique valley which the naturalist John Muir said was "the greatest of all God's places on earth". Wind and weather have played their part in carving bizarre formations from the cliff faces and the easily discernible rock strata are a record of various periods in Earth's geological history; fossils found here have revealed much about prehistoric life.

The Colorado River winds through the world's most famous canyon like a silver ribbon. The steep canyon sides feature cliffs, promontories, and platforms, and are punctuated by subgorges to either side. The rock strata can take on varying coloration, depending on the positions of the observer and of the sun.

BARRANCA DEL COBRE

Mexico   1,870 m (6,135 feet)

The Barranca del Cobre ("Copper Gorge") is a rock formation located in the Sierra Madre Occidental in the Mexican state of Chihuahua. The gorge complex worn away by the Río Urique and its tributaries extends for almost 30,000 sq. km (11,500 sq. miles) and is about 50 km (31 miles) long. It is one of the largest and most rugged gorge complexes in North America – the individual valleys, which can reach widths of 1,500 m (4,900 feet), fall away vertically to depths of 1,870 m (6,135 feet). The six deepest valleys in the Barranca del Cobre are:

Urique Canyon	1,870 m (6,135 feet)
Sinforosa Canyon	1,830 m (6,003 feet)
Batopilas Canyon	1,799 m (5,902 feet)
Copper Canyon	1,759 m (5,771 feet)
Tararecua Canyon	1,425 m (4,675 feet)
Oteros Canyon	983 m (3,225 feet)

Vertical, copper-hued cliffs tower majestically over the gorge complex.

CAÑÓN DEL COLCA
Peru   3,269 m (10,725 feet)

The scenery surrounding the Cañón del Colca near Chivay in southern Peru is a stunning sight. The Colca River has dug a 3,269-m (10,725-foot) deep gouge into the landscape – twice as deep as the Colorado River in the Grand Canyon.

The majestic Cañón del Colca.

Parts of the Cañón del Colca are habitable and the local farmers still tend terraces laid out by the Inca; the canyon is even named after the granaries (*colcas*) that the Inca excavated in the sides of the cliffs. The morning thermal winds at Cruz del Condor, located between Cabanaconde and Chivay, allow Andean condors, with wing-spans that can reach 2–3 m (6–10 feet), to glide along beside the valley walls; the clifftops of the Cañón del Colca lie about 1,200 m (4,000 feet) above the valley floor here.

Cactuses growing on a mountain slope
in the Cañón del Colca. Ichu, an Alpine
grass favored by vicuñas, llamas, and
alpacas, also manages to flourish here.

CAVES

The science of speleology exclusively defines caves as naturally created underground spaces with a length of at least 5 m (16 feet). The definition draws a distinction between primary caves, which are created at the same time as the rock surrounding them, and

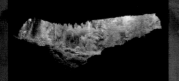

Honeycomb Hill Cave, New Zealand.

secondary caves, which are created at a later date by erosion or tectonic activity. Some of the most beautiful caves are those with the sometimes bizarre stalagmite and stalactite formations, and the images on these pages show just a few of the most spectacular.

THE WORLD'S LARGEST CAVES

❶ Mammoth Cave		590 km
Kentucky, USA		(367 miles)
❷ Jewel Cave		233 km
South Dakota, USA		(145 miles)
❸ Optimisticheskaya		
Cave		230 km
Ukraine		(143 miles)
❹ Wind Cave		211 km
South Dakota, USA		(131 miles)
❺ Carlsbad Caverns		203 km
New Mexico, USA		(126 miles)
❻ Hölloch Cave		194 km
Switzerland		(121 miles)
❼ Fisher Ridge Cave		
System		180 km
Kentucky, USA		(112 miles)
❽ Sistema Ox Bel Ha		177 km
Mexico		(110 miles)
❾ Gua Air Jernih		175 km
Malaysia		(109 miles)
❿ Sistema Sac Actun		159 km
Mexico		(99 miles)

EUROPE'S LARGEST CAVES

Postojna Cave, Slovenia.

❶ Optimisticheskaya Cave		
Ukraine	230 km (143 miles)
❷ Hölloch Cave		
Switzerland	194 km (121 miles)
❸ Siebenhengste-Hohgant Cave		
Switzerland	154 km (96 miles)
❹ Schönberg Cave System		
Austria	128 km (80 miles)
❺ Ozernaya Cave		
Ukraine	123 km (76 miles)
❻ Ojo Guareña Caves		
Spain	110 km (68 miles)

ASIA'S LARGEST CAVES

Hang Sung Sot Cave, Vietnam.

❶ Gua Air Jernih (Gunung Mulu National Park)	
Malaysia	175 km (109 miles)
❷ Shuanghe Dongqun	
China	119 km (74 miles)
❸ Teng Long Dong Caves	
China	59 km (37 miles)
❹ Bol'shaya Oreshnaya Cave	
Russia	58 km (36 miles)
❺ Kap-Kutan/Promezhutochnaja	
Turkmenistan	57 km (35 miles)

AUSTRALIA/OCEANIA'S LARGEST CAVES

Waitomo Cave, New Zealand.

❶ Bullita Cave System (Burke's Back Yard)	
Australia	105 km (65 miles)
❷ Mamo Kananda	
Papua New Guinea	54 km (34 miles)
❸ Bulmer Caverns	
New Zealand	52 km (32 miles)
❹ Atea Kananda	
Papua New Guinea	34 km (21 miles)
❺ Exhale Air/Tomo Thyme	
New Zealand	32 km (20 miles)
❻ Old Homestead Cave	
Australia	28 km (17 miles)

NORTH AND CENTRAL AMERICA'S LARGEST CAVES

Lehman Caves, Nevada.

❶ **Mammoth Cave**
Kentucky, USA   590 km (367 miles)

❷ **Jewel Cave**
South Dakota, USA   233 km
(145 miles)

❸ **Wind Cave**
South Dakota, USA   211 km
(131 miles)

❹ **Carlsbad Caverns**
New Mexico, USA   203 km
(126 miles)

❺ **Fisher Ridge Cave System**
Kentucky, USA   180 km (112 miles)

❻ **Sistema Ox Bel Ha**
Mexico   177 km (110 miles)

❼ **Sistema Sac Actun**
Mexico   159 km (99 miles)

AFRICA'S LARGEST CAVES

Cango Cave system, South Africa.

❶ **Sof Omar Caves**
Ethiopia   15 km (9 miles)

❷ **Cango Caves**
South Africa   4 km (2½ miles)

❸ **Arnhem Cave**
Namibia   4 km (2½ miles)

SOUTH AMERICA'S LARGEST CAVES

Caverna do Diabo.

❶ **Toca da Boa Vista**
Brazil   102 km (63 miles)

❷ **Toca da Barriguda**
Brazil   30 km (19 miles)

Ludi Yan, the "Reed Flute Cave" is situated north-west of the city of Guilin in the southern Chinese province of Guangxi. With its bizarrely shaped stalagmites and stalactites it is one of the world's most striking caves. The "Crystal Palace of the Dragon King" grotto is extensive enough to accommodate nearly a thousand visitors.

Mammoth Cave, which reaches an average depth of 115.5 m (379 feet) and has an aggregate length of 590 km (367 miles), is the world's largest and most convoluted cave system. Its passages lead visitors into a world of bizarre limestone formations which have been created over

A cave formation in the Drapery Room of the Mammoth Cave.

millions of years by the steady dripping of water from the porous rock. These giant chambers with their striking stalactites, stalagmites, and crystallized layers of gypsum were created more than 300 million years ago during the Carboniferous period, when water seeped through a porous layer of sandstone into the limestone strata beneath. Chemical processes created hollow spaces which dried out when the water table dropped, allowing subsequent dripping water to deposit its mineral content and create columnar limestone formations. Home to such strange animals as the eyeless cave fish, cave crickets, and the Kentucky cave shrimp, the caves have also become an important refuge for several endangered species of bat. The cave system's name derives from the outsize dimensions of its individual chambers and cavities, and not from the prehistoric animal.

The speleologist's flashlight reveals
the full variety of the Mammoth Cave's
underground scenery.

Carlsbad Caverns National Park
in the US state of New Mexico
is world-renowned for the
beautiful formations in its
spectacular caves. The cave

Stalactites against a blue "sky".

Researchers brave the Yo Acres Caves.

system also forms one of the
world's largest underground
spaces: the floor of the Big
Room covers 52,000 sq. m
(560,000 sq. feet). The Selenite
Chandelier Chamber in the
Carlsbad Caverns is decorated
with translucent white "crystal
chandeliers" made of selenite,
and the Bat Cave is indeed
home to an astonishing number of these small flying mammals, which hang in crowds
from the ceiling during the day.

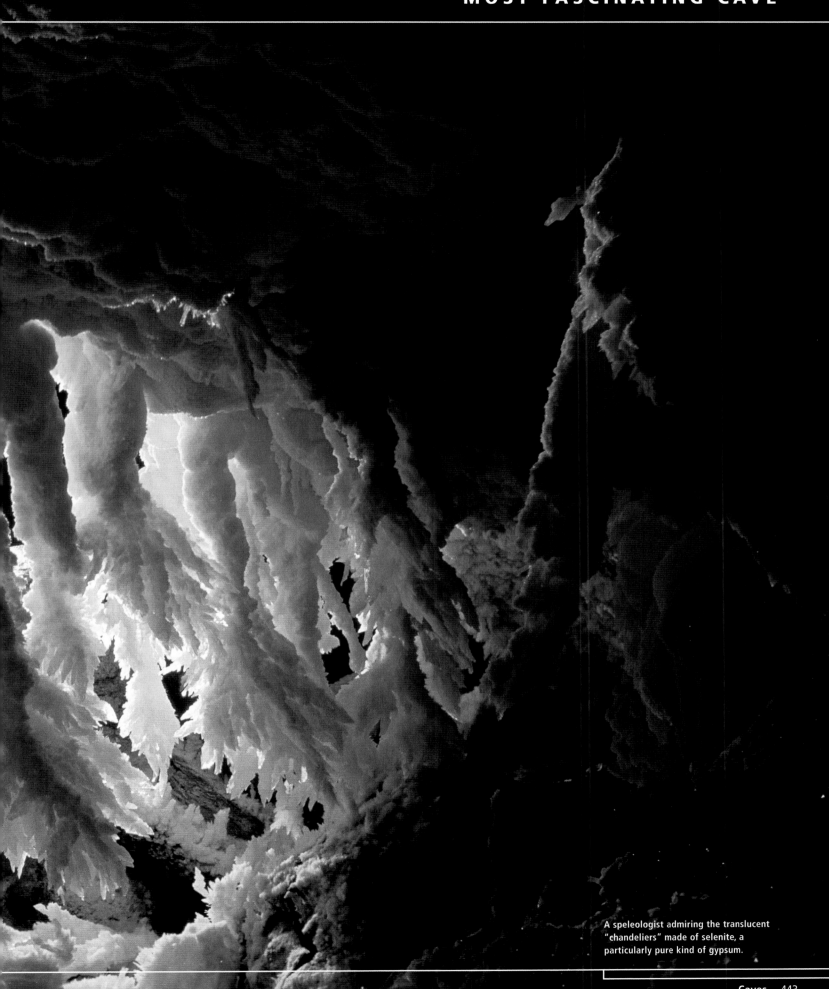

"chandeliers" made of selenite, a
particularly pure kind of gypsum.

A speleologist admiring the translucent

ICE FIELDS AND GLACIERS

During the most recent period of glaciation of the last ice age, known as the Würm or Vistulian glacial period, large parts of northern Europe were covered with a sheet of ice originating in Finland and Scandinavia, and the Alps lay beneath a mighty cap of ice. However, these ice

San Rafael Glacier, Patagonia.

caps and sheets have been retreating for the last 10,000 years, and, unlike glaciers, whose direction of flow is usually determined by the surrounding landscape, they simply roll over and shape the geological relief beneath them. The two mightiest ice sheets currently cover the world's largest island (Greenland) and an entire continent (Antarctica). Ice fields, which are similar in size to ice caps, are reclassified as ice sheets when they grow to an area larger than 50,000 sq. km (19,000 sq. miles).

THE WORLD'S LONGEST GLACIERS

1 **Lambert Glacier**
Antarctica 400 km (249 miles)
2 **Bering Glacier**
Alaska 190 km (118 miles)
3 **Beardmore Glacier**
Antarctica 160 km (99 miles)
4 **Lillie Glacier**
Antarctica 160 km (99 miles)
5 **Byrd Glacier**
Antarctica 140 km (87 miles)
6 **Nimrod Glacier**
Antarctica 135 km (84 miles)
7 **Hubbard Glacier**
Alaska/Canada 122 km (76 miles)
8 **Nabesna Glacier**
Alaska 120 km (75 miles)
9 **Vatnajökull**
Iceland 100 km (62 miles)

THE WORLD'S LARGEST ICE FIELDS

1 **Antarctic** *c.*12 million sq. km
ice sheet (4.6 million sq. miles)
2 **Greenland** *c.*1.7 million sq. km
ice sheet (656,000 sq. miles)
3 **Kluane** 18,000 sq. km
ice field (6,950 sq. miles)
4 **Southern** 16,800 sq. km
Patagonian (6,500 sq. miles)
ice field
5 **Devon ice cap** 12,000 sq. km
(4,600 sq. miles)
6 **Barnes ice cap** 6,000 sq. km
(2,300 sq. miles)
7 **Penny ice cap** 4,400 sq. km
(1,700 sq. miles)
8 **Northern** 4,400 sq. km
Patagonian (1,700 sq. miles)
ice field

An aerial photograph of Vatnajökull,
Iceland's largest glacier with an area of
8,300 sq. km (3,200 sq. miles). Reaching
a thickness approaching 1,000 m (3,300
feet), it is also Europe's largest glacier,
measured by volume.

THE ANTARCTIC ICE SHEET

The Antarctic ice sheet is the world's largest continuous ice field, with an area of some 12 million sq. km (4.6 million sq. miles) and a volume of 26 million cu. km (6.2 million cu. miles). This enormous mass of ice contains some 90% of all the fresh water on Earth and were it to melt, worldwide sea levels would rise by more than 60 m (200 feet). The Antarctic ice sheet is surrounded by wide ice shelves – expanses of thick ice floating in the sea – which are connected to the mainland by glaciers known as "grounding lines". The largest of the ice shelves are the Ross, Filchner-Ronne, and Amery.

A glacial fissure in Antarctica.

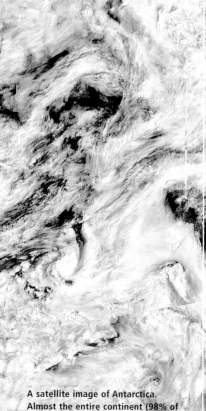

A satellite image of Antarctica. Almost the entire continent (98% of its surface area) is covered with ice. The darker region to the south is the Ross ice shelf.

The Ross and Filchner-Ronne ice shelves in the Antarctic are the world's largest floating expanses of ice. Where they connect to the Antarctic ice sheet, whose glaciers feed the ice shelves, they reach thicknesses of about 800–1,500 m

Ice formations in the Ross ice shelf.

(2,600–4,900 feet). The ice fronts at the Ross and Weddell Seas are only about 100–200 m (330–660 feet) thick, principally as a result of the melting of their undersides.

These images of the Ross ice shelf's ice front, towering 20–50 m (66–165 feet) above the Ross Sea, were taken from a helicopter.

ROSS ICE SHELF
Antarctica   487,000 sq. km
                    (188,000 sq. miles)

The Ross ice shelf – which is named after James Clark Ross, the Briton who discovered it in 1841 – covers about half the surface area of the Ross Sea. It is the largest expanse of shelf ice in the Antarctic and indeed in the world. The shelf's ice front, known as the Ross Barrier, is a sheer wall of ice, with a length of some 600–800 km (370–500 miles) and rising to heights of 20–50 m (66–165 feet) above the water. The greatest portion of the ice (up to some 90%) is below sea level.

FILCHNER-RONNE ICE SHELF
Antarctica   449,000 sq. km
                    (173,000 sq. miles)

The second largest permanent ice shelf on the Antarctic ice sheet is situated in a large bay in the Weddell Sea. It was named after the German geographer Wilhem Filchner and Edith Ronne, the wife of a Norwegian polar researcher. A German research station was established on the Filchner-Ronne ice shelf in 1982, but when a 150x50-km (93x31-mile) section known as A-38 broke away from the shelf in October 1998, the station went with it; fortunately, it was possible to rescue the inhabitants.

THE WORLD'S
LARGEST ICEBERG

An enormous iceberg known as B-15, which broke away from the Ross ice shelf in March 2000 and drifted off into the open sea, was the world's largest iceberg, with an area of about 11,000 sq. km (4,250 sq. miles). Initially blocking the McMurdo Sound and causing it to ice over still further, the iceberg later broke up during a violent storm, whereupon a section known as B-15A collided with the Drygalski Ice Tongue. As GPS probes had been placed on the iceberg, it is still possible to track the movements of various fragments of B-15A as they move around the area.

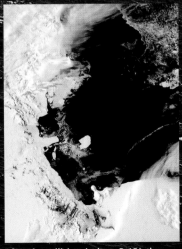

After the collision: iceberg B-15J, the other large fragment of B-15.

The Drygalski Ice Tongue, which measures 14–24 km (8½–15 miles) in width, juts out some 70 km (43 miles) into the Ross Sea from the Scott Coast of Antarctica.

GREENLAND ICE SHEET

Five-sixths of the world's largest island (2,166,086 sq. km/ 836,330 sq. miles) is covered by the Greenland ice sheet. With an area of 1.7 million sq. km (656,000 sq. miles), it extends some 2,400 km (1,500 miles) from north to south and measures about 1,100 km (680 miles) across at its widest point. The sheet of ice is on average more than 2 km (1½ miles) thick, with the inland ice reaching thicknesses of 3,400 m (11,150 feet) and a volume of 2.5 million cu. km (600,000 cu. miles). Only mountain peaks known as *nunataks*, jutting out of the ice, break the monotony of the white landscape. Mighty glaciers force their way to the sea through mountainous regions at the edge of the sheet, breaking off abruptly and giving birth to icebergs. The Humboldt Glacier, some 100 km (62 miles) across, is especially impressive, as are the steep cliffs of Melville Bay, which extend for 300 km (190 miles).

Rugged, partly glaciated mountains tower over estuaries filled with pack ice in this satellite image of eastern Greenland.

LAMBERT GLACIER

THE WORLD'S LARGEST GLACIER

The Lambert Glacier is the principal source of ice for the Amery ice shelf on the coast of Ingrid Christensen Land. The inland ice is fed down U-shaped valleys in a series of glaciers along the eastern edge of continental Antarctica, moving towards the ice shelf at speeds averaging about 2.5 m (8 feet) per day. The light from the low sun picks out even the smallest fissures and cracks. Many of these structures are formed by strong winds, although individual peaks jutting out of the ice and known as *nunataks* (an Inuit word) also steer the flow of ice.

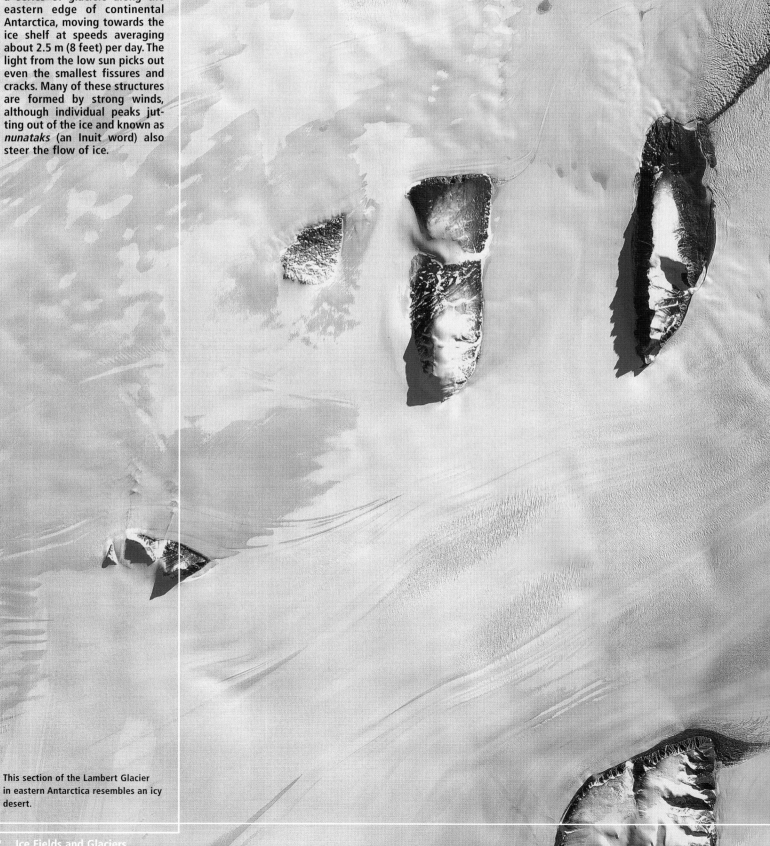

This section of the Lambert Glacier in eastern Antarctica resembles an icy desert.

THE WORLD'S LONGEST AND LARGEST GLACIER

ANTARCTICA'S LONGEST GLACIERS

The Beardmore Glacier in Queen Maud Mountains, the world's third longest glacier.

❶ Lambert Glacier   400 km (249 miles)
❷ Beardmore Glacier   160 km (99 miles)
❸ Lillie Glacier   160 km (99 miles)
❹ Byrd Glacier   140 km (87 miles)
❺ Nimrod Glacier   135 km (84 miles)
❻ Shackleton Glacier   100 km (62 miles)
❼ Leverett Glacier   80 km (50 miles)
❽ Minnesota Glacier   65 km (40 miles)

AUSTFONNA

Spitsbergen   **8,492 sq. km**
(3,279 sq. miles)

More than 2,600 sq. km (1,000 sq. miles) of mainland Norway are covered with extensive ice fields, including 60% of the Svalbard archipelago (once known as the Spitsbergen islands). The Austfonna ("eastern") glacier located on Nordaustlandet, which is part of Spitsbergen and therefore also Norwegian territory, is the largest ice field in Europe by area. The ice front of the Austfonna glacier is 200 km (125 miles) long and is only occasionally interrupted by rocky peaks. The ice has a thickness of some 230–560 m (750–1,840 feet) and reaches an elevation of 783 m (2,569 feet) at its highest point. The glacier forms a contiguous ice field with Vegafonna, although the latter has an ice cap of its own and is in fact separated from its neighbor Austfonna by a long, ice-filled fissure. The Vestfonna ("western") glacier, which extends out a little to the north-east of Austfonna, is the third largest glacier in Norway, covering an area of some 2,445 sq. km (945 sq. miles).

The ice front of the Austfonna.

VATNAJÖKULL

Iceland   **8,300 sq. km**
(3,200 sq. miles)

Situated in the south-east of the island, Vatnajökull ("water glacier") is Iceland's largest glacier. Its volume of 3,000 cu. km (720 cu. miles) is far greater than Austfonna's 1,900 cu. km (455 cu. miles), making it Europe's largest glacier by volume. Vatnajökull's ice sheet reaches thicknesses of up to 1,000 m (3,300 feet) and its highest point is known as Öræfajökull. It has been shrinking for several years now, however, and possible causes for this include global warming and the active volcano beneath this massive sheet of ice. Volcanic eruptions can cause glacial run-off (meltwater floods).

Vatnajökull in Iceland is surrounded by snow-capped mountains.

GREAT ALETSCH GLACIER –
THE LARGEST GLACIER IN THE ALPS

With an area of 117 sq. km (45 sq. miles), the Great Aletsch Glacier in the Bernese Alps is more than 23 km (14 miles) long and rises at Concordia near the Jungfrau, an almost flat sheet of ice, in places reaching close to 900 m (2,950 feet) thick, where four tributary glaciers, the Aletschfirn, Jungfrau-firn, Ewig-schneefeld, and Grünegg-gfirn converge to form the Great Aletsch Glacier. The Jungfraujoch, which can be accessed by the Jungfrau funicular railway, enjoys a magnificent view of the upper sections of this river of ice, which reaches its southern end in the Massa Valley.

CONTINENTAL EUROPE'S LARGEST GLACIERS

1 **Jostedalsbreen**
   Norway   487 sq. km (188 sq. miles)

2 **Vestre Svartisen**
   Norway   221 sq. km (85 sq. miles)

3 **Folgefonna**
   Norway   214 sq. km (83 sq. miles)

4 **Østre Svartisen**
   Norway   148 sq. km (57 sq. miles)

5 **Great Aletsch Glacier**
   Switzerland   117 sq. km
                              (45 sq. miles)

6 **Blåmannsisen**
   Norway   87 sq. km (34 sq. miles)

7 **Hardangerjøkul**
   Norway   73 sq. km (28 sq. miles)

Jökulsárlón ("glacier river lagoon"), Iceland's largest glacial lake and also the deepest lake in the country, lies at the southern edge of Vatnajökull.

The Hispar and Biafo Glaciers in the Karakoram Mountains together form continental Asia's longest glacier complex. The Biafo Glacier in northern Pakistan is about 63 km (39 miles) long, making it the third longest ice field beyond the poles after the Fedchenko and Siachen Glaciers. It is connected to the 49-km-long (30-mile) Hispar Glacier by the Hispar Pass, which rises to a height of 5,128 m (16,824 feet). The Baltoro Glacier, also located in northern Pakistan, has an area of 754 sq. km (291 sq. miles) and numerous sub-glaciers. At 70 km (43 miles) in length, the Siachen Glacier in the south-eastern Karakoram Mountains is the longest expanse of ice in India.

ASIA'S LONGEST GLACIERS

1 Fedchenko Glacier
Tajikistan   77 km (48 miles)

2 Siachen Glacier
India   70 km (43 miles)

3 Biafo Glacier
Pakistan   63 km (39 miles)

4 Baltoro Glacier
Pakistan   57 km (35 miles)

5 Batura Glacier
Pakistan   57 km (35 miles)

6 Hispar Glacier
Pakistan   49 km (30 miles)

Main image: climbers surveying the majestic mountain scenery of the Baltoro Glacier in northern Pakistan.

The Fedchenko Glacier in the Pamir Mountains.

The Baltoro Glacier in northern Pakistan.

The Siachen Glacier in the Karakoram Mountains.

THE "THIRD POLE" – THE GLACIERS OF THE KARAKORAM MOUNTAINS

Situated just to the north of the main range of the Himalayas in Central Asia, the Karakoram Mountains boast four peaks reaching over 8,000 m (26,250 feet) in height, including K2, which at 8,611 m/28,251 feet is the world's second highest mountain after Mount Everest. Some of the largest and longest glaciers beyond the polar ice caps are to be found in the Karakoram Mountains – more than a third of the mountains are glaciated, and the Biafo, Baltoro, and Hispar Glaciers in Pakistan, and the Siachen Glacier in India are of special interest.

Snow- and ice-covered summits in Karakoram and Pamir.

FRANZ JOSEF GLACIER
New Zealand   9.6 sq. km
(3½ sq. miles)

The Franz Josef Glacier on New Zealand's South Island was named after the Emperor Franz Josef I of Austria. The glacier rises in the New Zealand Alps

Franz Josef Glacier, New Zealand.

but its meltwater drains into the Waiho River, which in turn flows into the Tasman Sea. The glacier was once so large that it reached all the way to the river estuary. In contrast to almost all other glaciers on Earth, the Franz Josef is growing, currently by about 80 m (260 feet) per year.

The Franz Josef Glacier flows into the lush green forests of the Westland National Park on New Zealand's South Island.

The tip of the Fox Glacier.

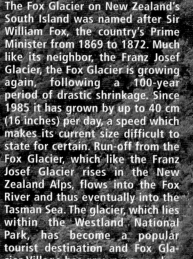

The Fox Glacier at dusk.

FOX GLACIER
New Zealand   13 km (8 miles)

The Fox Glacier on New Zealand's South Island was named after Sir William Fox, the country's Prime Minister from 1869 to 1872. Much like its neighbor, the Franz Josef Glacier, the Fox Glacier is growing again, following a 100-year period of drastic shrinkage. Since 1985 it has grown by up to 40 cm (16 inches) per day, a speed which makes its current size difficult to state for certain. Run-off from the Fox Glacier, which like the Franz Josef Glacier rises in the New Zealand Alps, flows into the Fox River and thus eventually into the Tasman Sea. The glacier, which lies within the Westland National Park, has become a popular tourist destination and Fox Glacier Village has grown up nearby.

HOOKER GLACIER
New Zealand   11 km (6½ miles)

Nunataks in the Hooker Glacier.

Like the Tasman Glacier, the Hooker Glacier is located on the slopes of Mount Cook on New Zealand's South Island. It is also the source of the Hooker River, a tributary of the Tasman River which eventually flows into Lake Pukaki. The Hooker Glacier is considered New Zealand's most easily accessible glacier.

TASMAN GLACIER
New Zealand   27 km (16½ miles)

Ice-covered rock formations.

This is the largest of a group of glaciers in the New Zealand Alps. In contrast to the Franz Josef and Fox Glaciers, the 4-km-wide (2½-mile) Tasman Glacier is shrinking rapidly. Recent decades have seen the glacier retreat by up to 180 m (590 feet) per year, and the current level could be as much as 800 m (2,600 feet) per year.

Africa's highest peak, Kilimanjaro (the meaning of the name is not known for certain but might be "white mountain") in Tanzania, is actually a chain of three volcanoes: Shira (3,962 m/12,999 feet), Mawensi (5,148 m/16,890 feet), and Kibo (5,895 m/19,340 feet). Kibo's frozen sum-

Stepped glacier, Kilimanjaro.

mit is covered with any number of steep hanging glaciers at elevations above 4,300 m (14,100 feet). According to American geologists who have examined Kilimanjaro's ice fields and discovered shrinkages of at least 50 cm (20 inches) per year, global warming will have melted away these millennia-old glaciers to nothing by the year 2020.

The summit of Kilimanjaro with its circular caldera is still covered in ice and snow, but its glaciers are slowly receding.

Stepped sections of the Rebmann Glacier.

The Kersten Glacier on the crater of Kilimanjaro.

ICE FIELDS AND GLACIERS
IN CANADA AND ALASKA

Several of North America's largest ice fields and glaciers are to be found on the west coast of the continent, from the Kenai Peninsula in Alaska (Harding ice field) along the border of the "Panhandle" (Kluane and Juneau ice fields) to the Coast Mountains in Canada's British Columbia (Homathko ice field). Only 5% of Alaska is covered with ice, but the ice fields here and in northern West Canada feed numerous glaciers, including the Columbia, Exit, and Hubbard Glaciers. The Canadian Arctic Archipelago lying just off the northern coast of the North American mainland also features considerable ice fields; the southern reaches of the islands are covered in barren plains and gently rolling plateaus which seldom exceed elevations of 400 m (1,300 feet) above sea level, but the northern areas are mountainous. The Arctic Cordillera chain of mountain ranges features innumerable glaciers, with the highest points being Barbeau Peak (2,616 m/ 8,583 feet) and others on Ellesmere Island, and peaks on Baffin Island rising to over 2,100 m (6,890 feet). Baffin Island is also the home of the Penny and the Barnes ice caps. The largest ice cap to be found in the region is the Devon ice cap on Devon Island.

Ice Fields and Glaciers

NORTH AMERICA'S LARGEST
ICE FIELDS AND GLACIERS

The Exit Glacier seen from Harding ice field, with the Kenai Mountains as a backdrop.

Columbia Glacier in the Chugach ice field.

A plane flies high over the Juneau ice field.

Kaskawulsh Glacier in the Kluane ice field.

LeConte Glacier in the Stikine ice field.

MAINLAND CANADA AND ALASKA'S LARGEST ICE FIELDS

❶ **Kluane ice field** Canada	18,000 sq. km	(6,950 sq. miles)
❷ **Stikine ice field** Canada	7,510 sq. km	(2,900 sq. miles)
❸ **Juneau ice field** Alaska	3,900 sq. km	(1,500 sq. miles)
❹ **Ha-Iltzuk ice field** Canada	3,610 sq. km	(1,390 sq. miles)
❺ **Homathko ice field** Canada	2,000 sq. km	(770 sq. miles)
❻ **Harding ice field** Alaska	1,770 sq. km	(680 sq. miles)

THE CANADIAN ARCTIC ARCHIPELAGO'S LARGEST ICE FIELDS

❶ **Devon ice cap** Devon Island	12,000 sq. km	(4,600 sq. miles)
❷ **Barnes ice cap** Baffin Island	6,000 sq. km	(2,300 sq. miles)
❸ **Penny ice cap** Baffin Island	4,400 sq. km	(1,700 sq. miles)

Large image: majestic glaciers forge a path from the remains of an ancient ice field down to Scott Inlet on Baffin Island.

BERING GLACIER – NORTH AMERICA'S LONGEST GLACIER

Alaska   **5,200 sq. km (2,000 sq. miles)**

With an area of 5,200 sq. km (2,000 sq. miles) and a length of 190 km (118 miles), the Bering Glacier is North America's longest glacier, stretching from the Saint Elias Mountains to Vitus Lake, 10 km (6 miles) short of the Gulf of Alaska. The glacier's sheet of ice is more than 800 m (2,600 feet) thick in places. Global warming has reduced the Bering Glacier by a length of 12 km (7 miles) since 1900, and this has had an interesting side effect – as the weight of the ice and thus the pressure on the Earth's crust is reduced, the convergence zone between the Pacific and the North American Plates has become less stable and as a result volcanic activity has increased in the region.

The Bering Glacier in southern Alaska is the largest in North America. Much like the Bagley ice field, it flows into Vitus Lake south of Wrangell–St Elias National Park.

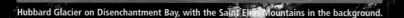

Hubbard Glacier on Disenchantment Bay, with the Saint Elias Mountains in the background.

Taku Glacier in the Boundary Ranges.

Ruth Glacier in the Denali National Park.

NORTH AMERICA'S LONGEST GLACIERS

1. **Bering Glacier**
   Alaska   190 km (118 miles)
2. **Hubbard Glacier**
   Alaska/Canada   122 km (76 miles)
3. **Nabesna Glacier**
   Alaska   120 km (75 miles)
4. **Taku Glacier**
   Alaska   92 km (57 miles)
5. **Seward Glacier**
   Alaska   80 km (50 miles)
6. **Klutlan Glacier**
   Alaska/Canada   64 km (40 miles)
7. **Ruth Glacier**
   Alaska   64 km (40 miles)

Kahiltna Glacier beside Mount McKinley.

Nabesna Glacier beside Mount Blackburn.

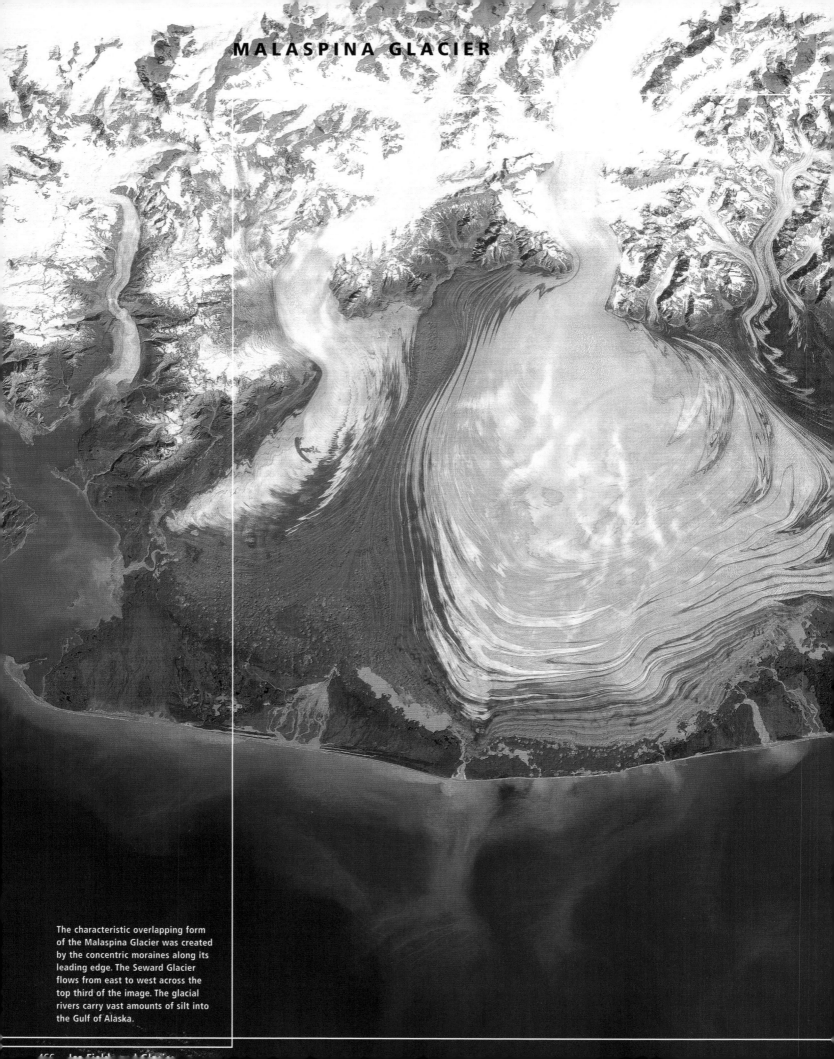

The characteristic overlapping form of the Malaspina Glacier was created by the concentric moraines along its leading edge. The Seward Glacier flows from east to west across the top third of the image. The glacial rivers carry vast amounts of silt into the Gulf of Alaska.

The Malaspina Glacier in the Saint Elias Mountains on the southern Pacific coast of Alaska is 45 km (28 miles) long, 65 km (40 miles) wide and up to 600 m (1,970 feet) thick. Although its tip is to be found at Yakutat Bay in the Gulf of Alaska, it never quite reaches the water; with its area of 3,900 sq. km (1,500 sq. miles), it is the world's largest Piedmont glacier, the name given to glaciers descending from a chain of mountains onto a plain to form a fan-shaped or circular ice field. The Malaspina Glacier is composed of a series of smaller glaciers which combine to form a large mass of ice at the foot of the Saint Elias Mountains. The largest single glacier in the complex is the 80-km-long (50-mile) Seward Glacier. One peculiar characteristic of the Malaspina Glacier is to be found in Oily Lake and Malaspina Lake, two icy lakes which have formed at the edge of the glacier above the glaciated valley. Between 1980 and 2000, the glacier's ice layer shrank by approximately 20 m (66 feet), and the sheer volume of water that this loss entailed had the effect of raising sea levels by about half a centimeter (½ inch). The Malaspina Glacier is located in its entirety in the Wrangell–St Elias National Park.

The Malaspina Glacier carries unimaginable amounts of ice and sediment.

CAMPO DE HIELO PATAGÓNICO SUR (SOUTHERN PATAGONIAN ICE FIELD)

The Campo de Hielo Patagónico Sur (Southern Patagonian ice field) is situated in the Andes between Chile and Argentina. This huge glaciated area measures some 350 km (220 miles) in length and has an area of about 16,800 sq. km (6,500 sq. miles), of which 14,200 sq. km (5,500 sq. miles) is on Chilean territory and the remaining 2,600 sq. km (1,000 sq. miles) is in Argentina. It represents South America's single greatest reserve of fresh water and is also one of the largest on Earth.

The ice field feeds a number of extensive Piedmont glaciers, all of which are shrinking; the largest are the Pio XI and the Viedma Glaciers, although the most famous is the 30-km-long (19-mile) Perito Moreno Glacier, whose 5-km-wide (3-mile) terminus advances over Lago Argentino. One of the few remaining glaciers that is still growing, it is slowly edging its tip towards a peninsula on the opposite side of the lake. This action acts like a dam and blocks a side channel of Lago Argentino every three or four years, raising the water level to some 30 m (100 feet), at which point the wall of ice is no longer able to resist the pressure and a magnificent natural spectacle results: the pent-up mass of water breaks through the front of the glacier, forcing its way into the other half of the lake.

THE LARGEST GLACIERS IN THE SOUTHERN PATAGONIAN ICE FIELD

❶ Pio XI Glacier	1,265 sq. km	(488 sq. miles)
❷ Viedma Glacier	987 sq. km	(381 sq. miles)
❸ Upsala Glacier	902 sq. km	(348 sq. miles)
❹ Perito Moreno Glacier	258 sq. km	(100 sq. miles)

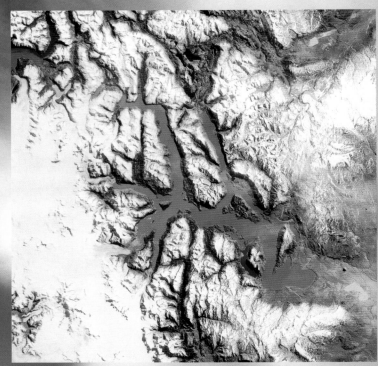

Glacier tips in the fjord-like sounds of Lago O'Higgins.

Still a challenge for the adventurous: an expedition on the Southern Patagonian ice field. One brave soul has left his tracks on the Viedma Glacier (main image).

Frontal view of the Perito Moreno Glacier in Argentina's Los Glaciares National Park.

RIVERS

Rivers are a striking feature of any landscape, carving deep valleys, irrigating plains, and changing barren deserts into fertile oases. As small and large rivers converge and eventually flow into the sea, they represent an essential part of the water cycle.

Qutang Gorge on the Yangtze River in the Three Gorges Region of China.

The longest rivers are not necessarily the biggest by volume: the Nile is an allochthonous river and during the journey to its delta loses so much water through evaporation that only about 2,800 cu. m (99,000 cu. feet) per second flow into the Mediterranean – far shorter rivers often discharge many times this amount. Such quantities pale into insignificance when compared with the world's largest rivers by volume, especially the Amazon, which has the greatest total river flow by several orders of magnitude.

THE WORLD'S LONGEST RIVERS
with their principal sources

1 Nile (incl. the Kagera)
Africa   6,671 km (4,145 miles)
2 Amazon (incl. the Ucayali/ Apurímac)
S. America 6,448 km (4,007 miles)
3 Yangtze (incl. the Tongtian)
Asia   6,380 km (3,964 miles)
4 Mississippi/Missouri (incl. the Red Rock River)
N. America 6,051 km (3,760 miles)
5 Yenisei/Angara (incl. the Selenga and Ider)
Asia   5,940 km (3,691 miles)
6 Ob/Irtysh
Asia   5,410 km (3,362 miles)
7 Amur/Argun (incl. the Kherlen)
Asia   5,052 km (3,139 miles)
8 Yellow River
Asia   4,845 km (3,011 miles)
9 Congo/Luvua (incl. the Luapula and Chambeshi)
Africa   4,835 km (3,004 miles)
10 Mekong
Asia   4,350 km (2,703 miles)
11 Lena River
Asia   4,400 km (2,730 miles)
12 Mackenzie (incl. the Peace/ Finlay)
N. America 4,241 km (2,635 miles)

THE WORLD'S LARGEST RIVERS BY VOLUME
(average flow)

1 Amazon (incl. the Ucayali/ Apurímac)   180,000 cu. m/s
S. America   (6.3 million cu. feet/s)
2 Congo   39,160 cu. m/s
Africa   (1.4 million cu. feet/s)
3 Yangtze (incl. the Tongtian)   31,900 cu. m/s
Asia   (1.1 million cu. feet/s)
4 Río Madeira (incl. Río Mamoré/ Río Grande)   31,200 cu. m/s
S. America   (1.1 million cu. feet/s)
5 Orinoco   29,000 cu. m/s
S. America   (1 million cu. feet/s)
6 Río Negro   26,700 cu. m/s
S. America   (942,000 cu. feet/s)
7 Brahmaputra   25,000 cu. m/s
Asia   (883,000 cu. feet/s)

8 Yenisei   19,600 cu. m/s
Asia   (692,000 cu. feet/s)
9 Paraná (incl. the Río Grande)   19,500 cu. m/s
S. America   (689,000 cu. feet/s)
10 Japurá   17,960 cu. m/s
S. America   (634,000 cu. feet/s)
11 Lena   17,100 cu. m/s
Asia   (604,000 cu. feet/s)
12 Río Tocantins   16,300 cu. m/s
S. America   (576,000 cu. feet/s)

The Jialing River flows into the Yangtze River in the Chinese city of Chongqing, a metropolis of skyscrapers built on a comma-shaped peninsula. As the mighty Three Gorges Dam reservoir was built nearby, large ships have been able to navigate as far as Chongqing's port since 2006. The city is located to the east of the central province of Sichuan, close to the seat of the government and on the edge of the fertile Red Basin.

THE NILE –
THE WORLD'S LONGEST RIVER

The Nile is an artery and a myth – its source was discovered only at the end of the 19th century. The Nile is considered an allochthonous river: its flow originates in the rains falling on its upper reaches and it takes on no further water on its journey to the delta.

The Nile, the world's longest river, is 6,671 km (4,145 miles) long with a drainage basin covering an area of 3 million sq. km (1.1 million sq. miles), which is approximately 10% of continental Africa. The river's source is the White Nile, which is fed from the Kagera River. The White Nile, the longer of these two source rivers, rises in Burundi, on the slopes of Luvironza, the highest mountain (2,700 m/8,860 feet) in this tiny African country; rising in Rwanda, the Kagera Rivera runs along the border between Tanzania and Uganda before becoming just one of the rivers flowing into Lake Victoria, an important source of water for the Nile. As the Albert Nile, the river cascades down the Murchison Falls before flowing further north through Uganda and Sudan. The Blue Nile flows into the White Nile at Khartoum and is joined by the Atbara River further north. Both of these tributaries rise in the Ethiopian Highlands. No further rivers join the Nile on its journey through the Nubian Desert into Egypt, where it forms a wide delta north of Cairo before finally flowing into the Mediterranean.

The Nile at Aswan, with the Aga Khan Mausoleum, which was built at the end of the 1950s, in the background. An oasis has formed on the banks of the river, but the barren desert begins immediately beyond this (below). A traditional felucca beside Elephantine Island, in Aswan (left).

THE AMAZON – THE WORLD'S LARGEST RIVER BY VOLUME

There is so much water in the Amazon that even ocean-going vessels can navigate it for some 1,500 km (900 miles), from its mouth at the Atlantic as far as Manaus in the middle of Brazil; smaller ships between 3,000 and 9,000 tons can penetrate as far as the port of Iquitos in Peru, 3,600 km (2,200 miles) away.

The Amazon is by some margin the world's largest river by volume: every second, 180,000 cu. m (6.3 million cu. feet) of water flow from its mouth into the Atlantic, with the river's ten longest tributaries providing about 150,000 cu. m (5.3 million cu. feet) of this flow rate. The Amazon lies close to the equator, and because the sun crosses the zenith between the two Tropics twice a year at this point, the Amazon Basin has two distinct rainy and dry seasons: there is heavy rain in the northern regions between April and August, and in the southern regions between October and April. The Amazon is thus topped up with water on a regular basis, flooding large areas of the forests on the surrounding plains. The Amazon's largest tributaries are to be found in the south, and when it rains there, the river swells to considerable proportions, reaching depths of up to 17 m (56 feet) in February or March. The Amazon forms a 330-km (205-mile) delta as it flows into the Atlantic at Macapá and provides about a fifth of all the freshwater flowing into the world's oceans.

Large areas of the Amazon Basin are flooded during the rainy season between October and June (left). Sandoval Lake lies surrounded by tropical rainforest in the Amazon Basin in Peru (below left). The Anavilhanas archipelago, the world's largest freshwater archipelago, is located on the Río Negro, 70 km (43 miles) upstream from Manaus (main image).

THE AMAZON –
THE WORLD'S LARGEST RIVER SYSTEM

At 2,250 km (1,400 miles) in length, the Río Negro is one of the Amazon's largest tributaries. Its name, which means "black river", is derived from the high content of partially decomposed plant material that the river leaches from the sandy floor of the *terra firme*, the

The black and white water sections.

areas which escape the flood-water all year round. This black water is extremely clean and low in nutrients. The forests flooded by the white water section of the river are known as Várzea, and those flooded by the black water section as Igapó. The low nutrient content of the black water has other advantages: with no mosquito larvae, there is thus no malaria.

THE AMAZON'S LONGEST TRIBUTARIES
(with country of origin)

1 **Juruá**
Peru   3,283 km (2,040 miles)

2 **Río Madeira/Mamoré;**
Río Grande
Bolivia   3,239 km (2,013 miles)

3 **Purús**
Peru   3,210 km (1,995 miles)

4 **Japurá**
Colombia 2,816 km (1,750 miles)

5 **Río Ucayali (incl. the Apúrimac)**
Peru   2,670 km (1,659 miles)

The sinuous Juruá River.

6 **Río Tocantins**
Brazil   2,640 km (1,640 miles)

7 **Tapajós (incl. the Teles Pires)**
Brazil   2,291 km (1,424 miles)

8 **Río Negro**
Colombia 2,250 km (1,400 miles)

9 **Xingú**
Brazil   1,980 km (1,230 miles)

10 **Marañón**
Peru   1,905 km (1,184 miles)

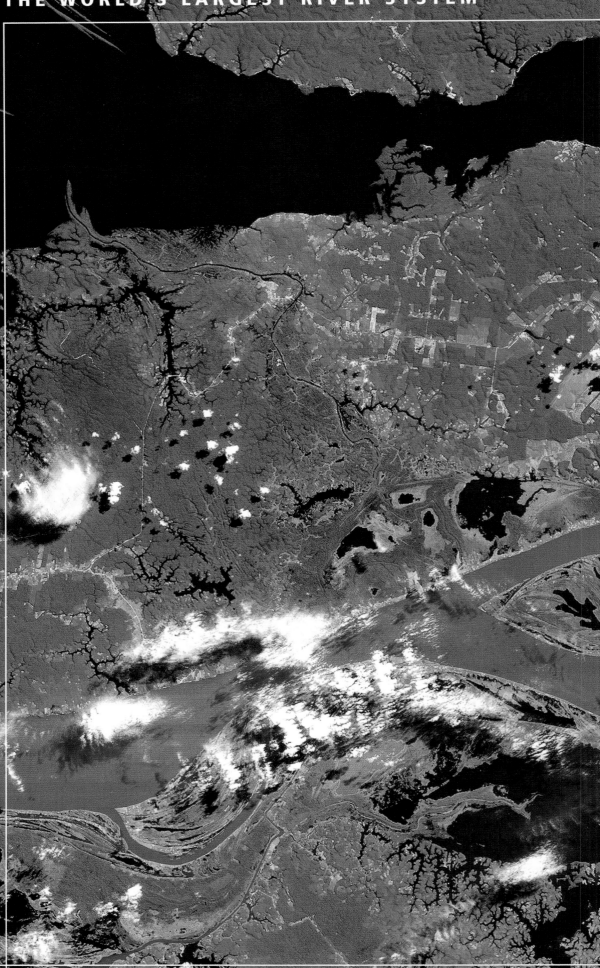

As it reaches the border between Peru and Brazil, the river is known as the Río Solimões, only regaining the name Amazon at the confluence of the dark waters of the Rio Negro and the white of the Río Solimões at Manaus in Brazil. The satellite image shows how the Rio Negro and the Río Solimões merge only gradually; the dark waters of the Rio Negro and the milky-brown of the Río Solimões can still be distinguished a considerable distance downstream.

EUROPE

The Volga River occupies 25th place on the list of the world's longest rivers. The Danube, however, flows through the most countries in Europe, followed by the Rhine. No less than six of Europe's ten longest rivers flow through the European part of Russia.

VOLGA
3,534 km (2,196 miles)

Europe's longest river rises in the Valdai Hills about 300 km (190 miles) north-west of Moscow. It is also the continent's largest river by volume, with an average flow of more than 8,000 cu. m (282,000 cu. feet) per second. The Volga initially flows east past Rybinsk before heading south-east at Kazan. It eventually turns slightly to the south-west at Volgograd and makes a brief excursion to the south-east through the steppes of the Caspian Depression south of Astrakhan before flowing into the Caspian Sea. The drop between the river's source and its mouth amounts to 256 m (840 feet). Its largest tributary is the Kama, which rises in the Kama Hills west of Perm. The Kama and Volga were both first dammed in the 1930s and there are now 12 large plants on their banks. The largest, the Kuibyshev reservoir to the west of Samara, was dammed between 1955 and 1957 and its area of 6,450 sq. km (2,490 sq. miles) makes it Europe's largest reservoir and the third largest in the world.

DANUBE
2,888 km (1,795 miles)

Rising in the Black Forest, the Danube flows through six countries and provides a border for a further four before reaching the Black Sea south of Odessa in Ukraine. The Breg, rising to 1,078 m (3,537 feet) above sea level north of Furtwangen, is thought to be its source, but the river becomes navigable only past Kehlheim. The Main-Danube Canal allows river traffic to reach the Black Sea from the North Sea.

The Danube valley in the Upper Danube Nature Park in Baden-Württemberg.

DON
1,870 km (1,162 miles)

Rising about 150 km (90 miles) south of Moscow, the Don, one of Russia's major rivers, first flows south before turning south-east and passing through the Zimlyansk reservoir west of Volgograd. The mouth of the river is located at Rostov on the Sea of Asov, which is linked to the Black Sea. The banks of the river Don are the traditional homelands of the Don Cossacks, a discrete tribe of Cossacks who raised an armed yeomanry to fight the Tatars in the 15th century and whose later opposition of the Bolsheviks resulted in execution or exile for many in 1919.

URAL RIVER
2,428 km (1,509 miles)

The Ural Mountains and the eponymous river are considered the border between Europe and Asia – the western bank is European, the eastern Asian. The source of the Ural is located in the southern Ural Mountains about 150 km (90 miles) from Magnitogorsk. It flows south to Orsk and makes an almost right-angled turn to the west before eventually continuing south at Urlask through the Kazakh Steppe and on to Atyrau, where it flows into the Caspian Sea.

PECHORA
1,809 km (1,124 miles)

The Pechora River flows west from its source in the northern Ural Mountains before turning north towards the city of Pechora and its confluence with the Ussa, which joins it from the north-east. The river then describes a 300-km (190-mile) arc to the west before heading north and flowing into the Barents Sea. The Pechora River is iced over for almost all of the year.

The Pechora flows through the Virgin Komi Forests, designated a UNESCO World Heritage Site in 1995.

DNIEPER
2,285 km (1,420 miles)

The Dnieper rises north-east of Smolensk before flowing south-west past the city and through Byelorus. It turns south into Ukraine towards Kiev and Dnepropetrovsk before looping round east of Odessa to flow into the Black Sea. The Ukrainian portion of the Dnieper is now a series of giant reservoirs whose power plants supply electricity to the region's densely populated industrial areas.

The Dnieper at Kiev, overlooked by the chapel of the Kiev Cave Monastery.

DNIESTER
1,352 km (840 miles)

The source of the Dniester lies at about 1,000 m (3,300 feet) in the Carpathian Forests and it is Ukraine's second longest river after the Dnieper. The Dniester flows through Ukraine and Moldavia before reaching its estuary south of Odessa on the Black Sea. Its name is derived from a Sarmatian form meaning "the near river". The Dniester is usually frozen over between January and March and though its upper mountain streams are fast-flowing, the central and lower portions of the river flow at a more leisurely pace due to the minimal drop of the river.

The monastery at Rybinsk on the upper reaches of the Volga (far left). A railway bridge crosses the Volga at Rybinsk just before the river reaches the Rybinsk reservoir (left). A system of canals links the reservoir with the White Sea and the Baltic near St Petersburg.

RHINE
1,320 km (820 miles)

The Rein da Medel flowing through the Swiss cantons of Ticino and Graubünden is the source river of the Rhine that is furthest removed from its mouth, and its largest tributaries are the Aar, the Mosel, and the Main. One of the world's busiest watercourses, the Rhine is also the largest river flowing into the North Sea. Passing through Switzerland, Austria, Germany, and the Netherlands, it also forms a border with France and Liechtenstein.

The Rhine at Cologne, with Cologne Cathedral to the left and the Hohenzollern Bridge to the right.

ELBE (incl. the Vltava)
1,252 km (778 miles)

The source of the Elbe is at 1,386 m (4,547 feet) in the Giant Mountains of the Czech Republic, and the length stated above includes the Vltava, which flows into the river 30 km (19 miles) north of Prague, as one of the Elbe's sources. Passing through much beautiful scenery, including sandstone mountains in the Czech Republic and the mudflats of Germany, the Elbe is the only watercourse linking Bohemia with the North Sea.

Brühl Terrace ("Europe's balcony"), overlooking the Elbe in Dresden.

VISTULA
1,047 m (651 miles)

The streams forming the source of the Vistula rise at an elevation of 1,100 m (3,600 feet) in the Beskids in Silesia before entering the Zbiornik Czernianski reservoir only a short distance away. The river flows east through the old royal city of Kraków and then heads north to Warsaw before discharging into the Baltic Sea through a delta with two branches near Gdańsk; an older one to the immediate west of the city and a more recent one further to the east.

The Vistula passing Wawel Castle in the UNESCO World Heritage City of Kraków.

ASIA

Asia, the world's largest continent, also contains some of the mightiest rivers. Most of the rivers in the Asiatic part of Russia drain into the northern Polar Sea and the rivers of South and East Asia drain into the oceans lying to the south or east.

YANGTZE RIVER
6,380 km (3,964 miles)

The official Chinese name for the world's third longest river is Chiang Jiang, the "long river". Although the river rises in an extensive area at an elevation of 5,400 m (17,700 feet) in the sparsely populated northern Tibetan Highlands, the Tuotuo He is considered the principal source river. The upper courses of the river are known as Tongtian He, the "river that crosses heaven", and flow to the south-east before encountering a solid limestone massif at Shigu which diverts the river in a sharp curve to the north-east. The "Great Bend of Shigu", as it is known, prevents the Yangtze from continuing to flow south like the nearby Mekong. After making a few further detours, the river finally flows east. The upper and central reaches of the river flow through numerous gorges, of which the most famous are the Three Gorges (with their controversial dam) between Chongqing and Yichang. The Yangtze flows into the East China Sea north of Shanghai.

YENISEI
5,940 km (3,691 miles)

The Yenisei crosses Siberia from south to north before flowing into the Kara Sea and thus the Arctic Ocean. The river's length includes the Angara, the Selenga (into which the Ider flows as a source river), and the bay of the estuary. The source of the river system is located in the Changhai Mountains south-west of Lake Baikal. The first ice floes begin to form in the fall, after which the river is completely frozen until May.

The Yenisei at Dudinka, Siberia, 350 km (215 miles) south of Yenisei Bay.

OB AND IRTYSH
5,410 km (3,362 miles)

The Irtysh ("white" river) rises in the Altay Mountains of Mongolia, an area known as Dzungaria in the Chinese province of Xinjiang. It flows through Kazakhstan into Russia before reaching its confluence with the Ob at Khanty-Mansiysk. The Ob continues north through western Siberia before reaching the Kara Sea via an estuary 800 km (500 miles) long and 70 km (43 miles) wide.

The Irtysh at Khanty-Mansiysk, just before its confluence with the Ob.

AMUR
(incl. the Argun and Kherlen)
5,052 km (3,139 miles)

The Kherlen River, which is also known as the Kerülen, rises to the north of Ulan Bator in Mongolia and flows through the steppes of China to reach the Hulun Lake. In years that have a high level of rainfall, the lake floods and drains north into the Argun, a river which forms the Sino-Russian border as it flows north to discharge into the Strait of Tartary at Nikolayevsk-on-Amur, opposite the island of Sachalin. The river supports a rich stock of fish.

Boats moored on the banks of the Yangtze River at the 44-km-long (27-mile) Wu Gorge. The Witch's Gorge (wu means "witch") is the middle one of the Three Gorges and is considered the most beautiful (far left). A pagoda, built high above the Yangtze River to represent Buddhism, one of the three sources of Chinese philosophy, along with Taoism and Confucianism (left).

YELLOW RIVER
4,845 km (3,011 miles)

The Yellow River (Huang He), China's second longest river after the Yangtze, also rises in the Tibetan Highlands; from its source in the Bayan Har Mountains in Qinghai province it flows through nine further Chinese provinces on its journey to the Bohai Gulf in the Yellow Sea, south of Beijing. It was named after the large quantities of *loess* present in its waters, which, though useful for agriculture, also causes erosion and sedimentation.

The source of the Yellow River lies in the mountainous Qinghai province (left).

MEKONG
4,350 km (2,703 miles)

The Mekong rises somewhere in the Tibetan Highlands, although the exact source is still disputed. Flowing south, it forms the border between Laos and Burma (Myanmar) and between Laos and Thailand. The Mekong then flows through Vientiane (Viangchan), the capital of Laos, before passing through Cambodia near its capital, Phnom Penh. Crossing the border into Vietnam, the river finally forms a broad delta at the South China Sea.

The Mekong at Luang Prabang, the old royal city in northern Laos (above).

LENA
4,400 km (2,730 miles)

The Lena, a river in Russia lying on the borders of central and eastern Siberia, rises in the Baikal Mountains, 5 km (3 miles) to the west of Lake Baikal. After flowing west, the Lena describes an arc to the north towards Ust-Kut, beyond which it becomes navigable. The river then continues east to Yakutsk, the capital of the Russian Sakha Republic, before flowing north and breaking up into a wide delta (the largest protected area in Russia) at the Laptev Sea on the edge of the Arctic Ocean. The Lena freezes between October and June.

EUPHRATES AND MURAT
3,380 km (2,100 miles)

The Murat, the source of the Euphrates, rises near Turkey's highest mountain, Mount Ararat (5,165 m/16,946 feet) in the highlands of Eastern Anatolia. Flowing west, it joins the Euphrates at Malatya, the capital of the eponymous Anatolian province, before descending through Syria and Iraq. Here it combines with its sister river the Tigris in Mesopotamia to form the Shatt al-Arab, which marks the Iran-Iraq border as it flows down to its mouth on the Persian Gulf. Ancient Mesopotamia is considered the "cradle of civilization".

THE INDIAN SUBCONTINENT'S LONGEST RIVERS

INDUS

3,180 km (1,976 miles)

The Indus is the longest river on the Indian subcontinent. Its source (a confluence of several glacial streams) is situated at an elevation of 5,350 m (17,550 feet) in the Tibetan

A footbridge over the Indus.

county of Gar in the Trans-Himalayas. From here it flows north-west along the southern edge of the Karakoram range before taking a detour to the south-west, leaving the moun-

tains and entering Pakistani territory. The Indus flows through the Tarbela reservoir about 50 km (31 miles) north-west of Islamabad before continuing its journey across Pakistan to the south-west, punctuated by numerous reservoirs and canals used for agri-

Disguised as a heron, a hunter works the Indus.

cultural irrigation. South-west of Hyderabad, not far from the Tropic of Cancer, the river forms a delta and discharges into the Arabian Sea.

This aerial photograph shows the Indus as it passes through the peaks of Karakoram, a mountain chain which eventually joins the main range of the Himalayas to the north and includes K2, the world's second highest mountain (8,611 m/28,251 feet). Karakoram makes up part of the disputed region of Kashmir between India, Pakistan, and China.

The Brahmaputra in Tibet.

Pilgrims on the Ganges at Varanasi.

There is plenty of river traffic at Dahka.

The Yamuna, a Ganges tributary at Agra.

Fishermen on the Brahmaputra in Assam.

GANGES
2,511 km (1,560 miles)

The Ganges, the sacred river of all Hindus, is created at the confluence of its two source rivers in the Indian district of Garhwal in the south-western Himalayas. It initially flows south-east through the Indo-Gangetic Plain before joining the Brahmaputra in Bangladesh and draining into the Gulf of Bengal through the Ganges Delta.

BRAHMAPUTRA
2,896 m (1,799 miles)

The Brahmaputra rises some 6,000 m (19,700 feet) above sea level in a glacier on the northern slopes of the Himalayas near the holy mountain of Mount Kailash. It flows east for 1,500 km (900 miles) across Tibet before negotiating the Dihang Gorges to the south. Having joined the Ganges, the river finally flows into the Bay of Bengal.

The nearby islands of Tasmania and Papua-New Guinea and the island chains of Oceania are all counted as part of the fifth continent. Mainland Australia has an extremely dry interior, with few rivers that are constantly in flow.

DARLING RIVER
(incl. Murray River)

3,370 km (2,094 miles)

At 2,739 km (1,702 miles), the Darling is the longest river in Australia. Its confluence with the 2,589-km-long (1,609-mile) Murray River at Wentworth in New South Wales creates a river system with a combined length of 3,370 km (2,094 miles) from source to mouth at the Indian Ocean. Both rivers rise in the Great Dividing Range, a mountain chain on the west coast of Australia: the Murray rises south of Canberra in the Snowy Mountains, and the Darling further north in the same latitudes as Brisbane. The Darling follows a sluggish path through dry grassland to the west and south, often drying out and leaving just a series of ponds, but when it floods, it immediately inundates large areas. The Murray flows west and is navigable for almost 2,000 km (1,250 miles) – houseboat trips are very popular here. Four dammed reservoirs, including Lake Hume, prevent all but a little of the water reaching the sea, and the river mouth is threatening to silt up.

MURRUMBIDGEE
1,579 km (981 miles)

The tributary east of the Murray in New South Wales rises on the northern slopes of the Snowy Mountains near Mount Kosciuszko, mainland Australia's highest peak at 2,228 m (7,310 feet). In the Aboriginal language, Murrumbidgee means "great river". The river initially flows north from its source for a short distance before crossing the pastureland to the west and reaching its confluence with the Murray River north of Swan Hill. Canberra, the Australian capital, lies on the banks of the Murrumbidgee.

A dead tree in the Murrumbidgee near Hay.

Flowing sleepily past its tree-lined banks, the torpid Murray River (left) is the longest watercourse in mainland Australia. The Sepik – seen here at dusk – is the second longest river in New Guinea and one of the world's largest river systems (large image).

SEPIK
1,125 km (700 miles)

The Sepik is the second longest river on the island of New Guinea, found mostly within the independent state of Papua New Guinea, which occupies the eastern half of the island. Rising in the Victor Emanuel Range at an elevation of 2,170 m (7,120 feet), the river first flows north-west before leaving the mountains in a wide arc to the northeast and flowing into the Bismarck Sea. The river's extremely extensive drainage basin is characterized by swamps and tropical rain forest, with very few inhabitants.

On the Sepik in Papua New Guinea.

COOPER CREEK
1,420 km (882 miles)

Cooper Creek rises to the south of the Australian town of Killarney Park and west of the Carnarvon Range, a chain of foothills of the Great Dividing Range to the west. The initial course of the river, which is known at this point as the Barcoo River, flows north-west before turning south at Blackall and its confluence with Thomson Creek. Now known as Cooper Creek, the river flows on through the desert to reach its mouth at Lake Eyre North, a salt lake. Cooper Creek flows only intermittently.

Water lilies and eucalyptus trees at Cooper Creek.

MAMBERAMO
(incl. the Taritatu and Tariku)
1,175 km (730 miles)

The Mamberamo is found in the Papua province of Indonesia on New Guinea, the world's second largest island after Greenland. Its two source rivers are the Taritatu and the Tariku, which rise in the mountain ranges on the north half of the island. The Taritatu River (once known as the Idenburg) flows north-west and crosses extensive mangrove swamps before emerging as the Mamberamo River, at the point where it joins the Tariku River. It now takes a sharp turn to the north through a deep valley before forming a large estuary delta as it reaches the Pacific.

FLY
1,120 km (696 miles)

The Fly River is the third longest river on the island of New Guinea, mostly in the country of Papua New Guinea. It rises on the southern face of the Victor Emanuel Range, and for a short distance forms the border with Indonesia on the western half of the island. The Fly continues its journey to the south-east through broad reaches of swampland before reaching the Gulf of Papua and forming a 56-km-wide (35-mile) estuary. The gulf contains numerous inhabited islands with extremely fertile soil.

THE WORLD'S
LARGEST CROCODILES

With its characteristic double row of nodules on the head and upper jaw, the saltwater crocodile (*Crocodylus porosus*) is not only the world's largest living reptilian but also – along with Africa's Nile crocodile – the most aggressive and feared on Earth. Although equally at home in salt or fresh water, the reptile prefers the brackish zones around river mouths.

A crocodile's staple diet...

...includes fish and mammals.

During the rainy season the animals can penetrate deep into the interior, and caution is advised not only at the coast, but near any river or pond. These ancient reptiles can easily reach lengths of 5–7 m (16–23 feet) and can go without food for exceptionally long periods – subsisting only on their own body fat, they can slow their metabolism to the extent that their hearts beat only three times a minute. Known as "salties" in Australia, the animals can survive for months without feeding and still be strong enough to attack with explosive force. The freshwater crocodile (*Crocodylus johnsoni*), known as a "freshie", is found in the tropical north of the country, especially in the McKinley River in the Northern Territory. It can reach lengths of 3 m (10 feet) including its long snout, but is considered extremely shy, and no attacks on humans have ever been recorded.

Saltwater crocodiles are identifiable by the two raised nodules just behind their eyes.

Ordering African rivers by length after the Nile still attracts some debate, not least due to the extreme differences in water volume between the dry and rainy season. Measurements can vary wildly.

CONGO AND LUVUA
(incl. the Luapula and Chambeshi)
4,835 km (3,004 miles)

Africa's second longest river is also the world's second largest after the Amazon. Its drainage basin of 3.7 million sq. km (1.4 million sq. miles) is even larger than that of the Nile. The Congo river system includes a number of other rivers, but the Chambeshi, the source of the Luapula, is situated the furthest from the river's mouth. Rising west of Lake Malawi in northern Zambia near the Tanzanian border, it flows south-west through the Bangweulu Swamps, which then drain into the Luapula River. The Luapula, which forms the border between Zambia and the Democratic Republic of the Congo, flows from south to north into Lake Mweru which in turn discharges into the Luvua to the north. The Luvua continues on as the right-hand of the two tributaries flowing into the Congo at the town of Ankoro. The river then describes a mighty arc to the west through the Congo Basin. As it turns to the south-west, the Congo marks the border

NIGER
4,184 km (2,600 miles)

Africa's third longest river rises in Guinea near the border with Sierra Leone. It flows east in an arc through Mali, passing through the city of Timbuktu and continuing east before taking a sharp turn to the south-east. It flows through Niger, passing close to the border with Benin, before passing through the Kainji reservoir and eventually draining into the Gulf of Guinea through a wide delta in Nigeria.

The Niger flows through the desert: sand dunes at Gao, Mali.

ZAMBEZI
2,574 km (1,599 miles)

The largest river in Africa, with a mouth on the east coast, the Zambezi rises in north-western Zambia at 1,500 m (4,900 feet) and flows through Angola and Zambia before draining into the Indian Ocean via a vast delta in Mozambique. The Victoria Falls on the Zambezi on the border between Zimbabwe and Zambia was designated a UNESCO World Heritage Site in 1989.

The Victoria Falls, seen here at dusk, was discovered by David Livingstone.

ORANGE
2,160 km (1,340 miles)

Known as the Oranjerivier in Afrikaans, the Orange River is the largest river in southern Africa. From its source in the Lesotho highlands it flows west through South Africa, then its lower course forms the border with Namibia, before it drains into the Atlantic at Oranjemund. The Orange River also marks the boundary of the Richtersveld, which has been a UNESCO World Heritage Site since 2007.

The Orange River plunges 60 m (200 feet) at the Augrabies Falls.

between the Democratic Republic of the Congo and the Republic of the Congo – their respective capitals, Brazzaville and Kinshasa, lie on opposite sides of a lake-like bulge in the river known as the Pool Malebo. The river then passes through Matadi on the Angolan border before eventually flowing into the Atlantic 135 km (84 miles) to the west.

The Congo winds its way through mangrove swamps near its mouth, as can be seen from this aerial photograph (far left). Large pirogues are used to transport goods along the Congo (left).

The Okavango flows through the swamps of Botswana's inland Okavango Delta.

OKAVANGO
1,800 km (1,118 miles)

The Okavango rises in the Bié Highlands of Angola in south-western Africa, where its upper course is known as the Cubango. Flowing south through the highlands, it forms the border between Namibia and Angola for some 400 km (250 miles) before reaching north-western Botswana beyond Andara. Here it runs into the swampy Okavango Delta, an inland delta of some 15,000 sq. km (5,800 sq. miles) in the north-eastern Kalahari Desert.

JUBBA
1,658 km (1,030 miles)

The streams which form the source of the Jubba River rise in the mountains of Ethiopia and combine at Doolow on the border with Somalia to form the Jubba. This then flows south through Somalia before reaching its mouth at Kismayo on the Indian Ocean. The Jubba Basin is really a savanna which has been turned into fertile agricultural land by the river. There is a great variety of plant and animal life, including giraffes, leopards, lions, cheetahs, buffalo, and other big game. Heavy rainfall has often resulted in devastating flooding of the Jubba.

LIMPOPO
1,750 km (1,087 miles)

The Limpopo, forming South Africa's north-eastern border with Botswana and Zimbabwe and draining into the Indian Ocean, is Africa's second longest river after the Zambezi. Its source, known as the Crocodile River, lies north-east of Johannesburg at about 1,800 m (5,900 feet) in the peaks of the Witwatersrand. The river then follows an arc to the south-east through Mozambique before reaching the Indian Ocean north of Mabuto. Its largest tributary is the Olifants, which flows through the Kruger National Park.

VOLTA
(incl. the Black Volta)
1,600 km (994 miles)

The Volta, which flows through West Africa, is fed by three streams rising in Burkina Faso (formerly Upper Volta): the Black (Mouhoun), Red (Nazinoun), and White (Nakambé) Voltas. Just after their confluence, the river's progress is blocked near Salaga in Ghana by the Akosombo Dam to form Lake Volta, the world's second largest reservoir after Lake Victoria. The Volta then continues on in a south-easterly direction, flowing into the Gulf of Guinea between the Ada and Keta lagoons.

CHARI
(incl. the Ouham)
1,740 km (1,080 miles)

The Chari (or Shari) is the main tributary of Lake Chad, which is situated on the southern edge of the Sahara on the borders of Chad, Cameroon, Nigeria, and Niger. The lake receives 90% of its water from the Chari River and its water level is determined by the changing amounts of precipitation at the river's origin. The Ouham River, the river's principal source, rises in the Central African Republic before crossing Chad and flowing into the Chari at Sarh; the combined rivers then flow on into the lake.

SÉNÉGAL
(incl. the Bafing)
1,430 km (889 miles)

The Bafing, the source of the Sénégal, rises in the mountains of Fouta Djallon in Mali near the border with Guinea. It then flows north until it is dammed at Manantali, and after its confluence with the Bakoyé it is known as the Sénégal. The river forms the border between Mauritania and Senegal (the country) as it flows west before reaching the Atlantic near the UNESCO World Heritage Site, the city of Saint-Louis. The area surrounding the river's mouth is a national park where many European white storks spend the winter.

HIPPOPOTAMUSES

The hippopotamus is the world's heaviest land mammal after the elephant. Although part of its name means "horse", it is not an odd-toed ungulate like many equines; it forms a separate suborder of the even-toed ungulates, a group which includes cows,

Daily dose: up to 60 kg (132 lb) of greenery.

goats, pigs, gazelles, and many other mammals. The hippo are found in the wild only in sub-Saharan Africa and genetic analysis has shown that its nearest relative is the whale. Weighing up to 4 tonnes (4.4 short tons) and measuring up to 5 m (16 feet) from snout to tail, the hippo is herbivorous and spends most of its day in the water, foraging only at night. Hippos exhibit a range of social behavior: some lead solitary lives but others live in herds of up to 150 animals, presumably in areas where there is enough vegetation to sustain such a population.

Hippos usually spend the day in the water as they have sensitive skin; the Hippo Pool in the Serengeti National Park in northern Tanzania can get a bit crowded during the dry season.

The North American subcontinent is surrounded by three of the world's oceans. The rivers of Canada and the northern USA flow into the Arctic Ocean, those in the west flow into the Pacific Ocean, and the eastern rivers flow into the Atlantic and its various seas.

MISSISSIPPI RIVER
(incl. Missouri and Red Rock Rivers)
6,051 km (3,760 miles)

The origins of the river system which includes the Mississippi are to be found in the Rocky Mountains in the American Mid-West. The Red Rock River rises to the west of Yellowstone Park in the state of Montana, not far from the border with Idaho. Of the two source rivers which form the Jefferson River it is the longer, and the Jefferson is the longest of the three rivers which come together at Three Forks to form the Missouri. The Missouri River continues north through rocky canyons before leaving the mountains east of Great Falls and flowing south-east, eventually joining the Mississippi near St Louis on the Illinois state line. The source of the Mississippi lies west of Lake Superior in Minnesota; from here the river flows south, forming state borders as it crosses vast tracts of America. After its confluence with the Missouri it continues south towards New Orleans, forming a wide delta at the Gulf of Mexico.

MACKENZIE RIVER
(incl. Pearce and Finlay Rivers)
4,241 km (2,635 miles)

The source of the Finlay River lies in western Canada to the east of the continental watershed in the Rocky Mountains. The river flows south-east to Williston Lake, into which the Peace River also drains. The Peace River joins the Athabasca further to the east before flowing north-west through the Great Slave Lake and reaching its mouth as the Mackenzie River at Beaufort Lake.

The delta at the mouth of the Mackenzie River in northern Canada.

RIO GRANDE
3,034 km (1,885 miles)

The Río Grande rises at the confluence of a number of smaller streams at some 3,000 m (9,800 feet) at the foot of Canby Mountain in Colorado. From here it flows south through San Luis Valley into New Mexico, passing Albuquerque on its way to El Paso, Texas. Further south, it leaves the mountains and follows a wide arc to the north-east before heading south-east to the Gulf of Mexico. The Río Grande forms the US-American border downstream from El Paso.

The Río Grande flows through a valley in Big Bend National Park, Texas (right).

YUKON
(incl. the Teslin and Nisutlin)
3,185 km (1,979 miles)

Made famous by gold prospectors, the Yukon's source, the Nisutlin, rises in Canada's Pelly Mountains before flowing south into Teslin Lake and then into the Teslin River, which reaches its confluence with the Yukon near Hootalinqua to the north-west. The Yukon continues west through the US state of Alaska and drains into the Bering Sea.

Dawson City, once the heart of the Gold Rush, and the Yukon River.

NELSON RIVER
(incl. Saskatchewan River)
2,671 km (1,660 miles)

The sources of the twin arms of the Saskatchewan both lie in the Rocky Mountains: the North Saskatchewan rises here at about 1,800 m (5,900 feet) and the South Saskatchewan first appears further to the south, in the Canadian province of Alberta. The two arms combine to form a single river east of Prince Albert before flowing into Lake Winnipeg. The Nelson is the only outflow of the lake and, having traveled east for some 664 km (413 miles), it reaches its mouth at Hudson Bay.

ST LAWRENCE
RIVER (incl. North River)
3,058 km (1,900 miles)

If the linked Great Lakes are included, the North River, a source of the St Louis, which flows into Lake Superior at Duluth, is the river which rises furthest from its eventual mouth at the Atlantic. The actual St Lawrence River begins as an outflow from Lake Ontario and drains into the Atlantic at Québec; its upper course forms the border between the USA and Canada.

The St Lawrence River near St Irenée north of Québec.

COLORADO RIVER
2,333 km (1,450 miles)

The streams which combine to form the Colorado River rise in the Rocky Mountains National Park in the US state of Colorado. Initially flowing south-west through Colorado, Utah, and then Arizona, the river turns south in the same latitude as Las Vegas and eventually drains into the Gulf of California near Mexicali in Mexico. The river is famed for the unique canyons it has eroded into the surrounding rock, including the Grand Canyon.

The Vermilion Cliffs on the Colorado (right) can reach heights of 900 m (2,950 feet).

The Mississippi River set against the skyline of St Louis in the US state of Missouri, including the 192-m-high (630-foot) Gateway Arch, the city's emblem, which was officially opened in 1968.

COLUMBIA RIVER
(incl. Snake River)
2,240 km (1,392 miles)

The Columbia River is an outflow of Columbia Lake, which lies at a height of 820 m (2,690 feet) in the Canadian province of British Columbia. Flowing south through Washington state, the river turns to the west at the Blue Mountains before being joined by its tributary, the Snake River, which rises in Yellowstone National Park. The river then flows into the Pacific Ocean, west of Portland, Oregon.

The Columbia River seen from Crown Point (below).

CHURCHILL RIVER
1,600 km (1000 miles)

The Churchill River, which rises near Beaver Lake in Alberta, Canada, was named after John Churchill, the governor of the Hudson Bay Company from 1685 to 1691. The Churchill River negotiates a series of lakes in Saskatchewan and Manitoba before flowing into Hudson Bay near the town of Churchill. Its most important tributaries are the Beaver and Reindeer Rivers, which are fed from Wollaston and Reindeer Lake respectively. The Nistowiak Falls on the Churchill River is the largest set of falls in Saskatchewan.

COLORADO RIVER (TEXAS)
1,438 km (894 miles)

Although it shares its name with the river in the Grand Canyon, both the source and the mouth of this Colorado River are to be found in the US state of Texas. Rising to the south of Lubbock on the Llano Estacado, a dry plateau in north-western Texas, the river flows south-east through several canyons before reaching the state capital Austin. Here it leaves the mountains to cross flat floodplains near the coast before reaching its mouth on the Gulf of Mexico at Matagorda Bay, which lies to the south of Houston.

The Amazon River's drainage basin covers 7 million sq. km (2.7 million sq. miles), an area the size of Australia, and many of its tributaries have record-breaking lengths in their own right. The list here includes the rivers which drain into a sea rather than the Amazonian river system.

AMAZON
(incl. the Ucayali and Apurímac)
6,448 km (4,007 miles)

The Marañón, Huallaga, and Ucayali Rivers, the principal sources of the Amazon, all rise in the Peruvian Andes. The Marañón is the northernmost of these and also has the greatest flow, but the Ucayali is the longest. The Apurímac, which rises at 5,597 m (18,363 feet) in the Nevado Mismi mountains in Peru, is considered to lie furthest from the river's mouth, although its source is only about 200 km (125 miles) from the Atlantic. The Apurímac reaches its confluence with the Ucayali at Atalaya, Peru, before continuing north and flowing into the Amazon at Nauta. The river is initially known as the Río Solimões as

PARANÁ
(incl. the Río Grande)
3,998 km (2,484 miles)

The Río Grande, the longest of the Paraná's tributaries, rises in the Brazilian state of Minas Gerais in the Serra da Mantiqueira. It flows west through a series of reservoirs before joining the Paranaíba to become the Paraná. This acts as the Argentine-Paraguayan border as it flows south through the La Plata basin and drains into the Atlantic north of Buenos Aires.

The Iguaçu, a tributary of the Paraná, and the falls at Foz do Iguaçu.

SÃO FRANCISCO
3,199 km (1,988 miles)

The Rio São Francisco rises in the Serra da Canastra in eastern Brazil and then flows through a number of Brazilian states before eventually draining into the Atlantic some 200 km (125 miles) south of Recife. It passes through two large dammed lakes en route: the Três Marias reservoir and, further to the north, the Sobradinho, one of the world's largest reservoirs. The river also passes through a picturesque canyon of rocks and cliffs between Paulo Afonso and the town of Penedo.

RIO TOCANTINS
2,640 km (1,640 miles)

The streams which feed the Río Tocantins, the Río Paranã, and the Río das Almas all rise in the Brazilian state of Goiás to the west of Brasilia, the capital. From here, the Tocantins flows north, marking the state line between Tocantins and Maranhão. The Río Araguaia, Tocantins' largest tributary, joins the river near S. João do Araguaia and the combined rivers subsequently flow into the Tucuruí reservoir. Upon leaving the reservoir the Río Tocantins drains into the Atlantic via a wide, funnel-shaped estuary at Belem.

it enters Brazil, only gaining the name Amazon after its confluence with the Río Negro at Manaus. The world's largest river (by a considerable margin) has no fewer than 10,000 tributaries, of which 1,100 are of a considerable size and 13 more than 1,000 km (620 miles) long. The river, which at this point is several kilometers (more than a mile) wide, flows through Brazil for 3,100 km (1,926 miles) before reaching the Atlantic at Macapá. More than 3,500 plant and animal species have been recorded in the water, including the Amazon river dolphin, which is now endangered. The region's forests are threatened by increased logging and increasingly pollutants are finding their way into the river, including mercury, a by-product of gold mining.

Clouds over the Anavilhanas archipelago on the Río Negro, one of the Amazon's largest tributaries. The giant archipelago, which is composed of a great number of islands, is located just before Rio Negro's confluence with the Amazon north of Manaus (left).

ORINOCO
2,140 km (1,330 miles)

The source of the Orinoco is to be found close by the Brazilian border in the Sierra Parima, Venezuela. It follows a wide arc to the west, skirting the Guayana uplands, and marks the border with Colombia as it flows east through the expanses of the Orinoco Basin on its way to a wide delta on the Atlantic coast. The river interconnects with the Río Negro in Brazil via the Casiquiare, a natural fork in the river's upper course.

The Orinoco's leisurely pace makes it ideal for canoeists (right).

PARNAÍBA
1,716 km (1,066 miles)

The Río Parnaíba, the second longest river in northern South America after the Río São Francisco, marks the border between the Brazilian states of Maranhão and Piauí. The upper course of the river is largely navigable, apart from a couple of waterfalls, and its source is located in the Serra das Mangabeiras, a chain of mountains whose territory is shared between both states. The Río Parnaiba separates into five arms, forming a delta that covers an area of some 2,700 sq. km (1,040 sq. miles) as it flows into the Atlantic Ocean.

URUGUAY
1,790 km (1,112 miles)

The Uruguay River combines with the Paraná to form the Río de la Plata estuary. Rising in the Serra Geral to the west of Tubarão in the south Brazilian highlands, the river flows south, forming the border first between Brazil and Argentina and then between Uruguay and Argentina. The river's many rapids make it somewhat difficult to navigate, but the Saltos del Moconá, a 2-km-long (1½-mile) waterfall, is the only one in the world where the water drops down along the length of the course of the river.

AMAZON DELTA – THE WORLD'S LARGEST RIVER MOUTH

The Amazon is not only the world's largest river by volume, it also has the largest delta. The exact dimensions are difficult to determine, but it is unquestionably number one: including the Pará, which drains into the Atlantic to the south, and the river island of Marajó, which in itself is almost as big as Denmark, the delta at the mouth of the river is 330 km (205 miles) wide. Although the Amazon carries a lot of sediment, the delta has not built up out into the sea, as is the case with many other rivers, and this is thought to be due to the action of waves caused by periodic high tides, which can reach a height of up to 4 m (13 feet). During the high tides at new and full moon in February and March, the waves can penetrate from the sea for several kilometers (over a mile) into a number of the Amazon's tributaries. Although feared by the local population for their destructive power, the waves attract surfers from all over the world.

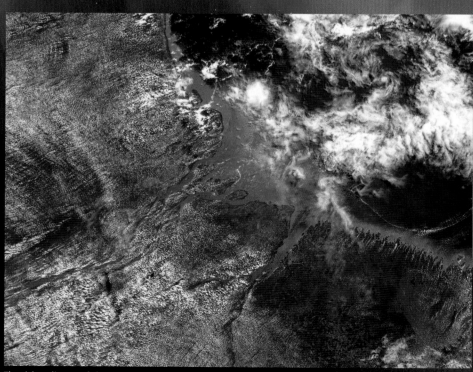

The rich sediment of the river water is carried far out into the Atlantic before finally mixing with seawater.

DELTAS – THE WORLD'S LARGEST RIVER MOUTHS

A delta is a landform which builds up at the mouth of a river due to the gradual deposition of sediment. Deltas are usually formed by slow-flowing rivers and the tides in the seas

The Lena delta in summer.

into which they drain tend to be quite weak. A delta forms when a river spreads out to flow into a lake or sea and the resulting area of deposited sediment resembles a triangle standing on its tip; this can most clearly be seen at the Nile. The 5th-century BC Greek historian Herodotus called the feature a "delta" for its close resemblance to the upended Greek letter. It is often quite difficult to determine exactly where a delta begins and ends as dry periods or floods can bring about short-term but drastic variations. The list on this page generally uses the most recent satellite measurements; the areas have been rounded but still give an idea of the order of magnitude.

THE LARGEST RIVER DELTAS

1. **Amazon delta**
   121,000 sq. km (46,700 sq. miles)
2. **Ganges delta**
   106,000 sq. km (41,000 sq. miles)
3. **Yukon/Kuskokwim delta**
   70,000 sq. km (27,000 sq. miles)
4. **Lena delta**
   45,000 sq. km (17,400 sq. miles)
5. **Mekong delta**
   39,000 sq. km (15,000 sq. miles)
6. **Huang He delta**
   36,000 sq. km (13,900 sq. miles)
7. **Irrawaddy delta**
   30,000 sq. km (11,600 sq. miles)
8. **Mississippi delta**
   29,000 sq. km (11,200 sq. miles)
9. **Volga delta**
   27,000 sq. km (10,400 sq. miles)
10. **Orinoco delta**
    22,500 sq. km (8,700 sq. miles)
11. **Song Hong delta**
    22,000 sq. km (8,500 sq. miles)
12. **Niger delta**
    19,000 sq. km (7,300 sq. miles)

The Mississippi, which regularly floods and deposits material to form its banks, has also created an imposing delta at the Gulf of Mexico which progresses a further 100 m (330 feet) into the sea every year. Some 17,500 cu. m of water (618,000 cu. feet) flow into the Gulf every second, about eight times as much as the Rhine discharges into the North Sea. As the river's speed drops, it deposits more and more sediment in the delta, leaving impressive fans of sedimentary material which reach far out into the open sea. Protected by levees, the banks of the main arm of the river are cultivated but the dark green areas are all swampland.

WATERFALLS

Geological faults or other suitably shaped ground formations can cause flowing water to fall many dozens or even hundreds of meters. This can occur in one fell swoop – which is rarely the case – or as a series of cascades in several stages. If the speed of the flow is increased by the falls or a narrowing of the river channel, rapids can result. If the continued course of the agitated water is through rocky cliffs, this is then known as a cataract. Rapids and waterfalls are among the world's most impressive natural spectacles.

THE WORLD'S MIGHTIEST RAPIDS AND WATERFALLS

❶ Chutes d'Inga
Democratic Republic of the
Congo (DRC)   42,500 cu. m/s
(1.5 million cu. feet/s)

❷ Chutes de Livingstone
DRC   35,000 cu. m/s
(1.2 million cu. feet/s)

❸ Boyoma Falls   17,000 cu. m/s
DRC   (600,000 cu. feet/s)

❹ Chutes de Khone 11,600 cu. m/s
Laos   (410,000 cu. feet/s)

❺ Salto Pará   3,500 cu. m/s
Venezuela   (124,000 cu. feet/s)

❻ Cachoeira de Paulo Afonso
Brazil   2,800 cu. m/s
(99,000 cu. feet/s)

❼ Niagara Falls   2,500 cu. m/s
USA   (88,000 cu. feet/s)

❽ Saltos do Iguaçu
Argentina/Brazil   1,750 cu. m/s
(62,000 cu. feet/s)

❾ Saltos dos Patos e Maribondo
Brazil   1,500 cu. m/s
(53,000 cu. feet/s)

❿ Victoria Falls
Zimbabwe/Zambia   1,100 cu. m/s
(39,000 cu. feet/s)

⓫ Virginia Falls   1,000 cu. m/s
Canada   (35,300 cu. feet/s)

⓬ Churchill Falls   990 cu. m/s
Canada   (35,000 cu. feet/s)

THE WORLD'S HIGHEST WATERFALLS

❶ Salto Angel
Venezuela   979 m (3,212 feet)

❷ Tugela Falls
South Africa   948 m (3,114 feet)

❸ Cataratas las Tres Hermanas
Peru   914 m (2,999 feet)

❹ Olo'upena Falls
USA   900 m (2,953 feet)

❺ Catarata Yumbilla
Peru   896 m (2,940 feet)

❻ Vinnufossen
Norway   860 m (2,822 feet)

❼ Balåifossen
Norway   850 m (2,789 feet)

❽ Pu'uka'oku Falls
USA   850 m (2,789 feet)

❾ James Bruce Falls
Canada   840 m (2,756 feet)

❿ Browne Falls
New Zealand   836 m (2,743 feet)

⓫ Strupenfossen
Norway   820 m (2,690 feet)

⓬ Ramnefjellsfossen
Norway   818 m (2,684 feet)

The Iguaçu Falls, found where the Brazilian, Argentine, and Paraguayan borders converge, is one of the largest and most impressive waterfalls on Earth. The surrounding area on the Argentine and Brazilian sides has been declared a national park, and these parks, including the waterfall, have been inscribed on the UNESCO Natural Heritage list since the 1980s.

CHUTES D'INGA

About 40 km (25 miles) north of Matadi, the Democratic Republic of the Congo's principal port, the Congo River narrows to form rapids, dropping 96 m (315 feet) over the course of 15 km (9 miles). An average of 42,500 cu. m (1.5 million cu. feet) of water race through these rapids every second on their way to the coast, and this can sometimes rise to as much as 70,000 cu. m (2.5 million cu. feet). The Chutes d'Inga is thus the largest set of falls on Earth, and these gigantic volumes of water already provide energy for two giant power plants, with a third in the planning stage. The plants are considered "white elephants", however; economically unviable prestige projects dating back to the dictator Mobuto Sese Seko, who died in 1997.

The rapids at the Inga Falls have spelled disaster for many – this image was taken from a helicopter searching for possible survivors from a French expedition in 1985.

BOYOMA FALLS

CHUTES DE LIVINGSTONE

The Chutes de Livingstone was named after David Livingstone (1813–1873), a Scottish missionary who explored Africa. Located about 35 km (21 miles) from the Chutes d'Inga, it is thought to be the world's second largest set of falls, with an average flow of 35,000 cu. m (1.2 million cu. feet) per second. The Congo River separates to form several mighty waterfalls to the south-west of the cities of Brazzaville (in the Republic of the Congo) and Kinshasa (in the Democratic Republic of the Congo). Here the river breaks through the "Guinean Backbone", one of the five great highlands of continental Africa; these watersheds are composed of extensive tracts of land which have often been folded to form mountain ranges. River basins are often to be found at their edges, and the Congo falls into this category, dropping a total of 274 m (899 feet) through a series of rapids on its 350-km (217-mile) journey to the delta.

The seven cataracts of the Boyoma Falls, the world's third largest set of falls, discharge some 17,000 cu. m (600,000 cu. feet) of water every second into a bend of the Lualuba River, the largest tributary of the Congo. The falls, which are about 60 m (200 feet) high, are spread out over a width of about 1.4 km (1 mile) and a length of 15 km (9 miles) of the river between the cities of Ubundu and Kisangani (Democratic Republic of the Congo). The falls mark the transi-tion between the whitewater upper course of the Congo and the navigable middle course through the Congo Basin, which ends above the Chutes de Livingstone.

SALTO ANGEL

The Canaima National Park, near the Guyanese and Brazilian borders in south-eastern Venezuela, is the country's second largest

The Salto Angel in Venezuela's deep forest.

national park and contains the Salto Angel, the world's highest free-falling waterfall at 979 m (3,212 feet). It was named after Jimmie Angel (1899–1956), the American bush pilot and gold prospector who discovered it in 1933, or rather rediscovered it; it had first been sighted by a Venezuelan in 1910, but Angel brought it to a wider public. The largest single drop of this mighty natural spectacle is 805 m (2,641 feet) high, and is immediately followed by a second of about 200 m (660 feet). The water plunges down from an outcrop of the Auyantepui, a plateau of 700 sq. km (270 miles), to form a tributary of the Río Carrao. The Salto Angel is fed from precipitation on the plateau, which often takes the form of violent storms.

The great height and the strong updrafts often cause much of the Salto Angel's water to form an aerosol of tiny droplets, especially during the dry season when water levels are low.

EUROPE'S GREATEST AND HIGHEST WATERFALLS

When compared with the giants elsewhere on the globe, European waterfalls seem to be rather modest affairs; the Rhine Falls, the continent's largest, only stands at number 23 in the world rankings.

RHINE FALLS

Switzerland   **370 cu. m/s**
                         (13,000 cu. feet/s)

About 4 km (2½ miles) to the west of Schaffhausen there is a rocky cliff where the Rhine plunges into a 23-m (75-foot) chasm. Every second, an average of 370 cu. m (13,000 cu. feet) of water pours over a waterfall that is about 150 m (490 feet) wide, making this Europe's largest. During the rainy summer months the water volume can average up to 700 cu. m (24,700 cu. feet) per second. The Rhine has followed its modern course along a bed of hard blue-gray limestone since the Würm glacial period, and the Rhine Falls was created some 14,000 to 17,000 years ago at the junction of this hard limestone and a softer gravel bed dating back to the Riss glacial period 200,000 years before. The outcrop of the Rhine Falls is the remains of the originally much steeper lip of the limestone, and the large cliff can be climbed by visitors. Over the millennia, the channel has not eroded as much as might have been expected, principally as the Rhine above Lake

Dettifoss Waterfall, Iceland.

Hafragilsfoss, a little distance to the north of Dettifoss.

The water plunges over Selfoss in northern Iceland with great force.

DETTIFOSS

Iceland   **200 cu. m/s**
                    (7,000 cu. feet/s)

The gray-brown water of the Jökulsá á Fjöllum glacial stream in the south of the Jökulsárgljúfur National Park in north-eastern Iceland plunges over a cliff 100 m (330 feet) wide into a chasm 45 m (148 feet) deep, before draining into the Norwegian Sea 30 km (19 miles) further north. Its average flow of 200 cu. m/s (7,000 feet/s) generates more potential energy than the Rhine Falls as the drop is twice as high, but the volume of water varies with the season.

HAFRAGILSFOSS

Iceland   **200 cu. m/s**
                    (7,000 cu. feet/s)

Only 2 km (1½ miles) north of Dettifoss, the Jökulsá á Fjöllum plunges a further 27 m (89 feet) down Hafragilsfoss, a 91-m-wide (299-foot) cliff on the south-eastern fringe of the Jökulsárgljúfur National Park. To visit Hafragilsfoss, the second highest waterfall on the river, visitors must follow a demanding circular route – which at some points is little more than a steep rocky path equipped with a safety rope – through the gorge. The roads in the park are nigh on impassable in winter.

SELFOSS

Iceland   **200 cu. m/s**
                    (7,000 cu. feet/s)

Selfoss, where the Jökulsá á Fjöllum (meaning "glacial river from the mountains") narrows, is located only a short distance south of Dettifoss. The river's gray-green waters plunge over a cliff that is 183 m (600 feet) wide and 11 m (36 feet) high before traveling the short distance to Dettifoss and Hafragilsfoss. The Jökulsá á Fjöllum, at 206 km (128 miles) the second longest river on the island, rises at Vatnahökull, Iceland's largest glacier, which has covered the south-east of the island with a sheet of ice up to 1,000 m (3,300 feet) thick.

STORFORSEN

Sweden   **186 cu. m/s**
                    (6,570 cu. feet/s)

This large set of rapids lies some 38 km (24 miles) north-west of Älvsbyn in the northern Swedish province of Noorbottens. The water drops some 80 m (260 feet) over the course of about 5 km (3 miles), with the steepest drop of 60 m (197 feet) occurring over the last 2 km (1½ miles). The Piteälven, a small tributary, is in spate during June, boosting the flow to 870 cu. m/s (30,700 cu. feet/s). The area surrounding the rapids is now a nature reserve but is accessible to visitors via paths and wooden walkways.

Constance carries only small amounts of gravel and sand, known as alluvium. The power of the Rhine was exploited in the past to drive mills and a small power plant near Neuhausen now generates 4.4 megawatts of electricity without reducing the river's output unduly. The Rhine Falls is a Mecca for tourists and is accessible via well-made paths on both sides.

Left: The cascades, pool, and characteristic cliffs of the Rhine Falls, seen from the Neuhausen side. On the Zurich side, Laufen Castle towers above the falls in the background.

The Grande Cascade de Gavarnie in the French part of the Pyrenees divides into three sections before reaching the valley floor of the Cirque de Gavarnie gorge.

Giessbach Falls, Switzerland.

Krimmler Falls, Austria.

NORWAY'S HIGHEST WATERFALLS

No European country has more or higher waterfalls than Norway. The following list is based on the World Waterfall Database, although the names and heights given are often not recorded in other sources.

Ramnefjellsfossen, Norway.

❶ Vinnufossen	860 m (2,822 feet)
❷ Baläifossen	850 m (2,789 feet)
❸ Strupenfossen	820 m (2,690 feet)
❹ Ramnefjellsfossen	818 m (2,684 feet)
❺ Mongefossen	773 m (2,536 feet)
❻ Kjelfossen	755 m (2,477 feet)
❼ Ølmäafossen	720 m (2,362 feet)

❽ Kjeragfossen	715 m (2,346 feet)
❾ Dantefossen	700 m (2,297 feet)
❿ Brufossen	698 m (2,290 feet)
⓫ Spirefossen	690 m (2,264 feet)
⓬ Krunefossen	660 m (2,165 feet)
⓭ Mardalsfossen	657 m (2,156 feet)
⓮ Tyssestrengene	646 m (2,119 feet)

EUROPE'S HIGHEST WATERFALLS
(outside Norway)

❶ Slapovi Levo Savice
Slovenia 600 m (1,969 feet)
❷ Cascade du Gietro
Switzerland 564 m (1,850 feet)
❸ Engstligen Falls
Switzerland 500 m (1,640 feet)
❹ Walcher Falls
Austria 500 m (1,640 feet)
❺ Rothbach Falls
Germany 469 m (1,539 feet)
❻ Grande Cascade de Gavarnie
France 422 m (1,385 feet)
❼ Duenden Waterfall
Switzerland 400 m (1,312 feet)

❽ Geltenfall
Switzerland 400 m (1,312 feet)
❾ Cascade du Moulin Marquis
France 400 m (1,312 feet)
❿ Giessbachfall
Switzerland 391 m (1,283 feet)
⓫ Krimmler Wasserfälle
Austria 380 m (1,247 feet)
⓬ La Cascade d'Arpenaz
France 365 m (1,198 feet)
⓭ Cascata del Serio
Italy 315 m (1,033 feet)
⓮ Faulenbachfall
Switzerland 305 m (1,001 feet)

ASIA'S GREATEST AND HIGHEST WATERFALLS

Asia's gigantic waterways have many mighty cascades and rapids, but the Chutes de Khone on the Mekong River top any list of waterfalls.

KHONE FALLS

**Laos/Mekong   11,600 cu. m/s
(409,650 cu. feet/s)**

The Khone Falls (Chutes de Khone) are a series of cataracts near the Cambodian border on the Mekong River in the Laos province of Champasak. The Chutes form a cascade-like waterfall south of the inland Si Phan Don delta, whose name translates as "4,000 islands". The Chutes are almost 11 km (7 miles) wide, of which more than 10 km (6 miles) is waterfall, with a drop of more than 21 m (70 feet). The Chutes de Khone are the largest waterfall in Asia and the widest and fourth-largest in the world. The average flow of 11,600 cu. m (409,650 cu. feet) per second can increase in the rainy season to 50,000 cu. m (1,765,700 feet) per second. The Chutes de Khone prevent the Mekong River from being navigable as far as China, although French colonists in the 19th century tried in vain to get ships past. It took a railway, which transports boats past the falls, to make it possible for ships to negotiate the cataracts.

HUKOU FALLS

**China/Huang He   1,000 cu. m/s
(35,300 cu. feet/s)**

The Hukou Falls lie in the middle reaches of the Yellow River (Huang He) between Shaanx and Shanxi provinces. The falls vary between 30–50 m (100 and 170 feet) in width during the year, with a drop of 30 m (100 feet). When the river is swollen the flow can reach 8,000 cu. m/s (282,500 cu. feet/s). The falls have given their name to the Huang He Hukou Pubu National Park.

The Huang He waters are stained yellow by the sediment they carry (right).

CAUVERY FALLS

**India/Cauvery River   940 cu. m/s
(33,200 cu. feet p/s)**

The Cauvery Falls, also known as the Shivanasamudra Waterfalls, are located on the Cauvery River in southern India, a Hindu sacred river. The river separates around the island of Shivanasamudra, east of Mysore, and the Cauvery Falls plunge 90 m (290 ft) into a chasm on each side. The falls are about 850 m (2,800 feet) wide, and their highest flow was recorded at 19,000 cu m/s (671,000 cu. feet/s).

The Cauvery Falls and islands in Tamil Nadu (large image, above).

The mighty cataracts of the Chutes de Khone in Laos, seen from the air (far left); one of the main cascades is called "Khong Phapheng" ("the roar of the Mekong") (left).

ASIA'S HIGHEST WATERFALLS

The highest waterfall in Asia is the Hannoki-no-taki near Tateyama in Japan, although these 500-m (1,640-feet) falls only carry water when the snow melts between April and July. They are a sister formation to the nearby Shomyo-daki, which is 350 m (1,160 feet) high and falls throughout the year. India has any number of high falls, and the Kunchikal Falls at Agumbe are the second-highest in Asia. Southern Thailand has a similar number of falls, all drawing their water from the Nakhon-Si-Thammarat Mountains. The Allwagwag Falls in the Philippines are located on the island of Mondanao, near Davoa. The Baizhang-Pu Falls in eastern China are fed from the Huangshan mountains.

❶ **Hannoki-no-taki**
  Japan   500 m (1,640 feet)
❷ **Kunchikal Falls**
  India   455 m (1,492 feet)
❸ **Barehipani Falls**
  India   399 m (1,309 feet)
❹ **Karom, Nam Tok**
  Thailand   396 m (1,299 feet)
❺ **Shomyo-daki**
  Japan   350 m (1,148 feet)
❻ **Allwagwag Falls**
  Philippines   338 m (1,110 feet)
❼ **Langshiang Falls**
  India   337 m (1,107 feet)

Shomyo-daki and the nearby Hannoki-no-taki (right) in Japan.

AUSTRALIA AND OCEANIA'S GREATEST
AND HIGHEST WATERFALLS

Australia is 29 times larger than New Zealand, but the smaller island state has a clear lead when the heights of the waterfalls in this part of the world are compared – no less than 16 of its falls have drops of 300 m (990 feet) or more. New Zealand has ideal geographic conditions: its islands are mountainous, there is a network of numerous rivers and streams, and the coast to the south-west features steep fjord cliffs. Most of its territory is located in a rainy temperate zone, whereas large portions of Australia's outback are desert, with many of its rivers carrying water only intermittently. Only the south and south-west coast of Australia lies in the temperate zone. The first waterfall on Oceania's many islands to feature in the list occupies 13th place: the Vaipo Falls on Nuku Hiva, the largest island in the Marquesa Group in French Polynesia, with a drop of 350 m (1,148 feet).

THE HIGHEST WATERFALLS

1. **Browne Falls**
   New Zealand   836 m (2,743 feet)
2. **Lake Chamberlain Falls**
   New Zealand   700 m (2,297 feet)
3. **Lake Unknown Falls**
   New Zealand   680 m (2,231 feet)
4. **Hidden Falls**
   New Zealand   660 m (2,165 feet)
5. **Bluff Falls**
   New Zealand   600 m (1,969 feet)
6. **Wishbone Falls**
   New Zealand   600 m (1,969 feet)
7. **Sutherland Falls**
   New Zealand   580 m (1,903 feet)
8. **Douglas Falls**
   New Zealand   540 m (1,772 feet)
9. **Wollomombi Falls**
   Australia   424 m (1,391 feet)
10. **Tin Mine Falls**
    Australia   421 m (1,381 feet)
11. **Gerard Falls**
    New Zealand   420 m (1,378 feet)
12. **Hirere Falls**
    New Zealand   420 m (1,378 feet)
13. **Vaipo (Ahuii) Falls**
    French Polynesia
    350 m (1,148 feet)

Main image: Sutherland Falls is located in the Fiordland National Park on New Zealand's South Island.

BROWNE FALLS
836 m (2,743 feet)

Browne Falls in the south-west of New Zealand's South Island tumbles from the Fiordland cliffs into the waters of Doubtful Sound in the Tasman Sea.

BLUFF FALLS
600 m (1,969 feet)

Bluff Falls is also to be found in the Fiordland National Park in south-western New Zealand, the largest park in the country and a UNESCO Natural Heritage Site since 1990.

WOLLOMOMBI FALLS
424 m (1,391 feet)

Located in the Oxley Wild Rivers National Park about 450 km (280 miles) north of Sydney in New South Wales, Australia's highest waterfall occasionally dries up.

VAIPO FALLS
350 m (1,148 feet)

Vaipo Falls (also called Ahuii) is to be found about 15 km (9 miles) south-west of the town of Taiohae on the volcanic island of Nuku Hiva in French Polynesia.

WALLAMAN FALLS
268 m (879 feet)

The impressive spectacle of Australia's highest single-drop waterfall in the wet tropics of Queensland has been a UNESCO World Heritage Site since 1988.

AFRICA'S GREATEST AND HIGHEST WATERFALLS

Tugela Falls, where water plunges down five rocky steps with a combined height of 948 m (3,114 feet), is second in magnitude only to the Salto Angel in Venezuela, the highest waterfall in the world. Tugela Falls is located in the northern Drakensberg, a range of peaks

The first sections of the Tugela Falls.

running parallel to the south-eastern coast of South Africa which can sometimes exceed 3,000 m (9,800 feet) in height. The area is enclosed within the Royal Natal National Park and the falls draw their water from the Tugela ("sudden" in Zulu) River, which rises only a short distance away in the Mont-Aux-Sources mountains.

THE HIGHEST WATERFALLS

1 **Tugela Falls**
South Africa   948 m (3,114 feet)
2 **Mutarazi Falls**
South Africa   762 m (2,500 feet)
3 **Cascades de Trou de Fer**
Réunion   725 m (2,379 feet)
4 **Cascade Blanche**
Réunion   640 m (2,100 feet)
5 **Ndedema Falls**
South Africa   460 m (1,509 feet)
6 **Vivienne Falls**
Kenya   460 m (1,509 feet)
7 **Gura Falls**
Kenya   305 m (1,001 feet)
8 **Cascade de Fleurs Jaunes**
Réunion   300 m (984 feet)
9 **Rianbavy**
Madagascar   250 m (820 feet)
10 **Chutes de Kambadaga**
Guinea   249 m (817 feet)
11 **Pungwe Falls**
Zimbabwe   243 m (797 feet)
12 **Elands River Falls**
South Africa   228 m (748 feet)

THE GREATEST WATERFALLS BY VOLUME

1 **Chutes d'Inga**
Democratic Republic of the Congo
(DRC)   42,500 cu. m/s
(1.5 million cu. feet/s)
2 **Chutes de Livingstone**
DRC   35,000 cu. m/s
(1.2 million cu. feet/s)
3 **Boyoma Falls**
DRC   17,000 cu. m/s
(600,000 cu. feet/s)
4 **Victoria Falls**
Zimbabwe/Zambia   1,100 cu. m/s
(39,000 cu. feet/s)
5 **Kongou Falls**
Gabon   900 cu. m/s
(32,000 cu. feet/s)
6 **Epupa Falls**
Namibia   500 cu. m/s
(18,000 cu. feet/s)
7 **Augrabies Falls**
South Africa   310 cu. m/s
(11,000 cu. feet/s)
8 **Murchison Falls**
Uganda   300 cu. m/s
(10,600 cu. feet/s)
9 **Ruacana Falls**
Namibia/Angola   280 cu. m/s
(9,900 cu. feet/s)

The longest single drop of the five stages making up the Tugela Falls sees water tumbling down a sheer cliff 411 m (1,348 feet) high.

KONGOU FALLS

Gabon   900 cu. m/s
(32,000 cu. feet/s)

Spanning more than 3 km (2 miles), Kongou Falls is one of the highlights of the Ivindo National Park. Islands and tropical forests divide the falls into several cataracts as they plunge some 56 m (184 feet) into the depths.

EPUPA FALLS

Namibia   500 cu. m/s
(18,000 cu. feet/s)

This waterfall on the Namibian-Angolan border is fed by the 500-m-wide (1,640-foot) Kunene River, which drops 60 m (197 feet) over 1.5 km (1 mile); the greatest drop is about 20 m (66 feet). The river and waterfall never dry up.

AUGRABIES FALLS

South Africa   310 cu. m/s
(11,000 cu. feet/s)

The Augrabies Falls National Park was named after its principal attraction, a waterfall with a drop of some 60 m (200 feet). The gorge cut deep into the cliff is proof that even granite cannot withstand the power of water.

RUACANA FALLS

Namibia/Angola   280 cu. m/s
(9,900 cu. feet/s)

Ruacana Falls is situated in northern Namibia on the Angolan border, about 135 km (84 miles) upstream of the Epupa Falls. The falls are 120 m (394 feet) and about 700 m (2,300 feet) across when in spate.

VICTORIA FALLS – AFRICA'S MIGHTIEST WATERFALL

The spectacular Victoria Falls lies within a number of conservation areas spread across several countries. It is thus easily accessible to tourists, and when the river is in spate, the thunder of the falling water can be heard for miles around.

Situated near the towns of Victoria Falls and Livingstone on the border between Zimbabwe and Zambia, Victoria Falls has been designated a UNESCO World Heritage Site since 1989. The waters of the Zambezi River plunge some 110 m (360 feet) into the depths from a cliff 1,708 m (5,604 feet) wide, forming the world's largest contiguous curtain of water. The flow rate can vary wildly – for example, in the dry season it amounts to only 170 cu. m/s (6,000 cu. feet/s), while at the height of the rainy season up to 10,000 cu. m/s (350,000 cu. feet/s) of water thunders into the chasm. The average flow is about 1,100 cu. m/s (39,000 cu. feet/s), making it the tenth largest waterfall on Earth. The Scottish missionary and African explorer David Livingstone (1813–1873) is thought to have been the first European to glimpse the falls, which he named Victoria Falls as a tribute to the incumbent British queen, and Zimbabwe still uses this name officially. Zambia, however, has retained the pre-colonial name of Mosi-oa-Tunya, which means "the smoke that thunders".

Below: A dramatic light is cast over the Victoria Falls at dusk, seen from the Zimbabwean side. Far left: The aerial photograph shows the water falling from the 1,708-m-wide (5,604-foot) cliff as a solid sheet. Rainbows often form in the fine mist (left).

NORTH AND CENTRAL AMERICA'S GREATEST AND HIGHEST WATERFALLS

The waterfalls of North America generally have a greater flow rate and are higher than those in Central America. The highest waterfalls are to be found on the volcanic island of Hawaii, the 50th state of America, which in fact is geologically distinct from continental North America.

VIRGINIA FALLS

Canada   **1,000 cu. m/s (35,300 cu. feet/s)**

Located approximately 500 km (300 miles) west of Yellowknife in the Mackenzie Mountains of the Northwest Territories, the Nahanni National Park has preserved its isolation since its establishment in 1972. The park was designated a UNESCO World Heritage Site six years later. Virginia Falls is situated at the southern tip of the park, where the wild South Nahanni River plunges over a cliff 250 m (820 feet) wide into a chasm some 96 m (315 feet) deep. The falls, called Nailicho in the Dene language, were renamed after the daughter of their discoverer, Fenley Hunter, a member of both the Royal Geographical Society of London and the New York Explorers' Club, who had been commissioned to explore the South Nahanni in 1928. Skilled in the use of a sextant for surveying, Hunter was an expert cartographer. He discovered and measured the Virginia Falls on 21 August 1928, his daughter's birthday, and when he handed over his

A heron hunting for prey at the Churchill Falls in Canada.

CHURCHILL FALLS

Canada   **990 cu. m/s (35,000 cu. feet/s)**

Once known as the Grand Falls or Hamilton Falls, Churchill Falls is located in McLean Canyon (originally Bowdoin Canyon) in Newfoundland. Ever since the majority of the water was diverted to a power plant, the falls have not looked quite so "grand", except when in spate. The waters of the Hamilton River fall in two stages for a total distance of 92 m (302 feet); the longer stage measures 75 m (246 feet). The waterfall averages 46 m (151 feet) in width.

WILLAMETTE FALLS

USA   **874 cu. m/s (31,000 cu. feet/s)**

The Willamette River, a tributary of the Columbia River, encounters a horseshoe-shaped cliff, 460 m wide (1,509 feet), near Oregon City in the US state of Oregon before plunging into a chasm 12 m (39 feet) deep. Willamette Falls is considered the largest set of falls in the American north-west, although a large proportion of the water is held back by sluice gates and the flow rate is especially limited in late summer. The riverbanks are lined with industrial plants. The original Native American

The Willamette Falls near Oregon City.

population once believed that the gods had placed the waterfall here to provide them with sustenance throughout the winter; there was an abundance of salmon, as the fish could only climb the waterfall when the river reached a certain level.

GREAT FALLS

USA   **323 cu. m/s (11,400 cu. feet/s)**

Rising in Preston County in West Virginia, the Potomac River flows down the eastern seaboard of America before reaching its mouth at Chesapeake Bay in the state of Maryland, about 60 km (37 miles) south of Washington D.C. Over a series of steps, the river plunges down a cliff about 46 m (150 feet) wide to a valley 24 m (79 feet) below. The surrounding reaches of the Potomac are popular with whitewater rafters and canoeists. The Great Falls Park is located on the southern banks of the river, in Virginia.

maps and sketches to the Geological Survey of Canada, he requested that the falls be named after her; his wish was granted in recognition of the great services he had rendered. The region is similarly obliged to Pierre Trudeau (1919–2000), the former prime minister of Canada, who made great efforts in the founding of the national park.

At 96 m (315 feet), Virginia Falls in north-western Canada is about twice as high as Niagara Falls; the central rocky island is known as Mason's Rock after Bill Mason, a Canadian naturalist, ecological activist, film-maker, and author (left).

Yosemite Falls seen from the valley floor.

Yosemite Falls is one of the principal attractions in the national park of the same name in the Sierra Nevada, California.

YOSEMITE FALLS
USA   **739 m (2,425 feet)**

Yosemite Falls in the Yosemite National Park in California's Sierra Nevada is the highest waterfall in the USA to have been officially measured (two in the North Cascades National Park in Washington State may be higher, but have not yet been officially confirmed). The water crashes down over three steps, of which the first and highest measures 436 m (1,430 feet). The original Native Americans who lived in the Yosemite Valley called the waterfall "Cholock" and believed that "Fallkolk", the plunge pool at the base of the falls, was inhabited by the spirits of witches.

Basaseachic Falls (312 m/1,024 feet), Mexico's highest permanent waterfall.

NORTH AMERICA'S HIGHEST WATERFALLS

❶ **Olo'upena Falls**
Hawaii   900 m (2,953 feet)
❷ **Pu'uka'oku Falls**
Hawaii   850 m (2,789 feet)
❸ **James Bruce Falls**
Canada   840 m (2,756 feet)
❹ **Waihilau Falls**
Hawaii   792 m (2,598 feet)
❺ **Yosemite Falls**
USA   739 m (2,425 feet)
❻ **Mana'wai'nui Falls**
Hawaii   719 m (2,359 feet)
❼ **Avalanche Basin Falls**
USA   707 m (2,320 feet)

NIAGARA FALLS –
NORTH AMERICA'S MIGHTIEST WATERFALL

The mighty Niagara Falls can be explored from both the American and the Canadian sides. Put on waterproof oil-skins and you can even go into the so-called Cave of the Winds directly behind the falls.

Niagara Falls, two-thirds of which lies in the Canadian province of Ontario and a third in New York state in the US, is one of the most famous waterfalls in the world. Some 2,500 cu. m/s (88,000 cu. feet/s) of water crash over its steep lip every second, making the Niagara Falls the world's seventh largest waterfall. On the 792-m-wide (2,598-foot) Canadian side (known as the Horseshoe Falls), the Niagara River, which links Lakes Ontario and Erie, falls into a chasm 52 m (171 feet) deep; on the American side, which is only 363 m (1,191 feet) wide, a rock-fall has reduced the drop to 21 m (69 feet). The two sections are separated by Goat Island, an uninhabited outcrop of rock which is part of New York State. Niagara Falls has a well-developed tourist infrastructure and newly-weds often used to honeymoon here, even inspiring screenwriters – in the sinister 1953 film *Niagara*, a honeymoon couple unwittingly became involved in a murder plot.. However, very little water flows out of season or at night now – up to 90% of the flow is diverted by dams to a number of power plants to generate electricity.

The atmospheric illumination of Niagara Falls is best seen at dusk; the Canadian side is in the foreground (left). So-called *Maid of the Mist* boats are used to explore the Canadian side; calling this section of the waterfall Horseshoe Falls seems not to have required too great a leap of the imagination (main image).

SOUTH AMERICA'S GREATEST AND HIGHEST WATERFALLS

SALTO PARÁ
Venezuela   3,500 cu. m/s
(124,000 cu. feet/s)

Salto Pará is South America's largest waterfall by volume. The waters of the Caura River, a large tributary of the Orinoco, crash down a drop of 60 m

The Salto Pará deep in the jungle.

(197 feet) in the middle of the rainforest about halfway along the river's length, before its confluence with the Orinoco. The waterfall, shaped like a crescent moon, extends in a 7-km-long (4½-mile) funnel which eventually finishes in a large sandbank.

CACHOEIRA DE PAULO AFONSO
Brazil   2,800 cu. m/s
(99,000 cu. feet/s)

The waters of the Río São Francisco cascade down 84 m (276 feet) in two stages, the larger of which is 59 m (194 feet). Although only 18 m (59 feet) across, the waterfall discharges a great amount of water. The falls are located where the river breaches Brazil's coastal mountain range in the state of Bahia.

THE GREATEST WATERFALLS BY VOLUME

1. **Salto Pará**   3,500 cu. m/s
   Venezuela   (124,000 cu. feet/s)
2. **Cachoeira de Paulo Afonso**
   Brazil   2,800 cu. m/s
   (99,000 cu. feet/s)
3. **Saltos do Iguaçu**   1,750 cu. m/s
   Brazil/Argentina (62,000 cu. feet/s)
4. **Saltos dos Patos e Maribondo**
   Brazil   1,500 cu. m/s
   (53,000 cu. feet/s)
5. **Kaieteur Falls**   660 cu. m/s
   Guyana   (23,300 cu. feet/s)
6. **Cascada da San Rafael**
   Ecuador   400 cu. m/s
   (14,100 cu. feet/s)
7. **Salto Hacha/Salta Sapo**
   Venezuela   (unknown)

KAIETEUR FALLS
Guyana   660 cu. m/s
(23,300 cu. feet/s)

Kaieteur Falls is located in the national park of the same name in Central Guyana. The Potarò River, which is a tributary of the Essequibo, Guyana's largest river, falls

Kaieteur Falls plunges 251 m (823 feet) in a single drop.

from a cliff 113 m (371 feet) wide into a chasm 251 m (823 feet) deep – approximately five times the height of the Niagara Falls – creating the world's 19th largest waterfall by volume.

SALTO HACHA/ SALTO SAPO
Venezuela   (flow rate unknown)

The Salto Angel, the world's highest waterfall, is not the only reason to visit the Canaima National Park; the Salto Hacha and the smaller Salto Sapo in the north-west of the

The lagoon surrounding the Salto Hacha.

park are just as popular. Both waterfalls are most easily reached by boat on the lagoon, whose waters are stained a noticeable red by the solution of tannic acid they contain. The smaller Salto Sapo has one peculiarity – squeezing between slippery rock cliffs, visitors can actually walk through the waterfall at the bottom, although you tend to get very wet. During the dry season, the Salto Sapo is little more than a rivulet.

THE HIGHEST WATERFALLS

Water from the "hanging glacier" – the Cascada de Ventisquero Colgante in Chile.

1. **Salto Angel**
   Venezuela   979 m (3,212 feet)
2. **Cataratas las Tres Hermanas**
   Peru   914 m (2,999 feet)
3. **Catarata Yumbilla**
   Peru   896 m (2,940 feet)
4. **Catarata Gocta**
   Peru   771 m (2,530 feet)
5. **Salto Kukenaam**
   Venezuela   674 m (2,211 feet)
6. **Salto Yutajá**
   Venezuela   671 m (2,201 feet)
7. **Salto Roraima**
   Venezuela   610 m (2,001 feet)
8. **Salto del Iguapo**
   Venezuela   600 m (1,969 feet)
9. **Cataratas la Chinata**
   Peru   580 m (1,903 feet)
10. **Cachoeira do Pilao**
    Brazil   524 m (1,719 feet)

CASCADA DE SAN RAFAEL

Ecuador   400 cu. m/s
(14,100 cu. feet/s)

The Cascada de San Rafael, which is also known as the Cascada del Coca, is a mighty waterfall of several stages in the Napo-province in Ecuador. It is located about 40 km (25 miles) south of the equator on the eastern slopes of the Andes in the Cayambe-Coca Ecological Reserve. The crystal-clear waters of the Río Coca, a tributary of the Río Napo (and thus also of the Amazon), cascade through a narrow gap into a 131-m (430-foot) deep chasm. A short distance to the north-west there is an active volcano called Reventador (3,562 m/ 11,686 feet).

The thick cloud of mist formed by the Cascada de San Rafael, one of South America's most striking waterfalls.

SALTOS DO IGUAÇU – SOUTH AMERICA'S MIGHTIEST WATERFALL

It may only be the third largest set of falls in continental South America, but it is by far the most beautiful, reason enough for UNESCO to inscribe it on their list of natural World Heritage Sites.

Close to the junction of the borders of Brazil, Argentina, and Paraguay, the Iguaçu River (known as the Iguazú in Argentina) flows over a cliff 2,700 m (8,860 feet) wide to form a waterfall which averages 62 m (203 feet) in height. In contrast to the solid sheet of water of the Victoria Falls in Africa, more than 270 individual waterfalls can be identified along the course of the cliff. The largest single set of falls is the Garganta do Diabo (or Garganta del Diablo in Spanish), the "Devil's Gullet", a U-shaped gorge some 150 m (492 feet) wide and 82 m (269 feet) high, into which a 400-m-wide (1,300-foot) curtain of water plunges. The Devil's Gullet lies right on the Brazilian-Argentine border. The Saltos do Iguaçu's flow rate of 1,750 cu. m/s (62,000 cu. feet/s) makes it the eighth largest waterfall on Earth, with two-thirds of the falls lying on Argentine territory and the remaining third in Brazil. The surrounding area in both countries has been declared a national park and has been run as a UNESCO World Heritage Site since 1984 in Argentina and 1986 in Brazil. The falls are easily

reached from the nearby border towns of Foz do Iguaçu in Brazil and Puerto Iguazú in Argentina. There is even a route from the town of Ciudad del Este in Paraguay. The Brazilian side leads tourists to the falls along an extended path, while in Argentina there is a narrow-gauge railway to transport visitors to various tracks that lead to the river.

The mist formed by the scattering of water droplets acts as a prism to break up the sunlight into all the colors of the rainbow (main image). The many islands in the Iguaçu reach almost to the lip of the falls (left).

The Iguaçu Falls seen from the Brazilian side, with the "Devil's Gullet" just visible through the mist in the background.

LAKES

A lake is defined as a large body of still water completely surrounded by land, whether watercourses flow into it or not. In contrast with an inland sea, such as the Mediterranean, a lake generally has no direct connection with the world's oceans. Most lakes are freshwater, but

The Vänern in southern Sweden is Europe's third largest lake.

there are also salt lakes, including the Caspian Sea, the largest lake in the world. To be regarded as a lake, as opposed to a pool or a pond, a body of water should be of a certain size, and this is generally considered to be a hectare (2½ acres).

THE WORLD'S LARGEST LAKES

❶ Caspian Sea
Russia, Kazakhstan, Azerbaijan, Iran, Turkmenistan 371,000 sq. km (143,245 sq. miles)

❷ Lake Superior
USA, Canada   82,414 sq. km (31,820 sq. miles)

❸ Lake Victoria
Tanzania, Kenya, Uganda 68,870 sq. km (26,590 sq. miles)

❹ Lake Huron
USA, Canada   59,596 sq. km (23,010 sq. miles)

❺ Lake Michigan
USA   58,000 sq. km (22,400 sq. miles)

❻ Lake Tanganyika
Democratic Republic of the Congo (DRC), Tanzania, Zambia, Burundi 32,893 sq. km (12,700 sq. miles)

❼ Lake Baikal
Russia   31,492 sq. km (12,159 sq. miles)

❽ Great Bear Lake
Canada   31,328 sq. km (12,096 sq. miles)

❾ Lake Malawi
Malawi, Tanzania, Mozambique 30,044 sq. km (11,600 sq. miles)

❿ Great Slave Lake
Canada   28,568 sq. km (11,030 sq. miles)

⓫ Lake Erie
USA, Canada   25,745 sq. km (9,940 sq. miles)

⓬ Lake Winnipeg
Canada   24,341 sq. km (9,398 sq. miles)

THE WORLD'S DEEPEST LAKES

❶ Lake Baikal
Russia   1,637 m (5,371 feet)

❷ Lake Tanganyika
DRC, Tanzania, Zambia, Burundi 1,470 m (4,823 feet)

❸ Caspian Sea
Russia, Kazakhstan, Azerbaijan, Iran, Turkmenistan   995 m (3,264 feet)

❹ Lake Malawi
Malawi, Tanzania, Mozambique 706 m (2,316 feet)

❺ Lake Vostok
Antarctica   670 m (2,198 feet)

❻ Lake Issyk-Kul
Kyrgyzstan   668 m (2,192 feet)

❼ Great Slave Lake
Canada   614 m (2,014 feet)

❽ Crater Lake
USA   594 m (1,949 feet)

❾ Lago General Carrera
Chile, Argentina   590 m (1,936 feet)

❿ Hornindalsvatnet
Norway   514 m (1,686 feet)

⓫ Lake Tahoe
USA   501 m (1,644 feet)

⓬ Lago Argentino
Argentina   500 m (1,640 feet)

THE WORLD'S LARGEST LAKES BY VOLUME

❶ Caspian Sea
Russia, Kazakhstan, Azerbaijan, Iran, Turkmenistan   78,200 cu. km (18,760 cu. miles)

❷ Lake Baikal
Russia   23,000 cu. km (5,500 cu. miles)

❸ Lake Tanganyika
DRC, Tanzania, Zambia, Burundi 18,900 cu. km (4,530 cu. miles)

❹ Lake Superior
USA, Canada   12,100 cu. km (2,900 cu. miles)

❺ Lake Malawi
Malawi, Tanzania, Mozambique 8,400 cu. km (2,015 cu. miles)

❻ Lake Vostok
Antarctica   5,400 cu. km (1,300 cu. miles)

❼ Lake Michigan
USA   4,918 cu. km (1,180 cu. miles)

❽ Lake Huron
USA, Canada   3,540 cu. km (849 cu. miles)

❾ Lake Victoria
Tanzania, Kenya, Uganda 2,750 cu. km (660 cu. miles)

❿ Great Bear Lake
Canada   2,236 cu. km (536 cu. miles)

⓫ Great Slave Lake
Canada   2,090 cu. km (500 cu. miles)

⓬ Lake Issyk-Kul
Kyrgyzstan   1,738 cu. km (417 cu. miles)

Lake Superior, which spans the border between the USA and Canada, is the world's second largest lake after the Caspian Sea, and the largest freshwater lake of all – the Caspian is a salt lake. The historic Split Rock lighthouse, which is located on the American side about 34 km (21 miles) from Two Harbors in Minnesota, was built in 1910 after violent storms had caused several bad shipwrecks in the area.

CASPIAN SEA – THE WORLD'S LARGEST LAKE

Millions of years ago, the Caspian Sea was part of a giant ocean. As the Earth's crust was compressed and folded to form the Alps, the Pyrenees, and the Carpathians, a gigantic basin was also separated from the open sea, creating a vast lake.

Although estimates of total surface area vary, the Caspian Sea covers an area of some 371,000 sq. km (143,245 sq. miles) making it, by some margin, the world's largest enclosed body of water. Located in south-western Asia, this endorheic lake (one that does not drain outwards to a river or sea) is about 1,200 km (750 miles) long and up to 435 km (270 miles) wide in places.

Five countries line its shores: Iran to the south, Turkmenistan to the east, Kazakhstan to the north and north-east, Azerbaijan to the west, and Russia. The lake holds 78,200 cu. km (18,760 cu. miles) of water – 40% of the volume of all the lakes worldwide. The Caspian Sea can be divided into three zones. To the north, the lake is only 6 m (20 feet) deep. The central zone, which begins

about level with the Chechen Peninsula, reaches depths of around 190 m (625 feet), and the zone south of Baku is up to 995 m (3,265 feet) deep. The water is saline, averaging a salt content of about 1% (seawater is 3.5%), and its largest tributary is the Volga. Fishing is of great economic importance – especially for sturgeon, valued for their caviar – as well as oil and gas mining.

The northern section of the lake can freeze over in winter.

The size of the Caspian Sea has always been subject to dramatic variation – at the beginning of the 1930s, its area is said to have approached no less than 420,000 sq. km (162,000 sq. miles) – but from then into the 1970s more water was required to irrigate arable land than the Volga, Ural, and Kura could provide. Water levels have been rising again since the end of the 1970s, but this has nothing to do with human activity: it is the result of increasing geological activity on the sea floor.

Main image: A view from space of the northern section of the Caspian Sea, where the Volga forms a wide delta.

There are large deposits of natural gas and oil beneath the Caspian Sea, but mining these is bad for the environment and has also caused conflict among the states bordering the lake. The image shows a drilling rig near Baku (left).

LAKE BAIKAL – THE WORLD'S DEEPEST AND LARGEST LAKE BY VOLUME

Lake Baikal is the world's deepest lake, the largest freshwater lake, and at an age of more than 25 million years, also the oldest lake on Earth.

Lake Baikal, which lies not far from the city of Irkutsk in southern Siberia, is 673 km (418 miles) long and in places up to 82 km (51 miles) wide. The region around the lake has been designated a UNESCO World Heritage site since 1996. The lake, lying 455 m (1,493 feet) above sea level, has a total surface area of 31,492 sq. km (12,159 sq. miles). A depth of 1,637 m (5,371 feet) having

been recorded at its deepest point, it is officially the world's deepest lake. Lake Baikal contains some 23,000 cu. km (5,500 cu. miles) of water and its only outflow, the Angara River, a headwater of the Yenisei, flows into the Kara Sea, part of the Arctic Ocean. The area around the lake is geologically active, with frequent earthquakes, and spa resorts have been established at min-

eral springs along the lake's shores. Lake Baikal, meaning "rich lake" in the Buryatic language, has an extraordinarily diverse animal and plant life – more than 1,200 different animal species live in the lake alone. The majority of this wealth of animal life, including such species as the Baikal seal and the golomyanka, a fish which gives birth to live young, is endemic.

Peschanaya Bay ("Sand Bay", far left) near Bolshoi and Aya Bay (left) on Lake Baikal. The Svyatoy Nos ("holy nose") Peninsula, shown here in the main image, is the only peninsula in the lake; it is some 53 km (33 miles) long and 20 km (12 miles) wide. Some 80 bears are said to live here.

More than 1,500 of the 1,800 species of animal and plant life in and around Lake Baikal are endemic; they are found only here. These include the Baikal seal, a species of seal which lives exclusively in fresh water. The seals tend to lead solitary lives and mainly eat fish. Reaching a length of 1.2 m (4 feet) and weighing up to 72 kg (159 lb), it is one of the smaller species of seal. There are said to be only about 60,000 Baikal seals in the area, and hunting them is now restricted.

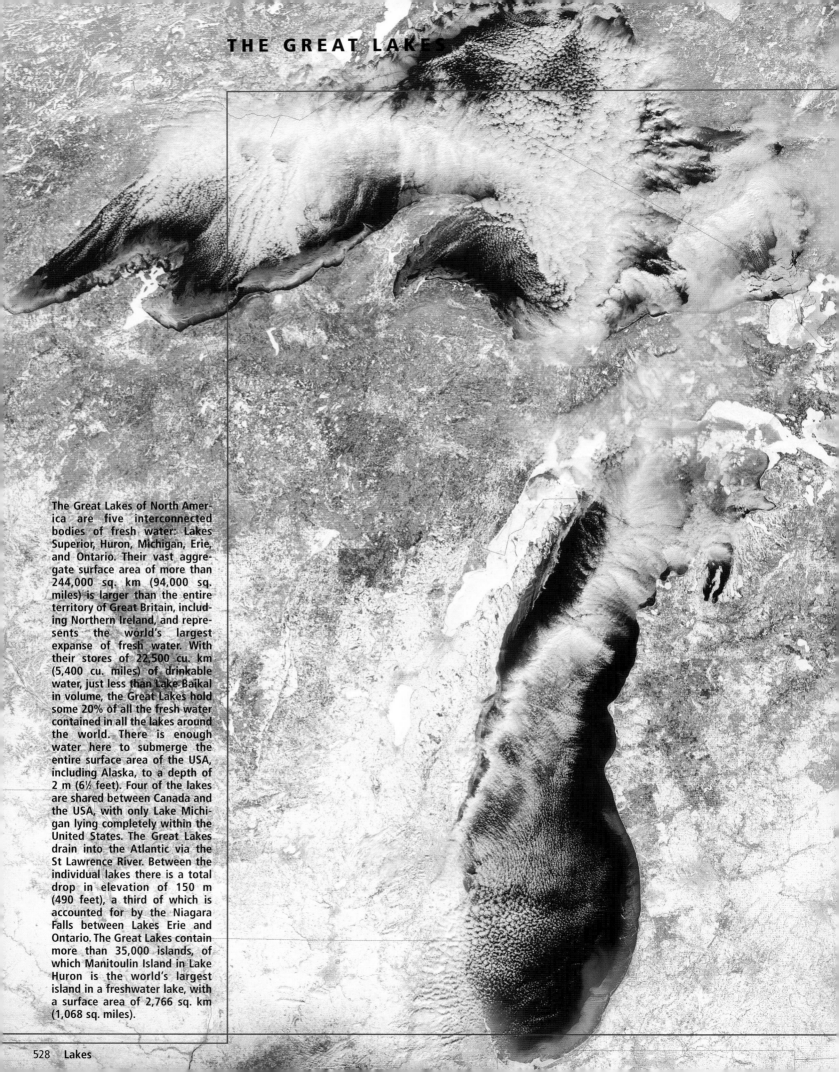

The Great Lakes of North America are five interconnected bodies of fresh water: Lakes Superior, Huron, Michigan, Erie, and Ontario. Their vast aggregate surface area of more than 244,000 sq. km (94,000 sq. miles) is larger than the entire territory of Great Britain, including Northern Ireland, and represents the world's largest expanse of fresh water. With their stores of 22,500 cu. km (5,400 cu. miles) of drinkable water, just less than Lake Baikal in volume, the Great Lakes hold some 20% of all the fresh water contained in all the lakes around the world. There is enough water here to submerge the entire surface area of the USA, including Alaska, to a depth of 2 m (6½ feet). Four of the lakes are shared between Canada and the USA, with only Lake Michigan lying completely within the United States. The Great Lakes drain into the Atlantic via the St Lawrence River. Between the individual lakes there is a total drop in elevation of 150 m (490 feet), a third of which is accounted for by the Niagara Falls between Lakes Erie and Ontario. The Great Lakes contain more than 35,000 islands, of which Manitoulin Island in Lake Huron is the world's largest island in a freshwater lake, with a surface area of 2,766 sq. km (1,068 sq. miles).

THE WORLD'S LARGEST BODY OF FRESH WATER

Anglers in Killarney Provincial Park on Georgian Bay in the northern reaches of Lake Huron (top); the historic Split Rock lighthouse, built on Lake Superior in 1910 (bottom).

From top: The skyline of Chicago, Illinois, on Lake Michigan; Mo'town – Detroit, Michigan – on the Detroit River between Lakes Huron and Erie; Toronto, Canada, on Lake Ontario.

The image shows the five Great Lakes covered by clouds and snow in the winter. At the top of the image, the vast outline of Lake Superior can just be made out. Directly below is Lake Michigan, and to the right, in the middle of the image, is Lake Huron with Georgian Bay attached on its right. In the bottom right-hand corner of the image, there is Lake Ontario on the right, and Lake Erie on the left. Apart from Lake Superior, which rarely freezes, the other four lakes ice over and become impassable to shipping between December and April.

Europe's greatest lakes are all to be found in the north of the continent. Geologically, they are all relics of the last Ice Age, which left its deepest marks at these latitudes.

LAKE LADOGA
Russia   **17,703 sq. km**
(6,835 sq. miles)

Lake Ladoga, Europe's largest lake, is located in north-western Russia about 50 km (31 miles) from St Petersburg. It is 220 km (137 miles) long, almost reaching the Finnish border, and in places up to 120 km (75 miles) wide.

The lake drains into the Baltic Sea at the Gulf of Finland via the Neva River and has an average depth of 52 m (171 feet), reaching 225 m (738 feet) at its deepest. The lake lies about 4 m (13 feet) above sea level and holds some 840 cu. km (202 cu. miles) of water. The lake, which contains more than 500 islands, was formed in the Vistula period of the last ice age about 12,000

to 15,000 years ago, making it relatively young in geological terms. It boasts rich stocks of fish, including several endemic species, some of which, such as the freshwater sturgeon, have become quite rare. One species of freshwater seal, a cousin of the ringed seal, has also found a habitat here. Increasing eutrophication has had a detrimental effect on water quality in recent years.

LAKE ONEGA
Russia   **9,616 sq. km**
(3,713 sq. miles)

Lake Onega, located some 160 km (100 miles) to the east of Lake Ladoga, is 248 km (154 miles) long, up to 92 km (57 miles) wide, and reaches depths of 127 m (417 feet). Europe's second largest lake, it flows into Lake Ladoga via the Svir River. The remarkable 18th-century wooden churches of Kizhi, one of its many islands, have been a UNESCO World Heritage Site since 1990.

The island of Kizhi in Lake Onega, with a typical wooden church on its shore.

LAKE PEIPSI-PIHKVA
Estonia/Russia   **3,555 sq. km**
(1,373 sq. miles)

Forming the border between Estonia and Russia, Lake Peipsi-Pihkva extends for 143 km (89 miles) along a north-south axis, reaching widths of 50 km (31 miles). Some 1,570 sq. km (606 sq. miles) of its total surface area belong to Estonia, the rest to Russia. The lake is shallow, with a maximum recorded depth of 15 m (49 feet) and an average depth of about 8 m (26 feet). It flows into the Baltic via the Narva River.

The Estonian shores of Lake Peipsi-Pihkva near the town of Mustvee (right).

LAKE VÄNERN
Sweden   **5,648 sq. km**
(2,181 sq. miles)

Lake Vänern, Europe's third largest, is located in south-western Sweden. Up to 106 m (348 feet) deep, it has an average depth of 27 m (89 feet) and a total volume of 150 cu. km (36 cu. miles). As many as 22,000 islands have been recorded in the lake. The Djurö National Park was established on the Djurö archipelago in the lake's centre in 1991.

One of the many little islands of Lake Vänern, Sweden's largest lake.

LAKE VÄTTERN
Sweden   **1,912 sq. km**
(738 sq. miles)

Lake Vättern, Sweden's second largest lake, flows into the Baltic via the Motala River. To the north the lake averages a depth of only 25 m (82 feet) but to the south this can reach more than 110 m (360 feet) with an average of 39 m (128 feet). This extensive body of water has a north-south length of some 140 km (87 miles) and reaches 30 km (19 miles) at its widest near the municipality of Motala. The water is of excellent quality and is used as drinking water by local communities.

LAKE SAIMAA
Finland   **4,370 sq. km**
(1,687 sq. miles)

Lake Saimaa, in south-east Finland, drains to the east into the Vuoksi River and thence into Lake Ladoga in Russia. The lake is composed of a host of smaller pools with a shoreline of almost 15,000 km (9,300 miles). The lake averages a depth of 7 m (23 feet), and is only 85 m (279 feet) at its deepest. The Saimaa ringed seal, which is found here, is acutely endangered.

A rowing boat at Loikansaari near Savonlinna in the Saimaa region.

LAKE BELOYE
Russia 1,290 sq. km (498 sq. miles)

Lake Beloye (Russian: *beloye ozero*, "white lake") in Vologda Province is Europe's ninth largest lake and is located about 110 km (68 miles) south-east of Lake Ladoga in north-western Russia. It is 46 km (29 miles) long, 33 km (21 miles) wide, and reaches a depth of 20 m (66 feet); on average it is only 5.5 m (18 feet) deep. It provides water for the Volga-Baltic Waterway by draining into the Rybinsk Reservoir via the Sheksna, a tributary of the Volga.

Typical Russian wooden huts on the shores of Lake Beloye (right).

Left: The deceptive calm before the storm: this cloud formation appears over Lake Ladoga before a violent squall. The diffuse light of dusk only intensifies the effect.

LAKE PÄIJÄNNE
Finland　　　　**1,081 sq. km (417 sq. miles)**

Lake Päijänne is Finland's second largest lake, and at 120 km (75 miles) it is also its longest. Averaging a depth of only 16 m (52 feet), the lake bed can lie up to 95 m (312 feet) below the surface. It holds a total of 18 cu. km (4 cu. miles) of water. The River Kymi drains the lake into the Gulf of Finland. An underground aqueduct connecting Lake Päijänne with Helsinki provides water for the capital and its hinterland. There are plenty of holiday cottages along the banks of the lake and it is a popular destination for weekend breaks.

LAKE INARIJÄRVI
Finland　　　　**1,040 sq. km (402 sq. miles)**

Lake Inarijärvi, also known as Lake Inari, lies 1,100 km (684 miles) to the north of Helsinki in the Finnish part of Lapland. The lake is north of the Arctic Circle and is often iced over until June. Its deepest point is 92 m (302 feet) below the surface. Surrounded by pine forests, the lake has more than 3,300 islands and flows via the Paatsjoki River into the Arctic Ocean.

Numerous, forested islands are scattered over Lake Inarijärvi in northern Finland.

LAKE TOPOZERO
Russia　986 sq. km (381 sq. miles)

Lake Topozero is located in the post-Soviet Republic of Karelia in north-western Russia, approximately 90 km (56 miles) south of the Arctic Circle. It is 75 km (47 miles) long and 30 km (19 miles) wide, but no more than 50 m (164 feet) deep. The lake has about 100 islands. Human use of the lake includes fishing and transporting lumber. The lake drains into Lake Pjaozero to the north, where the Kovda River also rises. This flows across the Kola Peninsula south of Murmansk before finally draining into the White Sea at the Kandalaksha Gulf.

ASIA

Many of Asia's large lakes are terminal basins, located in very arid areas, with few tributaries. Such endorheic lakes have no outflow and their water levels are determined only by evaporation. Human intervention has meant that many of these lakes are now under threat of drying up completely.

ARAL SEA

Kazakhstan, **17,160–27,000 sq. km**
Uzbekistan **(6,625–10,425 sq. miles)**

A few decades ago, the Aral Sea was the world's fourth largest lake. It has since shrunk to approximately a tenth of its original volume, from 708 cu. km (170 cu. miles) to a mere 75 cu. km (18 cu. miles). Intensive agriculture, including the cultivation of cotton and rice, has removed such volumes of water from the Amudarja and Syrdaja Rivers, which flow into the lake, that meltwater and precipitation have been unable to compensate, and large areas have dried up; the salinity has risen from 14 g per liter (0.1 oz per gallon) to more than 100 g per liter (0.9 oz per gallon), far too high for fish to survive.

Several of the shore towns are now separated from the lake by wide, barren steppes. A dam took the pressure off the smaller northern lake, preventing it from draining into abandoned canals. The water level has now risen and the salinity has dropped to 10 g per liter (0.07 oz per gallon). The lake continues to shrink to the south, and no change is in sight there.

LAKE BALKHASH

Kazakhstan **18,428 sq. km**
(7,115 sq. miles)

Lake Balkhash, Asia's second largest lake, is under threat of drying up. This lake in the Caucasus steppes is supplied by the Ili and the Karatal, and there is no outflow river. The lake is 620 km (385 miles) long, up to 70 km (43 miles) wide, with a maximum depth of 26 m (85 feet), although it averages only 5.8 m (19 feet). The lake narrows in the middle; the eastern section of the lake has a salt content of more than 7%, but the western section is only slightly brackish.

LAKE ISSYK-KUL

Kyrgyzstan **6,236 sq. km**
(2,408 sq. miles)

Kyrgyzstan's largest lake lies at 1,609 m (5,279 feet) above sea level in the Tian Shan Mountains and is the world's second largest mountain lake (after Lake Titicaca in South America). It is 182 km (113 miles) long and 60 km (37 miles) wide, with a maximum depth of 668 m (2,192 feet). It has a salinity of 6 g per liter (0.04 oz per gallon) and never freezes over, even in temperatures approaching -20°C (-4°F).

The majestic backdrop of the Tian Shan Mountains frames Issyk-Kul, the largest lake in the Central Asian republic of Kyrgyzstan.

LAKE URMIA

Iran **5,470 sq. km**
(2,112 sq. miles)

Iran's largest body of water has a salt content approaching 30%, almost as much as the Dead Sea. Lake Urmia lies 1,280 m (4,200 feet) above sea level, 60 km (37 miles) west of Tabriz in northwestern Iran. It is 140 km (87 miles) long and up to 55 km (34 miles) wide, with an average depth of just 7 m (23 feet). Very few animal and plant species survive here.

The mouth of the Zarin Rud at Lake Urmia in north-western Iran.

LAKE TAYMYR

Russia **4,560 sq. km**
(1,761 sq. miles)

Lake Taymyr lies on the north Siberian Taymyr Peninsula near the southern foothills of the Byrranga Mountains (Russian: Gory Byrranga). The lake has an irregular shape, its longest east-west axis measuring about 250 km (155 miles), with an average depth of 2.8 m (9 feet), rising to 26 m (86 feet). Its main tributary, the Taymyr, crosses the lake before flowing into the Kara Sea, part of the Arctic Ocean. The lake lies about 800 km (500 miles) north of the Arctic Circle and is usually covered with ice between September and June.

Turned milky-white by salt deposits, this whole area was covered by the waters of the Aral Sea only 30 years ago (left). The island visible in the middle was once much smaller and used by the Soviet military for biological warfare experiments (far left).

KOKO NOR (QINGHAI HU)

China   **4,538 sq. km (1,752 sq. miles)**

This salt lake, one of the world's largest, is known as Koko Nor in Mongolian and Qinghai Hu in Chinese (both mean "gray-blue sea"). The province of Qinghai is named after the lake, which lies at 3,195 m (10,482 feet) and freezes over in the winter. Fish manage to breed here despite the high salinity. Its largest tributary river is the Buh He – some 108 rivers are once said to have drained into the lake, but most have now dried up. The lake is considered sacred by Tibetan Buddhists, and it takes 23 days for pilgrims to walk around it.

KHANKA LAKE

Russia, China   **4,380 sq. km (1,691 sq. miles)**

Khanka Lake lies in eastern Siberia on the Sino-Russian border: about three-quarters of the lake is Russian territory and a quarter Chinese. The lake averages a depth of 4.5 m (15 feet), with a maximum of 10.6 m (35 feet). The area around the lake, which lies 68 m (223 feet) above sea level, is a wetland of international importance which has been protected as a nature reserve on both sides of the border. The lake is part of the Ussuri River system lying between Russia and China, and this in turn drains into the Amur River system.

LAKE VAN

Turkey   **3,740 sq. km (1,444 sq. miles)**

Lake Van (Turkish: Van Gölü) is the largest lake in Turkey. It is situated in Bitlis province in East Anatolia and lies about 150 km (93 miles) south-east of Ankara. The lake's longest axis is 120 km (75 miles) long and it is 80 km (50 miles) wide, with a depth of more than 450 m (1,476 feet). It lies 1,640 m (5,381 feet) above sea level. Its 576 cu. km (138 cu. miles) of water are heavily alkaline as the old outflow on its western shore has been blocked by the Nemrut volcano. Lake Van is endorheic, losing water only by evaporation.

POYANG HU

China   **3,585 sq. km (1,384 sq. miles)**

Poyang Hu, China's largest freshwater lake, lies in Jiangxi province in south-eastern China. It is 170 km (106 miles) long and 17 km (11 miles) wide, with an average depth of 8.5 m (28 feet). The maximum depth of this lake is no more than 25 m (82 feet) and its total volume is 25 cu. km (6 cu. miles). Its size can vary greatly: during the rainy season it expands to an area of 4,400 sq. km (1,700 sq. miles) but during droughts it can shrink to 1,000 cu. km (380 sq. miles). The lake is an important breeding ground for storks.

The largest lakes on the African continent are all located south of the equator near the East African Rift. The valley is lined with chains of high mountains and the lakes here are some of the deepest on Earth.

LAKE VICTORIA

Tanzania, Uganda, Kenya
68,870 sq. km (26,590 sq. miles)

Lake Victoria is the world's third largest lake, and of the freshwater lakes, only Lake Superior is larger in area. Lying 1,134 m (3,720 feet) above sea level on the East African plains, its longest axis measures 335 km (208 miles) and it is 250 km (155 miles) wide. Lake Victoria contains nearly 2,750 cu. km (660 cu. miles) of water, making it the world's ninth largest lake by volume. It has an average depth of 40 m (131 feet), although in places can be as deep as 80 m (262 feet). It is fed from the west by the Kagera River and drains into the Victoria Nile. The largest section of the lake is Tanzanian territory, and the second largest Ugandan. The lake has a wealth of fish life, especially cichlids, but the concentration of human population on the lake's shores has had some negative consequences. Massive pollution, resulting in eutrophication and a lack of oxygen, is a threat to the survival of both animal and plant life, and may well have repercussions for the local human population as well.

LAKE TANGANYIKA

Tanzania, Zambia, Burundi, Dem. Rep. of the Congo (DRC)
32,893 sq. km (12,700 sq. miles)

Lake Tanganyika in Central Africa is the world's sixth largest lake and at 1,470 m (4,823 feet) the world's second deepest, averaging a depth of 570 m (1,870 feet). It is Africa's largest fresh water lake with a volume of 18,900 cu. km (4,530 cu. miles). The lake, 673 km (418 miles) long and 72 km (45 miles) wide, lies 782 m (2,566 feet) above sea level.

Children play beside a boat on the Tanzanian shore of Lake Tanganyika.

LAKE ALBERT

Uganda, DRC   **5,347 sq. km (2,064 sq. miles)**

The lake was named in 1864 by the British explorer Samuel White Baker, in honor of the Prince Consort of Queen Victoria. In the Congo it is known as Mobuto Sese Seko after the late dictator. The lake is 160 km (99 miles) long, 30 km (19 miles) wide, and reaches a depth of 48 m (157 feet), although averages only 25 m (82 feet). It contains about 132 cu. km (32 cu. miles) of water. The lake is fed by two great tributaries: the Victoria Nile to the northeast and the Semliki to the south. The lake drains into the Albert Nile.

LAKE MALAWI

Tanzania, Malawi, Mozambique
30,044 sq. km (11,600 sq. miles)

Lake Malawi in East Africa is 560 km (348 miles) long and on average 50 km (31 miles) wide, although at its widest point it measures 80 km (50 miles). Its maximum depth is 706 m (2,316 feet), making it the world's fourth deepest lake. Lying 474 m (1,555 feet) above sea level, it is thought to contain more species of fish than any other lake on Earth.

A baobab tree on Likoma, an island within Lake Malawi.

LAKE MWERU

DRC, Zambia   **5,120 sq. km (1,977 sq. miles)**

"Mweru" means "lake" in various Bantu languages, and the lake is often called just that. Lying about 150 km (93 miles) west of Lake Tanganyika, Mweru is 931 m (3,054 feet) above sea level, 131 km (81 miles) long, and 56 km (35 miles) wide. It averages only 7.5 m (25 feet) in depth, although to the north-east it reaches depths of 27 m (89 feet). It contains about 38 cu. km (9 cu. miles) of water. Its main tributary is the Luapula and its principal outflow the Luvua, a tributary of the Congo.

LAKE TURKANA

Kenya, Ethiopia   **6,405 sq. km (2,473 sq. miles)**

The largest lake in Kenya (although a small portion to the north lies in Ethiopia) is 305 km (190 miles) long and 32 km (20 miles) wide. It is on average 30 m (100 feet) deep, measuring 73 m (240 feet) at its deepest. It contains 204 cu. km (49 cu. miles) of water. It has only one tributary, the Omo, and no outflow, which is why the lake's salt content continually rises. The surrounding land boasts a wealth of animal species, as well as three UNESCO World Heritage national parks.

LAKE TANA

Ethiopia   **3,000 sq. km (1,158 sq. miles)**

Africa's highest lake lies 1,830 m (6,004 feet) above sea level in the Ethiopian Highlands. Lake Tana is 84 km (52 miles) long and, in places, 66 km (41 miles) wide. The average depth is 8 m (26 feet), with a maximum of 14 m (45 feet). During the rainy season the water can rise some 1.6 m (5½ feet) flooding large areas of the shore. The lake is fed by a number of watercourses; the Blue Nile is its largest outflow.

Taking a break on a papyrus boat known as a *tankwa* on Lake Tana (left).

Cattle drinking at Winum Gulf on the Kenyan side of Lake Victoria; behind them a traditional sailboat built by the Luo, one of the tribes living on Lake Victoria (far left). Rock formations at Mwanza, Tanzania, Lake Victoria's largest port (left).

LAKE KIVU

DRC, Rwanda   **2,650 sq. km (1,023 sq. miles)**

Lake Kivu is 1,462 m (4,797 feet) above sea level and forms the border between the two countries. It is 89 km (55 miles) long and 48 km (30 miles) wide. It averages a depth of 240 m (787 feet), reaching 450 m (1,476 feet) in places, and is some 500 cu. km (120 cu. miles) in volume. It is fed by the Kalundura and drained by the Rusizi. Due to volcanic springs in its bed, both the water temperature and salinity increase at depth.

Several of the small islands in the eastern part of Lake Kivu, belonging to Rwanda.

LAKE EDWARD

DRC, Uganda   **2,325 sq. km (898 sq. miles)**

Lying 912 m (2,992 feet) above sea level, this lake lies mostly in the Congo, with only a small north-eastern portion belonging to Uganda. The lake is 77 km (48 miles) long and 40 km (25 miles) wide. Its average depth is 17 m (56 feet), but in places it can reach 117 m (384 feet). It is fed by the Rutshuru and the Rwindi, among other rivers, and its major outflow is the Semliki.

Cape buffalo beside Lake Edward in the Queen Elizabeth National Park.

LAKE MANZALA

Egypt   1,710 sq. km (660 sq. miles)

Lake Manzala lies in the north-east of the Nile Delta near Port Said. The Suez Canal runs to the east and only a 300-m-wide (990-foot) sandbank divided this 47-km-long (29-mile), 30-km-wide (19-mile) lake from the Mediterranean to the north. The lake is only 1.3 m (4½ feet) deep. The salinity varies greatly, depending on the water level, and the lake bed consists of soft clay. The lake, under considerable ecological pressure, is a rich source of fish.

A boy playing with a model fishing boat in the shallow water.

Most of the great lakes are to be found in the north of the American continent; this is partly a result of the ice age, although some of these deep scars in the land date back to earlier tectonic movement during the Tertiary period.

LAKE SUPERIOR

Canada, USA   **82,414 sq. km (31,820 sq. miles)**

The largest of North America's five Great Lakes is not only the world's second largest lake (after the Caspian Sea), it is also the largest freshwater lake by area. At an elevation of 184 m (604 feet), it is 563 km (350 miles) long and 257 km (160 miles) wide, with a volume of 12,100 cu. km (2,900 cu. miles) and an average depth of 149 m (489 feet) – its greatest depth being 405 m (1,329 feet). The lake lies on the border of the Canadian province of Ontario and the US states of Michigan and Wisconsin. It has a total shoreline of almost 4,400 km (2,734 miles) and more than 200 rivers and streams drain into it. The lake drains into Lake Huron via the St Mary's River; the 8-m (26-foot) difference in elevation is overcome with a series of locks. There is almost no industry on the banks of Lake Superior and as the first of the Great Lakes it receives no pollution from the other lakes; the water is extremely clean and the area is a popular tourist destination.

LAKE HURON

Canada   **59,596 sq. km (23,010 sq. miles)**

Lake Huron, the second in the Great Lakes chain, is the world's third largest freshwater lake by area. Some 332 km (206 miles) long and up to 245 km (152 miles) wide, it averages 59 m (194 feet) in depth, up to 230 m (755 feet) maximum. Containing 3,540 cu. km (849 cu. miles) of water, it drains into Lake Erie via the Niagara Falls and boasts the world's largest inland island.

Storm clouds gather over the northern tip of Lake Huron's Bruce Peninsula.

GREAT SLAVE LAKE

Canada   **28,568 sq. km (11,030 sq. miles)**

North America's deepest lake (614 m/ 2,014 feet) is named after the Slavey, a Native American tribe. The lake, which teems with fish, lies 156 m (512 feet) above sea level in north-western Canada. It is 480 km (298 miles) long, 109 km (68 miles) wide, and contains 2,090 cu. km (500 cu. miles) of water. The lake is fed by the Slave and Hay Rivers and drains into the Arctic Ocean via the Mackenzie River.

The Great Slave Lake freezes in winter; a camp can be seen in the background (right).

LAKE MICHIGAN

USA   **58,000 sq. km (22,400 sq. miles)**

Lake Michigan, the only one of the Great Lakes to lie completely within the USA, is 494 km (307 miles) long and up to 190 km (118 miles) wide in places. Containing 4,918 cu. km (1,180 cu. miles) of water, it has a maximum depth of 281 m (922 feet) and an average of 85 m (279 feet). Four US states share its 2,600 km (1,600 miles) of shoreline.

The skyline of Chicago, the largest city on Lake Michigan, at dusk.

LAKE ERIE

Canada, USA   **25,745 sq. km (9,940 sq. miles)**

The fourth largest Great Lake (the world's eleventh largest lake) is also the southernmost and the most shallow, with an average depth of only 19 m (62 feet) and a maximum depth of 64 m (210 feet). It thus contains only 480 cu. km (115 cu. miles) of water. The lake is 388 km (241 miles) long and 92 km (57 miles) wide and, due to its limited depth, it is also the warmest of the Great Lakes. Its largest tributary is the Detroit River and its principal outflow is the Niagara Falls.

GREAT BEAR LAKE

Canada   **31,328 sq. km (12,096 sq. miles)**

The Great Bear Lake, the largest lake to lie entirely within Canada, is near the Arctic Circle in the Northwest Territories. It contains almost 2,236 cu. km (536 cu. miles) of water and has more than 2,700 km (1,678 miles) of shoreline. Its deepest point is 446 m (1,463 feet) but it averages depths of only 72 m (236 feet) and ices over from the end of November until well into July.

Shoreline coniferous forest reflected in the waters of the Great Bear Lake.

LAKE WINNIPEG

Canada   **24,341 sq. km (9,398 sq. miles)**

Lake Winnipeg, in the province of Manitoba, is the third largest lake to lie completely within Canada. Located 55 km (34 miles) north of the city of Winnipeg, the lake's north-south axis measures 416 km (258 miles) and it is 100 km (62 miles) from east to west. Its tributaries include the Winnipeg and Saskatchewan, and the lake drains into the Nelson River. The average depth is 12 m (39 feet), the maximum 36 m (118 feet).

The shoreline of Hecla Island, one of several islands in Lake Winnipeg (right).

The fall has left its mark on the vegetation lining the shores of Grand Island, one of the islands lying off the little port town of Munising on Lake Superior. The island is part of the US state of Michigan and is a National Recreation Area.

LAKE ONTARIO
Canada, USA   **19,477 sq. km (7,520 sq. miles)**

The smallest of the Great Lakes forms the border of the Canadian province of Ontario to the north and New York state to the south. Lake Ontario ("great lake" in the language of the First Nation Canadians) is 311 km (193 miles) long and up to 85 km (53 miles) wide. It has an average depth of 86 m (282 feet), up to 244 m (801 feet), and contains 1,640 cu. km (393 cu. miles) of water. Its most important tributary is the Niagara and its principal outflow is the St Lawrence. Because of its great depth, the lake hardly every freezes over.

LAKE NICARAGUA
Nicaragua   **8,264 sq. km (3,191 sq. miles)**

Central America's largest lake is 148 km (92 miles) long, 55 km (34 miles) wide, and up to 45 m (148 feet) deep, with an average of 13 m (43 feet). Its principal outflow, the Río San Juan, drains into the Caribbean Sea. There are more than 400 islands in the lake, including Ometepe, an islet with two volcanoes, one of which, Concepción, is still active. Sharks and rays have been sighted in the lake.

The Concepción and Madera volcanoes on the island of Ometepe, Lake Nicaragua.

LAKE ATHABASCA
Canada   **7,921 sq. km (3,058 sq. miles)**

Lying in north-western Saskatchewan, the lake is 283 km (176 miles) long and up to 50 km (31 miles) wide. It lies 281 m (922 feet) above sea level and is 243 m (797 feet) at its deepest point. Athabasca means "where there are reeds" in the local Native American language. The lake contains around 204 cu. km (49 cu. miles) of water and its main tributary is the Athabasca; it drains into the Arctic Ocean via the Slave River. Deposits of gold and uranium on the northern shore were mined commercially until the early 1980s.

Several of South America's lakes lie at great altitude in the wide highland valleys of the Andes, and many of these, such as Lake Titicaca, have almost mythical importance. Others again are endorheic salt lakes.

LAKE MARACAIBO

Venezuela   **13,300 sq. km**
                     (5,135 sq. miles)

Lake Maracaibo has a narrow inlet, a sound only 8 km (5 miles) wide which connects it to the Caribbean, but it is generally thought of as a lake. Its geology supports this classification: the lake, which was once much more definitively separated from the sea, is in fact one of the world's oldest lakes. The sea sound is spanned by the General Rafael Urdaneta Bridge, opened in 1962, which at 8.7 km (5½ miles) is one of the world's longest bridges. This cable-stayed bridge, almost 87 m (285 feet) high, was named after one of the heroes of the Venezuelan independence movement. To the north, near the sea, the lake's water is brackish, but elsewhere it is freshwater. Lake Maracaibo's north-south axis is 160 km (100 miles) long and it is about 120 km (75 miles) from east to west. The maximum depth recorded at the lake is 50 m (164 feet). The Chama, Santa Ana, and Catatumbo Rivers all flow into the lake, which in turn drains into the Caribbean. The

LAKE TITICACA

Peru, Bolivia   **8,135 sq. km**
                     (3,141 sq. miles)²

Lake Titicaca, one of the highest lakes in the world and the highest navigable lake, is to be found on a highland plain in the cordilleras at a dizzying 3,810 m (12,500 feet) above sea level. The lake is some

194 km (121 miles) long and approximately 65 km (40 miles) wide. The lake marks the border between Peru and Bolivia. Five rivers flow into Lake Titicaca, but its only outflow is the Río Desaguadero, which accounts for just 10% of its water loss – the rest evaporates or is carried away by the high winds.

Above: A woman of the Peruvian Uru tribe and her daughter in one of Lake Titicaca's typical reed boats. Main image: Lake Titicaca at Copacabana, Bolivia, with the snow-capped peaks of the Andes in the background.

LAGUNA MAR CHIQUITA

Argentina   **5,770 sq. km**
                     (2,228 sq. miles)

South America's third largest lake is the Laguna Mar Chiquita, an endorheic salt lagoon in the northeastern reaches of the Argentine province of Córdoba. The lagoon is fed by three rivers, the Río Dulce, Río Suquía, and Río Xanaes, but as it has no outflow and is extremely shallow (averaging 10–16 m/33–52 feet in depth), its size continually varies with rainfall levels. At low water, its salinity can reach 25% (the Dead Sea is 30%); when flooded, a mere 4%.

LAKE POOPÓ

Bolivia   **2,530 sq. km**
                     (977 sq. miles)

The actual size of this salt lake, into which the Río Desaguadero flows from Lake Titicaca, is still disputed, with estimates ranging from 1,000 sq. km (386 sq. miles) to 2,800 sq. km (1,080 sq. miles). It lies 3,686 m (12,093 feet) above sea level and is about 90 km (56 miles) long and 32 km (20 miles) wide. Its depth averages only 3 m (10 feet), which leads to wide variation in its size. The muddy waters of the lake are an ideal habitat for flamingos, but there are increasing levels of pollution from the local silver and tin mines.

Maracaibo Basin is rich in oil, and the largest deposits are located on the eastern shores, where commercial mining began in the early 20th century. The lake is also an important transport route, especially since it is partially navigable for ocean-going vessels. Unfortunately, there is a great deal of pollution located around the oil plants.

Large deposits of oil beneath the Maracaibo Basin are being exploited by Venezuela, a member of OPEC. A drilling rig can be seen in the foreground.

LAGO BUENOS AIRES
Argentina, Chile   **1,850 sq. km (714 sq. miles)**

The border of Argentina and Chile divides this lake, 217 m (712 feet) above sea level, in two halves. The Chileans call it Lago General Carrera and its deepest point (586 m/1,923 feet) lies in Chile. Several rivers flow into the lake but the only outflow is the Baker, which drains into the Pacific at the Golfo de Peñas. The lake occasionally floods into the Fénix Chico and Deseado Rivers before draining into the Atlantic.

The Lago Buenos Aires, seen from the Argentine side (left).

LAGO ARGENTINO
Argentina   **1,490 sq. km (575 sq. miles)**

The largest freshwater lake to lie completely within Argentina is located in the Los Glaciares National Park. Meltwater from the glaciers, including the Upsala, South America's largest, is sluiced into the lake by several rivers. The lake's outflow, the Santa Cruz River, drains into the Atlantic. The lake's deepest point is 500 m (1,640 feet), although it averages only 150 m (492 feet). The lake is teeming with fish.

Late summer on Lago Argentino; the beech trees are already changing to brown.

Salt lakes are usually endorheic bodies of water in very arid and hot areas. Their salt content is often considerably greater than that of seawater, even as high as 35%. Few creatures can survive such extreme conditions, although certain cyanobacteria and

The Salar de Uyuni in south-west Bolivia.

brine shrimp thrive here. The mineral and salt content is increased by constant evaporation and if the water supply is not sufficient, the entire lake can dry up. Such dried-out lake beds are known as salt pans or saline clay pans. This dry state can be periodic or permanent.

THE WORLD'S LARGEST SALT LAKES
(non-drying)

1. **Caspian Sea**   371,000 sq. km
   Russia,   (143,245 sq. miles)
   Kazakhstan, Azerbaijan,
   Iran, Turkmenistan
2. **Aral Sea**   17,160–27,000 sq. km
   Kazakhstan,   (6,625-10,425
   Uzbekistan   sq. miles)
3. **Lake Balkhash (eastern section)**
   Kazakhstan   7,740 sq. km
     (2,990 sq. miles)
4. **Lake Turkana**   6,405 sq. km
   Kenya, Ethiopia   (2,473 sq. miles)
5. **Lake Issyk-Kul**   6,236 sq. km
   Kyrgyzstan   (2,408 sq. miles)
6. **Laguna Mar Chiquita**
   Argentina   5,770 sq. km
     (2,228 sq. miles)
7. **Lake Urmia**   5,470 sq. km
   Iran   (2,112 sq. miles)
8. **Koko Nor (Qinghai Hu)**
   China   4,538 sq. km
     (1,752 sq. miles)
9. **Great Salt Lake**   4,400 sq. km
   USA   (1,700 sq. miles)
10. **Lake Van**   3,740 sq. km
    Turkey   (1,444 sq. miles)
11. **Lake Alakol**   2,650 sq. km
    Kazakhstan   (1,023 sq. miles)
12. **Lake Poopó** 2,530 sq. km
    Bolivia   (977 sq. miles)

THE WORLD'S LARGEST SALT LAKES AND SALT PANS
(periodically drying)

1. **Lop Nur**   21,000 sq. km
   China   (8,100 sq. miles)
2. **Makgadikgadi Pan**   16,000 sq. km
   Botswana   (6,200 sq. miles)
3. **Salar de Uyuni**   10,582 sq. km
   Bolivia   (4,086 sq. miles)
4. **Lake Eyre**   9,500 sq. km
   Australia   (3,700 sq. miles)
5. **Chott el Djerid**   7,700 sq. km
   Tunisia   (2,970 sq. miles)
6. **Lake Torrens**   5,700 sq. km
   Australia   (2,200 sq. miles)
7. **Etosha Pan**   5,000 sq. km
   Namibia   1,900 sq. miles)
8. **Lake Gairdner**   4,750 sq. km
   Australia   (1,830 sq. miles)
9. **Qattara Depression**   4,680 sq. km
   Egypt   (1,800 sq. miles)
10. **Lake Mackay**   3,500 sq. km
    Australia   (1,350 sq. miles)
11. **Salar de Atacama**   3,000 sq. km
    Chile   (1,160 sq. miles)
12. **Lake Frome**   2,600 sq. km
    Australia   (1,000 sq. miles)
13. **Tuz Gölü**   1,500 sq. km
    Turkey   (580 sq. miles)

A flap-necked chameleon (Chamaeleo dilepis) crossing one of the many salt flats in Botswana's Makgadikgadi Pan. Such barren salt pans are surrounded by grassland. Wild animal numbers in the area are determined by the season; after the spring rains, when the salt pans are partially flooded, the desert blooms and attracts plenty of wildlife to the area.

Many salt lakes and salt pans are located in extremely arid and hot regions. The water that infrequently fills them evaporates rapidly, leaving behind the salt that was in solution.

LOP NUR – A LAKE WITHOUT WATER

China   **21,000 sq. km (8,100 sq. miles)**

The Tarim Basin, the largest basin system in Central Asia at some 530,000 sq. km (205,000 sq. miles), is an enclosed depression in north-western China. Located in Xinjiang province, the basin lies on average 1,000 m (3,280 feet) above sea level and two-thirds of its surface area is covered by the sand dunes of the Taklamakan Desert. The depression's lowest point (780 m/2,560 feet above sea level) is occupied by Lop Nur, a lake which dried up in 1971. The lake bed is about 260 km (160 miles) long on its north-west to south-east axis and has a maximum width of 145 km (90 miles). It is circumscribed to the north by the Kuruktag Mountains, southern foothills of the Tian Shan chain, and to the south by the Altunshan Mountains. Lop Nur is one of the world's most remote and inhospitable areas and the Chinese use it as a nuclear testing ground. The soil consists of brown salt clay with a

MAKGADIKGADI PAN

Botswana   **16,000 sq. km (6,200 sq. miles)**

There was once a large, landlocked lake in north-eastern Botswana; the lake dried out about 10,000 years ago, leaving a crust of salt up to 5 m (16 feet) thick, to form the salt pans visible today. The rivers here flow only infrequently and the salt pans are usually dry. Salt and sodium carbonate are mined here for profit.

A lake forms in the northern section of the pan during the rainy season – ideal for birds.

CHOTT EL DJERID

Tunisia   **7,700 sq. km (2,970 sq. miles)**

The largest salt lake system in the Sahara is located in Tunisia, stretching from the Algerian border almost to the Mediterranean. The salt lakes are fed by streams and rivers rising in the mountains to the north. The water soon evaporates in the extreme heat and aridity, leaving its mineral salt content. The Chott dries out completely during the summer, but can flood or turn into a mudbath during the spring rains.

An abandoned sailboat in the Chott El Djerid salt lake in Tunisia (right).

SALAR DE UYUNI

Bolivia   **10,582 sq. km (4,086 sq. miles)**

At an elevation of 3,653 m (11,985 feet), this salt lake in south-western Bolivia looks like a frozen sea. Dry from early June to early December, in the rainy season it is covered with a film of water barely 30 cm (12 inches) deep, forming a lagoon that attracts flamingos. The Salar is a good source of salt and contains rich deposits of lithium.

Cactuses on the shores of the Salar de Uyuni in the Bolivian Highlands.

LAKE TORRENS

Australia   **5,700 sq. km (2,200 sq. miles)**

Lake Torrens is a generally dry salt pan located in the Lake Torrens National Park in the Australian outback some 430 km (267 miles) north-east of Adelaide. Only once in the last 150 years has water flowed in the salt lake, which runs for about 200 km (125 miles) along a north-south axis parallel to the peaks of the Flinders Range in South Australia. The lake, which is 50 km (31 miles) wide, is separated from the Spencer Gulf of the Indian Ocean by a spit of land only 30 km (19 miles) wide.

LAKE EYRE

Australia   **9,500 sq. km (3,700 sq. miles)**

Lake Eyre lies in a depression 700 km (435 miles) north of Adelaide, which at 15 m (49 feet) below sea level is also the lowest point in Australia. The lake is usually dry, but every three years or so enough rain falls to lift the water level to about 1.5 m (5 feet), and once a decade it may even rise to 4 m (13 feet). This desert lake is completely enclosed and loses its water through evaporation.

Salt flats with cell-like, raised edges on Lake Eyre.

ETOSHA PAN

Namibia   **5,000 sq. km (1,900 sq. miles)**

During heavy rainy seasons, this former lake in northern Namibia fills with a thin layer of water, attracting thousands of flamingos and other birds, but the salt pan beneath, a depression in the Kalahari some 120 km (75 miles) long and 70 km (43 miles) wide, is usually dry and barren. The cracked clay soil has a high salt content and a greenish-white crust. In the Ovambo language, *etosha* means "large white place".

A dead tree on the edge of the Etosha Pan in northern Namibia (right).

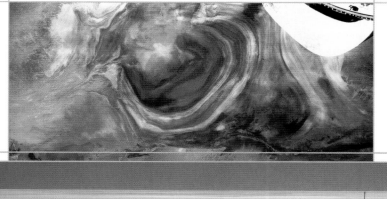

hard white salt crust. About 50 cm (20 inches) beneath this surface there is a salt marsh. Lop Nur is extremely arid and dusty, and plagued by strong north-westerly winds. Yardang is the name given to a typical local erosion formation – a combination of wind and water which has created abraded ridges with a broad face on the windward side and a narrower lee side.

Left: The "ear" formed by Lop Nur is visible from a space shuttle. These concentric rings are formed at various stages of the evaporation process. The view is from the south-east to the north-west.

LAKE GAIRDNER

Australia   4,750 sq. km
                            (1,830 sq. miles)

Lake Gairdner is located about 150 km (93 miles) north-west of Port Augusta in South Australia. It is 160 km (100 miles) long, 48 km (30 miles) wide at its broadest point, and covered with a layer of salt up to 1.2 m (4 feet) deep. The salt flats are periodically used in land speed record attempts. The Gawler Ranges to the south of the lake are around 1.5 billion years old and among the oldest volcanoes in the world.

Salt deposits in Lake Gairdner in South Australia.

QATTARA DEPRESSION

Egypt   4,680 sq. km (1,800 sq. miles)

The Qattara Depression is a desert basin in the Libyan Desert in north-western Egypt lying up to 133 m (436 feet) below sea level. About a quarter of this 18,000-sq.-km (7,000-sq.-mile) basin consists of a saline clay plain with a hard crust and thick mud which is occasionally covered in water. Salt swamps surround the area to the north and north-west. The Depression is more or less uninhabited, with just a few Bedouins proving the rule. Cheetahs have found a hunting ground here, preying on the local gazelles.

LAKE MACKAY

Australia   3,500 sq. km
                            (1,350 sq. miles)

Lake Mackay has a diameter of approximately 100 km (62 miles). The lake, which is located on Aboriginal territory, is the largest of the many hundreds of salt pans to be found in Western Australia and seems to retain a little residual moisture as satellite images reveal dark patches which may be simple desert vegetation or cyanobacteria. The lake plays an important role in Aborigine myth; it is known as Wilkinkarra and is said to have come about following a devastating bush fire.

Lake Assal (Lac Assal) is situated to the west of the Gulf of Aden in the middle of Djibouti, East Africa. Its salinity of 34.8% makes it the lake with the world's highest salt content – ten times as much as the world's oceans and even 10–15% more than the highest salinity

The lake and the Danakil Mountains.

Salt flats and peninsula on Lake Assal.

Weird gypsum and salt formations.

recorded for the Dead Sea. With an area of 54 sq. km (21 sq. miles), the lake lies considerably more than 150 m (492 feet) below sea level – measurements vary here, with some even going as low as 173 m (568 feet). What is certain is that the lake represents the lowest point and the deepest depression in continental Africa. You are more than likely to run across the occasional bizarre formation of salt or gypsum on the shores of Lake Assal. Underground springs supply the lake with water, some of which is seawater drawn from the Gulf of Aden. The extremely high level of salinity is the result of evaporation.

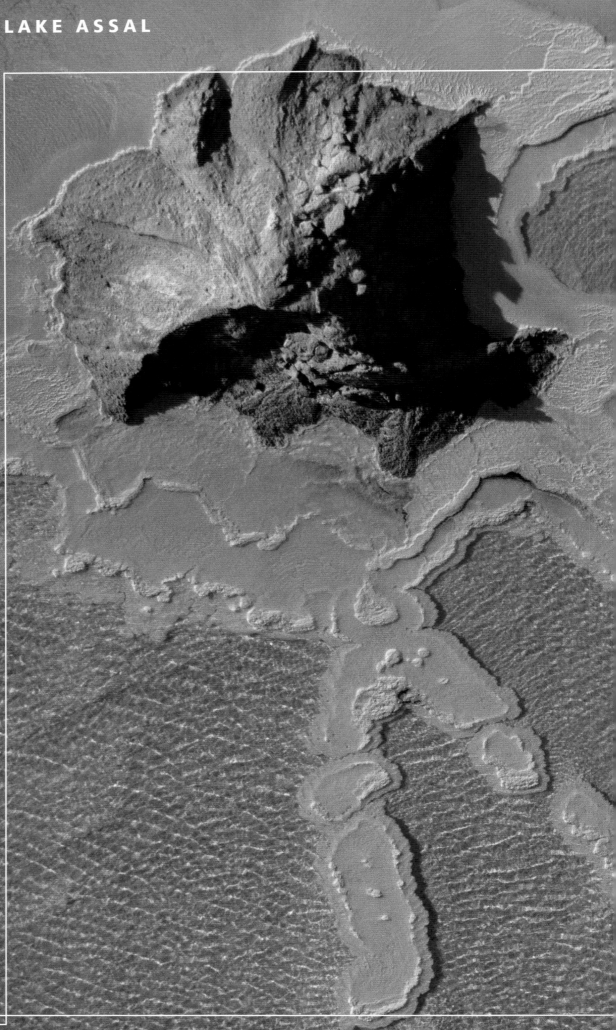

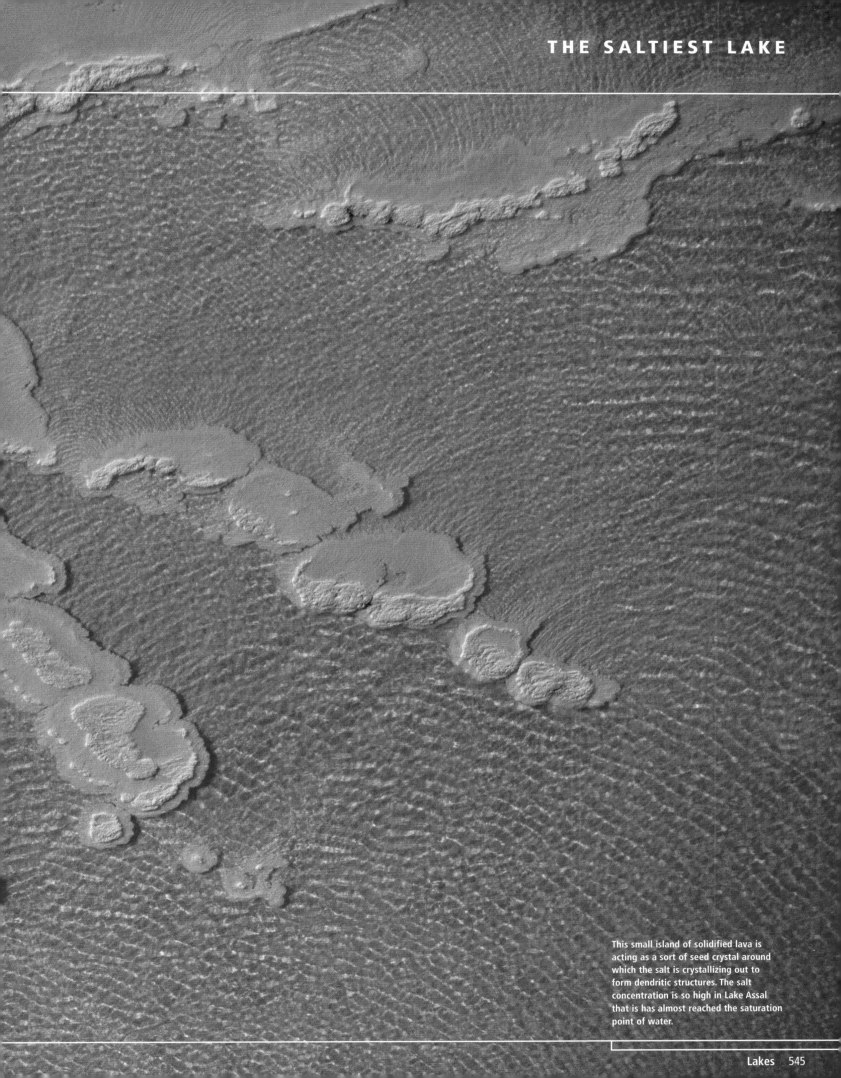

This small island of solidified lava is acting as a sort of seed crystal around which the salt is crystallizing out to form dendritic structures. The salt concentration is so high in Lake Assal that is has almost reached the saturation point of water.

WETLANDS

Certain areas in river valleys and around shallow lake shores can often be continually under water; this is usually fresh water, but salt water is also possible. The water level is typically low, and the surface is often broken by trees or islands covered in scrub. The footing is usually

Mangrove swamps in Florida.

muddy, and in contrast to moorland, turf is unlikely to form. Wetlands – usually created where a fluvial plain has only a slight incline or is lacking a natural outflow – provide a habitat for a wealth of flora and fauna; sedges are typically found, as are willows in northern latitudes. Excessive drainage to provide water for farming or drinking has threatened a number of wetlands, and many valuable biotopes could be lost forever.

THE WORLD'S LARGEST WETLANDS
(not including deltas and rivers which drain into the sea)

① Pantanal
Brazil, Paraguay, Bolivia
140,000–195,000 sq. km
(54,000–75,300 sq. miles)

② Sudd
Sudan   30,000–100,000 sq. km
(11,600–38,600 sq. miles)

③ Pripyat Marshes
Belarus, Ukraine, Poland
90,000 sq. km (34,800 sq. miles)

④ Vasyugan Swamp
Russia   53,000 sq. km
(20,500 sq. miles)

⑤ Shatt al-Arab
Iraq   35,600 sq. km
(13,700 sq. miles)

⑥ Asmat Swamp
Indonesia, New Guinea
30,000 sq. km (11,600 sq. miles)

⑦ Bangweulu Swamps
Zambia   15,000 sq. km
(5,800 sq. miles)

⑧ Okavango Swamp
Botswana   15,000 sq. km
(5,800 sq. miles)

⑨ Everglades
USA, Florida   6,000 sq. km
(2,300 sq. miles)

⑩ Big Cypress Swamp
USA, Florida   2,900 sq. km
(1,100 sq. miles)

The wetlands of the Pantanal provide a habitat for the largest water lilies. The genus known as *Victoria*, whose round leaves have a diameter approaching 3 m (10 feet), was named after the British Queen Victoria (1819–1901). The leaves have very fine pores and a notch at their edge to allow rainwater to run off. The portion of the leaves beneath the water is equipped with sharp spines to stop fish from nibbling them.

The Pantanal – Portuguese for "swamp" – is located in the middle of south-western Brazil and is the world's largest inland wetland. The swamp, which has a total surface area of 140,000–195,000 sq. km (54,000–75,300 sq. miles), was designated a UNESCO World

The Mato Grosso in the southern Pantanal.

Heritage Site in 2000. The Río Paraguay, the largest river in the area, drops only some 30 m (100 feet) on its 600-km (370-mile) course through the biotope, leading to widespread flooding; during the rainy season between November and March, many areas of the plain can lie up to 1 m (3 feet) under water. The area is a natural paradise with a wealth of animal and plant life, much of which is yet to be discovered. Although it has been recognized as a nature reserve, the Pantanal is under increasing threat from industrialization and logging.

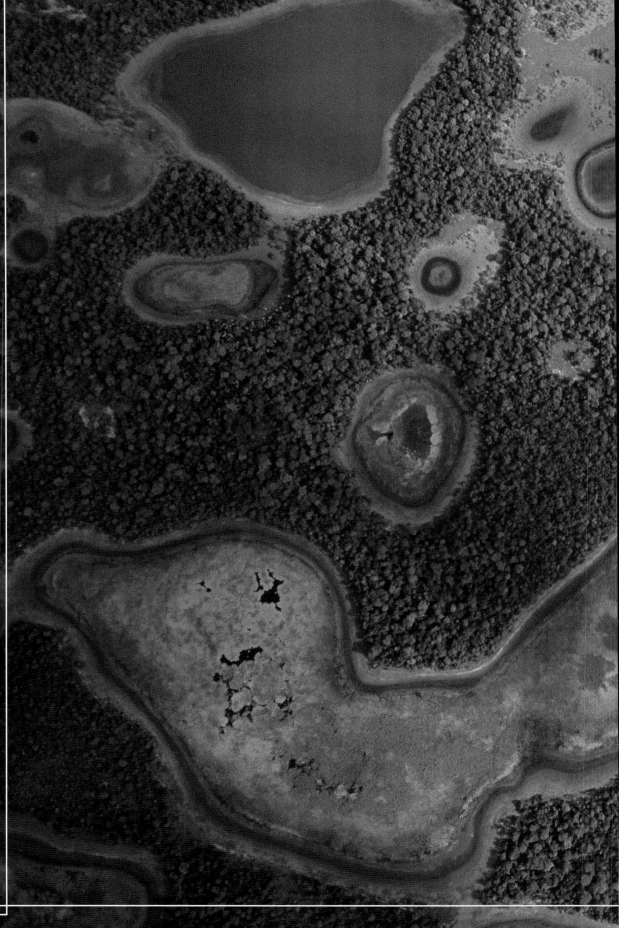

An aerial image of the Pantanal during the rainy season. Countless green lagoons have formed between the slightly raised forested areas.

Trees reflected in the Mutum River in the northern Pantanal.

The spectacled caiman (*Caiman crocodilus*) lives in the swamps.

CAPYBARAS

The capybara (*Hydrochoerus hydrochaeris*) is the world's largest living rodent. It is related to the guinea pig, although its lifestyle is more reminiscent of that of the hippopotamus. This mammal, which has found a habitat in the wetlands of South America

Capybaras are social animals.

and the Pantanal in particular, measures up to 1.3 m (4½ feet) from head to tail and stands about 60 cm (24 inches) high at the shoulder. A fully grown male weighs about 50 kg (110 lb) and a female 60 kg (132 lb). Capybaras have webbed folds of skin between their toes and are excellent swimmers. The animals typically come out at dusk, usually escaping the heat of the day by staying in shallow water. Capybaras live in large groups of up to 20 animals, and each group occupies a territory which can be up to 200 ha (500 acres) in size, although they tend to keep to a core area of about 10 ha (25 acres). The animals in a group mark their territory with their scent glands. They mostly live on grasses.

Capybaras take to shallow water to escape the heat of the day, only coming out when it gets dark. The cattle tyrant, a species of sparrow found only in South America, uses the heads of capybaras as a landing strip and departure lounge during its hunt for insects.

With an area of more than 20,000 sq. km (7,700 sq. miles), the Okavango Swamp is the world's largest inland delta and also one of the largest wetlands on Earth. As the Okavango, one of the longest rivers in Africa, fans out to form this delta, located in

A swampy area in the "panhandle".

north-western Botswana, much of its water evaporates and the rest trickles away into the Kalahari Desert. There are four separate zones: the so-called "panhandle", the lower course of the river near the mouth of the delta, which always carries water; the area at the end of the panhandle, which is swampy throughout the year; several areas at the edge of the delta which flood periodically; and the islands in the interior and to the south of the delta. The total drop from the beginning of the delta to its end, 250 km (155 miles) away, is just 60 m (200 feet), and the water thus runs off very slowly, further hampered by the dense vegetation. When the water levels in the panhandle are at their highest during the rainy season in spring, between October and April, it can take four months for the water to reach the delta's southern edge, and it arrives there at the height of the dry season. The local flora and fauna are thus able to survive throughout the year. Despite the high levels of evaporation, the water is still good to drink.

An aerial image of the Okavango Delta: the arms of the river fan out to form a giant swamp with a mosaic of watercourses and countless green islands. Such islands lie no more than 3 m (10 feet) above the surrounding swampland, although their areas can vary between just a few square meters to several square kilometers. There is a phenomenal variety of species in the delta; 122 mammal species alone have been recorded.

Elephants picking their way through the shallow swamp waters.   Large herds of zebras find a way through the flooded landscape.

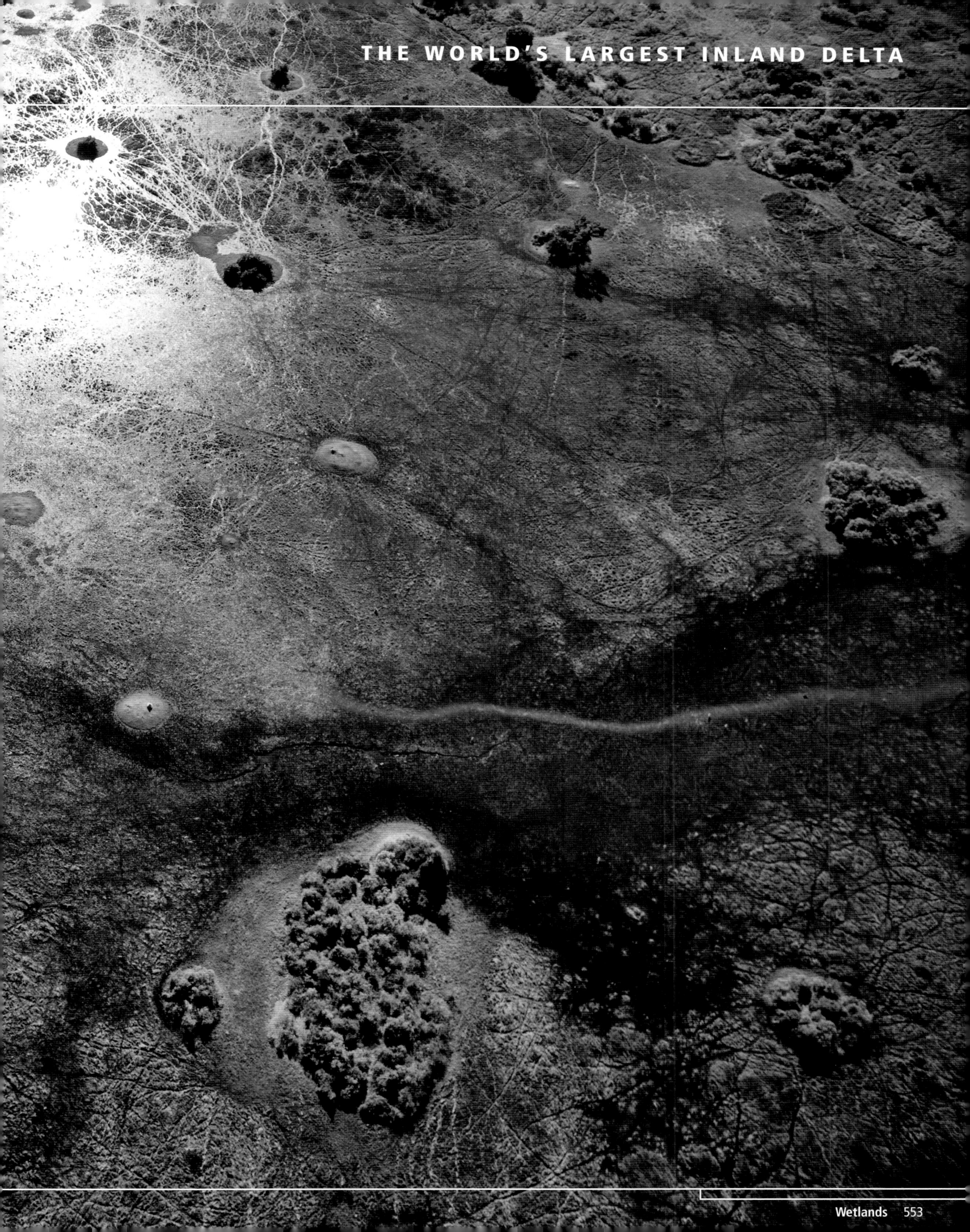

Abbreviations:
A = Alamy, C = Corbis, G = Getty, L = Laif,
M = Mauritius, Schapo = Schapowalow

l. = left, m. = middle, r. = right, t. = top,
b. = bottom

Front cover (large image): Mauritius;
from left to the right: laif/Hoa-Qui; Corbis/Schafer; seatops.com; Look/Per Andre Hofmann

2/3: Don Fuchs; 4/5: C/Momatiuk-Eastcott; 6/7: L/IML; 8/9: G/Banana Pancake; 10/11: G/Sutherland; 12/13: A1PIX/BIS; 13: M/A/Interfoto; 14 t. l. + m. l.: C/NASA; 14 b. l.: C/Bettmann; 14/15: 15 t., 15 m. 1–3: C/NASA; 15 m. 4: M/A/Saurer; 15 t. r.: G/Stocktrek; 15 b. r.: C/Benson; 16/17: M/A/Stocktrek; 17 t. + b.: M/A/Saurer; 18/19: C/Benson; 19 1 + 2: C/NASA; 19 3: C/Bettmann; 19 4: C/Stocktrek; 19 5: C/Morris; 19 6: C/Bettmann; 19 7: C/Benson; 19 8: C/Bettmann; 20: G/Stocktrek; 20/21: NN.; 21 t. l.: Premium; 21 b. l.: C/Allofs; 21 m.: C/Carter; 21 b. m.: G/Flood; 21 r.: C/Remi Benali; 22 t. l.: M/A/Eden; 22 t. r.: G/Stocktrek RF; 22/23: G/Sightseeing Archive; 23 t. + b.: G/World Perspectives; 24 t. l.: G/Simonsen; 24 t. r.: A/Robert Harding; 24/25: G/National Geographic; 25 t.: C/Lanting; 25 b.: SSPL/NASA; 26/27: Focus/Science Photo Library; 27 t.: dpa; 28: mcs/Dettling; 28/29: Geospace/EDC2002; 30: Premium/Minden; 30/31: M/A/Rotman; 32: A/Larionova; 32/33: G/Johnson; 33: G/Oomen; 34: C/Guttman; 34/35: G/Breiehagen; 35 (all): C/Bettmann; 36/37: G/Hellier; 37 1: G/Wilson; 37 2: C/Schafer; 37 3: www.deff.de; 37 4: G/Panoramic Images; 37 5: G/Peter Adams; 37 6: G/Macduff Everton; 37 7: C/Hellier; 38/39: Geospace/EDC 2002; 39: G/Stucky; 40 t. l.: C/Rellini; 40 b. l.: Huber/Graefenhain; 40/41: Erich Spiegelhalter; 41: Geospace/EDC 2002; 42: Zielske; 42/43: Geospace/Eurimage 2002; 44 l.: A/Wave Royalty Free; 44 b.: M/A/Chesire; 44/45: G/Blair; 45: L; 46 l.: G/Melford; 46 b.: G/Panoramic Images; 46/47: G/Johnston; 47 b. l.: G/pa; 47 t. r.: G/Jezierski; 47 b. r.: Don Fuchs; 48 t. l.: C/Ganci; 48 l. m.: A/Classic Stock; 48 b. l.: G/Melford; 48/49: Premium; 49: C/Bettmann; 50 l.: C/Lanting; 50/51: A/Conlin; 51 1 +2: C/Rotman; 51 3: C/Yin; 51 4: C/Rotman; 52: Premium; 52/53: Huber/Giovanni; 53 t.: Geospace/EDC 2002; 54: G/Sherman; 54/55: G/Chesley; 56 t. l.: G/Stanfield; 56 b. l.: G/Douwma; 56/57: Geospace/Spotimage 2002; 58 l.: G/Allen; 58/59: C/Stenzel; 59: G/Flood; 60/61: Premium; 61: Wildlife; 62 l.: M/A/digitalunderwater; 62/63: seatops/Howard; 63 1: C/Psihoyos; 63 2: A/Stock Connection; 63 3: C/Nachoum; 63 4: BA-online; 63 5: Wildlife; 64: C/Nachoum; 64/65: G/Westmoreland; 65 t.: A/Alaska Stock; 65 b.: C/Allofs; 66: L/Heeb; 66/67: Premium; 68: C/NASA; 68/69: G/Harding; 69 b.: Premium; 70: C/NASA; 70/71: L/Steinhilber; 71 b.: G/Noton; 72 t. l.: A/Aflo; 72 b. l.: G/Panoramic Images/Blackmore; 72/73: C/Radius Images; 73 t. l. + b.: G/Panoramic Images; 74 b. l.: sinopictures; 74 b. r.: G/Edwards; 74/75: blickwinkel/Gerth; 75 t. l.: C/NASA; 75 t. r.: M/A/Paterson; 75 t. l.: G/National Geographic; 75 b. l.: Westend61/Rietze; 75 b. r.: G/Sinibaldi; 76: C/NASA; 76/77: L/Hauser; 77: Premium; 78 l.: C/NASA; 78 r.: Premium/Wolfe; 78/79: G/Warburton-Lee; 80 t. l.: G/Baigrie; 80 b. l.: G/Bourseiller; 80 b. l.: A/Rietze; 80 b. r.: G/Peter; 80/81: C/Nomachi; 81 b. l. + r.: G/Peter; 82 l.: C/NASA; 82 b.: Ifa/Index Stock; 82/83: Ifa/Panoramastock; 84 l.: A/JupiterImages; 84 b. l.: C/Bettmann; 84 b. r.: C/Murat; 84/85: G/Balog; 85 1: C/Xinhua Press; 85 2: G/Solomon; 85 3: G/Mitidieri; 85 4: G/Yager; 85 5: G/AFP; 86: C/NASA; 86/87: C/Momatiuk-Eastcott; 87: G/Stone; 88: C/NASA; 88/89: G/Wiltsie; 89 b.: Premium/Hummel; 90 + 90/91: A/Bryan & Cherry Alexander Photography; 91 l.: C/Bettmann; 91 t. r.: C/Hulton; 91 r. m.: A/North Wind Picture Archives; 91 b. r.: C/Hulton; 92 l. 1: Klammet; 92 l. 2: G/Winter; 92 l. 3: A/look; 92 l. 4: Okapia; 92 t. r.: A/Cohen; 92 r. m.: L/Heeb; 92 b. r.: G/Flood; 92/93: C; 93 r.: G/World Perspectives; 94/95: C/Steinmetz; 95 t.: G/World Perspectives; 95 b. l.: G/Adams; 95 b. r.: M/A/Nathan; 96: G/Arctic-Images; 96/97: Tobias Hauser; 98: G/Bouseiller; 98/99: C/NASA; 99 t.: G/Stablefort; 99 b.: G/Adams; 100 t. l.: G/Rosing; 100 t. r.: M/A/ Noton; 100/101: C/Krahmer; 101 t.: G/Benson; 101 b. l.: C/Strand; 101 b. r.: G/Kobalenko; 102 t.: G/Wyman; 102 m.: G/Brynn; 102 b.: Premium; 103 t.: Look/Leue; 103 1: G/Everton; 103 2: G/Sonnet; 103 3: G/Nicklen; 104 b.: G/Mead; 104/105: G/Adams; 105 t.: M/A/Brianafrica; 106/107: Premium; 107 t.: M/A/Sylvia Corday Photo Library; 107 b.: G/Torckler; 108/109: blickwinkel/Rose; 109 b.: C/Leask; 110 l.: C/Souders; 110/111: G/Momatiuk; 112 l.: NN; 112/113: Premium; 113 t.: G/TCL; 113 b. r.: Premium/Minden; 114 t. l.: Premium; 114 b. l.: Wildlife/Cox; 114/115: C/Souders; 116 l.: G/Kim in Cherl; 116/117: G/Johannson; 117 t.: G/Hermansen; 117 b.: Blickwinkel/Hummel; 118 l.: G/Momatiuk-Eastcott; 118/119: G/Wolfe; 120 l.: G/Momatiuk-Eastcott; 120/121: G/Edwards; 121 t. r.: G/Sund; 121 r. m.: G/Rouse; 121 b. r.: A/Juniors; 122 l.: G/National Geographic; 122/123: Premium/Chrysanthu; 124 t.: M/imagebroker; 124 b.: C/Tidmann; 125 t.: Premium; 125 m.: C/Kaufmann; 125 b.: Premium/Tidmann; 126 t. l.: G/DC Productions; 126 b. l.: G/Nicklen; 126/127: G/Postma; 127 t.: Premium; 128/129: Geospace EDC 2002; 129 b.: G/van Oos; 130 l.: G/Kitchin & Hurst; 130/131: Junior Bildarchiv; 132 t. l.: G/Quinton/Gillan; 132 b. l.: C/Widstrand; 132/133: G/Conger; 134 l.: Premium; 134/135: G/Erwin; 135 t.: Premium; 135 b. 1: G/Panoramic Images; 135 b. 2: Premium; 135 r.: Rudolf König; 136/137: Geospace Eurimage 2002; 137 t.: DFA/Nimtsch; 138 t. l.: Premium; 138 b. l.: Premium; 138 b.: Ifa/Panstock; 138/139: Premium; 139 b.: Wildlife/Shipilenok; 140 l.: Panoramastock; 140 b.: Premium; 140/141: Panoramastock; 142 t.: G/Toft; 142/143: G/Gehman; 143 b.: G/Jordan; 144 l.: Blickwinkel/Huetter; 144/145: Blickwinkel/Linke; 146 l.: Helga Lade; 146/147: M/A/BL Images; 147 t.: G/Collins; 147 b.: M/A/Gibbons; 147 r.: M/A/Siepmann; 148 t. l.: Okapia; 148 b. l.: Wildlife; 148/149: M/A/tbkmedia; 149 t. r.: G/Oomen; 149 r. m.: M/A/BL Images; 149 b. r.: A; 150 l.: A/Juniors; 150/151: Premium; 151 b.: M/A/Blickwinkel; 152 t.: A/Monkiewicz; 152/153: G/Wittek; 154 l.: G/Osawa; 154/155: G/Iwamoto; 155 t. l.: M/A/Stamboulis; 155 t. m.: M/A/Panorama Media; 155 t. r.: A/View Stock; 155 t. r.: G/Tohoku Color Agency; 155 b. r.: G/Iwamoto; 156 l.: G/Krebs; 156/157: M/A/Falzone; 157 t.: G/Chiba; 157 b.: G/WIN-Initiative; 158 t. l.: G/Nature Expressions; 158 b. l.: G/Slade; 158/159: M/A/Bloom; 159 b.: Look/Wothe; 160 l.: G/Clay; 160/161: M/A/Delimont; 161 t.: M/A/Young; 161 r.: Okapia/Krabbe; 162 t. l.: C/Richardson; 162 t. r.: G/Panoramic Images; 162/163: G/Whaley; 164 l.: animal.affairs.com; 164/165: G/Parfitt; 166/167: M/A/Kikvidize; 167 t.: M/Morandi; 167 b. l.: A/Keller; 167 b. m.: photoplexus/Portrat; 167 b. r.: G/Wood; 168 t. l. + l. m.: Premium/Waldhäusl; 168 b. l.: M/A/imagebroker; 168/169: Premium/Waldhäusl; 170/171 + 171 t. l.: animal-affairs.com; 171 l. m.: C/Keren Su; 171 b. l.: NN; 171 t. r.: Stéphane Frances; 171 r. m.: Juniors; 171 b. r.: Premium/Wehrle; 172 t.: G/Edwards; 172 b.: G/Nagaoka; 172/173: Premium/Imagebroker; 173 b.: G/Ricard; 174 t. l.: Picture Press; 174 b. 1: A/Nature Picture Library; 174 b. 2: M/A/ Manjeet&yograi jadeja; 174/175: A/Nature Picture Library; 176 l.: mediacolors/Buck; 176/177: C/Kaehler; 178 t. l.: G/Allofs; 178 b. l.: G/visionandimagination.com; 178 r.: M/A/Donald; 178/179: M/A/Bachmann; 180 l.: Premium; 180/181: C/Gallo; 182 l.: G/Illig/Glover; 182/183: G/Robert Harding; 183 b.: M/A/Pearce; 184 t.: A/Bryan&Cherry Alexander Photography; 184/185: dpa/epa; 186 t.: C + W. Kunth; 186 b.: Premium/Lanting; 186/187: G/Gulin; 188: C/Harvey; 188/189: Premium; 190 t.: G/Woolfe; 190 b.: G/Wilkins/ Sneesby; 190/191: C/Zuckermann; 192 t.: G/Hornocker; 192/193: M; 194 t.: G/Warwick; 194/195: C/Davis; 196/197: G/Allofs; 197 b.: Premium; 198 t.: G/Shah; 198/199: G/Warwick; 200 t.: C. + W. Kunth; 200 b.: G/Gulin; 200/201: M/A/Top-Pics; 201 t.: A/Wildlife; 201 b. l.: G/Holt; 201 b. r.: Look/Franz Marc Frei; 202 t. l. + t. r.: Premium/Lanting; 202/203: C/Ripani; 204 l.: C/Johnson; 204/205: G/Poliza; 206/207: G/Laman; 207 b.: G/Harding; 208 l.: G/Oberle; 208/209: G/Jurak; 209 1 + 2: G/Postma; 209 3: G/Everton; 209 4: G/Panoramic Images; 210 t. l. + b.: Premium; 210/211: Premium/Brandenburg; 212 b. l.: dpa/epa; 212 b. r.: M/A/Pili; 212/213: M/A/Trinidade; 214 t. l.: G/van der Hilst; 214 t. r.: G/van Oos; 214/215: Premium/Heinrich; 216: Premium; 216/217: M/A/FAN; 218 l. 1 + 2: C/Lemmens; 218 l. 3: L/Hemis; 218 l. 4: G/TCL; 218/219 + 219: C/Nomachi; 220: Premium; 220/221: Geospace/Eurimage 2002; 222 t.: C/Phototravel; 222 m.: M/A/Clegg; 222 b.: BLW/Pohl; 223 1: G/Wiltsie; 223 2: C/Steinmetz; 223 3: C/Krist; 223 4: f1online/Panorama Media; 224 t.: A/Redling; 224 b., 224/225 + 225 b.: C/Steinmetz; 226 l.: C/Raga; 226 t. r.: G/Morandi; 226 b. r.: G/Panoramic Images; 226/227: C/Steinmetz; 228/229: G/The Image Bank; 229 t.: Visum/Wildlight; 230/231: Geospace/Acres 2002; 231 l.: Premium/APL; 231 r.: C/Allofs; 232 l.: Premium; 232/233: Image State/Mead; 233 t. l.: G/Gallo Images; 233 t. r.: G/Travel Ink; 233 r. t.: M/A/Duthie; 233 r. b.: Clemens Emmler; 234 t. l. + b. l.: G/Turner; 234/235: G/Beatty; 236/237: Geospace EDC; 237 l.: A/Arco; 237 r.: C/Steinmetz; 238/239: Premium; 240: Clemens Emmler; 240/241: Premium; 242 1: G/Photographer's Choice; 242 2: G/Don Smith; 242 3: G/Melford; 242 4: G/Footh; 243 t.: A/Hallstein; 243 m.: G/Footh; 243 b.: C/Darack; 244: G/Wiltsie; 244/245: G/Aguirre; 245 t.: Ifa/Panstock; 245 m.: Rainer Hackenberg; 245 b.: Premium; 246 t. l.: G/Veiga; 246 b. l.: G/DEA; 246/247: G/Hebert; 247 t. l.: G/Gulin; 247 t. r.: Bios/Cyril; 248 l.: A/Mainka; 248/249: M/A/Bachmann; 250 l.: A/Gonzales; 250/251: G/Slade; 251 b.: M/A/China Images; 252 l.: M/A/Urbanmyth; 252/253: M/A/China Images; 254 t. l.: M/A/Bloom Images; 254 b. l.: M/A/China Span; 254/255: M/A/Steve Bloom; 256 l.: C/Strand; 256/257: M/A/Friend; 257 t. r. + r. m.: M/A/Mainka; 257 b. r.: M/A/Smith; 258 b. l.: M/A/McKenna; 258 b. r.: M; 258/259: M/A/Delimont; 260 t. l.: M/A/Hallstein; 260 b. l.: Christian Heeb; 260 b. r.: G/Everton; 260/261: A/Hallstein; 261 b.: M/A/Gonzales; 262 b. l.: M/A/imagebroker; 262 b. r.: M/A/Milne; 262/263: M/A/Hellier; 263 l.: M/A/Hodges; 263 r.: M/A/Brad Perks Lightscapes; 264/265: Premium/ Lanting; 265 t.: wildlife/Carwardine; 266 t.: G/Graham; 266/267: G/Beltra; 268 t.: M/A/Anderson; 268/269: M/A/Art of Travel; 269 t.: M/A/Robert Harding; 269 b.: M/A/travelib prime; 270 l.: M/A/Csernoch; 270 t. m.: Arco/NPL; 270 m.: M/A/Ridley; 270 b.: C/Westmoreland; 270 r.: M/A/South America; 270/271: C/Macduff; 272 l.: G/Laman; 272/273: M/A/Noton; 273 1: M/A/Imagebroker; 273 2: M/A/Travel Ink; 273 3: A/Arco; 273 4: M/A; 274 t. l.: G/Kumar; 274 b. l.: M/A/Strigl; 274 b. r.: M/A/Top-Pics; 274/275: M/A/World Photo; 276 t.: M/A/Images&Stories; 276 b.: G/Lewis; 276/277: Geospace EDC; 278 t. l.: G/Packwood; 278 b. l.: M/A/Diniz; 278/279: Premium/Minden; 280 b. l.: G/Klum; 280 b. r.: C/Lanting; 280/281: M/A/Falzone; 281 t.: M/A/ Parker; 281 b. l.: C/Atlantide; 281 b. r.: M/A/Falzone; 282 t. l.: M/A/Slater; 282 b. l.: C/Lanting; 282 b. r.: G/Cox; 282/283: G/Laman; 284 l.: C/McDonald; 284 r.: Voller Ernst/Maske; 284/285: A/Morse; 286 l.: M/A/Greenberg; 286/287: M/A/ Long; 287 t. r.: M/A/Visage; 287 b. r.: L/Hoa Qui; 288/289: G/Noton; 289 t.: C/Steinmetz/Lord; 289 b. 1 + 2: Premium; 290 l. + b.: Wildlife; 290/291: G/ Edwards; 292 l. + 292: G/Nichols; 293 t. l.: M/A/blickwinkel; 293 t. m.: M/A/Christopher; 293 t. r.: M/A/Jangoux; 293 t. l.: M/A/Long; [repeat 293 t.l. might mean l. t. perhaps? haven't got PDF to check] 293 b. l.: M/A/Parker; 293 r.: M/A/van Zandbergen; 294 b.: G/Fay; 294/295: G/Nichols; 296 t. l.: A/Juniors; 296 b. l.: M/A/blickwinkel; 296 r. + 296/297: G/Nichols; 298 t. l.: G/Allan; 298 l. m.: M/A/Images&Stories; 298 b. l.: M/A/Barker; 298/299: G/Massey; 299: A/World Travel Library; 300 l.: C/Lanting; 300/301: Premium; 302/303: C/Schafer; 303 t. l.: A/Jon Arnold; 303 t. m.: A/Schafer; 303 t. r.: A/Delimont; 303 b.: G/Banana Pancake; 304 t. l.: G/Szaley; 304 b. l.: G/Hunter; 304/305: M/A/Bennett; 305 b.: M/A; 306 l.: Okapia; 306/307: Arco/NPL; 307 t. r.: M/A/Dalton; 307 r. m.: Okapia; 307 b. r.: M/A/Dalton; 308 l.: G/Jaccod; 308/309: A/Peter Arnold; 309 t.: A/Photoshot; 309 r.: M/A/Jangoux; 309 b. l.: M/A/BrazilPhotos; 309 b. r.: M/A/Images Etc.; 310 l.: C/Rotman; 310/311: G/Kenney; 312: G/Rafla; 312/313: C/Silver; 314/315: Geospace EDC; 315 b.: G/Astrumujoff; 316 t. l.: A/Royal Geographical Society; 316 b. l.: C/Bettmann; 316 b.: M/Krinnninger; 316/317: A/Preston; 318 1: G/Art Wolfe; 318 2: M/A/Wojtkowiak; 318 3: G/Klesius; 318 4: A/CuboImages; 318 5: G/Keren Su; 318 6: M/A/Roig; 318 7: M/A/Paterson; 318 8: C/Rowell; 318 9: G/Stockbyte; 318/319: M/A/MCS; 319 1: M/A/Golob; 319 2: M/A/Stockshot; 319 3: C/Rowell; 319 4: A/Koutsaftis; 320 l.: C/Rowell; 320 b.: Woodhouse; 320/321: NN; 322/323: G/Doerr; 323 t.: M/A/Toporsky; 324 t.: G/Slow Images; 324 b.: G/Tomlinson; 324/325: G/Stone; 325 l.: G/Walker; 325 r.: L/Heidorn; 326 t. l.: C/Nevada Wier; 326 b. l.: G/Dixon; 326/327: Mau/imagebroker; 327 t.: M/A/Don Davis; 327 t. r.: Mau/imagebroker; 327 b. r.: A/vario; 328 t.: G/De Agostini Picture Library; 328 b.: G/McManus; 328/329: A/Atmotu Images; 329 t.: G/Kaehler; 329 r.: M/A/Banana Pancake; 330 l.: A/CuboImages; 330/331: Mau/A/Imagebroker; 331 b.: f1online/JB-Fotografie; 332 t. l.: C/Rowell; 332 b. l.: G/Hatcher; 332 r.: A/Rowell; 332/333: G/Hatcher; 334 l.: C/Vikander; 334/335: C/Lowell; 335 t. l.: L/ChinaFotoPress; 335 t. r.: Panoramastock/Suichu; 335 b. l.: Premium/Panoramic Images; 335 b. r.: L/Engelhorn; 336 t. + b.: Premium; 336/337: M/A/Lockhart; 338 1: M/A/Noble; 338 2: C/Souders; 338 3: G/Travel Ink; 338 4: M/A/Donald; 338/339: G/Hellier; 339: C/Steinmetz; 340: G/Foott; 340/341: G/Schermeister; 341 l.: C/Craddock; 341 t. r.: G/Mayfield; 341 b. r.: C/Fleming; 342/343: Geospace EDC 2002; 343 t.: L/Martin; 343 b.: Premium; 344 t.: Look/Martin; 344 m.: G/National Geographic; 344 b.: A/Imagebroker; 345 1: Premium; 345 2: G/Panoramic Images; 345 3: Premium; 345 4: M/A/Wherrett.com; 346: G/Hook; 346/347: Geospace EDC 2002; 348 l.: G/Travel Ink; 348 r.: G/VisionsofAmerica; 348/349: M/A/Ebi; 349 t.: M/A/Arco; 349 b. l.: C/Ressmeyer; 349 b. r.: M/A/L3; 350 b.: Premium; 350/351: Premium/Prisma; 351 b. l.: C/Terrill; 351 b. r.: G/Fowlks; 352 l.: M/A/Dearing; 352/353: Premium; 354 l.: A/Scholpp; 354/355: G/DEA; 356/357: C/Radius Images; 357 t.: C/Stadler; 357 b.: C/Hummel; 358/359: G/Sartore; 359 t. l.: M/A/Etcheverry; 359 t. m.: Premium/Cavendish; 359 t. r.: Premium/Donadoni; 360 b.: C/Hellier; 360/361: C/McDonald; 362 l.: G/Image Source; 362/363: L/Meyer; 363 t.: A/Opitz; 363 m.: L/Meyer; 363 b.: A/Buntrock; 364 l.: A/Bryan&Cherry Alexander; 364 b.: G/Wiltsie; 364/365: G/Wiltsie; 365 b.: A/blickwinkel; 366/367: Look/Hofmann; 368 b.: G/Darack; 368/369: C/Science Faction; 370 l.: A/Skrypczak; 370/371: A/Till; 371 t.: A/Kaehler; 371 b.: A/Hancock; 372 b. l.: neuebildanstalt/Vogt; 372 b. r.: M/A/Fraser; 372/373: G/DEA; 373 t.: M/A/Filatov; 374 t.: G/Slow images; 374/375: Geospace Eurimage 2002; 375 t.: G/Wolfe; 375 b.: G/Peter; 376 t.: C/Setboun; 376 m.: C/Roth; 376 b.: Waterframe/Dirscherl; 377 t.: Argus/Schwarzbach;

PICTURE CREDITS

377 1: G/Allen; 377 2: M/A/A1pix; 377 3: M/A/Images Etc. Ltd.; 378 l.: A/Axelsson; 378 b. l.: M/A/Arctic Images; 378 b. r.: M/A/Stefansson; 378/379: Schapo; 379 t.: M/A/FLPA; 379 b. l.: M/A/Arctic Images; 379 b. r.: G/Taylor; 380/381: M/A/Cox; 381 t.: C/Lukassek; 381 b. l.: C/Arthus-Bertrand; 381 b. m.: C/Wood; 381 b. r.: BA-Geduldig; 382: G/Nigge; 382/383: G/Peter; 383 1+2: G/Bourseiller; 383 3: G/Kaehler; 383 4: G/Bourseiller; 384/385: C/Xinhua Press; 385 t.: C/Lawler; 385 t. r.: A/Westlake; 385 b. r.: M/A/MJ Photography; 386 b. l.: C/Gutman; 386 t. r.: Tobias Hauser; 386 b. r.: Clemens Emmler; 386/387: Premium/Schott; 387 t.: G/Wall; 387 b. l.: C/Steinmetz; 387 b. r.: Premium; 388 1: G/Allen; 388 2: C/Goodshot; 388 3: G/Bourseiller/Paice; 388 4: M/A/Greenslade; 388 5: G/Yamashita; 388 6: C/Sanbagan; 388 7: Premium/Minden; 388/389: C/Premium; 389 1: M/A/Dembinsky; 389 2: G/Sund; 389 3: C/Schafer; 389 4: C/Vega; 389 5: C/Bettmann; 389 6: G/Adamus; 389 7: C/Radius Images; 389 8: G/Balaguer; 390: C/Cook&Lenshel; 390/391: G/Wolfe; 391 t.: G/Panoramic Images; 391 m.: G/Severns; 391 b.: M/A/Lowry; 392 l.: G/Mobley; 392 m.: A/Purestock; 392 b.: C/Nowitz; 393 t.: G/Osolinski; 393 1: M/A/Wall; 393 2: A/van Zandbergen; 393 3: M/A/van Zandbergen; 394 l.: Look/Dressler; 394 t. r.: G/Turner; 394 b. r.: C/Arthus-Bertrand; 394/395: Geospace EDC 2002; 396 t.: M/A/Lovell; 396 m.: G/Bourseiller; 396 b.: G/Pfeiffer; 396/397: C/Derda; 397 t.: G/Johns; 397 b.: C/Bettmann; 398 1 t.: G/Bourseiller; 398 b. l.: L/Hemis; 398 b. r.: C/Arthus-Bertrand; 398/399: L/Hemis; 399 b.: M/A/Osborne; 400 t.: G/Herben; 400 m.: A/Brian&Cherry Alexander Photography; 400 b.: L/Warter; 401 t.: C/Hirschmann; 401 b.: G/Pefley; 402 l.: M/A/Ebi; 402 t. r.: Premium; 402 b. r.: M/A/Donnelly; 402/403: C/O'Rear; 403 b. l.: G/Stefko; 403 b. r.: C; 404 b. l.: A/Carrasco; 404 b. r.: G/Touzon; 404/405: G/Gray; 405 t.: A/Taylor; 405 b.: C/Ressmeyer; 406/407 t. + b.: C/Hummel; 407: G/Darack; 408 b.: M/A/Csernoch; 408/409: G; 409 t.: C/Allofs; 410/411: Geospace EDC 2002; 411 t.: C/Stadler; 412 l.: M/A/Harris; 412/413 + 413 b.: C/Steinmetz; 414/415 C/Everton; 415: M/A/Ebi; 416 l. 1: C/Bettmann; 416 l. 2: G/Freeman; 416 l. 3: C/Bettmann; 416 l. 4: Look/Hoffmann; 416 l. 5: G/Maudsley; 416/417: G/Bourseiller; 418: blickwinkel/Lohmann; 418/419: G/Melford; 420 l.: M/A/Svensson; 420/421: G/Wiltsie; 421 t. l.: M/A/Interfoto; 421 t. r.: M/A/Diniz; 422 l.: C/LiuLiquin; 422/423: M/A/Lehne; 424 l.: M/A/Ehlers; 424 t.: M/A/Ward; 424 b.: G/Ehlers; 425 t.: G/Kennedy; 425 m.: A/Ehlers; 425 b.: Premium/Sisk; 425 r.: M/A/Crabbe; 426 l.: M/A/Edwards; 426/427: Schapo/Sime; 428 t. l.: G/Evans; 428 b. l.: A/Image Source Pink; 428 r.: M/A/Panorama Stock; 428/429: C/LiuLiquin; 430/431 t.: G/Simeone Huber; 430/431 b.: C/Garvey; 432/433: L/Heeb; 433 t.: M/A/Schneider; 433 b.: Premium/Waldhäusl; 434 l.: C/Randklev; 434/435: Ifa; 435 b.: G/Frerck; 436: M/A/Bowes; 436/437: M/A/Lattes; 438 l.:

A/Delimont; 438 b. l.: G/Harding; 438 b. m.: M/A; 438 b. r.: Tobias Hauser; 438/439: G/Saloutos; 439 b. l.: M/A; 439 b. m.: G/Schermeister; 439 b. r.: M/A; 440 l.: A/Farlinger; 440/441: G/Alvarez; 442 t. l.: G/Altrendo; 442 b. l.+ 442/443: G/Nichols; 444: M/A; 444/445: M/A/Degginer; 446: G/Sue Flood; 446/447: C/NASA; 448: M/A/Leeth; 448/449: A/Imagebroker; 449 b. l.: M/A/Stocktrek Images; 449 b. r.: A/Bryan&Cherry Alexander Photography; 450/451: Geospace Eurimage 2002; 452/453: Geospace EDC 2002; 453 b.: C/Rowell; 454 b. l.: G/Schafer; 454 b. r.: G/Panoramic Images; 454/455: G/Breiehagen; 455: mcs; 456 l.: M/A/Images &Stories; 456 t. r.: A/Novosti; 456 b. r.: C/Rowell; 456/457: M/A/Giffard; 457 t.: G/World Perspectives; 458 l.: M/A/Wall; 458/459: G/Schlenker; 459 l.: M/A/Wall; 459 t. m.: C/Webster; 459 b. m.: G/Souders; 459 r.: M/A/Horisk; 460 l.: Premium/Imagebroker; 460/461: C/Nomachi; 461 b. l.: Premium/Imagebroker; 461 b. r.: Premium; 462/463: G/Ryan; 463 t.: transit/Haertrich; 463 m. l.: G/Reid; 463 m. r.: G/Bean; 463 b. l.: G/Farlow; 463 b. r.: G/Thad Samuels Abell II; 464/465: M/A/Dembinsky; 465 1: G/Gendler; 465 2: A/Delimont; 465 3: G/Pincham; 465 4: G/Reid; 465 5: G/Herben; 466/467: Geospace; 467: M/A/Bull; 468 t.: Geospace EDC 2002; 468 b.: G/Sessa; 468/469: M/A/Percy; 470: L/China Tourism Press; 470/471: L/ChinaFotoPress; 472/473: Huber/Zoom; 473 t. + 474/475: G/Panoramic Images; 475 t.: DFA/Meyer; 475 b.: G/Graham; 476 t.: C/Nomachi; 476 b.: C/Collart Herve; 476/477: Geospace EDC 2002; 478 t.: Romeis; 478 m.: Okapia; 478 b.: Peter Arnold; 479 1. l. + t. r.: C/Sergei; 479 t.: Bilderberg; 479 m.: Zielske; 479 b.: C/Boisvieux; 480 t.: A/Kaehler; 480 m.: Visum/Ludwig; 480 b.: G/Alex Cao; 481 t. l.: G/Evans; 481 t. r.: G/China Tourism Press; 481 m.: M/A/Interfoto; 482 t. l.: C/Rowell; 482 b. l.: G/Olson; 482/483: dpa/epa; 483 t.: C/Wright; 483 m. l.: C/Nomachi; 483 m. r.: M/A/Pitt; 483 b. l.: C/Harrington III; 483 b. r.: Majority World/Alam; 484 b.: M/A/Jackson; 484/485: M/A/Smithers; 485 t.: G/Hay; 485 t. l.: Look/Fuchs; 485 b. l.: A/Photodisc; 485 r.: G/Gebicki; 486/487 + 487 t. r.: C/Conway; 487 b. r.: C/Harvey; 488 t.: C/Arthus-Bertrand; 488 m.: C/Skyscan; 488 b.: G/Souders; 489 t. l.: G/Caputo; 489 t. r.: M/A/Wilson-Smith; 489 b.: C/Lanting; 490 t.: Premium/Ellis; 490/491: C/Benali; 492 t.: A/All Canada Photos; 492 m.: M/A/Sylvester; 492 b.: G/Marcoux; 493 t. (small): G/Panoramic Images; 493 t.: G/Panoramic Images; 493 m.: G/Corvin; 493 b.: G/Hopkins; 494 t.: G/Medioimages; 494/495: G/Lebowski; 495: G/Altrendo; 496 b.: M/A/NASA; 496/497: C/NASA; 497: Peter Arnold; 498/499: C/Allofs; 500/501: C/Langevin; 501 t.: G/AFP; 501 b.: M/A/Wilson-Smith; 502 t.: G/Fisher; 502 b.: A/moodboard; 502/503: A/Schafer; 504 t. l.: M/A/blickwinkel; 504 b. l.: A/Icelandic photo agency; 504: M/A/Percy; 505 t.: alimdi/Keller; 505 m.: A/dfwalls; 505 b. l.: BA-online; 505 b. m.: M/A/BL Images; 505 b. r.: M/A/Owston; 506 t.:

Visum/The Image Works; 506 b.: A/View Stock; 507 t.l.: M/A/Atmotu Images; 507 t. r.: M/A/Iconotec; 507 l. + r.: A/JTB Photo; 508 b.: M/A/Wall; 508/509: Look/Johaentges; 509 b. 1: M/A/Wall; 509 b. 2: A/Wildlight; 509 b. 3: C/Wheeler; 509 b. 4: A/Radius Images; 510 l. + 510/511: M/A/The Africa Image Library; 511 1: G/Nichols; 511 2: L/Emmler; 511 3: f1online/ Prisma; 511 4: L/Emmler; 512/513: G/Gallo Images; 513 t. l.: G/Wyman; 513 t. r.: G/Sheppard; 513 b.: G/Cumming; 514 t.: G/Brown; 514 b.: M/A/Jenny; 515 t.: Peter Arnold; 515 m.: G/Art Wolfe; 515 l.: G/Falconer; 515 b.: G/Hoehn; 516/517: G/Merten; 517 t.: G/Palmisano; 518 t. l.: M/A/Jangoux; 518 t.: M/A/Wilson; 518 t. r.: M/A/Dalton; 518 b.: A/imagebroker; 518/519: C/Schafer; 520/521: Premium; 521 t.: C/Lanting; 521 b.: G/Panoramic Images; 522: A/Pixonnet.com; 522/523: C/Bibikow; 524: C/NASA; 524/525: C/Encyclopedia; 525 t.: C/Garanger; 526/527: Look/Wothe; 527 t. l.: Look/Hoffmann; 527 t. r.: A/Imagebroker; 527 b.: M/A/Visage; 528/529: C/NASA; 529 t. l.: G/Watts; 529 t. r.: G/Panoramic Images; 529 m. l.: G/Sohm; 529 m. r.: A/Bibikow; 529 b.: G/Cralle; 530 t.: M/A/Marka; 530 m.: M/A/Schwanke; 530 b.: f1online/Siepmann; 531 t.: A/Shuldiner; 531 1: A/imagebroker; 531 2: C/Yamashita; 531 3: A/Interfoto; 532 b.: vario; 532/533: A/Hellier; 533 t. l.: C/Ludwig; 533 t. r.: C/Reuters; 534 t.: M/A/MJ Photography; 534 m.: G/Baigrie; 534 b.: C/Steinmetz; 535 t. l.: M/A/Images of Africa Photobank; 535 t. r.: M/A/MJ Photography; 535 t. l.: L/VU; 535 m.: A/Ariadne von Zandbergen; 535 b.: M/A/Egeland; 536 t.: G/Meleg; 536 m.: G/Reese; 536 b.: M/A/Michael DeFreitas North America; 537 t.: C/Sohm; 537 1: G/Wiltsie; 537 2: Look/Richter; 537 3: A/Ken Gillespie; 538 t.: G/Hellier; 538 b.: L/RAPHO; 538/539: G/Panoramic Images; 539 t.: C/Friedman; 539 b.: Still Pictures/ Moreiras; 540 l.: C/Adams; 540/541: C/Lanting; 542 t.: M/A/Newton; 542 m.: C/Nomachi; 542 b.: Look/Fuchs; 543 t.: C; 543 1: L/Gil; 543 2: G/Edwards; 543 3: M/A/AfriPics; 544 t.: M/A/ Kaplan; 544 m.: M/A/Dirscherl; 544 b.: G/Peter; 544/545: G/Haas; 546: C/Frei; 546/547: C/Allofs; 548 l.: G/Haas; 548/549: G/Sartore; 549 t. r.: C/Atlantide; 549 b. r.: G/Sartore; 550: G/Weise; 550/551: G/Allofs; 552 l.: C/Arthus-Bertrand; 552 b. l.: C/Lanting; 552 b. r.: G/Balfour; 552/553: Afripics.

MONACO BOOKS is an imprint of Verlag Wolfgang Kunth

© Verlag Wolfgang Kunth GmbH & Co.KG, Munich, 2010
Text: Thomas Horsmann (pp. 330–333, 336–337, 350–353, 358–359), Heiner Newe (pp. 30–65, 96–109), Dr Reinhard Pietsch (pp. 10–29, 470–553), Linde Wiesner (pp. 66–95, 110–329, 334–335, 338–349, 354–357, 360–467).

English translation: JMS Books LLP (translation Malcolm Garrard; editing Jo Murray, David Harding, Jenni Davis; design Kathie Wilson, cbdesign)

Monaco Books
c/o Verlag Wolfgang Kunth, Königinstrasse 11
80539 Munich, Germany
Tel: +49.89.45 80 20-0
Fax: +49.89.45 80 20-21

www.monacobooks.com
ww.kunth-verlag.de